ESSENTIAL Jazz The First 100 Years

ESSENTIAL Jazz

The First 100 Years

Henry Martin RUTGERS UNIVERSITY

Keith Waters UNIVERSITY OF COLORADO

THOMSON ™

SCHIRMER

Australia ■ Canada ■ Mexico ■ Singapore ■ Spain ■ United Kingdom ■ United States

THOMSON
SCHIRMER

Executive Editor: Clark Baxter
Senior Development Editor: Sharon Adams-Poore
Senior Assistant Editor: Julie Yardley
Editorial Assistant: Anne Gittinger
Technology Project Manager: Michelle Vardeman
Marketing Manager: Mark Orr
Marketing Assistant: Annabelle Yang
Advertising Project Manager: Brian Chaffee
Project Manager, Editorial Production: Kirk Bomont
Art Director: Rob Hugel
Print/Media Buyer: Lisa Claudeanos

Permissions Editor: Stephanie Lee
Production Service: Ideas to Images
Text Designer: Gary Palmatier, Ideas to Images
Photo Researcher: Cheri Throop
Copy Editor: Elaine Brett
Autographer: Ernie Mansfield, Mansfield Music-Graphics
Cover Designer: Roger Knox
Cover Image: Roger Knox
Compositor: Robaire Ream, Ideas to Images
Printer: Transcontinental Printing/Louiseville

For more information about our products, contact us at:

Thomson Learning Academic Resource Center
1-800-423-0563
For permission to use material from this text or product, submit a request online at
http://www.thomsonrights.com
Any additional questions about permissions can be submitted by e-mail to
thomsonrights@thomson.com

Library of Congress Control Number: 2004106597

ISBN 0-534-63810-4

Thomson Schirmer
10 Davis Drive
Belmont, CA 94002-3098
USA

Asia
Thomson Learning
5 Shenton Way #01-01
UIC Building
Singapore 068808

Australia/New Zealand
Thomson Learning
102 Dodds Street
Southbank, Victoria 3006
Australia

Canada
Nelson
1120 Birchmount Road
Toronto, Ontario M1K 5G4
Canada

Europe/Middle East/Africa
Thomson Learning
High Holborn House
50/51 Bedford Row
London WC1R 4LR
United Kingdom

Latin America
Thomson Learning
Seneca, 53
Colonia Polanco
11560 Mexico D.F.
Mexico

Spain/Portugal
Paraninfo
Calle Magallanes, 25
28015 Madrid, Spain

BRIEF CONTENTS

CONTENTS

CHAPTER *4*

The Bebop Era

Revolution Versus Evolution   135
Characteristics of the Bebop Style   137
A Recomposition: Dizzy Gillespie's "Groovin' High"   138

CHAPTER **6**

The Sixties   **189**

PREFACE

WITH OUR NEW TEXT, *ESSENTIAL JAZZ,* we hope to provide students and instructors with a briefer, more concise version of *Jazz: The First 100 Years*. In *Essential Jazz*, we abridge the overall treatment of jazz history, eliminate most of the written musical examples, and omit all technical discussions involving music theory beyond what is normally found in music-appreciation texts. Our goal in writing *Jazz: The First 100 Years* was to present a fresh history of jazz that would serve both music majors and non-majors. As a result, there is some technical discussion of the music. Aside from these discussions, the goals are similar in *Essential Jazz* and *Jazz: The First 100 Years*, so let us begin by pointing out the changes we have made in developing the "essentials" version of the text before reviewing our overall philosophy of jazz history.

▶ We reduced the length of the text. While trying to keep the most important material, we have omitted some artists in order to focus limited class time on the most significant. We also shortened discussion, particularly of recordings that are not on the CDs included with the text.

▶ The number of chapters is reduced. In particular, we tightened up the material on jazz in the 1920s (initially presented in three chapters), so it now spans a single chapter. The swing-era discussion is now concentrated into one chapter as well, as is jazz of the 1960s.

▶ We added an Introduction on the elements of jazz. The Introduction is keyed to the ⓐ Audio Primer recordings and outlines many of the basic principles of both jazz and music in general.

▶ The content of the CDs is modified. In the first text, our goal was to avoid, as much as possible, duplicating material found on the *Smithsonian Collection of Classic Jazz*. That collection had become ubiquitous—even canonical—during the 1980s and early 1990s, and we felt that instructors were likely to have it handy for additional classroom examples. Moreover, during the later 1990s, as we were working on the first book, rumors abounded that the Smithsonian collection was to be picked up and reissued by another record company. Since then, this possibility has become increasingly remote, nor can we count on instructors' having access to those recordings. Hence, for *Essential Jazz* we decided to include a few of the significant pieces from the Smithsonian collection that we feel are exemplary of certain trends or artists.

▶ Continuing our goal of reducing the total amount of material, we shortened the contents of the historical recordings so that both these selections and the 🅿 Audio Primer recordings fit onto two CDs. This enables the CDs to be bound into the book rather than sold separately. We have also taken the liberty of excerpting more of the historical selections to conserve space on the CDs.

▶ Despite the reduced size of the text, we have included additional material on Latin jazz and women as jazz performers and composers.

▶ Where appropriate, we have updated the ancillary material, such as Suggested Readings.

As in *Jazz: The First 100 Years*, we continue to focus principally on the stylistic development of jazz and its most important artists. In addition, *Essential Jazz* relates the music to relevant aspects of social and intellectual history, including the Harlem Renaissance, the status of women in jazz, racism, the counterculture revolutions of the 1960s, and the contributions of Latino culture. Finally, we tried to include the most up-to-date information possible, taking advantage of the fine scholarly work on jazz that has appeared during the past several years.

Our chronological presentation of jazz history preserves the customary divisions of the music into stylistic periods because we feel that this is the clearest method of introducing the material to the student. Nevertheless, throughout the text we acknowledge the arbitrariness of the stylistic divisions and emphasize that many (if not most) artists have produced significant work beyond the era in which they first came to public attention.

As with any history, we sometimes must stray outside the time frame of a given era to complete the narrative of an important figure. For the most part, however, an artist is treated in the era in which he or she exerted the greatest influence. The two main exceptions to this practice are Miles Davis and Duke Ellington. Although Ellington was prominent and influential throughout his career, he played an especially important role in early jazz and the swing era (Chapters 2 and 3). Davis's work influenced the disparate styles of 1950s cool jazz, 1960s mainstream jazz, and 1970s jazz-rock, so his story is related in Chapters 5, 6, and 7 to clarify these distinct contributions.

Features

▶ **The two-CD set**, packaged free with the book, features a variety of jazz recordings from 1917 to 1999 as well as brief examples of some of the music that gave rise to jazz.

▶ The 🅟 **Audio Primer recordings**, prepared by the authors, are also included on the two-CD set. These recordings demonstrate basic musical concepts (scales, syncopation, blues, rhythm changes, inside/outside playing, and so forth), as well as the instruments of jazz (the four principal saxophones, trumpet and trombone with different mutes, electric and acoustic guitars, the different sounds of the drum set, and so on). Many of the Audio Primer recordings are keyed to the Introduction. Where appropriate, the definitions of key terms in the text refer to the Audio Primer recordings so that the student can hear what is being defined.

▶ **Listening Guides for each CD** track appear in the text, with CD timings keyed to events in the music and the work's overall form.

▶ The book features a historical focus on the evolution of significant trends, key figures, and the changing role of instrumental and improvisational style. It also includes relevant ideas in twentieth-century U.S. social and intellectual history, including the Harlem Renaissance and the countercultural movements of the 1960s. Many issues relating to contemporary U.S. political and social history appear in the photographs and their captions.

▶ We include a balanced view of jazz since 1960. One-quarter of our book chronicles jazz since 1960, covering significant trends and performers of the 1960s through the 1990s.

▶ Current scholarly and critical work is reflected throughout. The text takes into account some of the groundbreaking jazz research of the previous two decades. The presentation attempts to illuminate and amplify current historical and musical controversies rather than assert unqualified truths.

▶ Questions at the end of each chapter are given for class discussion or assignments.

▶ Key terms are listed at the end of each chapter.

▶ A glossary containing definitions presented in the text is included.

▶ The back matter includes a recommended discography and a bibliography listing extensive sources for further listening, study, and research.

▶ The instructor has Web site access with a protected link to the electronic instructor's manual. The manual contains suggestions for additional recordings to play in class and information about other important artists relevant to each chapter. The Web site also includes notes to the additional recordings and will include updated information as it becomes available. Visit the Schirmer Music site to access quizzing, our interactive audio dictionary, and streaming audio from our library of links to musical performances available online.

Accompanying Two-CD Set

The recordings selected for the CDs attempt to give a general overview of jazz in the twentieth century. We could not include all of the many important artists in a brief two-CD presentation, of course, but the selections nevertheless sample a broad cross-section of significant jazz artists and styles. The text includes Listening Guides for each track, which readers may refer to while working through the material. These Listening Guides contain commentary, highlighting aspects of form, instrumentation, and improvisation. In choosing our selections, we followed these criteria:

▶ The recordings are representative of the artists' work generally.

▶ The recordings are well known, unless there is reason to include something more obscure.

▶ The choice and arrangement of the selections should work aesthetically. We hope that students will enjoy listening to the CDs for pleasure rather than just focus on each selection as it is discussed in the text.

Acknowledgments

The text of *Essential Jazz* was developed from *Jazz: The First 100 Years*, which itself began as an expanded second edition of Martin's *Enjoying Jazz* (Schirmer Books, 1986). We acknowledge the wise guidance of the staff at Schirmer Books in developing *Enjoying Jazz* and overseeing the early development of *Jazz: The First 100 Years*.

We have benefitted from the advice of Latin jazz expert Christopher Washburne in our discussion of Latin jazz and in the selection of "Manteca" for the two-CD set. Charles "Tad" Turner went beyond the call of duty in locating "Daniel," "Dere's No Hidin' Place Down Dere," and "Field Hands' Call" for the two-CD set. Thanks, Tad, for providing items from your extensive collection of folk and ethnic music! Both Sherrie Tucker and Janna Saslaw provided expert advice on women in jazz. We thank them for their thoughtful critiques of our additional material and the suggestion of "Vi Vigor" for the two-CD set. Thanks to Rosalind Cron for her photo of the International Sweethearts of Rhythm. We thank Craig Wright for the selection "Kasuan Kura" from his text *Listening to Music* (4th ed., Wadsworth/Schirmer).

The environment and support provided by the Special Interest Group in Jazz (SMT-Jz) of the Society for Music Theory have helped make this book a reality. Many thanks to the members of SMT-Jz who encouraged us to pursue the project of an abridged text and offered suggestions throughout the composition of the manuscript.

We thank Clark Baxter, publisher for music at Thomson Learning, who, in pointing out that our original text could be made accessible to a wider audience, conceived of *Essential Jazz*. We owe Clark and his colleagues a tremendous debt for their tireless work in uncovering the photographs, sheet music covers, and other pictorial material used in the text. Clark's commentary for all the pictures provides an important dimension to the book, particularly by placing the development of jazz within the larger context of U.S. social and political history. We thank Sharon Adams-Poore, our development editor on this project, who reviewed the final manuscript in detail to make sure it was consistent and balanced and suggested numerous improvements. She was a pleasure to work with in every way.

For the Audio Primer recordings, many thanks to the excellent Denver-based musicians who agreed to perform on it. They include Rich Chiaraluce, Mark Harris, Bill Kopper, Ron Miles, Todd Reid, and Ken Walker. We would also like to thank our assistant engineers, Ty Blosser, Jerry Wright, and John Romero. A special thanks to Joe Hall, the principal engineer as well as trombonist. Thanks also go to Paul Rinzler for creating the Active Listening Tools.

We thank Tom Laskey of Sony Music Special Projects, who worked with us on the production of the two CDs. Tom's patience in locating the best possible audio sources for each selection was admirable. The engineer who helped assemble the CDs from the various audio sources was Jeff Zaraya of SoundByte Productions in New York.

We would also like to thank the readers engaged by Thomson to critique the manuscript, comment on the two-CD set, and provide overall guidance on abridging *Jazz: The First 100 Years*. We gained excellent insights and suggestions from David Borgo, University of California, San Diego; Jean A. Boyd, Baylor University School of Music; Michael J. Budds, University of Missouri–Columbia; Scott Cowan, Western Michigan University; Clarence Henry, University of Kansas; Richard Hermann, University of New Mexico; Kip Lornell, George Washington University; Jim Lovensheimer, Blair School of Music, Vanderbilt University; Brad Madson, Jefferson College; Frederick Moehn, State University of New York, Stony Brook; Michael Pagan, University of Colorado, Boulder; Paul Rinzler, California Polytechnic State University, San Luis Obispo; Thomas Smialek, Pennsylvania State University, Hazleton; Alexander Stewart, University of Vermont; and Yolanda Williams, University of Minnesota.

Thanks to Kirk Bomont of Thomson, who oversaw the details of final design and production. The striking cover is the work of Roger Knox. Interior design was provided by Gary Palmatier, the layout by Robaire Ream, both of Ideas to Images, the company that produced the final pages. Elaine Brett did the meticulous copy editing. Elaine caught many inconsistencies and played a pivotal role in clarifying and focusing our prose. We thank her profusely. The beautiful music examples were prepared by Ernie Mansfield of Mansfield Music-Graphics. The comprehensive index was prepared by Edwin Durbin.

We thank Robert Sadin, who commented on Marsalis's "Express Crossing" from the experience of having conducted it in concert. Our historical and analytical insights are profoundly indebted to the explosion of recent first-rate scholarly and critical studies on jazz. Many have proven invaluable, including but not limited to Lewis Porter's excellent studies of Lester Young and John Coltrane, Mark Tucker's work on Duke Ellington, Scott DeVeaux's writings on bebop, Stuart Nicholson's book on jazz-rock fusion, and Enrico Merlin's material on Miles Davis's electric period. We would like to thank Tom Riis for his input on late-nineteenth-century American music in general. Bill Kirchner offered excellent advice in the early stages of the process, as did Greg Dyes, formerly of the University of Colorado, and Michael Fitzgerald. Carl Woideck suggested several improvements and clarifications for which we are grateful. Brian Fores's unpublished master's thesis on John Zorn contributed material not available elsewhere. John Galm provided excellent insights into the retention of African music in the United States and helped us clarify the summary of African music in Chapter 1.

The graduate students in the master's degree program in Jazz History and Research at Rutgers University–Newark read earlier drafts of many sections and provided valuable feedback; we thank them for their time and comments. We particularly acknowledge the staff of the Institute of Jazz Studies at Rutgers University–Newark: Dan Morgenstern, Ed Berger, and Vince Pelote were extremely generous with their time and advice.

ABOUT THE AUTHORS

Henry Martin

Henry Martin is professor of music at Rutgers University–Newark. With a Ph.D. from Princeton University and degrees from the University of Michigan and Oberlin Conservatory, he has pursued a dual career as a composer-pianist and as a music theorist specializing in jazz and the Western tonal tradition. His compositions have won several awards, including the 1998 Barlow Endowment International Composition Competition and the National Composers Competition sponsored by the League of Composers–International Society for Contemporary Music, and are published by Margun Music (distributed by Shawnee Press). A CD of his *Preludes and Fugues* was released by Bridge Records in 2004 (Bridge 9140).

Martin teaches in the master's degree program in Jazz History and Research at Rutgers University–Newark, the country's only program granting a degree in jazz scholarship. He is co-editor of the *Annual Review of Jazz Studies,* which is published by Scarecrow Press and the Rutgers Institute of Jazz Studies. His book *Charlie Parker and Thematic Improvisation* was published by Scarecrow Press in 1996. Scarecrow Press is also publishing his book *Counterpoint* in 2005. *Enjoying Jazz* was published by Schirmer Books in 1986. He has published numerous reviews and articles on music theory in such journals as *Perspectives of New Music, Music and Letters,* and *In Theory Only.* He is also the founder and chair of the Jazz Special Interest Group, an organization of music theorists devoted to advancing scholarship in jazz theory.

Keith Waters

Keith Waters is associate professor of music theory at the University of Colorado at Boulder. He received a Ph.D. in music theory from the Eastman School of Music, a master of music degree in jazz piano from the New England Conservatory of Music, and a bachelor of music degree in applied piano from the University of North Carolina–Greensboro. He has published articles on Herbie Hancock, Booker Little, Miles Davis, Keith Jarrett, and other topics related to jazz analysis and improvisation, as well as a book on twentieth-century composer Arthur Honegger.

As a jazz pianist, Waters has performed in concerts, jazz festivals, and clubs throughout the United States and Europe, appearing in such venues as the Blue Note and the Village Corner in New York, and Blues Alley and the Kennedy Center in Washington, D.C. He has performed in concert with numerous jazz artists, including James Moody, Bobby Hutcherson, Eddie Harris, Chris Connor, Sheila Jordan, Keter Betts, Buck Hill, and Meredith D'Ambrosia. He has recorded for VSOP Records, and his playing has been featured in *Jazz Player* magazine. His most recent recording is a Chet Baker tribute with former Baker sideman Phil Urso and West Coast trumpeter Carl Saunders.

The authors welcome suggestions for subsequent editions. Comments may be posted to the book's Web site at *www.wadsworth.com* or e-mailed directly to the authors:

Henry Martin
martinh@andromeda.rutgers.edu

Keith Waters
keith.waters@colorado.edu

INTRODUCTION: JAZZ BASICS

IN THIS INTRODUCTION, we provide a guide to some of the elements necessary for understanding jazz as musical experience. Much of the material discussed here is keyed to the Audio Primer tracks of CD 1 (listed inside the book's front cover). They demonstrate fundamental principles, the most common instruments of jazz, and basic ideas of form. When the Audio Primer is referred to, you will find the track number to listen to, as well as the Audio Primer logo 🎧.

Note that this overview of the elements of music is highly condensed; to understand the subject thoroughly, you would need to consult and work through a jazz theory text. This introduction is designed to give you the basic vocabulary you need to listen to and talk about jazz. To help you master this terminology, there is a list of key terms at the end of this introduction (and at the end of each chapter), along with the number of the page on which the term is discussed. You will also see that some key terms are shown in *bold italic* when they come up in text; this means that the term's definition is included in the glossary at the back of the book. Try to get the general idea of the terms in the introduction and return to them when necessary.

The Three Fundamentals of Western Music

What do we do when we listen to music? When we listen to music or think of it analytically, it is customary to separate music—at least the music in Western culture—into three fundamental aspects: rhythm, melody, and harmony. We will discuss these three elements in turn, then examine other factors, including the instruments of jazz and aspects of form. The introduction ends with an overview of strategies for listening to jazz and ways of discussing it in various contexts.

RHYTHM

Jazz is known for its rhythm, but rhythm in a general sense pervades all music. When notes follow one another in time, they are necessarily in some kind of *rhythm,* so we can think of rhythm as the experience of music through time. A familiar aspect of rhythm is more abstract, however, and that is the music's beat. When you listen to much of the world's music, you feel a steady *pulse* to which you may clap your hands or dance. That pulse is known as the *beat.* In much jazz (and in other music as well), the drummer keeps the beat. However, music without drums (such as a solo piano performance) may still project a strong beat even though there is no drummer keeping time or (in a synonymous phrase) keeping the beat. This is why we describe the beat as abstract.

Our innate attraction to music may have developed through the experience of rhythm before we were born: the perception, while still in the womb, of our mother's heartbeat. The beat of music is roughly equal to the beating of the human heart, which is normally around 72 beats per minute. Music's beat ranges from somewhat slower to considerably faster, but within the same basic range: from about 40 beats per minute to about 200 beats per minute. After birth our first actual experience of music is likely to be our mother's singing, especially the lullabies that calm us as infants and lull us to sleep. In listening to our mother's lullabies, virtually from birth, we experience the overwhelming power of music and its effect on our emotions.

We just noted that music in general projects a range of beat speeds from very slow to very fast. The speed of the beat is an important musical factor and is known as *tempo.* Slower tempos tend to be moodier, while faster tempos are livelier.

In music, beats are organized according to **meter.** Meter arises when the music groups the beats into strong and weak pulses. When we feel the music alternating between strong and weak pulses, the meter is *duple;* when two weak pulses separate strong pulses, the meter is *triple.* Meter can also be *irregular* when the strong pulses are unpredictable. Most jazz uses duple meter.

The duple meter heard in most jazz is represented in musical notation by what we call the *time signature.* Music Example I-1 shows a musical *staff* (the five horizontal lines) with a *treble clef* followed by a time signature, in this case 4/4, the most common of all time signatures. The upper 4 means that there are four beats in a *measure,* or *bar* of the music; the lower 4 means that a certain note, called a *quarter note,* receives one beat. The bars are separated by lines (called *barlines*) running vertically through the staff. The four quarter notes correspond to the four beats in the bar. In a bar of 4/4 time, we feel structural accents on the first and third beats. By *structural* we mean that the music is generally organized in reference to those beats. The weaker beats

Music Example I-1
The basic elements of musical notation.

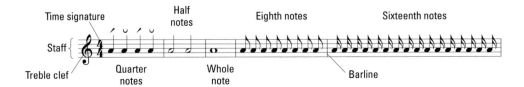

(two and four) may receive dynamic accents because drummers, as well as people who clap their hands to the music, may emphasize them.

The second bar of Music Example I-1 shows two notes; these are *half notes* and they each receive two beats. The third bar shows one *whole note,* which fills the whole measure by receiving four beats. The fourth bar shows eight *eighth notes,* which receive ½ beat. The fifth bar shows sixteen *sixteenth notes,* each of which receives ¼ beat. These types of notes are the most common in jazz, although even smaller note values that further subdivide the beat are often heard at slow tempos (because there is more space for players to fill between the slowly occurring beats). Beats can also be divided into threes, but we will not discuss that topic here.

The disruption of regular meter, an important musical effect, is very common in jazz and is known as **syncopation**. Syncopation occurs when the weaker portions of a metrical grid receive dynamic accents. Music that normally includes syncopation sounds static or stiff without it. To hear the effect of removing syncopation from a familiar piece that features it, listen to Track 4 of CD 1 🎧.

The jazz ensemble often includes accompanying rhythm instruments (piano, banjo or guitar, bass, and drums) that provide backup to the primary melodic instruments (cornet or trumpet, trombone, clarinet, or saxophone). This backup group from the ensemble is called the **rhythm section**.

Other aspects of jazz rhythm are traceable to the African contribution to our musical heritage. These features are discussed more thoroughly in Chapter 1.

MELODY

The second fundamental of music is *melody.* The building blocks of melody are *notes,* or *tones.* The human voice, the first musical instrument, can create tones by simply sustaining a sound. Let us consider several musical terms that will help you understand the various aspects of melody.

The distance between any two notes is called an *interval.* Of particular importance (and present in all cultures) is a crucial interval called the *octave,* in which notes vibrate in a 2:1 ratio. When notes do this, they sound the same, but higher or lower. We acknowledge this property by giving notes that are an octave apart the same name. The property of notes' being higher or lower is referred to by the word *pitch,* as in a low or high pitch. For example, women's voices typically have a higher pitch than men's voices. Musical notes are sometimes called pitches.

We name the notes of music by using the letters of the alphabet and arranging them into *scales* that are defined by the octave. *Scale* is from the Italian *scala,* or ladder, because the notes move up and down by step, as on a ladder. Notes that are next to one another in a scale are thus related by *step.* In the music of Western culture, the note names take on the first seven letters of the alphabet: A, B, C, D, E, F, and G. The next note of this ascending scale would again be A, but this new A would be an octave higher than the original A. This second A is the eighth note above the initial A, which explains the origin of *octave* from the Latin *octo,* or eight. To hear examples of scales, listen to Track 1 of CD 1 🎧, in which different scales are played on the piano.

The seven basic notes, A to G, of Western music correspond to the white notes of the piano keyboard. There are five additional notes that are variants of the basic seven white notes and are arranged as the black notes of the keyboard. These black

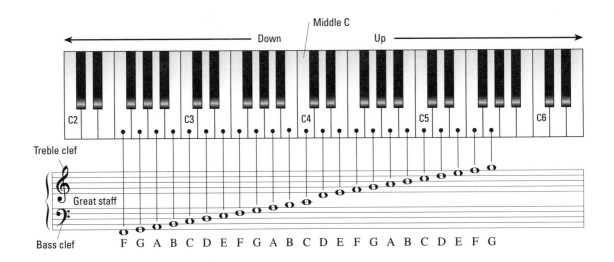

Music Example I-2
Musical notes on a staff designate specific keys on a piano keyboard.

notes are normally named relative to the white notes. For example, a black note just to the right of C is called C#, or C sharp. The same black note is to the left of D and has the additional name of D♭, or D flat. It is not necessary for us to get into the complex issues of why the notes of music can have more than one name (the white notes can take on different names as well!), but you should be aware that the black notes are usually called *sharps* or *flats* depending on their relationship to adjacent white notes. Together, these twelve notes, repeating in lower and higher versions related by the octave, form the basis of Western music.

As seen in Example I-2, notes in Western culture are often diagrammed on the musical staff in musical *notation*. Each line and space on the staff corresponds to a white note on the keyboard. Flats and sharps on the same lines and spaces refer to the black notes. The clefs, treble clef and *bass clef* (also called G and F clefs), show which notes correspond to positions on the staff. In piano and keyboard writing, the staff with the F (bass) clef usually corresponds to music played by the left hand and is lower in pitch, while the G (treble) clef usually corresponds to the higher music played by the right hand.

Scales in Western music are combinations of white and black notes, ascending and descending. The simplest scale—one that is often taught first—is the C major scale, which consists of the white notes only and is named after the note C, which is the *tonic* of the scale. The tonic is of primary importance to the scale and forms a "center of gravity" to which the other notes in the scale are seen to relate. The use of tonics gives rise to the sense of *key*, or **tonality**, which we discuss in the following section on harmony.

To create melodies, we arrange the notes of the scale into patterns that are more interesting than scales, which merely ascend or descend. Melodies are coherent patterns of notes; that is, they are not random notes that occur unpredictably. Melodies are made coherent by the use of patterns that combine predictability on the one hand and surprise on the other hand. Too much predictability is boring, while too much surprise is incoherent. Jazz musicians often base their playing on songs, which generally consist of notes coherently arranged in a melody. Jazz musicians also create spontaneous melodies, a process called *improvisation*. Part of the education of a jazz musician is learning to create improvised melodies that are coherent and emotionally engaging.

Melodies are usually divided into *phrases*. These are subgroups of melody that form self-contained units that are often sung in one breath. Think of the U.S. national anthem, "The Star-Spangled Banner": Its first phrase would be "O say can you see by the dawn's early light." At that point, if you were singing it, you would probably want to take a breath. Similarly, "Take Me Out to the Ballgame" would probably have an opening phrase of "Take me out to the ballgame, take me out with the crowd."

In a most basic sense, we think of the phrases that constitute melodies as built on scales in which successive notes are often related by step. This can be seen in the familiar Irving Berlin songs "White Christmas" and "God Bless America." The first phrase in each song is built on stepwise notes. Interestingly, the first phrase of "The Star-Spangled Banner" is not built on stepwise notes but on *leaps* or *skips,* which are intervals between notes that are larger than steps. Leaps give rise to harmony, the third fundamental of music.

Different cultures have different notes and scales. Because jazz is a Western music (although a significant part of its history is non-Western), most of its notes, scales, phrases, and other musical building blocks are Western in origin.

HARMONY

In addition to melody, *harmony* is another important feature of Western music—a feature most prominently developed in jazz. We noted in the previous section that melodies make frequent use of stepwise notes. Harmony, on the other hand, is based on skips between notes. We can create a simple harmony by taking a scale and playing every other note for three or four notes. If we play them simultaneously, we hear a *chord,* the basic unit of harmony. In a C major scale (C-D-E-F-G-A-B-C), we create a C major *triad,* which is a three-note chord, by playing C-E-G, that is, by skipping over D and F. We can also create a D minor triad by playing D-F-A, or skipping over E and G. In similar fashion, we can build numerous triads by including the black notes and beginning on various notes, both white and black.

By linking triads together successively in music, we get a flow of basic harmony, which often serves as *accompaniment* to the melody. Harmony adds richness and context to a basic melodic flow. In Western music a singer often performs a song's melody while the accompanying instruments play chords that provide harmony. The piano has long been the basic instrument of Western music because it can function as a kind of one-man band in which the performer can provide melody and harmony simultaneously: A player's right hand might play the melody while the left hand plays chords that provide harmony. Track 3 of CD 1 🎵 is a melody played on the piano—first without chords, then with chords.

We conceptually separate melody and harmony, but in fact melodies sometimes duplicate harmonies or chords by skipping around and avoiding stepwise notes. Consider the opening notes of "The Star-Spangled Banner": "O say can you see by . . ." is based entirely on skips and in fact duplicates the opening harmony of the piece. For example, if the song were performed in the key of C, the opening of the first phrase would consist of the notes G-E-C-E-G-C-E, which outline a C major triad. In the opening notes of that tune, there are Cs and Es that occur in different octaves.

When we move through chords one note at a time, up and down, as in the beginning of "The Star-Spangled Banner," it is called *arpeggiation,* a word deriving from the Italian for harp. In addition to the triads (the most basic chords) already discussed, harmonies with more notes are also possible. Jazz, for example, often exploits *seventh chords,* which have four notes. Listen to Track 2 of CD 1 🅟 for examples of the arpeggiation of seventh chords.

Music can be said to be a collection of chords and melodic lines used in an idiomatic way and related to the scale they are derived from. A chord can be built on each note of a given scale. As mentioned earlier, the scale and chords occurring in a piece of music determine its key. If the notes of a melody keep the same relative positions, a piece can be *transposed* from one key to another without changing the nature of the musical piece. This is often done for a vocalist whose best singing range is higher or lower than that of the published sheet music. For example, we cited the beginning of "The Star-Spangled Banner" with the notes from the key of C. The same song can be transposed to occur in twelve different keys, each corresponding to a note of the keyboard.

The musical keys that are derived from the notes of the keyboard have two common forms, *major* and *minor.* There is the key of C major, the key of C minor, the key of B♭ major, the key of B♭ minor, and so on. When composers write songs or when jazz improvisers create melodies spontaneously, they work with the key system of twenty-four major and minor keys, the basis of Western tonality. In later jazz (from the 1950s on), a system called *modality* both extends and partially supplants the major-minor system.

As shown in Example I-3, Roman numerals are often used to designate a chord relative to the key that contains it. In general, the seven notes of the scale can each take a Roman numeral that helps specify what that chord does in the context of the key determined by the scale. The set of chordal usages for a given chord in a key is referred to as its *function.*

The chordal element of jazz is so pervasive that a system of *slash notation* describing chords has become standard in most jazz styles, as shown in Example I-4.

The succession of chords in music is usually not random, but is often based on standard conventions. The chordal sequence is then called a *chord progression* or *progression.*

Music Example I-3
Roman numerals designate the harmonies relative to the key.

In the key of C major, the C major triad is a tonic or I chord.

In the key of G, the same C major triad is a subdominant IV chord.

Music Example I-4
Slash notation.

Another feature of jazz harmony is called **harmonic substitution**. The original progression is altered by using new chords that function similarly to the original chords. On Track 6 of CD 1 you can hear a standard jazz chord progression (ii7-V7-I) modified by the use of *extensions* (extra notes added to the chord) and *substitution*. The chord substitution used here is the *tritone substitution,* which was popularized during the bebop era.

When improvisers choose to adapt their melodic improvisations to the underlying chords, they are said to be playing *inside*. When the melody and harmony do not quite match, the improviser is playing *outside*. Listen to Track 8 of CD 1 for the difference between inside and outside playing.

Although there is much more that could be said about rhythm, melody, and harmony, the material here should help you understand most of the references in the text.

Texture and Timbre

The **texture** of music is what you are hearing at a given moment: the combination of instruments playing and the manner in which they are being played. The specific quality of the sound of a given instrument is an example of *timbre*. For example, the timbre of a violin is quite different from the timbre of a trumpet. While you are listening to a piece of music from any culture, you can ask yourself, "What am I hearing *now?*" The answer is likely to be a summary of the music's timbres and textures at that moment in time.

Textures are often described in dualities, such as thick or thin, high or low, or fast or slow. A thin texture, for example, has few notes and/or instruments, such as a human voice singing without accompaniment. A thick texture may have many notes and/or instruments, such as a large symphony orchestra with all members playing. Some very flexible instruments, such as a piano, can project many different textures by themselves.

To focus on the texture when you listen to music, think of:

▶ What instruments am I hearing? Can I distinguish them?

▶ How are they being played? (Lots of notes, few notes, fast, slow, soft, loud, high, low, and so on.)

Dynamics and Articulation

Music ranges from very soft to very loud. This is most obvious when you listen to recorded music: You can make the playback softer or louder through the volume control.

However, musical sounds themselves have subtly varying degrees of softness and loudness within the same performance. The notes of a melody can sound very mechanical when all are played at the same volume. On the other hand, a melody can vary from soft to loud within a few notes. The way performers vary the softness and loudness of the notes they play greatly affects their performances and their emotional impact on listeners. The softness and loudness of musical sounds are referred to as *dynamics*.

Trumpet

Cornet

Flugelhorn

Notes can be attacked, or played, in numerous ways. We refer to the ways that notes are played as *articulation*. For example, the articulation of notes proceeding smoothly from one to the other is *legato*. Short, detached notes are *staccato*.

Dynamics and articulation are often included under the category of *expression* because the way a performer varies the dynamics and the articulation of notes greatly affects the overall expressiveness of that performance.

Instruments of Jazz

First, we shall describe the *wind instruments* most often heard in jazz. Wind instruments are normally divided into two families, brass and reeds.

Among the brasses, the most important jazz instrument is the **trumpet**. Its close cousin, the **cornet**, is common in early jazz and sounds like a trumpet but is mellower and more restrained. Another trumpet-like instrument is the *flugelhorn*, which is even mellower than the cornet.

The trumpet can be played open—that is, without mutes—or with various mutes. The characteristic sound of the open trumpet is heard on Track 12 of CD 1 . Mutes are placed into the trumpet bell (the flared end of the horn) to change its timbre, or quality of sound. Cup and harmon mutes are demonstrated on Tracks 13–15 of CD 1 .

The *saxophone* is the most important reed instrument in jazz. There is a whole family of saxophones in various sizes. The most common saxophones are heard on Tracks 16–19 of CD 1 , ranging from high (the soprano) to low (baritone).

Soprano saxophone

Alto saxophone

Tenor saxophone

Photos courtesy of G. Leblanc Corporation www.gleblanc.com

Clarinet

The *clarinet* is a reed instrument that was more common in early jazz than the saxophone. The clarinet has receded in popularity since its heyday in the 1930s, but is recently making a comeback. Tracks 20 and 21 of CD 1 🅟 show two common clarinet stylizations: the swing-style lines of the 1930s and the *obbligato* lines heard in Dixieland in the 1920s.

Trombone

After the trumpet, the *trombone* is the most important jazz brass instrument. Like the trumpet, it can be played open or with mutes, as shown on CD 1 🅟. Track 22 demonstrates a trombone with an open sound, and Track 23 with a cup mute. The growl sound on Track 24 is a common brass technique that can also be performed on the trumpet. The tailgate effect of Track 25 is sometimes heard in Dixieland jazz; it is created by moving the slide while holding a note, a feature technically called a *glissando*.

Tracks 10 and 11 of CD 1 🅟 feature a common jazz ensemble, called a *piano trio*, which usually consists of piano, acoustic bass, and drum set. A less common piano trio consists of piano, bass, and guitar.

The *piano*, developed in the early 1700s, soon became the most common of all Western instruments. (Electronic keyboards and guitars may be overtaking the piano more recently.) Because the keys can be operated independently by the ten fingers to produce simultaneous sounds, it can play both melody and harmony. In fact, solo piano can mimic a larger ensemble because of the piano's ability to supply the functions of numerous instruments. Larger pianos, called grand pianos, have longer strings, resulting in a richer, more powerful sound than upright pianos.

The acoustic *bass* should be distinguished from its cousin, the horizontal electric bass guitar, which is more common in rock and jazz-rock. The acoustic bass was originally played without amplification, but nowadays is usually amplified. The acoustic bass is commonly heard in the jazz ensemble, but can be

Piano

heard alone on Track 43 of CD 1 . There, it *walks*—that is, the player provides a note for each beat in mostly stepwise fashion.

The drum set is like a piano in that the drummer can play a number of instrumental parts simultaneously. Unlike a piano, however, the drums cannot play specific pitches to create chords. *Drums* are examples of *percussion instruments*—instruments that are generally struck with either the hand or a stick or mallet. The most common drums of the drum set are featured on the solo tracks of CD 1. (To play the various instruments of the drum set, we assume a right-handed, right-footed drummer; this arrangement is sometimes reversed for drummers who favor their left side.)

Let us summarize the percussion instruments most commonly found in the drum set, demonstrated on Tracks 26–35 of CD 1. Track 26 shows the snare drum, usually played with the left hand (if the right hand is otherwise keeping the beat). Tracks 27 and 28 feature high and low tom-toms, which can be played with either hand. The bass drum (Track 29) is sometimes articulated on each beat of the bar, especially in older jazz; it is played by the right foot through the use of a pedal. The ride cymbal (Track 30) is usually played with the right hand; the track features what is called a swing beat. The hi-hat (Track 31) consists of a pair of cymbals, top and bottom. It is usually played by the left foot pedal, which closes and opens the cymbal pair, thus producing a "chick" sound. The top cymbal of the hi-hat can also be played by hand, usually the right. Track 32 shows the simultaneous foot pedal and hand playing of the hi-hat, which produces a familiar swing rhythm sound. Crash cymbals (Track 33) add color and accents to the drum texture; they are most commonly played by the right hand. On

Copyright PhotoDisc

Acoustic bass

Cymbals

Tom-toms

Hi-hat

Snare drum

Ludwig

Kick bass drum

Drum set

Courtesy of Ludwig Drums, a division of Conn-Selmer, Inc.

Acoustic guitar

Electric guitar

Track 34 all the drum set parts are combined into a swing beat; try to distinguish the different sounds made by each element of the set. Finally, Track 35 shows how the drum set can be played with wire brushes instead of sticks; this creates a lighter, softer sound, but one that can still generate considerable rhythmic drive.

The *guitar* comes in both electric and acoustic versions, demonstrated on Tracks 36–42 of CD 1 🎧. The older acoustic guitar was very much a rhythm instrument in classic jazz because it played chords on each beat; this effect is heard on Track 36 of CD 1. The acoustic guitar was not very loud, but in a small-group setting it could play occasional melodies, as heard on Track 37. Track 38 features bossa nova–style acoustic guitar, a sound that became popular in the 1960s.

The electric guitar was developed during the 1930s. The use of the amplifier enabled it to be heard in any setting. The early electric sound of the guitar is featured on Track 39 of CD 1; this is the basic sound associated with the jazz electric guitar in non-rock settings. After rock became popular in the 1950s and 1960s, the electric guitar underwent a sonic revolution. Electronic effects were introduced that radically augmented the sounds the instrument could produce. Some of these sounds, typical of jazz-rock and jazz-funk fusion, can be heard on Tracks 40–42.

Form and Organization

Musical *form* is the layout of the music in time. Earlier we discussed how a melody combines predictable patterns with moments of surprise to create a coherent and hopefully engaging organization. Form operates similarly, but over longer spans of time; it too combines predictability and surprise. An important aspect of uncovering the organization of music is to be aware of its repetitive aspects. Because music operates on a number of levels, repetition can be found from the lower level of notes to the higher level of long spans of time.

We often describe the form of a musical work by enumerating and labeling its self-contained parts, frequently by the letters A, B, C, and so on, although some analysts use lowercase letters. Letters can stand for small units, such as phrases, as well as much longer parts of compositions and performances.

An important musical unit, typically present in jazz performances, is a *section,* which is a self-contained melodic and harmonic grouping, often consisting of two phrases. Eight-bar sections are very common in jazz, though larger sections are possible. Examples of forms that show sections are AABA, a common song form, and ABACA, which is more often heard in classical music. If a section repeats but is modified, the repeated section is often denoted by one or more primes added to the letter: AA'BA" shows that the initial A section returns twice but is modified at each repetition.

In general, to uncover the basic form of a piece of music, count the number of bars that create self-contained sections. The easiest way to count bars is to keep track of them systematically through the beat of the music. For example, to count bars of 4/4 time, you should proceed:

ONE-two-three-four,

TWO-two-three-four,

THREE-two-three-four,

FOUR-two-three-four,

FIVE-two-three-four,

SIX-two-three-four, and so forth

As you near the end of a phrase (often four bars) or a section (often eight bars), listen to how the music creates a *cadence,* which is a harmonic progression supporting an appropriate melody that signifies closure of that phrase or section. The signifying of closure enables the preceding part of the music to feel self-contained. The more important the sectional division, the more conclusive will be the cadence that helps create that closure.

Almost all jazz before the 1950s is based on symmetrical sections with the numbers of bars occurring in multiples of four, the common phrase length. We typically find sections of eight or sixteen bars that combine to create larger groups of thirty-two bars. After 1950 symmetrical forms continued to dominate jazz performance, but irregular forms became more common.

FORM IN EARLY JAZZ

Early jazz (c. 1917–28) is characterized by forms that maintain the 8-, 16-, and 32-bar symmetrical sections of European popular songs and marches. We will discuss the march form, which can be heard in the important early jazz style known as ragtime, in Chapter 1.

SONG FORMS

European song form became especially prominent as jazz matured through the 1920s. Two basic formats, *AABA* and *ABAC,* have been mainstays of the music ever since. Each section is eight bars, so these are examples of 32-bar song form. In each of these forms, the A section is often called the **head** and the B section the **bridge.** (Two older terms for the B section, *channel* and *release,* are now uncommon.) We will point out examples of these forms later when we discuss specific musical pieces.

RHYTHM CHANGES

Rhythm changes are an important vehicle for jazz performance. George and Ira Gershwin's song "I Got Rhythm," published in 1930, provides the basis of the form and harmony for rhythm changes. Listen to Track 10 of CD 1 for a brief demonstration of rhythm changes. (The final two-bar tag of the original song is omitted, so a symmetrical 32-bar AABA plan results for rhythm changes as customarily performed.) A hit in the 1930s, "I Got Rhythm" is still a familiar song, and jazz musicians still use its form and harmonies for improvisation and composition.

BLUES CHANGES

Another important musical form in jazz is the **blues.** (We discuss the meaning and historical significance of the blues in Chapter 1; here we summarize its formal aspects.) In its regularized format (the kind most commonly used by jazz musicians), the **blues form** consists of twelve bars comprising three four-bar phrases. Example I-5 shows a classic form with a single 12-bar chorus and a typical harmonic progression. The harmonic progression of the blues is quite regular, but there are many variants. One of its most significant harmonic moves is to the IV chord of the key at measure 5.

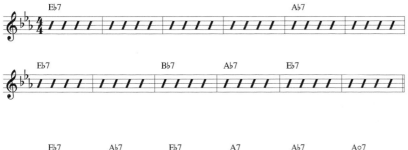

Music Example I-5
Classic blues form with a single 12-bar chorus and a standard harmonic progression. This is typical of the many ways a blues progression may be varied.

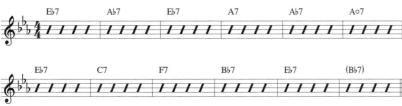

The general phrasing of the blues follows a sharply defined format. If A and B represent two four-bar phrases of the original 12-bar song, AAB denotes the form. This form is ideal for improvisation because the singer can think ahead for a rhyming third phrase during the repetition of the first. Adding to the ease of improvisation, each A and B phrase usually falls within the first two or three bars of each four-bar phrase. The concluding part of each phrase can be filled with a response from the instrumental accompaniment while the singer ponders the next phrase.

A. *I was with you, ba-by, when you did not have a dime.*

A. *I was with you, ba-by, when you did not have a dime.*

B. *Now since you've got plenty money, you have brought your good gal down.*

Early blues was less regular than the 12-bar format. Because folk musicians often perform very informally, simplifying the harmony, embellishing the melody, and freely interpolating extra bars, country blues exhibited great flexibility of form. Once we reach the classic blues of the 1920s, however, we can represent the blues form as a single 12-bar chorus with a strict basic harmonic progression. Within the framework of standard chord changes, we can construct variants. Blues forms can occur in minor keys as well. Listen to Track 11 of CD 1 🄟 for a demonstration of blues changes.

THE BLUES SCALE

Earlier we discussed the major scale but referred to the use of other scales in jazz. One particular form often heard in jazz is the ***blues scale***, which incorporates notes commonly heard in blues melodies. Some of these notes, not part of the major scale, are called ***blue notes***. In many instances, these blue notes suggest pitch inflections or slurred pitches rather than discrete pitches. If, however, we consider blue notes as discrete pitches, we can construct a blues scale (Example I-6).

Music Example I-6
A blues scale can contain blue notes that are slurred pitches.

Sometimes the blues scale has incorporated other pitches. For example, the jazz style bebop, which evolved in the 1940s, featured extensive use of a flatted fifth that can take on the quality of a blue note. More generally, it is possible to inflect any note of the scale in such a way that it becomes a blue note, but the blue third and seventh are by far the most pervasive.

Jazz Performance Terms

Tracks 44–49 of CD 1 🄟 summarize the material we have discussed so far in this introduction. They feature a jazz quintet performing the basic blues form. As we describe these tracks, we will define a few other important jazz terms.

On Track 44 we hear the first blues chorus. Each time a band or soloist plays through the complete changes of a song or of a given chord progression, it is called a *chorus*. For this first chorus, all we hear is the bass player walking and accompanied by the drums. Count the bars of the chorus to follow the 12-bar blues structure.

Continuing to Track 45, the band adds the pianist comping chords for the group's second chorus. *Comping*, probably derived from *accompanying*, is a style of playing in which the pianist provides chords that follow the chord progression but in a rhythmically irregular fashion.

For the third chorus (Track 46), the trumpet player takes solo breaks on bars 1–2, 5–6, and 9–10. *Solo breaks* are moments in which the rhythm stops while the soloist remains featured.

On the fourth chorus (Track 47), the trumpet player and the saxophonist trade twos. *Trading twos, trading fours,* and *trading eights* are improvisational formats in jazz, common since the swing era. In trading twos, for example, each soloist improvises for two bars before the next soloist takes over for two bars. Any number of soloists may participate, but two to four are most typical. Trading solos is often used to create climactic moments in performances. It is also an example of *call-and-response*, a common technique in which players take turns answering one another. In classic call-and-response, a single voice or instrument states a melodic phrase—the *call*—while a group of voices or instruments follows with a responding or completing phrase—the *response*.

Stop time is featured on the fifth chorus (Track 48). In *stop time*, the rhythm section or band punctuates distinct beats, often to accommodate a soloist's improvisation between the band's chords. Here stop time provides a background texture to the saxophone solo.

For the sixth and final chorus (Track 49), the trumpet player provides a background riff while the saxophonist continues to solo. A *riff* is a short melodic idea, usually one to two bars long, which is repeated as the core idea of a musical passage.

Ways of Listening to Jazz

Listening analytically is an important way to broaden your understanding of how jazz works. However, we do not always listen analytically, nor should we. The enjoyment of music need not always be an intellectual activity, but it can be heightened through some understanding of its technical bases.

While much of the focus on listening in this book will be through commentary, it is important to understand that jazz—and all music—can be appreciated through its relationship to culture in general and not just through analysis of the technical bases of the music. This more sociological approach to understanding is emphasized by *ethnomusicology*, which is the study of music in its cultural context. This approach examines the role that music plays within society. For example, in many cultures music is used to accompany religious ceremonies or important social rituals that mark births, weddings, and deaths.

Much of the text in this book emphasizes jazz history and places the music in a cultural perspective, whereas the Listening Guides focus more on the music from a technical perspective. From time to time, you may want to refer to this introduction to clarify points that come up in the Listening Guides.

Key Terms

AABA song form 13

ABAC song form 13

Accompaniment 5

Arpeggiation 6

Articulation 8

Bar 2

Barline 2

Bass 9

Bass clef 4

Beat 2

Blue note 14

Blues 13

Blues form 13

Blues scale 14

Bridge 13

Cadence 12

Call-and-response 15

Chord 5

Chord progression 6

Chorus 15

Clarinet 9

Comping 15

Cornet 8

Drums 10

Duple meter 2

Dynamics 7

Eighth note 3

Ethnomusicology 15

Expression 8

Extension 7

Flats 4

Flugelhorn 8

Form 11

Function 6

Glissando 9

Guitar 11

Half note 3

Harmonic substitution 7

Harmony 5

Head 13

Improvisation 5

Inside playing 7

Interval 3

Irregular meter 2

Key 4

Leap 5

Legato 8

Major key 6

Measure 2

Melody 3

Meter 2

Minor key 6

Modality 6

Notation 4

Note 3

Obbligato 9

Octave 3

Outside playing 7

Percussion instruments 10

Phrase 5

Piano 9

Piano trio 9

Pitch 3

Progression 6

Pulse 2

Quarter note 2

Rhythm 2

Rhythm changes 13

Rhythm section 3

Riff 15

Saxophone 8

Scale 3

Section 12

Seventh chord 6

Sharps 4

Sixteenth note 3

Skip 5

Slash notation 6

Solo break 15

Staccato 8

Staff 2

Step 3

Stop time 15

Substitution 7

Syncopation 3

Tempo 2

Texture 7

Timbre 7

Time signature 2

Tonality 4

Tone 3

Tonic 4

Trading twos, trading fours, or trading eights 15

Transposed 6

Treble clef 2

Triad 5

Triple meter 2

Tritone substitution 7

Trombone 9

Trumpet 8

Walking bass 10

Whole note 3

Wind instruments 8

ROOTS

1

WHAT IS JAZZ? It seems proper to begin our historical discussion of jazz by defining it, but this is a famous dead end: Entire articles have been written on the futility of pinning down the precise meaning of *jazz*. Proposed definitions have failed either because they are too restrictive—overlooking a lot of music we think of as jazz, or too inclusive—calling virtually any kind of music "jazz." Surely Louis Armstrong, the first jazz mega-star, should be able to characterize the music. Yet when asked to define jazz, Armstrong supposedly replied: "If you have to ask, you'll never know."

Jazz is difficult to define, in part because of its complex history, because jazz has African, European, and even Caribbean roots. Although the precise contributions of various cultures and subcultures remain controversial, without their blending jazz would not have come into being. This much is clear: Jazz arose not in Africa, not in Europe, and not in the Caribbean, but in the United States, thanks to the importation of nonnative musical elements into the dominant European culture of U.S. society.

Because African and European cultures have contributed the most to jazz, we begin with a brief examination of these cultures and the elements that they contributed. More specifically, we discuss the following:

- Genres of folk and popular music from the African tradition, including:
    - ▶ Spirituals
    - ▶ Early African-American folk songs

- European culture, including:
    - ▶ Tonality
    - ▶ Instruments
    - ▶ Marches and other important genres

- The rise of minstrelsy and its stereotypes of African-American music

- Ragtime

- The blues

Ragtime and the blues are the direct predecessors of jazz.

To **transcribe** a piece of music is to write in standard, European musical notation what the listener, or transcriber, hears. The transcriber's notated version is called the **transcription**. Transcriptions of the same piece of music can vary widely, depending on the quality of the original sound source, the skill of the transcriber, and what the transcriber chooses to include in the notation. (See the box "The Problem of Transcribing African-American Music" on page 23.)

African-American Music in the Nineteenth Century

The story of African-American music in the nineteenth century can be told only partially. It is the story of the stevedores on the wharves of Savannah, the tobacco pickers in the Piedmont of North Carolina, the cotton pickers on the plantations of rural Alabama, the worshipers at camp meetings in Kentucky, the Methodist ministers of Philadelphia, the oarsmen of the Sea Islands in South Carolina, the dance hall performers of New York, the riverboat minstrels on the Mississippi, and the conservatory-trained musicians of Boston. Most of their music was not written down but transmitted orally from musician to musician. Except for a few collections of *transcriptions*, the only tangible sources of information are diaries, letters, newspapers, and novels, as well as paintings and pictures—but these do not always depict African-American music clearly or reliably.

SOURCES OF MUSICAL DIVERSITY

Countless, mostly nameless individuals contributed to a rich African-American musical heritage before, during, and after the Civil War. This diverse musical culture varied over time and from region to region. There were clear musical differences between the North and the South; among the East, Midwest, and West; between urban and rural areas; and before and after the Civil War. Despite these distinctions, the African-American heritage provided a foundation for jazz when it began to develop around the end of the nineteenth and the beginning of the twentieth centuries.

Much of this musical heritage emerged from African music and culture. The earliest slaves came to the New World at the beginning of the seventeenth century, and the tyranny of slavery continued for more than two hundred years. Uprooted from their homelands, especially from the rain forests of the west coast of Africa— including Senegal, the Guinea coast, and the Niger delta—the slaves witnessed the destruction of their families and the elimination of their well-defined social structures. Nonetheless, many West African musical traditions persevered and ultimately blended with American and Western European traditions.

Geography strongly influenced the degree to which African slaves preserved their musical traditions. In regions where whites lived separately from African Americans, slaves tended to retain their African traditions. For example, the relative inaccessibility of the coastal Sea Islands of Georgia and South Carolina allowed the resident Gullah blacks to preserve several musical as well as linguistic elements from African culture, some of which survive to this day. But in the northeastern United States, where farms were relatively small and the number of slaves fewer, blacks and whites interacted more often. As blacks in the North converted to Christianity and gained literacy and early emancipation, they had more difficulty preserving their African traditions. In contrast, on larger plantations in the Southeast, dependent as they were on large numbers of slaves who lived together in separate quarters, it was possible for some African traditions to survive intact. Furthermore, many owners encouraged slaves to perform their music as well as learn European musical styles.

THE PRESERVATION OF AFRICAN TRADITIONS

When we look at the preservation of African musical traits in the New World, several questions arise: What characteristics of African music took root on American soil?

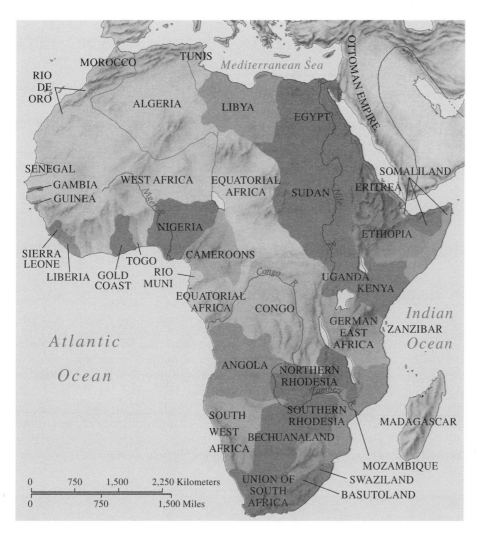

Africa in 1914

How were they preserved, and how were they adapted? More specifically, which of these elements influenced jazz?

Most slaves came to the New World from the tribes of western, sub-Saharan Africa. These tribes exhibited numerous and varying musical cultures in the eighteenth and nineteenth centuries. These cultures were not studied much at the time, but we can assume that the same musically significant traits that exist today in these regions also characterized African music in the eighteenth and nineteenth centuries and therefore must have been part of the musical culture of U.S. slaves. As such, we need to examine twentieth-century African musical cultures to see which African musical features likely contributed to jazz.

Above all, African music today plays an important social function: It accompanies work, forms an essential part of religious and social events, and is often accompanied by dance. Thus African music is highly functional. There are six characteristics shared by the various tribes that distinguish their functional musical cultures from the European tradition:

Call-and-response is a musical procedure in which a single voice or instrument states a melodic phrase—the *call*—and a group of voices or instruments follows with a responding or completing phrase—the *response*.

▶ *Metronomic sense.* African musicians tend to maintain a steady, underlying pulse throughout a performance. The regularity of the beat can be compared to a metronome, a mechanical device that enables musicians to maintain a steady beat while practicing. The dancers' motions generally show the pulse.

▶ *Overlapping call-and-response.* In *call-and-response,* a solo vocalist sings one line (often improvised), then a group responds. In African traditions, the group response tends to overlap the original solo part.

▶ *Off-beat phrasing of melodic accents.* This is the unexpected accenting of weaker notes within the melody, or what many scholars describe as **syncopation**.

▶ *Dominance of percussion.* In African music, percussion instruments are plentiful and used more widely than melodic ones, with some exceptions. The melodic instruments themselves are sometimes played percussively.

▶ *Singing that stresses nasal textures, with bending of pitches and colorful effects.* (This will be described more completely later in this chapter.) These effects are sometimes used to imply more than one musical part (for example, a change between falsetto and natural voice).

▶ *Polyrhythm.* This is an intricate web of rhythms heard among the different parts.

Although the first five attributes of African music are fairly straightforward, polyrhythm is more complex. The rhythmic layering of the different instruments in an African ensemble is typically founded on a single ground beat, which Western ears usually hear as in duple or triple meter. Africans themselves often think of their music's rhythm as projected along a time line in which patterns may be based on large numbers of beats, perhaps as many as twelve. In addition, many of the rhythms arising from this layering can seem independent though they are not played separately. Thus African music is often described as rhythmically polyphonic.

Drummers from Dagomba, Ghana, performing on dondons and gongons

John Miller Chernoff, Pittsburgh.

"Kasuan Kura"

CD **1** Track **50**

The People of Dagomba, Ghana: "Kasuan Kura" (traditional).
Field recording in Ghana by John Miller Chernoff.

This recording and the next two are examples of "field recordings"—which folklorists and ethno-musicologists often make on-site with performers in their familiar cultural settings. An advantage of field recordings for folk material is that scholars are able to capture the works in context. The performers themselves, who very likely are not professionals, may be more comfortable in their usual surroundings than in formal recording studios. As a result, we are likely to obtain freer, less self-conscious performances. A disadvantage of such recordings is that audio quality may suffer. Still, it is certainly better for us to glimpse these pieces in their usual settings.

The Dagomba are from northern Ghana and are known for their sophisticated oral culture. Indeed, oral culture has served the role of professional historian. "Kasuan Kura," for example, is a praise-song, telling the story of an honored ancestor. His name forms the answer in this call-and-response format.

We first hear dondons, or talking drums, whose pitch can be varied by pulling on leather thongs that connect the two drumheads on each drum. We also hear gongons in the ensemble. These are larger drums that have a string stretched over the drumhead to produce a rattle as the drum is played. As the performance develops, the rhythmic relationships between the different types of drums and the singing grow more complex.

0:00   Dondons begin the excerpt, followed closely by gongons. The feeling of the beat is irregular at first, then becomes more regular as the voices enter.

0:12   Voices enter with call-and-response figures. Notice that the response figures remain roughly the same, as is usually the case with a chorus. This type of chorus singing is called *heterophonic*—there is a kind of spontaneous harmony, but not a European-oriented chord progression. A *groove,* or repeating rhythm pattern, underlies the performance, but the dondons engage in a conversation with the lead singer. That is, both dondons and gongons accompany the calls, but usually only gongons accompany the responses.

1:24   The drumming becomes more intense, as does the singing of the leader. Nevertheless, the singers continue with roughly the same answering figures.

We assume that these six traits were true of African music in the eighteenth and nineteenth centuries; certainly, many of these elements appear in African-American music today. Religious and secular music retained the *metronomic sense.* Call-and-response patterns, nearly universal in West African culture, formed the basis of work songs and spirituals in the United States and became a significant component of blues and jazz. African-American music in the nineteenth century retained the offbeat phrasing of melodic accents, a key characteristic that became part of the jazz tradition. African slaves brought their tradition of drumming to the United States. Slave owners, however, suspected that the drums allowed slaves to communicate over long distances. Moreover, drumming and dancing were forbidden by Methodists and Baptists, the Protestant denominations that most actively worked to convert slaves to Christianity. Hence, throughout most if not all of the American South, slave owners outlawed drums and thus eliminated an important percussive element of West African music.

Lacking drums, the slaves adapted in ingenious ways. They used stringed instruments in a percussive manner. They added percussion by clapping and

Metronomic sense is a steady rhythmic pulse, often associated with drums and with music from Africa.

Originally derived from African religious practice, a **ring shout** is a rhythmic dance performed in a circular figure. Worshipers moved counterclockwise while singing spirituals and accompanying themselves by clapping and stamping. The worshipers ingeniously circumvented the prohibition against dancing—strictly speaking, to lift and cross the feet—by shuffling. Some historians describe the ring shout as contributing the essence of African song, dance, and spirit to African-American music.

Polyphony describes music with at least two distinct and simultaneous melodic lines. Another name for a polyphonic texture is *counterpoint*.

Cross-rhythms refer to the performance of simultaneous and contrasting rhythms, such as patterns with duple and triple groupings. By superimposing one rhythmic pattern on another, we create a cross-rhythm.

stamping, for example, when performing the *ring shout* in religious worship. Finally, "patting juba" (clapping, stamping, and slapping thighs) provided percussive dance accompaniment, frequently without any other instruments.

The survival of rhythmic *polyphony* is more difficult to trace. In African music, percussion parts are typically played on different drums and rattles, each with its own rhythm, creating a complex overlay of contrasting patterns. African Americans did not retain this practice in the United States, most likely due to the proscription against drums. Instead, they expressed percussive rhythm in syncopated melodies and *cross-rhythms*. In this way, African rhythmic complexity survived in African-American music.

Clearly, rhythm played a prominent role in defining the African musical aesthetic, and it became crucial in shaping the African-American musical aesthetic as well. In discussing the relationship between West African and African-American music, one writer states:

> The approach to metrical organization with cross-rhythms as the norm, the percussive technique of playing any instrument resulting in an abundance of qualitative accents, the density of musical activity, the inclusion of the environmental factors as part of the musical event, the propensity for certain "buzzylike" musical timbres—all these are African features which have been consistently maintained in Afro-American music.[1]

European Music in the Nineteenth Century

The European tradition remains embedded in jazz. Indeed, throughout jazz history a particular mix of European and African elements often characterized a specific jazz substyle from the earliest days. The three main contributions of European music to jazz were instrumentation, form, and harmony.

INSTRUMENTATION, FORM, AND HARMONY

The **front line** described the lead (melody) instruments in early jazz bands and usually included trumpet (or cornet), trombone, and clarinet. The saxophone came later to jazz.

Many elements of the European tradition contributed to the formation of early jazz. The instruments of early jazz are virtually all European. The *front line* and rhythm section of a typical early jazz band included the following:

MELODY	RHYTHM
Trumpet or cornet	Piano (melodic also)
Clarinet	String bass or tuba
Trombone	Guitar or banjo
	Drums

The saxophone was not commonly heard in early jazz. The **banjo,** which lost favor in subsequent jazz styles, was common in early jazz and most likely has African roots, although its specific origins are controversial.

Despite the prominence of rhythm as a key ingredient of African music, the basic instruments of the jazz drum set—snare drum, bass drum, and cymbals—are those of the European marching band. Pioneering drummers in early jazz bands created the drum set by arranging these instruments so that one person could play them all at once. Modern additions to the basic drum set—gongs, wind chimes, hand drums, and so on—come from cultures the world over.

The European marching or brass band also contributed instrumentation that served as a model for many early jazz bands: We hear in the basic textural layout of the cornet (or trumpet) playing lead melody, the trombone playing countermelody, and the clarinet providing obbligato.

In addition to instrumentation, the most significant European contributions to jazz are its form—that is, the basic layout of the music—and harmony. These elements of the European tradition were transmitted to jazz through nineteenth-century popular songs, marches, and dance music. The basic aspects of form and harmony were discussed in the Introduction.

A constant dialogue between the written European and improvised African traditions runs throughout jazz history. The African musical tradition was oral, but jazz band members performing written arrangements had to be able to read their parts. Some jazz players learned to play "by ear" but then joined bands for which they needed to learn to read music. Such stories are especially common in early jazz.

Early African-American Music

Throughout the eighteenth and nineteenth centuries, African-American music drew on both European and African characteristics and appeared in both sacred and secular settings. This music was communal and woven into the daily rituals of life. The notion of the professional musician was largely unknown (a characteristic typical of folk music), as was the separation between performer and audience that we know today.

Although the music that evolved was rooted in African tradition, it soon took on European elements. Slaves who were called on as musicians to entertain whites at

The Problem of Transcribing African-American Music

Contemporary transcriptions of nineteenth-century African-American folk music emerged slowly in the second half of the century. Three white scholars collaborated in 1867 to produce the first published collection, *Slave Songs of the United States.* With this collection, we see an attempt to translate into European musical notation the African-American music that had, up until that point, been performed and transmitted orally. The process of transcription made clear how different were African-American and European performance practices. Transcription also made clear the limitations of European musical notation for African-American music.

The early transcribers frankly admitted

to the difficulty of notating African-American music. One of them, Lucy McKim Garrison, pointed to the problem of accurately rendering the vocal effects and the rhythmic qualities: "It is difficult to express the entire character of these negro ballads by mere musical notes and signs. The odd turns made in the throat, and the curious rhythmic effect produced by single voices chiming in at different irregular intervals, seem almost as impossible to place on the score as the singing of birds or the tones of an Aeolian Harp."*

Garrison's comments describe a number

* William Francis Allen, Charles Pickard Ware, and Lucy McKim Garrison, *Slave Songs of the United States* (New York: Peter Smith, 1951; reprint, Mineola, NY: Dover, 1995), vi.

of performance practices. The technique of vocal ornamentation, referred to by some writers as "trimming" and what Garrison calls "the odd turns made in the throat," points to a flexibility of interpretation and perhaps even alterations in vocal timbre. Although the transcriptions in the book suggest single-line melodies, Garrison implies that non-unison singing occurred in the original performances that either were not or could not be notated. Another point is that the music of the slaves often featured improvisation, in which the singers, when properly inspired, would alter established melodies or even compose new ones. Transcriptions are at best only an approximation of the actual musical practices.

From *Cabin and Plantation Songs* as sung by students of the Hampton Normal and Agricultural Institute of Virginia—now Hampton Sydney University—and published by G. P. Putnam's Sons in 1875 at the height of Reconstruction following the Civil War. To raise money for their college, the Hampton students toured the country with this booklet. In his introduction, Thomas P. Fenner, head of Hampton's music department, noted that although "slave music is . . . rapidly passing away, [i]t may be that this people who have developed such a wonderful musical sense in their degradation will, in their maturity, produce a composer who could bring a music of the future out of this music of the past." Note the use of black dialect in the lyrics, a feature of much African-American music of the time.

Courtesy Morgan Collection

dances and balls came to know the European tradition. Classified advertisements in newspapers of the period referred to slaves as highly skilled players on European instruments. An advertisement from as early as 1766 called attention to a slave proficient on the French horn; other advertisements announced slaves' skills on the violin or the fife.

Contemporary descriptions of the gatherings of slaves on Sundays and holidays in New Orleans' Place Congo (now called Louis Armstrong Park) reveal the mix of African and European instruments. The ban on drumming throughout much of the South was relaxed for these weekly performances. Performers used the long drums of the Congo, the *ndungu,* as well as other drums struck by hands, feet, or sticks; gourds filled with pebbles or grains of corn; and scrapers made from the jawbones of oxen, horses, or mules. Other instruments included a derivative of the African thumb piano, or *mbira,* which had several reeds stretched across a wooden board, and the four-string **banjo,** an instrument imported by West African slaves from Senegambia. One writer imagines the unique mix as it might have taken place in New Orleans in the mid-1800s:

> The tremendous creative energies released when Kongo-derived traditions combined in New Orleans with those from the equally sophisticated Malian, Nigerian, and Cameroonian traditional civilizations must have been amazing. That does not even take into account the final fillip: the blending of it all with the equally complex mix of musics—French, Spanish, English—in that culturally strategic city.[2]

Today we know very little about African-American music before the eighteenth and early nineteenth centuries. Songs and instrumental pieces passed from one individual to another almost completely through an oral tradition in which performers sang and played by ear. Over many years, as one person taught another, this music and its performance undoubtedly underwent gradual stylistic changes. Unfortunately, these changes have been lost to historians because there is little or no documentation.

CHRISTIANITY, SPIRITUALS, THE RING SHOUT, AND WORK SONGS

As many African-Americans converted to Christianity, they learned Protestant hymns and other religious songs that introduced them to the melodic, formal, and harmonic elements of European music. African-American religious music took on the practice of "lining out" psalms, a European tradition in which a leader read or chanted the psalm verse one or two lines at a time, and the congregation sang back the lines, often elaborating on the original tune. Introduced in New England in the mid-seventeenth century, the practice eventually took root in the rural South and West. Interestingly, although a European tradition, the practice closely resembled the call-and-response patterns of African music.

The first all-black churches appear to have developed near the end of the 1700s, and hymns and *spirituals* replaced the tradition of "lining out" psalms. Choirs or congregations sang the spirituals in the call-and-response form, alternating solo verses with refrain lines. Hymns and spirituals spread not only through church worship but also through open-air camp meetings, where thousands often gathered to worship for days at a time.

Observers at the camp meetings and churches described the use of the West African ring shout, which persisted in Christian ecstatic rituals in the Deep South. One writer witnessed a ring shout in Florida during the 1870s or 1880s:

> The shouters, formed in a ring, men and women alternating, their bodies close together, moved round and round on shuffling feet that never left the floor. With the heel of the right foot they pounded out the fundamental beat of the dance and with their hands clapped out the varying rhythmical accents of the chant; for the music was, in fact, an African chant and the shout an African dance, [a] whole pagan rite transplanted and adapted to Christian worship. Round and round the ring would go. One, two, three, four, five hours, the very monotony of sound and motion inducing an ecstatic frenzy.[3]

Spirituals were African-American songs that arose in the nineteenth century and consisted of religious lyrics with folk melodies. They were often harmonized for vocal choir.

"Daniel" (excerpt)
CD **1** Track **51**

Georgia Sea Island Singers: "Daniel" (traditional). Field recording by Alan Lomax, 1960.
New World Records 278. Willis Proctor, leader; Bessie Jones, Jerome Davis, John Davis, Peter Davis,
Joe Armstrong, Henry Morrison, Ben Ramsay.

The Sea Islands are located off the coast of the eastern United States, extending from Maryland to Florida. Because of their isolation from much of the rest of the country through the mid-twentieth century, these areas featured a vibrant black culture—sometimes called *Gullah*—with a remarkably close connection to the African roots of the inhabitants' ancestors.

An example of this close relationship can be heard in this recording of "Daniel"—a Christian spiritual in the form of a ring shout—as compared with "Kasuan Kura" (CD 1, Track 50). In "Kasuan Kura," we heard African drums accompanying a call-and-response performance by the leader and chorus. We hear a similar relationship in "Daniel," as performed by the Georgia Sea Island Singers. Rather than drums, the Sea Island singers use handclapping. The piece has been influenced by Western tonality as well.

The piece begins directly (0:00) with the leader and his call. The singers respond "Daniel" or "O, Daniel." The leader is shadowed by another singer, who sometimes sings along with him. The chorus response approximates a major triad that suggests a relationship to tonality. The clapping projects a syncopated accompaniment.

Because the piece is undifferentiated regarding form (other than the changing lyric of the call), there are no timing cues in this Listening Guide. Instead, the piece develops the story with each line repeated by the lead singer, followed by the response of the other singers. (Sometimes a line is repeated three times for a total of four calls.) This abbreviated form creates intensity and drive and is appropriate for the highly energetic circle dance that the music of the ring shout accompanies.

Cultural historian Sterling Stuckey has argued that the ring shout was one of the most significant and powerful elements of African culture to be retained in America.[4] In nineteenth-century New Orleans, accounts of voodoo ceremonies—a religion of Dahomean origin—similarly describe a circle dance. Such dances, especially the ring shout, clearly preserved several African musical elements and indicate a nineteenth-century link to jazz, from the "rhythms and blue tonality, through the falsetto break and the call-and-response pattern, to the songs of allusion and even the motions of the African dance."[5]

The link to African traditions is very evident in the ring shout, but the performance of spirituals could also take on characteristics more associated with European music. The European connection became prominent in the later nineteenth century, in particular through the concert tours of the Fisk Jubilee Singers, which began in 1871. Such practices helped establish spirituals as an art form that united African and European characteristics.

LISTENING GUIDE

"Dere's No Hidin' Place Down Dere"

CD **1** Track **52**

Marian Anderson: "Dere's No Hidin' Place Down Dere" (traditional). New York, September 9, 1941.
Marian Anderson, contralto; Franz Rupp, piano; Lawrence Brown, arranger.

With "Dere's No Hidin' Place Down Dere" we hear a more conventional spiritual. The harmony and melody are in the Western tradition. The use of the piano, one of the most important instruments in the Western tradition, together with the solo vocal evokes the atmosphere of a Western art song, particularly as the singer, Marian Anderson, performs with diction and execution that show her extensive training in Western classical music. In fact, Anderson sang with the New York Philharmonic in 1925, studied in Europe, and, in 1955, became the first black singer to appear with New York's Metropolitan Opera. Still, elements of the African and African-American traditions remain, such as the informal change to spoken text, lyrics in dialect ("dere" rather than "there"), and a reminiscence of a call-and-response pattern—all of which help impart a feeling of informality.

0:00	Piano introduction as a two-bar repeated-chord ***vamp***—a repeated melodic or harmonic idea.
0:03	First verse of the spiritual. The piece consists of an eight-bar melody in two four-bar phrases. The beginning of the second phrase (0:10) deviates from the title lyric of the first phrase to explain *why* "Dere's No Hidin' Place Down Dere," then the final two bars return to the title line. Thus, the eight-bar tune projects an ABA form, which, in this small-scale context, is partly reminiscent of the call-and-response pattern.
0:17	Second verse.
0:31	Third verse. Anderson introduces a minor variation on the theme. A broadening of the tempo and the amusing avoidance of the word *hell* bring the piece to an effective close.

Not all African-American music was associated with the church, of course. In rural areas, nonreligious music included occasional songs, field hollers, and work songs. Occasional songs accompanied various aspects of slave life, such as playing games or celebrating holidays. Work songs—nearly universal in African culture—accompanied different types of labor. Field laborers picked tobacco or cotton, threshed rice, husked corn, or harvested sugar cane to the sound of work songs. Up and down the eastern seaboard and on the Ohio and Mississippi rivers, stevedores loaded and unloaded boats and oarsmen rowed in unison to work songs. These songs enabled laborers to synchronize their tasks and movements to the call-and-response pattern. A group leader sang out the main phrases, while the rest of the workers responded together in time with their work. Field hollers were both a form of song and a means of communication; in half-sung, half-shouted language, the worker called for water or asked for help across long distances in the cotton fields.

L I S T E N I N G   G U I D E

"Field Hands' Call"

CD **1**   Track **53**

Annie Grace Horn Dodson: "Field Hands' Call" (traditional). Field Recording (central and western Alabama)
by Harold Courlander, January and February 1950. Folkways P417. Annie Grace Horn Dodson, vocal.

According to Harold Courlander's liner notes to Folkways P417, Annie Dodson's father, Josh Horn, was born a slave. Once free, he became a farmer, and Dodson's field calls are what she remembered hearing as a child on her father's farm in the late nineteenth century. This was an important time in U.S. music: the genesis of ragtime and the blues. Our example of a field hands' call shows the kind of material that may indeed have provided impetus for the blues.

Although performed by a solo singer, there is within Dodson's solo line an internal call-and-response pattern. Later blues artists, perhaps accompanying themselves on guitar, would also provide calls and responses within a solo performance—a practice that is sometimes heard in jazz musicians. Further, Dodson's solo melodic line uses a blue note, contributing to its bluesy effect. If her first note is taken as a tonic (the first note of the scale), the range of her melody extends outward through the second note of the scale to the third note, which is a blue third.

0:00	The call.
0:09	The call repeated.
0:18	The response.
0:25	Return to the call.
0:32	Response.
0:40	Call.
0:49	Response.
0:57	Call.
1:06	Response; for the final response, Dodson extends the phrase somewhat and adds a slight vocal embellishment.

BLUE NOTES AND SYNCOPATION

William Francis Allen, one of the transcribers of *Slave Songs of the United States,* recognized that African-American musicians "seem not infrequently to strike sounds that cannot be precisely represented by the gamut [scale]."[6] To the transcribers' perplexity, the singers used pitches *between* the natural and flatted versions of the third and seventh scale degrees, pitches not heard in the equal-tempered European system. In general, these pitches are often called "neutral" thirds and sevenths; in African-American practice, they are called *blue notes*. (We discussed this briefly in the Introduction.)

Nearly all types of African-American music used these blue notes—work songs, field hollers, ballads, spirituals, and hymns—yet historians still debate their origin and performance. Among the most intriguing theories is that African slaves manipulated their traditional and largely pentatonic (five-tone) melodies to fit the seven-note diatonic Western scale by adding blue notes.

A few of the transcriptions in *Slave Songs of the United States* show both natural and flatted thirds and sevenths in the same composition. The transcribers offer one song in a major key and an alternative version in a minor key, showing a further variability between major/minor thirds and sevenths. Even so, most songs appeared notated in a major key with many of their melodies emphasizing the five-note scale, which is found in folk music around the world.

The opening lines of the spiritual "Nobody Knows the Trouble I've Had" are built entirely on the B♭ pentatonic scale (see Music Examples 1-1 and 1-2).

Music Example 1-1
The B♭ pentatonic scale.

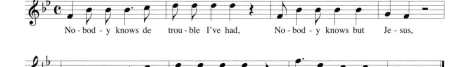

No - bod - y knows de   trou - ble I've had,   No - bod - y knows but   Je - sus,

No - bod - y knows de   trou - ble I've had.   Glo - ry   hal - le - lu!

Music Example 1-2
Measures 1–8 from "Nobody Knows the Trouble I've Had."

Notice that this spiritual features syncopation: The pattern eighth note–quarter note–eighth note (♪ ♩ ♪) occurs at the beginning of the third measure. Moreover, in practice the first, second, and fifth measures may also be performed with the same syncopated rhythm. In effect, this pattern enables the performer to avoid emphasizing the second beat. A faster version of syncopation was also common, featuring a sixteenth–eighth–sixteenth note rhythm:

Whatever the origins of these kinds of syncopation, minstrel songs adopted them, and they gradually became signature elements of the rhythmic language of ragtime at the turn of the twentieth century.

Syncopation is considered a small-scale rhythmic feature in a piece of music. In general, there are several different levels of rhythmic activity in a jazz piece, from the note-to-note progression to the overall form of a work. Examining these levels helps clarify the mixture of the African and European traditions:

▶ At the note-to-note level, we hear clear African influences: melodic accents fall in unexpected places, the music shows syncopated movement, and unusual vocal and instrumental timbres are evident.

▶ At the level of meter and phrase, we hear both European and African tendencies. The harmonic flow is European in origin, yet the syncopation, cross-rhythms, and call-and-response forms are largely of African origin.

▶ Finally, at the level of form, the European influence is strongest in such features as sectional structure, tonality, and instrumentation.

Minstrelsy

African-American folk music joined with the dominant European musical culture around the middle of the nineteenth century in the minstrel show—a hodgepodge of songs, comic sketches, dances, and melodrama. *Minstrelsy* was especially significant as the first distinctively U.S. musical genre, reflecting a decisive blend of European and African-American traditions.

Minstrel shows became a widespread form of entertainment in the United States between 1845 and 1900, especially on the emerging frontier. Initially, minstrel shows were performed by white troupes in blackface. But beginning in 1865, authentic black companies toured the United States and Europe, with the performers still appearing in blackface because audiences expected it.

On the one hand, minstrel shows were overtly derogatory, based on negative stereotypes of black characters such as the city slicker, sometimes called the "Zip Coon," or the lazy, shiftless Jim Crow. On the other hand, the success of this entertainment showed white America's deep fascination with African-American culture and allowed blacks the possibility of careers as professional entertainers.

Minstrel shows featured instruments that blacks played in the South—the banjo, tambourines, and bone-clappers. These instruments constituted American music's first rhythm section—the constant underlying beat that was derived from the African tradition and has given jazz and American popular music much of its characteristic sound. Nevertheless, it is difficult to gauge whether the music in minstrelsy was authentically African-American or was as caricatured as the minstrel figures themselves. Historian Thomas Riis notes:

> Trying to imagine sounds heard long ago, with only verbal descriptions to go on, obviously presents problems. We can be sure, however, that where black performers and composers were active a strand of authenticity resided. The vigorous, unsentimental tunes of 1840s minstrelsy, only rarely identified with known black composers, present persistent syncopations, asymmetrical note groups, and the call-and-response pattern. These features all point to the retention of African elements, although the evidence for direct African provenance is slim.[7]

One of the most famous minstrel figures was James Bland (1854–1911), a black performer who gained international fame in minstrelsy and who composed several famous songs, including "Carry Me Back to Old Virginny" and "Oh, Dem Golden Slippers." Many of the most famous songs of the first professional U.S. songwriter, Stephen Foster (1826–1864)—including "Old Folks at Home" ("Swanee River"), "Old Black Joe," and "My Old Kentucky Home"—were minstrel-type songs that incorporated black dialect.

Despite the initial exclusion of blacks from minstrelsy and the later pejorative portrayals of blacks, minstrel shows introduced many whites to black

Minstrelsy was a form of musical theater and variety show that flourished in the nineteenth century. Traveling troupes performed songs, dances, and skits based on caricatures of African Americans. Performed by both blacks and whites in blackface, minstrelsy is often considered the first distinctively U.S. musical genre.

Courtesy Morgan Collection

An early photograph of a minstrel from *Brainard's Ragtime Collection,* published in 1899.

music; provided employment for black actors, dancers, and musicians; and helped popularize various black dances. Among the most memorable dances was the *cakewalk*, which achieved considerable popularity with whites. Bert Williams, a well-known black entertainer and dancer in the early twentieth century, taught the dance to Edward VII of England.

In the late nineteenth century, minstrelsy was replaced by vaudeville, a touring entertainment form similar to minstrelsy but without self-contained troupes. Vaudeville often included much ethnic humor that we would now regard as offensive, but its stereotyping of African Americans was less overt than in minstrelsy. Great vaudeville performers, such as the blues singer Bessie Smith (discussed later in this chapter), helped popularize jazz in its early years.

Urban musical theater also developed out of minstrelsy. Turn-of-the-century New York developed a flourishing black theater community that included the composers Bob Cole, James Weldon Johnson, Ernest Hogan, and Will Marion Cook.

The *cakewalk* was more an exhibition than a dance. At the end of the evening, the most talented couple won a cake—hence the dance's name. Some believed that the exaggerated walking step was an imitation of the way members of the white "high society" comported themselves.

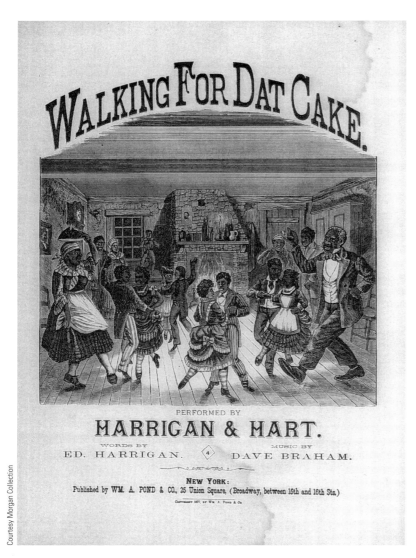

Courtesy Morgan Collection

Published in 1877, this sheet music is an early reference to the cakewalk. Here is a portion of the lyrics:

Twas down at Aunty Jackson's, there was a big reception
Of high-tone colored people full of sweet affection.
Such singing and such dancing, we made the ceiling shake,
The cream of all the evening was a'walking for dat cake.

Notice that although the art is not that skillful, it appears to be an honest attempt to capture the dance without undue caricature.

They built many of their works on African-American themes, and their songs served as important precursors to ragtime. With the decline of minstrelsy, many composers turned to ragtime and vaudeville. Yet the composers just listed also continued to work in black musical theater and greatly contributed to the rising consciousness of African-American culture.

Ragtime

The 1893 World's Fair in Chicago marked the beginning of the popular fascination with *ragtime.* For the first time, thousands of Americans heard a new type of music associated with black, itinerant piano players. Adapting African polyrhythms to piano, these players developed the use of syncopation that would become one of ragtime's central features. "Syncopation," Irving Berlin maintained, "is nothing but another name for ragtime."[8] As a sober observer of the London *Times* said, "In American slang to 'rag' a melody is to syncopate a normally regular tune."[9] The traditional ragtime piano figures, which often pivot around fixed notes, may have been taken from banjo playing. In time, Scott Joplin and other ragtime composers would formalize the genre to create the works we now call "classic ragtime."

Beginning in the 1890s and lasting two decades, ragtime swept the nation. The success of ragtime was unparalleled. It was especially significant because, for the first time, a specifically black musical genre entered and dominated the U.S. mainstream while also achieving notable popularity in Europe. Commercial ragtime made entrepreneurial fortunes as publishing houses for ragtime compositions sprang up throughout U.S. towns and cities. The first manual of ragtime performance, *Ben Harney's Ragtime Instructor,* appeared in 1897. Two years later "Maple Leaf Rag"— Scott Joplin's second published rag—became the most celebrated ragtime composition for piano.

During its heyday, however, ragtime was not strictly associated with piano music. Early ragtime probably derived from songs taken from minstrel shows and urban musical theater. Although many of these songs were unsyncopated, the early ragtime pianists worked up arrangements for solo piano or for piano and voice. The syncopated manner in which these songs were performed came to be described as ragtime.

Although the idea of "ragging" melodies was first associated with songs and solo piano, ragtime was quickly taken up by bands. In the late nineteenth century, brass bands were extremely common throughout the country and sometimes acted as a locality's cultural focus. A small city might have three or four bands; an average town usually had at least one. In larger cities such as New Orleans, there were numerous bands, both black and white, that competed through concerts, funerals, dances, parades, and other venues. The southern black bands served as training ensembles for many early jazz musicians and often performed marches from the white repertory (see Chapter 2). As ragtime grew in popularity, the practice of ragging marches— especially those by John Philip Sousa—became common. (Sousa, the country's premier march composer, was not especially fond of ragtime but did include it in his band concerts.) The sectional design and the key relationships of classic ragtime were taken from marches, and many ragtime composers, including Scott Joplin, named some of their rags "marches" or indicated "march tempo" as the speed and rhythm of a work.

Proficient ragtime pianists were expected to improvise ragtime versions of popular songs; and in the Ragtime Championship of the World competition, held in New York in 1900, the three semifinalists were required to improvise a version of the popular period piece "All Coons Look Alike to Me." (This song is not as racist as its title suggests. It is sung by a black woman lamenting the loss of her lover; because other black men do not interest her, they all "look alike.")

Ragtime versions of other types of music were also popular. *Ben Harney's Ragtime Instructor* included syncopated versions of hymns and folksongs. Patriotic songs were not immune; several pianists featured syncopated versions of "The Star-Spangled Banner" in their repertories. In another practice, called "ragging the classics," performers created ragtime renditions of classical compositions—Felix Mendelssohn's "Wedding March" was a particular favorite.

These practices show that ragtime began as an *improvised* music—a style of performance—and later became a written music, including both instrumentals and ragtime songs. The early players improvised, but the masters of ragtime worked over their pieces with much attention to compositional detail. Aside from Scott Joplin, whose life and work we shall examine, the finest instrumental ragtime composers included James Scott, Joseph Lamb, and Artie Matthews.

SCOTT JOPLIN

The solo piano rags of Scott Joplin became the pinnacle of the classic ragtime canon. Born in Texarkana, Texas, in 1868, Joplin worked as an itinerant musician in the Mississippi valley during his teens, settled in Sedalia, Missouri, in 1895, then relocated in St. Louis. In 1907 he moved to New York, where he died in 1917.

The success of "Maple Leaf Rag" allowed the composer to live comfortably after its publication in 1899 by John Stark, a music store owner trying to capitalize on the rising popularity of ragtime. Remarkably, Stark offered Joplin a publishing contract for "Maple Leaf" that included a penny royalty for each copy sold. This was a generous arrangement at the time: Although such contracts are commonplace now, a fair agreement between a white publisher and a black artist was virtually unheard of in the 1890s. The fame Joplin achieved through "Maple Leaf" increased the sales of his other rags. Joplin's music returned to vogue in the 1970s with the success of the movie *The Sting*, which featured several of Joplin's rags, including "The Entertainer."

A well-known photograph of Scott Joplin, c. 1900, dressed to reflect the respectability that he sought for his music.

L I S T E N I N G   G U I D E

"Maple Leaf Rag" (excerpt)

CD **1**   Track **54**

Scott Joplin: "Maple Leaf Rag" (Joplin). April 1916. Connorized piano roll 10265. Scott Joplin, piano.

Scott Joplin's "Maple Leaf Rag" quickly became a ragtime classic. Like many of the works of the ragtime piano repertory, the music was composed and written down for publication. Its jaunty rhythms were characteristic of the best ragtime compositions. As in most ragtime piano works, we hear the left hand usually alternating a bass note and a chord, while the right hand plays a syncopated melody.

The form of ragtime was derived from the march. In "Maple Leaf Rag" the form is AABBACCDD. The excerpt here includes only the first AAB sections, which in rags are called *strains*. The recording here is from a piano roll performed by Scott Joplin himself.

A strain (repeated)

0:00   The opening A strain is sixteen bars long. Typical for ragtime works, the left hand keeps time and provides the harmony, while the right hand plays syncopated "ragged" melodies. The section is repeated at 0:23.

B strain

0:45   The left hand is even more regular in the B strain, usually alternating a bass note with a chord. In addition, the right-hand part is more active in this section than in the previous section and is played in a higher register on the piano.

An early edition of "Maple Leaf Rag" by Scott Joplin, the "King of Ragtime writers," published in 1899. The sheet music cover advertises more recent Joplin rags. Notice that the Stark Music Company bills itself as "publishers of ragtime that is different" but does not show a picture of "King" Joplin on the cover—a cautious omission that was to continue for the next several decades.

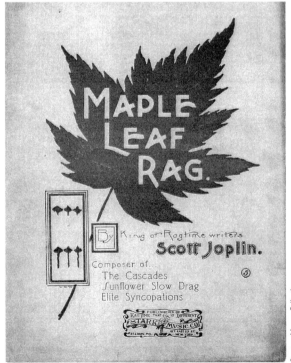

Courtesy Morgan Collection

Joplin sought to elevate ragtime to an art form. His earliest training included the study of European harmony. Later, his published ragtime compositions artfully combined the African-American tradition with techniques, forms, and principles derived from European music.

In addition to writing piano rags, Joplin incorporated ragtime within larger, more classically oriented musical forms, including the ballet *Ragtime Dance* and two operas. The first of these operas, *A Guest of Honor,* is now lost. Joplin financed a performance of the second, *Treemonisha,* in 1915, but it was unsuccessful. These works anticipated later attempts to merge European classical forms with jazz, as we shall see with the works of jazzmen James P. Johnson and Duke Ellington.

RAGTIME'S RELATIONSHIP TO JAZZ

Was *ragtime* just another name for early jazz? The boundaries between them were certainly never fixed. Whatever their differences, ragtime and early jazz mightily influenced each other during the early twentieth century, as the following time-line shows.

1885(?)–1900	1900–1917	1917–1930
Ragtime developing (almost entirely improvised)	**Ragtime flourishing** (written and improvised)	**Ragtime quickly declining**
	Jazz developing (largely improvised)	**Jazz flourishing** (largely improvised, also written)

Although the ragtimers must have improvised to some extent, evidence is generally lacking; in recorded ragtime, multiple strains often repeat their melodies verbatim. In part, this may have been because fairly well-known ensembles were the first to record and were expected to perform a "straight" version—the version they had made popular. More informal ragtime was surely improvised at least in part because so many of its practitioners played by ear.

As further evidence of the ragtime-jazz symbiosis, both forms were persistently associated with dancing. Published ragtime pieces frequently listed dances for the work: the cakewalk, the two-step, the slow drag, and the march. From this we can argue that jazz not only replaced ragtime but also *became* early jazz at a later stage. We can also argue the other side—that ragtime and jazz were distinct. According to this reasoning, a stricter, more vertical sense of rhythm characterized ragtime performance, while jazz rhythm was looser and more fluid. Furthermore, jazz incorporated more improvisation as a matter of course. Without further evidence, the debate remains open.

After 1913 jazz—or at least the use of the term—began to gain in popularity over ragtime. The works of the classic ragtime composers showed a shift toward simpler, sometimes fewer, syncopations. The use of dotted rhythms became commonplace, bringing about what scholar Edward A. Berlin described as the "erosion" of classic ragtime.[10] These dotted rhythms provided one of the links from ragtime to the more fluid rhythmic language of early jazz. Recordings of jazz-oriented treatments of ragtime compositions—such as Jelly Roll Morton's interpretation of

Joplin's "Maple Leaf Rag"—made clear the practice of "swinging" the eighth notes, that is, playing them either as dotted eighth–sixteenth notes or as triplets, as suggested in Music Example 1-3.

Music Example 1-3
Swinging the eighth notes.

LISTENING GUIDE

"Maple Leaf Rag" (excerpt)
CD **1**   Track **55**

Jelly Roll Morton: "Maple Leaf Rag" (Joplin). Washington, D.C., June 1938. Library of Congress Recordings
Disc 1654A ("Morton Style"). Jelly Roll Morton, piano.

A comparison of Jelly Roll Morton's version of the "Maple Leaf Rag" with Scott Joplin's piano-roll version of the same composition provides a fascinating glimpse into the shift from ragtime (Joplin) to early jazz (Morton). Not only is Morton's early jazz version slower, it is much lighter and has a looser, more swinging feel characteristic of jazz. This is in contrast to the very regular pulse heard in ragtime. Morton also incorporates more improvisation into his version by departing frequently from the written version of the piece. Morton's left hand is highly active, with syncopated melodic ideas that might be played by a trombone in the front line of a New Orleans band. Throughout you can hear Morton keeping time by tapping his foot.

Introduction and A strain

0:00   In contrast to the Joplin version, Morton includes an introduction. This eight-measure introduction is taken from the second half of the A strain.

0:12   The A strain begins. Listen for the difference in rhythmic feel compared with the Joplin version. The A strain is played only once (perhaps because eight measures of it have already been heard in the introduction).

B strain and return of the A strain

0:33   As in the A strain, the B strain is played only once here. Notice the active left hand throughout.

0:54   Morton embellishes his return to the A strain, compared with what he played at the beginning of the piece (0:12). The left hand plays less of the traditional ragtime style (alternating bass and chord), saving that for the following C strain.

C section (trio)

1:16   Morton plays this section in a more driving, hotter style. Listen for the more consistent ragtime left hand that alternates bass note and chord. He repeats the C section at 1:36.

The decline of ragtime paralleled, or gave rise to, early jazz styles that made greater use of these looser rhythms.

Additionally, the style of solo jazz piano known as *stride* evolved directly from ragtime. Stride pianists used left-hand techniques similar to those of ragtime but treated the melodic right hand in a freer manner with added blues elements. Pianists James P. Johnson, Fats Waller, Count Basie, and Duke Ellington were brought up in this style of piano playing, which owes its origins to ragtime but which clearly became part of the jazz tradition.

The Blues

The addition of blues to ragtime helped create jazz. More precisely, ragtime—both in its classic piano form and in songs and marches "ragged" by ensembles—gradually metamorphosed into jazz. It did so through an internal evolution alongside the infusion of the blues. Because the addition of this final ingredient was so significant, some claim that to improvise with authority and passion in the jazz tradition requires the ability to play the blues well.

An active musical genre to this day, the ***blues*** has roots in the nineteenth century. By the 1870s and 1880s, the diverse, formerly African slaves living in the United States had become African Americans and, thanks to emancipation, were now free citizens. The blues—from spirituals and work songs, through hollers and shouts—jumped out to celebrate black entrance into a world less repressive, less harsh, and more optimistic—but also far more uncertain, still tragic, and full of deprivation. The unique character of the blues projected sadness, guilt, and sometimes despair but also humor and bawdiness. Ironically, the blues could express joy, although this was less characteristic of the form as a whole.

The origins of the blues can be traced to the African-American secular and sacred music of the late nineteenth century. However, the classic form of the genre coalesced from its various antecedents rather suddenly at the dawn of the twentieth century; not until shortly after 1900 do examples of blues forms or written descriptions of what sounds to our ears like the blues surface. As discussed in the Introduction, the classic blues featured an AAB lyric pattern that fit regular chord changes:

> *The blues is a lowdown, achin' heart disease,*
> *The blues is a lowdown, achin' heart disease,*
> *It's like consumption, killin' you by degrees.*[11]

Where and how was the blues first performed? The music was originally vocal, usually accompanied by guitar, piano, or harmonica (although instrumentalists also played the blues). In the country blues tradition, singers often accompanied themselves. Groups of performers would gather informally in what were known as jook joints, barrelhouses, honky-tonks, or chock houses. These were simple wooden structures with a bar for drinking, perhaps a floor for dancing, and a few stools and tables. The "bandstand" might consist of a battered piano in the corner—used not only for the blues but also for ragtime. The musicians themselves were often non-professionals who substituted improvised, homemade instruments for the real thing: a washboard played with thimble became a snare drum, a jug blown on became a bass. The audience added clapping, call-and-response lines, and encouragement. From such humble beginnings grew what was to become one of the greatest and most influential folk traditions of the United States.

While local variations and styles of the blues proliferated throughout the country, the Mississippi Delta and Texas spawned the greatest number of early blues singers. As first performed by these folk artists, the blues was free in form, befitting its origins in the African-American vernacular tradition. Many of the early blues singers sang about a life of pain and despair and of the need to endure. Indeed, the great authority of their performances arose from vivid descriptions of tragic hardship yielding to the necessity of song. Among the great country blues performers were Charley Patton and Robert Johnson.

Unfortunately, the earliest recordings of the blues were not made in any quantity until the 1920s. By then the country blues form had acquired the professional sound of the classic blues as heard in the work of such artists as the incomparable Bessie Smith. Many of the best-known blues performers from the 1920s got their start in vaudeville, where most of the blues singers were women. These performers often recorded with jazz musicians, although blues singers were soon to be differentiated from jazz singers. Still, through their recordings we can view the blues as the first jazz vocal style.

Mamie Smith made the first blues recording, "Crazy Blues," for OKeh/Phonola records in 1920. Within a few weeks it sold more than 75,000 copies in Harlem alone and precipitated the blues craze and a demand for music by and for blacks. *Variety* magazine noted that "colored singers and playing artists are riding to fame and fortune with the current popular demand for 'blues' disk recordings."

A *race record* was a recording, usually of jazz or blues, typically performed by and marketed to African Americans.

These special recordings, known as *race records*, targeted black audiences that had expanded in the black neighborhoods of urban centers, particularly New York City. Throughout the twenties, recording companies such as OKeh, Paramount, and Vocalion released numerous blues and blues-oriented vocal recordings.

Until the end of the 1920s at least, many great jazz musicians worked as accompanists for blues singers. Record companies called on cornetists such as Louis Armstrong and Joe Smith, pianists such as Fletcher Henderson and James P. Johnson, and many others to make blues recordings. Later, the Dixieland style adapted various blues vocal techniques. Certainly, the interaction between the instrumentalists and the singers on these early blues recordings brought to bear a significant blues influence on instrumental jazz.

Ultimately, we can trace the story of the blues from its country origins in field hollers, spirituals, and folk ballads to the jook joints, circuses, minstrel shows, and vaudeville stages and finally to the center of U.S. song-writing in New York's Tin Pan Alley. No other artist more embodied the professional emergence of the blues than the composer and collector of several important blues compositions, W. C. Handy.

As a youngster, William Christopher Handy (1873–1958) was lucky to receive a solid education in his hometown of Florence, Alabama. Discouraged from pursuing music by his father, who was a minister, Handy felt that "becoming a musician would be like selling my soul to the devil."[12] After early successes, Handy moved to New York, where he worked to popularize the blues and devoted himself to the cause of black music and its recognition. Although he eventually became known as the "Father of the Blues," this was an overstatement.

Courtesy Morgan Collection

Composer W. C. Handy published this 1916 edition of "Saint Louis Blues." Unlike most composers of the time, Handy retained copyright and started his own publishing company. Notice that the music hall performer (later, the recording artist) was invariably pictured on early sheet music. The cityscape in the background is St. Louis; notice the riverboat approaching the bridge. The large cube in the foreground is a bale of cotton among cotton plants.

However, he did compose the first genuine blues to be published, "Memphis Blues" (1912), then followed its success with the most famous blues tune of all, "St. Louis Blues" (1914), as well as "Beale Street Blues" (1916). With such works, the various forms of the blues became fairly standardized and provided an interesting contrast to the looser performance practices of the original country blues.

BESSIE SMITH

In the early 1920s, before microphones, blues singers establishing their reputations needed volume and projection. Of all the fine blues singers of this period, the greatest was Bessie Smith (1894–1937). She is probably the most beloved of all classic blues singers. The richness and breadth of her tone are evident even on her oldest recordings. Her first blues recordings for Columbia, "Down-Hearted Blues" and "Gulf Coast Blues," were hits in 1923, but by the end of the decade her popularity waned as classic blues vocalists found themselves less in demand. Almost forgotten, she began to work in minor musical shows that toured the country. She was on such a tour when she died in a car crash in Clarksdale, Mississippi. With Smith's work we can begin to detect the qualities that later differentiated the jazz, pop, and blues vocal idioms.

An elegant publicity portrait of Bessie Smith (CD 1, Track 56) at about age thirty. Later images of Smith showed her dressed more flamboyantly, in keeping with her vocal power and musical standing as "Empress of the Blues."

Courtesy Morgan Collection

"Back Water Blues"
CD **1** Track **56**

Bessie Smith and James P. Johnson: "Back Water Blues" (Smith). Columbia 14195-D, New York, February 17, 1927. Smith, vocal; Johnson, piano.

James P. Johnson was Bessie Smith's favorite accompanist. Their superb performance of "Back Water Blues" is one of their finest joint efforts. The form and performance of the piece could not be simpler, but the power of the expression is clear throughout. Johnson's accompaniment provides a steady and beautifully wrought commentary to Smith's story.

After a two-bar introduction, the song unfolds in seven choruses of 12-bar blues. Practice counting the 12-bar choruses, with four beats to the bar, to determine where each chorus begins and ends.

Introduction—2 bars

0:00   Count this piece in a moderate four beats to the bar. Johnson provides a rolling introductory vamp before Smith comes in for her first chorus.

1st chorus

0:04   Smith's phrases generally fill the first two bars of each four-bar phrase. Johnson fills the remaining two bars. The first chorus sets the scene with its depiction of five days of rain.

2nd chorus

0:32   The song turns more personal. Note the despair of the line "Can't even get outta my door."

3rd chorus

1:00   The story continues with the description of the boat picking up Smith with her clothes to escape the flood.

4th chorus

1:28   A return to the nature description of the first chorus.

1:34   Note how Johnson's expressive bass answers Smith's phrases.

5th chorus

1:54   A return to the personal as Smith looks down on her flooded house.

6th chorus

2:21   "The blues" calls Smith to reflect on her loss.

7th chorus

2:49   Complete despair: Smith "can't move no more." Johnson ends the piece without a tag or any extra musical statement.

CHARACTERISTICS OF EARLY JAZZ SINGING

In the performance of "Back Water Blues," we can point to three features of Bessie Smith's style that will remain characteristic of subsequent jazz singing:

▶ Loosely constructed phrasing

▶ Offbeat, syncopated placement of notes and lyrics

▶ Use of slides, blue notes, and other vocal embellishments

First, in jazz singing, the phrasing of the song must be loose. For example, sometimes the phrase may begin at the beginning of the measure, the downbeat. At other times, the phrase may begin as a pickup—that is, at the end of the preceding bar. But the singer may move the phrase so that it fits its original placement only approximately. This practice of varying the placement of the phrase relative to the beat gives a free quality to the performance and contrasts with the on-the-beat feel sometimes heard in non-jazz singing. In later styles, beginning in the 1930s, such singers as Billie Holiday delayed the placement of the melody as much as a full bar. Slight delays and embellishments, as heard in Smith, are typical of 1920s blues singing. The loose placement of the phrase has become an element heard in much popular-song singing in our own time.

Second, jazz and blues singing is characterized by the offbeat, syncopated placement of important notes and their lyrics. Jazz singing epitomizes the freedom of loose phrasing allied with inventive syncopation.

Third, jazz and blues singers use slides, blue notes, and other melodic pitch inflections and ornaments. Although these features appear in all popular singing, they are especially prominent in the blues. In general, constant modification and the embellishment of various phrases play important roles in distinguishing jazz and blues singing from pop singing, which is usually less ornamental.

With the popularization of the blues in the 1920s, composers began to write songs in the 12-bar blues style. For example, during the swing era, blues pianists of the South and the Southwest developed a driving style of piano playing called boogie woogie that became extremely popular throughout the country. Such important songs as "In the Mood" (Garland) and "One O'Clock Jump" (Basie) were in fact blues tunes with riffs based on the melodic figures of the boogie-woogie pianists. Later, in such songs as "Rock Around the Clock" (Freedman-DeKnight) and "Blue Suede Shoes" (Perkins), we can hear blues harmony, form, and phrasing. These features of early rock offer evidence of its evolution from the blues and R&B (rhythm and blues).

In addition to the standard 12-bar blues form, by far the most common in jazz, there are 8- and 16-bar forms whose harmonic structures are somewhat more unpredictable. Although modern composers have written blues tunes with highly irregular structures, much classic blues retains the simpler 12-bar, rhyming lyric structure.

With ragtime's popularity waning in the late teens and the blues thriving as a separate genre, the necessary conditions were in place for jazz to become the primary musical medium of popular culture. The next chapter examines this breakthrough, which takes place largely during the late teens and the 1920s and is fully completed by the 1930s.

Key Terms

Questions and Topics for Discussion

1. How do the European and African musical traditions differ? Contrast both musical and cultural qualities.

2. In what ways was ragtime fresh and innovative?

3. What are some of the characteristics of the blues? How do these characteristics relate to the African tradition?

4. What are the important differences between blues and ragtime?

5. In what ways can ragtime be seen as a blend of African and European traditions?

EARLY JAZZ

2

IN THIS CHAPTER, we explore jazz as it became a mainstream music in the late teens and twenties, particularly in and around the cities of New Orleans, Chicago, and New York. Despite controversies surrounding the origins of jazz, which this chapter considers, the city of New Orleans figures prominently in any discussion of the music's early history. Much of what made early jazz exciting was the innovative way players approached traditional instruments, producing effects that were considered tawdry by traditionalists but brilliant and creative by early jazz fans.

The Shift from Ragtime to Jazz

New Orleans is popularly considered the birthplace of jazz, but the entire picture is much more complex and has produced a significant and ongoing controversy among historians. Some contend that jazz crystallized in New Orleans. Other scholars argue that jazzlike styles were evolving throughout the country but New Orleans musicians were the first to break through with the Dixieland style. Both positions are partially true. During the teens and twenties, in a decisive step toward the emergence of jazz, some prominent New Orleans musicians moved to Chicago, taking jazz styles with them. But jazz styles also developed in other urban centers such as New York and Kansas City. In fact, jazz styles developed wherever musicians, encouraged by the spontaneous performance practices of ragtime and turn-of-the-century popular music, took jazzlike liberties.

The origins of the word *jazz* are murky. The word first appeared in print in 1913 in the baseball column of a San Francisco newspaper, where it seems to have meant "pep" or "energy." The word gained currency by 1917, especially after the first recording labeled as jazz (from the Original Dixieland Jazz Band, to be discussed shortly). The etymology of the word *jazz* continues to be obscure. Some have pointed to a French origin from the verb *jaser,* which means to chatter or gossip; others have said that the word is a synonym for sexual intercourse. It is unlikely that the origins of its name will ever be precisely determined.

Around 1920, musicians performed and wrote compositions that highlighted the ragtime-to-jazz shift. Older New Orleans musicians played "jazz" based on the formal structure of ragtime. During the 1920s, however, musicians began moving away from the ragtime format. Instead of relying on multiple 16-bar strains, they took the popular songs that emerged from publishing houses, record companies, and musical theater and used them as vehicles for jazz—casting them primarily in a 32-bar AABA format. In addition, many of the New Orleans and Chicago musicians made the 12-bar blues a staple of their repertory. Jazz musicians such as Louis Armstrong and Fletcher Henderson accompanied blues singers on recordings as well. Lawrence Gushee summarizes these changes:

> Also obvious in the years after World War I was a shift from tunes with many articulated sections (several strains differing in character and often in key, along with introductions, transitions, interludes, codas) to the verse-chorus format, with the verse often disappearing in instrumental performance. The older pieces were routines that had to be played as such; the newer ones were repetitions of a chord progression that cried out for elaboration and enlivening through ingenious arrangement or solo extemporization.[1]

Despite the practice of improvisation in urban areas throughout the country, jazz musicians from New Orleans were especially skilled in "elaboration" or "extemporization." At the same time, these pioneers, both black and white, incorporated elements of the blues tradition in their treatment of ragtime forms. The next section describes the fertile musical environment of New Orleans, the "Crescent City."

New Orleans

By all accounts, music was omnipresent in New Orleans during the first two decades of the twentieth century. Anecdotes and remembrances by those who were present describe a constant flood of outdoor and indoor social events, nearly all of which required music. The legendary red-light district of Storyville, the section of town set off for legalized prostitution in 1897, flourished until the U.S. Navy Department closed it in 1917. Storyville's bordellos provided steady employment for pianists. The bars and sporting houses of "the District," as Storyville was known to musicians, hired dozens of bands. Clarinetist Louis "Big Eye" Nelson recalled that the four saloons on the corner of Iberville and Franklin had eight bands among them, and the saloons "changed bands like you change underclothes."[2]

Another participant, bassist Pops Foster, described the explosive musical activity in the city:

> There were always twenty-five or thirty bands going around New Orleans. There was all kinds of work for musicians from birthday parties to funerals. Out at the lake [Lake Ponchartrain] they had some bands in the day and others at night; Milneberg was really jumping. There were a lot of string trios around playing street corners, fish frys, lawn parties, and private parties. The piano players like Drag Nasty, Black Pete, Sore Dick, and Tony Jackson were playing the whorehouses. . . . There were tonks like Real Tom Anderson's at Rampart and Canal, and Tom Anderson's Annex at Iberville and Basin Street. Out in the country, like Breakaway, Louisiana, or Bay St. Louis, Mississippi, you played dances, fairs, picnics, and barbecues. We had plenty of fun together and there was music everywhere.[3]

Enshrined in the history of New Orleans jazz are the brass bands. The influence of brass bands and early jazz dance bands was probably reciprocal. Historian William J. Shafer suggests that the brass band influenced jazz bands in three ways: repertory, instrumentation, and technique. More specifically, the roles of the instruments in the brass band, in which the cornet performs the melody, the clarinet plays piccolo-like elaborations, and the trombone provides an independent voice of harmony notes and glissandi, suggest an origin for the front line of Dixieland instrumentation.[4]

In their role in New Orleans funerals, brass bands made a prominent contribution to jazz lore. New Orleans had numerous fraternal organizations—clubs, lodges, and benevolent associations—that would pay for the funeral of one of their members and provide a band to accompany the funeral procession to and from the burial site. One of New Orleans's most renowned drummers, Baby Dodds, described this tradition:

> Of course we played other numbers coming back from funerals. We'd play the same popular numbers that we used to play with dance bands. And the purpose was this: As the family and people went to the graveyard to bury one of their loved ones, we'd play a funeral march. It was pretty sad, and it put a feeling of weeping in their hearts and minds and when they left there we didn't want them to hear that going home. It became a tradition to play jazzy numbers going back to make the relatives and friends cast off their sadness. And the people along the streets used to dance to the music. I used to follow those parades myself, long before I ever thought of becoming a drummer. The jazz played after New Orleans funerals didn't show any lack of respect for the person being buried. It rather showed their people that we wanted them to be happy.[5]

CHARLES "BUDDY" BOLDEN

Many New Orleans musicians attributed the genesis of the rougher, improvised style to a single person: black cornetist Charles "Buddy" Bolden. Bolden never recorded, but he may have been an important influence on the emerging jazz style. For instance, see how one musician wistfully described the generational change between the older music readers and the younger improvisers of his time:

> Bolden cause all that. . . . He cause these younger Creoles, men like [Sidney] Bechet and [Freddie] Keppard, to have a different style altogether from the old heads like [Lorenzo] Tio and [Manuel] Perez. I don't know how they do it. . . . Can't tell you what's there on the paper, but just play the hell out of it.[6]

Buddy Bolden and his band, c. 1900. *Left to right:* Jimmie Johnson, bass; Buddy Bolden, cornet; Brock Mumford, guitar; Willie Cornish, valve trombone; Frank Lewis, clarinet; Willie Warner, clarinet. This famous photograph has been the subject of controversy, with various writers claiming that some of the players are holding their instruments incorrectly. Musicians have been known to do this as a practical joke.

Courtesy Frank Driggs Collection

Bolden was born in 1877. A plasterer by trade, he formed a band around 1895 that performed throughout New Orleans in the saloons of Storyville, in the dance halls, and in the parks. Said to be heard for several miles, the volume of Bolden's horn was legendary. Cornetist Peter Bocage claimed that Bolden "was powerful. Plenty of power. He had a good style in the blues and all that stuff."[7] Bolden was a heavy drinker, and his bouts of insanity led to his institutionalization in 1907. He died in a state institution in Jackson, Louisiana, in 1931.

Bolden's style of improvisation was based on "ragging" the melodies. As Wallace Collins noted, "He'd take one note [of the original] and put two or three to it."[8] Bolden was particularly remembered for playing the blues, and henceforth this folk idiom, imported from the Mississippi Delta, became a primary source for New Orleans musicians.

Was Bolden the first New Orleans jazz musician, the first "hot" jazz cornetist? That is probably impossible to answer. Banjoist Johnny St. Cyr claimed that Bolden inserted the same "hot lick" in each of his compositions but that other bands, such as the Golden Rule Band, were playing in a hotter style. (A *lick* or *formula* is a worked-out melodic idea that fits a common chord progression.) Clearly Bolden's six-piece band, along with his use of a ragged, improvised style and a reliance on the blues, strongly influenced an emerging New Orleans jazz style, instrumentation, and repertory.

SIDNEY BECHET

Although many, if not most, of the early woodwind players played clarinet, the saxophone did appear during the early jazz period. Sidney Bechet (1897–1959) began as a clarinetist, but he took on the soprano saxophone as his primary instrument and became one of its early virtuoso soloists.

Bechet's style on both clarinet and soprano saxophone was unique and unforgettable. The sound was rich and woody, modulated by a quick and surprisingly wide *vibrato*. On the clarinet, Bechet tended to be demure, whereas on the soprano sax he was more experimental and freewheeling.

Bechet was possibly the first jazz musician to be recognized as first-rate by the musical establishment. In one of the most famous pronouncements in jazz history, Swiss conductor Ernest Ansermet hailed a 1919 performance of Bechet's in Europe by referring to him as an "artist of genius."[9] Some historians interpret Ansermet's recognition of Bechet as evidence that Europeans accorded jazz respectability before Americans at home did. The actual story is more complex because numerous U.S. critics throughout the 1920s wrote of the greatness of jazz. Still, the Ansermet review is significant because it came from one of the most important musicians in Europe and probably represented the first high praise for artistic quality in a jazz performance and a jazz musician.

Returning to the United States in the early 1920s, Bechet recorded important sessions with Louis Armstrong in groups organized by pianist-composer and music publisher Clarence Williams (c. 1893–1965). At that time, Bechet was more established than Armstrong, but the latter's emerging excellence created a tension in the band that led to such fine recordings as "Mandy, Make Up Your Mind" (1924) and two versions of "Cake Walking Babies (from Home)" (1924 and 1925).

Vibrato is a method of varying the pitch frequency of a note, producing a wavering sound. It is heard mostly on wind instruments, strings, and vocals.

JELLY ROLL MORTON

One of the most influential of New Orleans musicians was a pianist and composer-arranger named Lemott Ferdinand Joseph "Jelly Roll" Morton (1890–1941). A pool hustler, braggart, and "ladies' man," he often made a living from gambling and pimping, which were far more lucrative than playing the piano. He was also a Creole of Color with a mixed ethnic background that included both black and white culture. (See the box "Creoles of Color" on page 48.) During the 1920s, Morton cut classic recordings in Chicago, including superb piano solos and the best-arranged ensemble numbers of early jazz. In his ensemble work, principally with the Red Hot Peppers' recordings of the mid-1920s, Morton shows a deft awareness of the balance between improvisation and worked-out arrangement. Because of this gift, Morton was undoubtedly the finest composer-arranger in early jazz and remains among the best in jazz to this day.

The wide variety of music Morton played points to the complexity of early jazz evolution. In a series of interviews recorded by folklorist Alan Lomax in 1938, Morton discussed playing not only rags, blues, and stomps but also selections from light opera, popular songs, and dances such as quadrilles. Morton also claimed to have invented jazz in 1902. Although this is an exaggeration, Morton's performance on a series of recordings produced by Alan Lomax for the Library of Congress (CD 1, Track 55)

Creoles of Color

Creoles of Color were people of mixed black and white ancestry who throughout the nineteenth century enjoyed a privileged status above that of blacks. Creoles of Color (as distinguished from the Creoles who were French-speaking people of white ancestry) formed a professional, skilled class and were usually well educated. Some Creoles of Color even owned slaves. Most of the Creoles of Color lived in downtown New Orleans in what is now known as the French Quarter. By comparison, the blacks of New Orleans lived uptown above Canal Street and were primarily unskilled workers. Throughout the 1880s, however, whites enacted increasingly restrictive legislation against the Creoles of Color and gradually reduced their status. By 1894 the segregation code removed the final legal distinctions between Creoles of Color and blacks. From that point on, Creoles of Color were segregated along with blacks.

Copyright © CORBIS

Jelly Roll Morton (CD 1, Track 55), the self-styled "inventor" of jazz, pictured here c. 1923. Morton was one of the most significant composer-arrangers and pianists to have emerged from New Orleans.

provides convincing evidence that he was part of the cutting edge of ragtime and early jazz musicians.[10] He was among the first pianists to transform traditional ragtime figures into a more linear jazz style. His informal performances of "Maple Leaf Rag" (from the Library of Congress recordings) demonstrate the liberties most early improvising pianists took with written compositions. These performances also reveal the close relationship between ragtime and early jazz.

Morton's early solo recordings for Gennett between 1923 and 1924 remain classics, equal in quality to the famous sides he soon recorded with the Red Hot Peppers. Throughout the 1920s, he recorded voluminously, both solos and small-band arrangements. During the 1930s, unable or unwilling to update his style to swing, he commanded less and less attention. When he died in 1941, relatively few people remembered him.

Some of Morton's performances include what he called the "Spanish tinge," which he claimed was an essential component of jazz. The Spanish tinge referred to the use of Latin American dance rhythms, which appear even in some ragtime works and in W. C. Handy's "St. Louis Blues." They are used to great effect by Morton in his solo piano recordings of "New Orleans Joys" (1923) and "Mamanita" (1924). Such works represent early examples of the fusion of Latin music and jazz, a trend we discuss further in Chapter 4.

Jelly's Last Jam

As one of the great characters in jazz history, Morton inspired a controversial Broadway show in the mid-1990s called *Jelly's Last Jam*. The show dramatized Morton's background as a Creole of Color who sought to deny the importance of his black heritage.

It is in fact true that Morton took pains to emphasize his French ancestry, but *Jelly's Last Jam* displayed an anachronistic understanding of the complexities of racial rela-tions. One of the greatest musicians in jazz history was reduced to a bigoted stereotype on the basis of late-twentieth-century atti-tudes and ethnic pride. While the difficulties of racial issues in jazz are dramatized by Morton's multiethnic background, his contri-bution to jazz must be considered on its own merits and in its own time period. We briefly explore issues of race and authenticity in jazz in future chapters.

The Evolution of the Early Jazz Band

Jazz ensembles evolved from different types of groups, including dance bands, brass bands, and string bands. As pointed out in Chapter 1, numerous ensembles featured three horns—usually trumpet, trombone, and clarinet; three rhythm players—drums, bass, or tuba; and a chordal instrument—piano, banjo, or guitar. Naturally, there were exceptions. For example, King Oliver's Creole Jazz Band featured the two cornets of Oliver and Louis Armstrong. And even though we associate the tuba with the bass voice in early jazz, the string bass was also common because it blended better with the violins of the New Orleans string bands. We even see a string bass in the only extant picture of the Buddy Bolden group (see page 46).

The early jazz style with the standard six- or seven-piece ensemble was called Dixieland, making clear its New Orleans origins. Although earlier prejazz bands probably featured melodies played in unison, perhaps by clarinet and violin, the jazz style moved toward polyphonic improvisation, in which the horns improvised simultaneously, creating an intricate web of rhythmic and melodic activity.

As defined in Chapter 1, *polyphony* describes distinct, simultaneous parts. Applying the term to the sound of the New Orleans ensemble, however, would be slightly inaccurate. Normally, polyphony refers to equally important parts or melodies, but in New Orleans style the lead cornet dominates the ensemble texture while the other instruments play parts similar to accompaniments.

The ensemble frequently used the technique of *breaks,* in which the band stopped and allowed a soloist to play alone but without losing the beat. In his dis-cussions of jazz, Jelly Roll Morton made it clear how important breaks were: "[W]ithout breaks and without clean breaks and without beautiful ideas in breaks, you don't even need to think about doing anything else, you haven't got a jazz band and you can't play jazz."[11]

Breaks not only featured soloists but also provided textural relief from the busy sound of collective improvisation. As soloists' improvisational prowess increased through the 1920s, collective improvisation became less frequent, especially in the highly competitive urban musical centers of Chicago and New York.

By the end of the late 1920s, as jazz developed in the major cities, some bands had as many as twelve or more players. Saxophones became common in these larger bands. In fact, the use of the saxophone in jazz in the late 1920s was an adaptation of its presence in earlier dance bands. These larger bands developed into swing bands, which we will discuss in Chapter 3.

Both large and small bands contrasted the texture of the ensemble versus soloists, who often improvised. However, it is important to distinguish our current conception of spontaneous improvisation from what occurred in early jazz. Listening to alternate takes of jazz recordings from the twenties confirms that "improvised" solos were in fact often worked out and repeated from take to take. Soloists most likely duplicated their efforts in live performances as well. Nonetheless, as the twenties proceeded, improvisation as we understand it was typically associated with "hot" style and became more often the norm. Hot soloists even played with more-commercial orchestras, adding spice to their often-conservative arrangements.

The 1920s also show a general shift from melodic to harmonic improvisation. At the beginning of the decade, so-called improvised solos often closely adhered to the melody of the composition, occasionally embellishing it. By the end of the decade, soloists were developing improvisational methods that reflected the harmonic framework of the composition. The development of individual soloists and their improvisational expertise gradually shifted the focus of jazz away from ensemble playing to music that heightened the importance of the individual soloist. As jazz historian Martin Williams wrote, this made jazz "a soloist's art."[12]

The Exodus from New Orleans

During the late teens, many of the best New Orleans musicians began leaving the city. It has been traditionally thought that the 1917 closing of Storyville, the well-known red-light district, cut down employment opportunities for New Orleans musicians, causing their departure, but this factor has probably been overstated. In fact, many musicians left earlier.

Musicians were probably drawn away from New Orleans by the allure of the road or the steadier employment conditions in bigger cities. The trombonist Kid Ory, whose New Orleans band had included many of the top musicians in the city (such as Louis Armstrong, King Oliver, Jimmie Noone, and Johnny Dodds), left for Los Angeles in 1919. (Ory's 1922 Los Angeles recording as the leader of Spikes' Seven Pods of Pepper was the first record cut by a black New Orleans band.) Joe "King" Oliver moved to Chicago in 1918, bringing with him many first-rate New Orleans musicians. White bands such as the Brown Brothers, the New Orleans Rhythm Kings, and the Original Dixieland Jazz Band caught the spotlight of national recognition after leaving New Orleans.

Many New Orleans musicians, of course, chose to stay in the Crescent City. Listeners and critics normally refer to the music associated with New Orleans—that is, small instrumental groups marked by collective improvisation—as New Orleans jazz or traditional jazz. The term *Dixieland jazz* is also used, although this term is

New Orleans jazz, often called *Dixieland*, originated in New Orleans and flourished in the late 1910s and 1920s. The New Orleans jazz band often had a front line of trumpet or cornet, trombone, and clarinet, accompanied by a rhythm section of piano, guitar or banjo, bass, and drums.

now often used to refer to music performed by white musicians. Throughout the 1920s and 1930s, New Orleans jazz was eclipsed by later developments that altered the musical style and instrumentation, although some of its repertory was retained.

The 1940s saw a revival of New Orleans jazz and the discovery—or rediscovery—of many of the original players. With the New Orleans revival, several of the players present in New Orleans during the inception of jazz— including Jimmie Noone, Baby Dodds, and Sidney Bechet—enjoyed a second career of performing and recording.

New Orleans jazz is still played today. There are entire newspapers devoted to New Orleans jazz, and numerous players specializing in the style continue to find work. In 1961, Preservation Hall was established in New Orleans to help focus attention on the contributions of the city to the founding of jazz. The Preservation Hall Jazz Band continues to tour worldwide and is probably the most prominent ensemble devoted to keeping the New Orleans tradition alive.

The Original Dixieland Jazz Band (ODJB) (CD 1, Track 57) formed in 1916 and published this song in 1921. Notice the billing that the band gives itself and the instrumentation. Sheet music promoted a star or band by featuring their publicity photographs.

The Migration North

The exodus of New Orleans jazz musicians was part of a much larger trend known as the Great Migration, in which many blacks abandoned rural life in the South for urban life in the North. The most important reason behind the Great Migration was probably the availability of city jobs that paid a fair wage. For example, Henry Ford had invented the automobile assembly line in 1914 and needed workers to manufacture the first mass-produced automobile—his Model T Fords. He guaranteed $5 a day—an astonishing wage at the time. As a result of opportunities like this, nearly half a million blacks moved from the South to the North between 1916 and 1919, the largest internal migration in the history of the United States.

Between 1910 and 1920, more than 65,000 blacks emigrated from the southern states of Louisiana, Mississippi, Alabama, Arkansas, and Texas to Chicago alone. Most northern cities developed black sections because whites refused to have blacks as neighbors. The presence of blacks and black neighborhoods changed the urban entertainment industry across the country. In Chicago, for example, the entertainment community responded enthusiastically to the resulting demand for black music: Cabarets and nightclubs sprang up along the South Side and created a glittering urban nightlife full of music for listening and, especially, dancing.

The newly transplanted black population could spend an evening seeing floor shows, dancing, and hearing live music at any number of dance halls. Chicago's so-called black-and-tan clubs allowed more interracial mingling than the clubs in New York did. Whites could take in the nightlife, and—important to the development of *Chicago jazz*—white musicians could hear the black bands. South Side clubs such as

Chicago jazz is a type of New Orleans–style jazz created by Chicago musicians in the 1920s.

the Elite #1 held up to 400 customers. According to one newspaper account, "The entertainers and the orchestra always hit it up pretty lively during evening hours."[13]

In 1914 the Dreamland Cafe opened with a capacity of 800 people. Even larger was the Royal Gardens Cafe, later renamed the Lincoln Gardens, on Thirty-First Street. This club sported a huge spotlighted mirror ball suspended from the ceiling and reflecting glittering light over the dancers. Other clubs that hosted live music during the 1920s include the Plantation Cafe, allegedly controlled by the Capone syndicate, and the Sunset Cafe, just across the street from the Plantation.

The enactment in 1919 of the Prohibition Amendment to the Constitution, which outlawed the sale of alcoholic beverages throughout the country, encouraged connections between nightlife and the underworld. Because Chicago was one of the principal centers of organized crime in the 1920s, Prohibition did little to curtail the nightlife or the consumption of alcohol in South Side bars and cabarets. Instead, organized crime expanded its smuggling and distribution networks to satisfy the demand for liquor. Despite alcohol's illegality, it was easily available in nightclubs, cabarets, and *speakeasies,* in which most of the jazz players of the time found ready employment.

Chicago's many performance opportunities attracted New Orleans musicians. Through extended engagements at cabarets and dance halls, they transplanted their music to a much more sophisticated venue. No longer were the musicians playing for street parades, fish fries, and the small saloons and wooden dance halls of New Orleans. Abandoning the open-air, folksy quality of New Orleans music, they adapted to the urbane musical professionalism of Chicago. The extended engagements and higher level of musical competition produced two important results:

▶ The creation of distinct ensembles with their own characteristic arrangements

▶ The development of individual, improvisational skill

The competition on the Chicago scene required a higher level of virtuosity from the players than before. Up-tempo compositions were expected. Banjoist Johnny St. Cyr recalled that "the Chicago bands played only fast tempo . . . the fastest numbers played by old New Orleans bands were slower than . . . the Chicago tempo."[14] In the push for moral respectability in Prohibition-era Chicago, organizations such as the Juvenile Protection Agency urged that fast tempos would eliminate "immoral," slower dances like the toddle and the shimmy. As a result, even the more respectable *sweet* white dance orchestras cultivated brisk tempos.

A *speakeasy* was a Prohibition-era nightclub in which liquor was sold illegally.

Courtesy Morgan Collection

Prohibition, which made the sale and public consumption of alcohol illegal throughout the United States, began on January 16, 1920. But Americans bought liquor illegally from smugglers and gangsters, hid it in their cellars, made their own "bathtub gin," and headed to speakeasies to enjoy lively jazz bands. Notice that the cover of this sheet music, published in 1919 in anticipation of Prohibition, features black and white hands.

Sweet bands played less syncopated, slower pieces, such as ballads and popular songs. *Hot bands* featured faster tempos and dramatic solo and group performances, usually with more improvisation than sweet bands had.

The Advent of Jazz Recording

Sound recordings began as a novelty and were not taken very seriously at first because their primary function in the late teens and early twenties was to publicize a band's live performances. As quality improved and dissemination broadened, however, recordings became a decisive step toward national prominence for artists and the popularizing of their work. They also became the most important evidence for later historians trying to present a coherent story of jazz. Yet, because bands that were physically present near the recording centers of New York and Chicago would naturally have had the opportunity to record first, such recordings taken out of context may present historians with a distorted view of how early jazz crystallized.

Until 1925, recordings were made acoustically instead of electrically. Musicians played into a large horn with a tapered end that connected to a cutting stylus. This stylus cut a groove into wax that covered a disc or cylinder. With this somewhat crude process, sound reproduction often suffered, but we must be thankful for the recordings we have. Jazz was the first musical genre to be so documented in its entirety.

By 1925, the advent of electric recording had improved sound fidelity. This method used microphones to capture the sound. At the standard speed of 78 rpm (revolutions per minute), recordings were normally about three minutes long for each song and remained so until long-playing records (LPs with 33⅓ rpm) appeared in the late 1940s.

Changes from ragtime to jazz appeared on recordings beginning around 1914. James Reese Europe's Society Orchestra, based in New York, performed music influenced by ragtime. Europe's orchestra accompanied the dance team of Irene and Vernon Castle, who demonstrated several new dances—the fox-trot, tango, and maxixe. Europe's 1914 recordings feature ragtime numbers, often played with violin lead, that seem well worked out and planned. By the time of Europe's 1919 recordings of the 369th Infantry ("Hell Fighters") Band, improvised breaks within the multiple-strain compositions show the growing influence of the New Orleans style. (Recall Morton's comment about breaks being a defining quality of jazz.)

THE ODJB AND THE FIRST JAZZ RECORDING

According to anecdotal legend, cornetist Freddie Keppard was the first New Orleans jazz musician given the opportunity to record. He turned down the offer for fear that others would steal his music. Instead, in early 1917 Victor Records released the first jazz record with Nick LaRocca, white cornetist and bandleader of the Original Dixieland Jazz Band (ODJB). The ODJB recorded two pieces, "Livery Stable Blues" and "Dixie(land) Jass Band One Step." These included humorous barnyard effects, with clarinetist Larry Shields crowing and cornetist Nick LaRocca imitating a horse's whinny. A white band from New Orleans, the ODJB achieved popularity performing at Schiller's Cafe in Chicago and Reisenweber's Restaurant in New York. The group, which included Shields, LaRocca, Tony Sbarbaro on drums, Eddie Edwards on trombone, and Henry Ragas on piano, brought the New Orleans style to national prominence. The brash and energetic barnyard effects of these pieces also made jazz synonymous with novelty or slapstick music.

After the ODJB's appearance at Reisenweber's, the band recorded prolifically through 1923 and helped spread the jazz craze outside the United States. They appeared in London in 1919—even performing for the royal family—then afterward in Paris. During the mid-1920s, the group broke up, but they later tried a comeback in 1936. Although they made several recordings for Victor, they never fully reestablished themselves.

Part of the novelty of early jazz bands such as the ODJB rested with the public's perception of a performance built on completely spontaneous improvisation. Bands played up their inability to read music and increased the mystique of the new music. For example, LaRocca quipped, "I don't know how many pianists we tried before we found one who couldn't read music."[15] Despite the band's pose of musical naiveté, they played repeated sections of compositions virtually note for note. A comparison of alternative versions of the same compositions reveals that the ODJB consistently played the same memorized arrangements for years.

L I S T E N I N G   G U I D E

"Tiger Rag"
CD 1 Track 57

Original Dixieland Jazz Band: "Tiger Rag" (Nick LaRocca). Victor 18472. New York, March 25, 1918.
Dominic James "Nick" LaRocca, cornet; Eddie "Daddy" Edwards, trombone; Lawrence "Larry" Shields, clarinet; Henry W. Ragas, piano; Antonio "Tony" Sbarbaro, drums.

"Tiger Rag" is probably the most famous traditional jazz composition, a piece that originated in the oral tradition of New Orleans music. (To highlight its continuity in the jazz tradition, this is the first of several performances of "Tiger Rag" on our two-CD set.) The ODJB recording of 1918 is one of the most famous of the early recordings and very much helped to popularize the piece. At the same time, it was one of the hit records that helped make the ODJB well known.

A strain (8 bars, repeated)

0:00   Without introduction, the piece begins right at the A strain for the opening eight-bar section. The instruments all play together, with the cornet taking the lead. The key is B♭ major.

0:08   Repeat of the eight-bar A strain.

B strain (8 bars)

0:15   The second strain acts as a kind of bridge between the repeated A strain and the return of the A strain. This second strain is in stop time. That is, the accompanying instruments play short repeated chords behind the soloist. The clarinet offers glissandos during the breaks in the rhythm.

A strain (8 bars)

0:23   Repeat of the A section.

C strain (32 bars, as C1 and C2)

0:31   At the C strain, the music changes key. As is typical in rags, marches, and other music associated with traditional jazz, the music moves to the subdominant (IV, i.e., E♭ major). The strain features clarinet breaks throughout and is divided into two equal 16-bar sections, C1 and C2.

0:46   Beginning of the second part of the C strain (C2), which is also 16 bars. In C2, the chord progression changes, but the music remains in the same key and finishes with a conclusive cadence.

D strain (32 bars), 1st chorus

1:01   The D strain is the most famous of the "Tiger Rag" sections. The music changes key again: this time to A♭ major, the subdominant of the preceding E♭ major. The strain divides into 16 + 16.

The first time through the strain, all the instruments play together, but you may be able to hear Sbarbaro with extra syncopated hits to the woodblock. The end of the first 16-bar half is punctuated by a clarinet break.

1:17   Second half of the D strain.

D strain (32 bars), 2nd chorus

1:32   The cornet and the trombone join in a repeated figure that provides a background for the more freewheeling clarinet riding above them. Again, this first half ends with a clarinet break. The cornet-trombone figure anticipates the "Hold That Tiger!" melody that will be featured in the third chorus.

1:47   The second half of the D strain. Toward the end of the strain, the trumpet and the trombone join the clarinet in a drive to the cadence as a conclusion to the chorus.

D strain (32 bars), 3rd chorus

2:02   For the D strain, third time, the trombone is featured with the famous lip glissando down to the low note (the tonic A♭) that initiates the chorus lyric ("Hold That Tiger!"), which is played instrumentally by the cornet and the clarinet. Yet again, the clarinet marks the halfway point of the chorus with a break.

2:18   The second half of the D strain. Toward the end of the strain, the trumpet and the trombone again join the clarinet in a drive to the cadence as a conclusion to the chorus.

D strain (32 bars), 4th (out) chorus

2:33   For the out (or final) chorus, the band picks up the intensity and improvises together. The cornet begins with a repeated, syncopated three-note figure. The clarinet again marks the halfway point of the chorus with a break.

2:48   The second half of the out chorus. At its conclusion, a short *tag* is added.

Even James Reese Europe's orchestra maintained a pose of musical illiteracy, despite the fact that they were all highly trained players. As William Howland Kenney points out:

> Orchestra leader James Reese Europe, in order to maintain the illusion of the "naturally gifted" black musician, would rehearse his band on stock arrangements, leave the scores behind, and, when taking requests for these thoroughly rehearsed tunes, ask customers to whistle a few bars, and then "confer" with the musicians "in order to work it out with the boys."[16]

In the early 1920s, numerous white bands in the tradition of the ODJB—such as the Louisiana Five, the Original New Orleans Jazz Band (with pianist Jimmy Durante), and the New Orleans Rhythm Kings (NORK)—issued recordings with the spirit and instrumentation of the ODJB. Many of these sides helped establish the Dixieland repertory. "Tin Roof Blues," recorded by the NORK for Gennett on March 13, 1923, is an early example of the excellence of some of these white groups. The rise of dance as a social craze augmented Dixieland's popularity and brought about a proliferation of jazz-influenced dance-band records by small groups as well as hotel-ballroom orchestras.

The year 1923, a seminal time for instrumental jazz recording, witnessed releases by King Oliver's Creole Jazz Band—the first recordings by a black Chicago jazz band. Gennett Records was setting out to enlarge its catalog of race records, and Oliver's band traveled from Chicago to Richmond, Indiana, to record nine numbers. (Drummer Baby Dodds later recalled that the band recorded all nine tunes in one day because none of them had a place to stay in Richmond.) That same year, Jelly Roll Morton produced the first interracial jazz recording by recording with the New Orleans Rhythm Kings. The band recorded several of Morton's own pieces, including "Wolverine Blues" and "Mr. Jelly Lord."

These early recordings led to the wide dissemination of jazz on a national scale and allowed musicians anywhere to imitate the solo and ensemble styles of New Orleans. Aspiring jazz musicians could now model themselves not only on local players but also on famous players' recordings; as a result, records helped break down or soften regional differences in jazz. Dispersed through phonograph players, jukeboxes, and eventually radio broadcasts, jazz became a nationwide phenomenon. Throughout the decade, the music evolved rapidly through both live performances and countless recordings.

King Oliver and the Creole Jazz Band

Joe Oliver's arrival on the Chicago scene in 1918 brought the flourishing of New Orleans music there to a climax. In 1920, he put together his own band, which played in California before returning to Chicago in 1922 and beginning an extended engagement at the Lincoln Gardens in June. His band, billed as King Oliver's Creole Jazz Band, featured first-rank New Orleans players—Johnny Dodds on clarinet, his brother Baby Dodds on drums, Honore Dutrey on trombone, and Bill Johnson on double bass and banjo. The pianist, Lil Hardin, was from Memphis, Tennessee. Oliver augmented his own cornet when he sent for cornetist Louis Armstrong a month into the Lincoln Gardens engagement. The popularity and success of the group earned Oliver the nickname "King."

The band recorded prodigiously—forty-three sides for the OKeh, Columbia, Gennett, and Paramount labels in 1923 alone. These recordings are important because they are some of the earliest and best works in the history of jazz. There were original compositions by Oliver, Armstrong, and Hardin, but also works by New Orleans musicians A. J. Piron and Alphonse Picou.

Oliver's fine personal performances greatly influenced the jazz cornet style of the times. He altered the sound of his instrument with *mutes*, often creating a wah-wah effect. In addition to mutes, he used cups and glasses to change the horn's tone. When Louis Armstrong joined them, the group became renowned for the breaks both cornetists seemingly improvised. According to a famous anecdote, Oliver in fact would silently finger the upcoming break so Armstrong could play along with him "spontaneously."

The group performed in a tightly knit fashion, with collective improvisation among the melody instruments. Their recordings are probably at best only an approximation of the group's live performance. For example, Baby Dodds was required to keep time on woodblocks instead of playing his usual drums. Certainly the three- to four-minute length of the recordings did little to capture the group's live sound—one listener described a live performance of "High Society" that ran to forty minutes! Although such reports are likely exaggerated, the band's live improvi-

Mutes are devices played in or over the bells of brass instruments to alter their tone. Different mutes create different kinds of effects, but a muted horn is usually less brilliant than an "open" one. Listen to the Audio Primer CD, Tracks 13, 14, 15, 23, and 24, for muted brass sounds.

Copyright © Bettmann/CORBIS

Joe "King" Oliver and his Creole Jazz Band (CD 1, Track 58) pose in their studio in Chicago, c. 1922. The band, which had a life span of just four years, was one of the most influential early jazz bands, and it became the launching pad for Louis Armstrong's brilliant career. Left to right, the members are Johnny Dodds, clarinet; Baby Dodds, drums; Honore Dutrey, trombone; Louis Armstrong, second cornet; King Oliver, lead cornet; Lil Hardin, piano; and Bill Johnson, banjo.

sations must have lasted longer than what we hear on their recordings. It is unfortunate that we cannot hear precisely how they did it.

Through their recordings and live performances, the group was profoundly influential, with a highly integrated ensemble sound that was more than the sum of its parts. Hoping to become jazz musicians, white teenagers were sometimes permitted into the clubs and became infatuated by the level of musicianship. Banjoist Eddie Condon attested to the powerful influence of the band when he and cornetist Jimmy McPartland heard them at the Lincoln Gardens: "Oliver and Louis [Armstrong] would roll on and on, piling up choruses, with the rhythm section building the beat until the whole thing got inside your head and blew your brains out. . . . McPartland and I were immobilized; the music poured into us like daylight running down a dark hole."[17]

After his initial successes, Oliver later led a group called the Dixie Syncopators, a ten-piece band with a reed section of two to three saxophones and arrangements that reflected a smoother and more refined commercial dance-band sound. The Syncopators held the gig at the Plantation Cafe until the club was bombed in 1927, a victim of gangster violence. After a two-week stint at the Savoy in New York, the band broke up, but Oliver remained in the city. Ailing, with gum problems that affected his playing, he continued to record and play as a leader, but his final recording was made on February 18, 1931. Despite his success in Chicago during the 1920s, Oliver's popularity had waned. After touring with a ten- and eleven-piece band for the next five years, he worked as a pool hall janitor in Savannah, Georgia, and died there of a stroke in 1938.

The late-1920s recordings of King Oliver show the trend toward more-arranged jazz, a trend that progressed through the decade. Louis Armstrong and, more conspicuously, the large New York ensembles of Fletcher Henderson and Duke Ellington continued to challenge the freewheeling New Orleans style.

"Dippermouth Blues"

CD 1   Track 58

King Oliver's Creole Jazz Band: "Dippermouth Blues" (Oliver). Richmond, Indiana, April 6, 1923. Gennett 5123.
King Oliver, leader and cornet; Louis Armstrong, cornet; Johnny Dodds, clarinet; Honore Dutrey, trombone;
Lil Hardin, piano; Bill Johnson, banjo and vocal break; Baby Dodds, drums.

"Dippermouth Blues," an example of New Orleans jazz, is one of King Oliver's finest recordings and probably his most influential cornet solo. Many cornet and trumpet players copied this solo throughout the 1920s. The New Orleans style is apt to sound cluttered, even a little chaotic at first, because of the thickness of the sound and the exuberance of its hot style. After several listenings, however, the three or four lead instrumental parts of the ensemble grow clearer and their distinct functions within the dense texture begin to separate.

When the entire New Orleans ensemble plays, the cornet carries the main melody. In Oliver's band, Louis Armstrong (playing second cornet) either harmonized the lead or added a **countermelody**. The trombone played a countermelody below the cornets, much like a melodic bass line, while the clarinet played an obbligato above the cornets. The obbligato, usually containing more notes than the cornet parts, was often quite virtuosic. The rhythm section in Oliver's band consisted of piano, drums, and banjo. In "Dippermouth Blues," the entire performance is structured as a series of 12-bar blues choruses that are arranged for various combinations of instruments.

Introduction

0:00   "Dippermouth Blues" begins with a four-bar introduction. The lead instruments all play an introductory figure together. The second chorus begins at 0:21.

Ensemble—1st 2 choruses

0:05   After a short pause, the main body of the piece begins. The rhythm section initiates a driving, on-the-beat pattern. Both the first and second choruses are played in classic New Orleans fashion: The horns' functions are separated as described above, while the rhythm section parts are accompanimental.

Clarinet solo—2 choruses

0:36   The clarinet solo plays two choruses in stop time; the rhythm instruments and the accompanying horns play a simple figure to accompany the soloist. The stop time figure heard in "Dippermouth Blues" consists of repeated groups of three chords, one on each beat, with a pause on the fourth beat. The second chorus begins at 0:51.

Ensemble—1 chorus

1:07   The entire ensemble plays a single chorus.

Oliver cornet solo—3 choruses

1:22   Oliver's three-chorus solo follows, accompanied by the other instruments in rhythm, not stop time as was heard during the clarinet solo. Oliver builds his solo very slowly through the three choruses. His use of a mute on his cornet gives the sound a *wah-wah* effect. The inclusion of the other horns during Oliver's improvisation typifies early New Orleans style, where at times all the instruments continue playing through the entire performance, even the solos. (In later small-group jazz, the horns usually lay out during each other's solo, except for occasional additional riffs.)

Ensemble: Final chorus

2:08   During this final ensemble chorus, the drummer plays more heavily, increasing the feeling of drive.

2:23   The group adds a final two bars, called a tag, to this final chorus.

Reviewing "Dippermouth Blues," we find that the following New Orleans characteristics are evident:

▶ Typical instrumentation of cornet(s), clarinet, trombone, piano, banjo, and drums

▶ Improvised ensemble sections with the first cornet on the lead melody and the other instruments providing countermelodies

▶ Hot style with exuberant performances by all the musicians

▶ Driving 4/4 meter with emphasis on the beat

▶ Simple rhythm-section parts with all the rhythm instruments articulating the beat

Chicago became a hotbed of jazz thanks to regular performances of groups like King Oliver's. But even as Oliver was enjoying great popularity, the New Orleans ensemble style was rapidly becoming passé as innovators began to claim attention. The most important of these was Oliver's former student, Louis Armstrong. He in turn influenced a group of young, white, midwestern jazz fans who converged on the city. One of them, Bix Beiderbecke, was a cornet player with a distinctive bell-like tone that would help him become a jazz legend. Beiderbecke and Armstrong were the two most important cornet players of the 1920s.

Louis Armstrong

Louis Armstrong was born in New Orleans on August 4, 1901 (not July 4, 1900, as Armstrong himself thought) and spent an impoverished childhood, first with his mother, Mayann, then, from age thirteen, at the Colored Waifs' Home, where he played cornet in the band. He soon befriended Joe Oliver, who became his mentor, and later replaced him in the Kid Ory group when Oliver left New Orleans for Chicago in 1918. Armstrong continued to develop alongside his mentor after joining the Creole Jazz Band in Chicago in 1922, but by 1924 it was clear that Armstrong was ready to direct his own career:

> I never did try to overblow Joe at any time when I played with him. It wasn't any showoff thing like a youngster probably would do today. He still played whatever part he had played, and I always played "pretty" under him. Until I left Joe, I never did tear out. Finally, I thought it was about time to move along, and he thought so, too.[18]

Once Armstrong left Oliver, he played a brief stint at the Dreamland Cafe with Ollie Powers, a vocalist and drummer. Then, late in the summer of 1924, Armstrong left for New York to take over (as cornet) the third trumpet chair in Fletcher Henderson's band. This second apprenticeship with Henderson on the East Coast earned Armstrong growing national attention as the leading hot cornet player in the country. After a year with the Henderson band, Armstrong returned to play at the Dreamland in Chicago in 1925. The pace of Armstrong's performing and celebrity increased: He played movie houses with the Erskine Tate Orchestra early in the evening before moving to the Dreamland for late-night sets.

Armstrong began recording under his own name almost immediately after returning to Chicago. Interestingly, the groups he recorded with were not working

Louis Armstrong and His Hot Five (CD 1, Track 59). *Left to right:* Johnny St. Cyr (banjo), Edward "Kid" Ory (trombone), Louis Armstrong (trumpet), Johnny Dodds (clarinet), and Lillian Hardin (piano) in New Orleans. Lillian Hardin, Armstrong's wife at the time, encouraged the trumpeter to take charge of his own career. Note the serious demeanor of Armstrong, seen here at about age 24. Within a few years, he would become the ebullient entertainer with the winning smile, trumpet in hand, and trademark handkerchief.

Louis Armstrong's Hot Five, Exclusive OKeh Record Artists

The ***plunger*** is a type of mute derived from a plumber's sink plunger. The rubber cup of the plunger is held against the bell of the instrument and manipulated with the left hand to alter the horn's tone quality.

Scat singing is a jazz vocal style in which the soloist improvises using made-up or nonsense syllables.

bands but were put together for the recording sessions. With these recordings Armstrong departed from the collective improvisation of the New Orleans style as heard in the Creole Jazz Band, altering it to feature a succession of solos with his own work as the climax. In other words, Armstrong redefined jazz as an art in which individual solos played a greater role than in the original New Orleans style.

The first recordings of Louis Armstrong and His Hot Five, one of the groups assembled for recording, were cut on November 12, 1925, for OKeh Records. In addition to Armstrong on cornet and Hardin on piano, the musicians included New Orleans players Johnny St. Cyr on banjo, Johnny Dodds on clarinet, and Kid Ory on trombone. By this time the Dixieland format was becoming quaintly archaic, but Armstrong continued to play cornet and use the *plunger* in the style of Joe Oliver.

The same band recorded again the following year on February 26. This session included "Heebie Jeebies," a vocal number for Armstrong in which he sang *scat*— nonsense syllables—over the chord changes. It is probably untrue, but jazz mythology claims that Armstrong was forced to make up the syllables when his lyric sheet dropped to the floor.

An important, forward-looking recording that showcases Armstrong's emerging solo virtuosity is "Cornet Chop Suey" (1926). In this vibrant, well-balanced performance, Armstrong shines through from beginning to end, with an apt mixture of the improvised and what was likely planned. His playing here anticipates much of the swing-era phrasing to follow in the 1930s. In these recordings Armstrong remained part of the band, acknowledging the communal, polyphony-based New Orleans jazz idea, but at the same time he loosened and heated up jazz phrasing through virtuosic brilliance and unprecedented technical command. Jazz would never be the same.

ARMSTRONG'S CLASSIC STYLE

Not only did Armstrong revolutionize cornet playing, but he also stands as the single most powerful, individual, and influential voice in early jazz. Although Armstrong's playing was deliberately restrained in his 1923 recordings with Oliver, his later recordings attained ever higher levels of musical, artistic, and technical advancements as the decade progressed.

Around 1927 or 1928, Armstrong switched from cornet to the more brilliant and penetrating trumpet, which helped showcase his newfound virtuosity. He extended the upper register of the instrument, cultivating a three-octave range with dazzling technical proficiency. Armstrong's playing showed an inventive improvisational skill, and his ability to create coherent musical relationships conveyed a dramatic depth and pacing. Why was Armstrong's the most powerful individual voice in early jazz? Among the most important factors were the following:

■ Instrumental virtuosity: Technically, Armstrong was head and shoulders above other trumpeters.

■ Emphasis on logical, brilliant solo improvisation: He was able to create coherent musical relationships and convey them with dramatic depth and pacing.

■ More than his peers, Armstrong had an ability to generate swing in his playing. He did this through the following techniques:

▶ Unequal eighth-note rhythms that implied an underlying 2 + 1 triplet organization

▶ Unexpected accents that were largely off the beat within the melodic line

▶ Control over placement of the notes just before or after the beat

▶ *Terminal vibrato* to add excitement and "movement" to notes at the ends of phrases

Armstrong had an overwhelming influence on his contemporaries. Max Kaminsky captured something of Armstrong's effect:

I felt as if I had stared into the sun's eye. All I could think of doing was to run away and hide till the blindness left me. . . . Above all—above all the electrifying tone, the magnificence of his ideas and the rightness of his harmonic sense, his superb technique, his power and ideas, his hotness and intensity, his complete mastery of his horn—above all this, he had the swing. No one knew what swing was till Louis came along.[19]

On returning to Chicago, Armstrong began a musical association with pianist Earl Hines that would have lasting repercussions. Armstrong met Hines shortly after the pianist went from Pittsburgh to Chicago in 1924; by mid-1926 both men were doubling in Carroll Dickerson's Band at the Sunset Cafe and in Erskine Tate's orchestra at the Vendome Theater. In Hines, Armstrong found a peer. Both had developed a level of musical virtuosity far above their contemporaries; both soloists were willing to take improvisational chances. Hines was an easterner who had trained in the classics and absorbed stride (discussed later in this chapter) and blues-based piano.

Armstrong's roots were more casual, grounded in the predominantly oral tradition of New Orleans and the King Oliver band. Together, they created a combination that produced some of the era's most exciting jazz records. Eventually, Armstrong accepted the leadership of Dickerson's band and made Hines the musical director.

ARMSTRONG IN CHICAGO AND HIS LATER CAREER

Hines and Armstrong first recorded together in 1927, but their primary collaborations came the following year. In the meantime Armstrong continued to use pianist Lil Hardin for the most important records of that year. His band the Hot Seven, which was the Hot Five augmented by Pete Briggs on tuba and Baby Dodds on drums, went into the studio on May 7, 1927, and again on May 13 in a session that included "S. O. L. Blues." Later that year, Armstrong recorded nine sides with the Hot Five in September and December. The latter session is especially notable for the versions of "Savoy Blues," "Struttin' with Some Barbecue," and "Hotter Than That." These recordings also marked a switch to the new technique and increased fidelity of electrical recording. Hines, meanwhile, had recently joined Jimmie Noone's five-piece band at the Apex Club; he would later record with Noone in spring 1928.

L I S T E N I N G   G U I D E

"Hotter Than That"

CD **1** Track **59**

Louis Armstrong and His Hot Five: "Hotter Than That" (Lil Hardin). Chicago, December 13, 1927. OKeh 8535.
Louis Armstrong, cornet and vocal; Kid Ory, trombone; Johnny Dodds, clarinet; Lil Hardin Armstrong, piano;
Johnny St. Cyr, banjo; Lonnie Johnson, guitar.

"Hotter Than That" is from the famous Armstrong Hot Five sessions of the later 1920s. In this recording, Armstrong both plays hot cornet and scat-sings. Lil Hardin, the pianist in the band and composer of the piece, married Armstrong in the early 1920s and was one of the few women of her time who was not a vocalist to make a career in jazz.

Introduction (8 bars)

0:00   Introduction. The instruments all play together, with the cornet taking the lead.

1st chorus: 32 bars, as 16 + 16

0:09   For the A strain, Armstrong is featured in a solo accompanied by the rhythm section. The first half of the strain concludes with a break (0:25).

0:27   Second half of the chorus. Armstrong's solo continues, but the last two bars feature a clarinet break, moving to the clarinet solo for the second chorus.

2nd chorus: 32 bars, as 16 + 16

0:45   For the second chorus, clarinetist Dodds is featured, accompanied by the rhythm section. As with Armstrong's chorus, Dodds concludes the first half of the strain with a break (1:01).

1:03   Second half of the chorus. Dodds's solo concludes with Armstrong's scat vocal break.

3rd chorus: 32 bars, as 16 + 16

1:21   Armstrong's scat chorus, accompanied by guitar alone. In adhering to the form of the first two choruses, Armstrong concludes the first half with a solo break (1:36).

1:38   The second half of Armstrong's scat chorus became famous for its continuous syncopation, which creates a cross-rhythm with the underlying pulse of the rhythm section.

Call-and-response interlude between Armstrong and Johnson

1:54   In keeping with the form of the preceding choruses, a break occurs at the end of Armstrong's scat chorus. This break, however, becomes a call-and-response duet between Armstrong and Johnson. What begins in rhythm becomes free: The two players answer each other with imitation.

Hardin brings in the beat

2:13   Lil Hardin enters with a piano bass riff that resets the tempo.

4th chorus: 32 bars, as 16 + 16; coda

2:17   Trombone solo for the first half.

2:32   Armstrong enters with a brilliant break that initiates the climactic second half of the fourth chorus of the performance. The whole band joins in for this passage.

2:43   A brief stop time passage featuring Armstrong.

2:50   A guitar break for Johnson becomes an additional call-and-response coda featuring Johnson and Armstrong. This coda ends surprisingly with Johnson arpeggiating a chord. This chord is a diminished-seventh chord, one not customarily used for endings. It is possible that as the recording approached three minutes, the engineer or producer could have signaled for the band to stop; hence, the impromptu conclusion.

We can summarize the Chicago-style features of "Hotter Than That" as follows:

▶ Typical instrumentation of trumpet, clarinet, trombone, banjo, piano, and drums (with tuba included)

▶ Group improvisation in which the trumpet carries the lead, accompanied by trombone and clarinet countermelodies

▶ Horn solos accompanied by the rhythm section

▶ Use of call-and-response

▶ Frequent use of expressive blues elements: slurs, slides, and blue notes

▶ Use of instrumental breaks

The 1928 collaborations between Hines and Armstrong spotlighted the two as the leading jazz instrumentalists of the day. Working primarily within a six-piece format, the group included alumni from the Carroll Dickerson Savoy Orchestra: Fred Robinson on trombone, Jimmy Strong on clarinet, Mancy Carr (not "Cara," as seen in old discographies) on banjo, and Zutty Singleton on drums. Their June–July recordings in summer 1928 were released as *Louis Armstrong and His Hot Five,* the last of Armstrong's Hot Five recordings. With Hines and the Dickerson musicians, though, this set clearly showed Armstrong's departure from the New Orleans format of the earlier Hot Five and Hot Seven records. Dickerson's band at the Savoy was using the arrangements of Bill Challis, Don Redman, and Fletcher Henderson, and these Hot Five recordings revealed more of the small big-band format than the collective improvisational Dixieland style. Furthermore, Armstrong by now had switched to trumpet permanently, imparting an even greater brilliance and flair to these sides.

The same group recorded again in December 1928; the records were released as *Louis Armstrong and His Orchestra.* Armstrong sang on "Basin Street Blues," which, while not a blues composition, would become a Dixieland standard. Several cuts from the sessions included saxophonist Don Redman, who had played with Armstrong in Fletcher Henderson's band in New York. Redman arranged "No One Else but You" and "Save It Pretty Mama." Alex Hill wrote and arranged "Beau Koo Jack," another superb number. Thus we see, in the evolution of Armstrong through the 1920s, an increasing focus on arrangement and larger ensembles. From the evenly distributed, collective improvisation of King Oliver—the essence, perhaps, of New Orleans style—we have seen an evolution through an increasing emphasis on solo playing to well-arranged works in which Armstrong is featured.

Hines and Armstrong parted ways in early 1929, shortly after these sessions were concluded. Hines went on to establish a major career as both soloist and bandleader (see Chapter 3). Armstrong struck out for New York with Dickerson's band, landing a gig at Connie's Inn for himself, and for the band a role on Broadway in *Hot Chocolates,* a show with music by Fats Waller and Andy Razaf. Armstrong's great success at singing "Ain't Misbehavin'," which would become one of Razaf and Waller's most popular songs, hinted at a gradual transformation of the traditional New Orleans jazz cornetist into an internationally famous entertainer.

Armstrong's manager, Joe Glaser, helped cultivate Armstrong's persona as an entertainer. By the end of the 1930s, Armstrong was appearing in feature films and would become the first black to have a major radio show.

As the swing era dawned in the 1930s, Armstrong spent more and more time fronting big bands as the feature attraction. His many superb performances included solo features on "Stardust" and "When It's Sleepy Time Down South," both from 1931. "Sleepy Time" became a trademark Armstrong number. Also noteworthy were the driving virtuosity of "Swing That Music" from 1936—in which Armstrong hits dozens of concert high Cs before a final flourish to high E♭—and the high-spirited chart "Jubilee" from 1938.

When the big-band era began to wane during World War II, Armstrong was well positioned to appear again with smaller groups. This profile fit his early work as a New Orleans Dixieland cornetist, so he was able to take full advantage of the New

Trombone Technique

Trombone technique had greatly advanced since the days of the New Orleans *tailgaters*, trombonists who used the technique of playing with a rapid up and down motion of the slide. One of the earliest trombonists to attain a high level of virtuosity was Miff Mole (1898–1961), whose recordings with Red Nichols had a profound effect on later trombonists. Jack Teagarden (1905–1964), originally from Vernon, Texas, arrived in New York in the late twenties. With his rich, full-toned sound and his relaxed virtuosity, Teagarden became one of the finest trombonists in jazz. During the New Orleans revival, he worked frequently with Armstrong.

Orleans revival in the 1940s. He played with a group known as the All Stars, which included a reunion with Earl Hines as well as the fine trombonist Jack Teagarden. (See the box "Trombone Technique" on the facing page.)

By the 1950s, Armstrong's career had peaked, but he continued to work as hard as ever. When Armstrong became an ambassador for U.S. goodwill during the cold war with the Soviet Union, the State Department sponsored many of his tours. In 1959, Armstrong suffered a heart attack, which forced him to cut back his performances—especially the physically exhausting, bravura trumpet playing he was known for in the 1930s and 1940s. Despite declining health, he continued working through the 1960s, though he was featured more as a singer than as a trumpeter. In fact, he played gigs right through 1971, the year in which he died on July 6.

Armstrong was a musical revolutionary in his youth and one of the two or three most important jazzmen ever. He also became a preeminent figure in twentieth-century popular culture. Amazingly, Armstrong had a Top 10 record in every decade from the 1920s to the 1960s—a span of fifty years.

The Chicagoans and Bix Beiderbecke

Transplanted New Orleans players in Chicago gave early jazz its strongest impetus, but the music soon attracted local musicians as well. During the twenties, as Chicago-based white players flocked to clubs such as the Lincoln Gardens to hear their idols Oliver and Armstrong play, the city provided a training ground for musicians cultivating a Chicago style. Listening to the original New Orleans players, a second generation of jazz instrumentalists fashioned their own improvisational and group styles. These players are collectively known as the "Chicagoans" and epitomize what has been called Chicago jazz.

These musicians included native Chicagoans as well as players from other parts of the country, drawn by the magnetic pull of Chicago's jazz world. Though Eddie Condon, Elmer Schoebel, Wild Bill Davison, Bix Beiderbecke, Hoagy Carmichael, Rod Cless, and Frank Trumbauer were born in the Midwest outside Chicago, many of them subsequently became associated with and made their careers in that city.

The relatively affluent suburb of Austin, on the far west side of Chicago, fostered the most influential group of musicians. Collectively known as the Austin High Gang, the players included Jimmy McPartland on cornet, his brother Richard McPartland on guitar, Bud Freeman on tenor saxophone, Frank Teschemacher on clarinet, Dave North on piano, and Jimmy Lannigan on bass. It is primarily this group, together with banjoist Eddie Condon, drummer Dave Tough, and William "Red" McKenzie, who became the self-styled "Chicagoans." Although the Austin High Gang's most significant performing and recording would take place after the twenties and in New York, the group helped articulate and define the notion of Chicago jazz.

Before hearing Oliver and Armstrong, the Chicagoans had learned from the recordings of white sweet dance bands and the Original Dixieland Jazz Band (ODJB). A more significant influence was the New Orleans Rhythm Kings (NORK), a white band made up of New Orleans and midwestern musicians (mentioned earlier). To a certain extent, the Rhythm Kings based their instrumentation and repertory on the ODJB's performances, but they were somewhat more successful at transforming the ragtime syncopations of the ODJB into a looser, more swinging approach.

MODERN MUSIC AND ITS MAKERS

BIX BEIDERBECKE

Courtesy Frank Driggs Collection

The well-known Bix Beiderbecke (CD 1, Track 60) portrait from The Wolverines' publicity photograph of 1923.

The NORK's extended engagement at the Friar's Inn in Chicago allowed teenage Chicagoans to hear them; their records, originally released under the name *Friar's Society Orchestra,* exercised enormous influence on fledgling Chicago jazzmen.

Cornetist Jimmy McPartland described how they learned from the NORK:

> What we used to do was put the record on—one of the Rhythm Kings', naturally— play a few bars, and then all get our notes. We'd have to tune our instruments up to the record machine, to the pitch, and go ahead with a few notes. Then stop! A few more bars of the record, each guy would pick out his notes and boom! we would go on and play it. Two bars, or four bars, or eight—we would get in on each phrase and then play it all. . . . It was a funny way to learn, but in three or four weeks we could finally play one tune all the way through—"Farewell Blues." Boy, that was our tune.[20]

Possibly the deepest influence on the Chicagoans came from a cornet player born in Iowa in 1903, who received his earliest musical experiences in Chicago— Leon Bix Beiderbecke. In contrast to the virtuosic flamboyance of Louis Armstrong, Beiderbecke had developed a style marked by introspection and refinement. Contemporaries strove to pinpoint Beiderbecke's restrained and uniquely lyrical sound: Mezz Mezzrow stated that every note sounded "like a pearl" and stood out "sharp as a rifle crack." Hoagy Carmichael described it as a mallet hitting a chime; to Eddie Condon, Bix's sound came out "like a girl saying yes."[21]

Bested only by Armstrong, Bix Beiderbecke was the second leading voice on the cornet during the twenties. Whereas Armstrong used differing timbres, a wider range, and consistent vibrato as expressive devices, Beiderbecke's sound had a more even timbre, a narrower range, and a straight tone, with only occasional vibrato.

Beiderbecke's unique tone color resulted partly from employing unusual trumpet fingerings. He also emphasized the ninths and thirteenths of the chords in his playing.

Although often associated with Chicago, Beiderbecke actually performed there infrequently. He began playing cornet in his hometown of Davenport, Iowa. With the exception of a few piano lessons, he was largely self-taught as a musician and learned by playing along with recordings of the Original Dixieland Jazz Band. His parents, unhappy about his jazz playing, sent him to Lake Forest Military Academy outside Chicago in 1921. But Beiderbecke's gigs and frequent trips into the city to hear the NORK created an alarming truancy rate, and he was expelled from the academy the following year. His dismissal freed him to become a full-time professional musician; he played gigs on an excursion steamer in Lake Michigan, at fraternity parties on campuses, and throughout the Midwest with a group of players who gradually became known as the Wolverines.

Beiderbecke was beginning to create an impact on the jazz world. When Beiderbecke left the Wolverines, he headed back to the Midwest from Manhattan, where the group had been playing. He picked up some jobs with Jean Goldkette, a Detroit-based bandleader, and in 1925 joined one of Goldkette's bands in St. Louis, under the leadership of Frankie Trumbauer. In the company of high-caliber musicians such as Trumbauer, who played C-melody saxophone, and Pee Wee Russell on clarinet, Beiderbecke's playing deepened. His reading improved; he played piano more frequently. Frankie Trumbauer (1901–1956) was an important white jazz player of the 1920s and one of few who played the C-melody saxophone. He became closely associated with Beiderbecke and significantly influenced Lester Young, the swing saxophone great (Chapter 3).

In 1926, Trumbauer and Beiderbecke graduated to Goldkette's first-string New York band, which recorded prolifically for a year or so. The next year, Bix also began to record with an orchestra under the direction of Trumbauer that mostly included members of the Goldkette band. After the latter group folded in September 1927, both Beiderbecke and Trumbauer, along with the arranger Bill Challis, moved to the famous Paul Whiteman band, Beiderbecke's last major ensemble. Unfortunately, the recordings made with the large Whiteman band contain only brief cornet solos by Beiderbecke.

Beiderbecke's recordings of 1927 made a lasting impact. His solo on "Singin' the Blues," recorded with Trumbauer's band, was imitated widely by other players. Beiderbecke also recorded as band leader—under the name of Bix and His Gang—including rerecordings of the Wolverines' "Royal Garden Blues" and "Jazz Me Blues." A unique item in the Beiderbecke catalog was recorded by the artist himself: his harmonically daring solo piano piece, "In a Mist."

Beiderbecke's drinking caused a rapid deterioration in his health, and he died in 1931 at age twenty-eight. Although largely unknown to the general public, Beiderbecke's legacy among musicians was profound. Other cornetists such as Jimmy McPartland, Red Nichols, Rex Stewart, and Bobby Hackett directly imitated his playing. Beiderbecke's improvisations, which were harmonically advanced, affected musicians of all instruments. His melodic ideas seemed to grow logically and organically from one into the other, giving the impression of improvisation as a unified whole—what Lester Young later referred to as "telling stories." To many who idealized his brief life, Beiderbecke served as the tragic hero of the Jazz Age, a romantic symbol of the Roaring Twenties. He became the model for Dorothy Baker's novel *Young Man With a Horn.*

"Singin' the Blues"
CD **1**   Track **60**

Frank Trumbauer and His Orchestra: "Singin' the Blues" (Robinson, Conrad). New York, February 4, 1927. OKeh 40772. Frank Trumbauer, C-melody (or alto) saxophone, leader; Bix Beiderbecke, cornet; Bill Rank, trombone; Jimmy Dorsey, clarinet; Paul Mertz, piano; Eddie Lang, guitar; Chauncey Morehouse, drums.

"Singin' the Blues" contains a famous Beiderbecke solo—in fact, one of his first solos to become widely known. The ensemble for this recording, under the nominal leadership of Frank Trumbauer, was assembled from the Jean Goldkette band specifically for the session. Trumbauer solos on the now-rare C-melody saxophone, an instrument pitched between the alto and the tenor saxophones in range. His solo, equally as famous as Beiderbecke's chorus at the time, greatly impressed and influenced Lester Young, who was said to keep a copy in his saxophone case. We also hear a brief Jimmy Dorsey solo on clarinet. He and his brother Tommy, best known as a trombonist, became two important bandleaders in the 1930s. Among the other musicians, Eddie Lang was a pioneering guitarist who often recorded with violinist Joe Venuti.

Introduction (4 bars)

0:00   For the introduction, the horns present block chords, accompanied only by the drums.

1st chorus: 32 bars, as 16 + 16, for Trumbauer

0:07   The first chorus features Trumbauer on the C-melody (or alto) saxophone, accompanied by Lang only. The sweet, unforced quality of his playing contrasted with the heaviness of much 1920s saxophone playing. A break (0:31) occurs in the last two bars of the solo's first half.

0:35   In the second half of the solo, we hear a particularly nice moment in Trumbauer's descending arpeggio (0:42), answered by a desending harmonic minor scale by Lang (0:43). After this, there occur several other moments in which Lang answers Trumbauer, all the while continuing to keep time. Trumbauer's break at the end of the second half (0:59) ushers in Beiderbecke's chorus.

2nd chorus: 32 bars, as 16 + 16, for Beiderbecke

1:02   For the second chorus, Beiderbecke is featured, accompanied yet again by Lang only. Although Beiderbecke's lyricism is a hallmark of his style, note that the actual melody he improvises has a surprising number of leaps. His improvisational style is "compositional," as he maintains much form and symmetry in the melodic line. As with Trumbauer's chorus, Beiderbecke concludes the first half with a break (1:27).

1:31   Second half of the chorus. Notice that the three repeated on-the-beat notes at 1:33 echo the repeated on-the-beat notes heard during the break (1:27). These parallels are partly what makes Beiderbecke's style so elegant. Paralleling the interplay between Lang and Trumbauer in the saxophonist's solo, both players play diminished-chord arpeggios in the opposite direction at 1:47—a remarkable and beautiful moment in the solo that was probably spontaneous.

3rd chorus: 32 bars with the whole band and Dorsey clarinet solo

2:00   The entire band enters with a free, almost New Orleans–style group improvisation for the first eight bars of the first half of the chorus.

2:13   For the second eight bars of the first half of the chorus, Dorsey is featured on clarinet, accompanied by piano and guitar only. He ends his solo with a break (2:25).

2:28   Beiderbecke's commanding entrance sets up the piece's climax, consisting of the song's second half. Lang's solo break at 2:45—yet another diminished-chord arpeggiation—provides a textural contrast to the strong ending by the entire ensemble.

"Singin' the Blues" is an excellent example of the genius of Bix Beiderbecke. His performance is both a brilliant solo on its own terms and representative of certain aspects of his general style:

▶ Concentration on the middle register

▶ A lyrical, mellow tone

▶ Rhythmic variety

▶ Extreme subtlety of melodic continuation

▶ Restrained use of blue notes

▶ Small but compelling emotional compass

▶ Little use of vibrato

▶ *Inside playing*

Beiderbecke seemed to synthesize all that Chicago had to offer New Orleans bands and styles in the twenties. He merged the tradition of the white New Orleans bands such as the ODJB and the NORK with the emerging solo emphasis pioneered by Armstrong in the context of larger bands. He helped solidify a Dixieland repertory, a group sound, and an improvisational style that the Chicagoans kept alive for the next several decades. Hundreds of later bands maintained the Dixieland tradition, and it continues to this day.

Jazz musicians are said to be playing ***inside*** when their melodic lines favor the principal notes of the harmonies. The more players depart from the notes of the harmonies, the more they are said to be playing ***outside***. (These terms are most commonly associated with modern jazz. Listen to Track 8 on CD 1 🅿 for an example.)

Jazz in New York

After World War I, jazz flourished in New York. The hot, improvisational New Orleans–Chicago school strongly influenced New York musicians. Combining the freewheeling approach of the out-of-towners with the professional commercialism long associated with the city, New York musicians took over the jazz vanguard and made New York the leading jazz city. Most significant were the innovations of Fletcher Henderson, Duke Ellington, and the stride pianists (discussed later in this chapter), but also important was the mainstream work of such popular artists as bandleader Paul Whiteman and composer George Gershwin. Together these artists, both black and white, helped set the stage for swing music in the 1930s.

Jazz in Europe

It is not surprising that Europeans quickly became enthusiastic about jazz, since in previous decades they had embraced ragtime as the first musical style associated with the United States. A number of American jazz groups and artists, such as Sidney Bechet and the ODJB, performed in Europe in the late 1910s and early 1920s. We have written earlier that European music critics wrote enthusiastically about jazz. This activity encouraged European musicians to try their hand at the music.

What *is* perhaps surprising is that fine players appeared in Europe as early as the 1920s. European musicians formed jazz bands in England, Belgium, and France. One of the most significant bands was the Quintette du Hot Club de France. The group formed in 1934 and featured violinist Stéphane Grappelli and guitarist Django

Stéphane Grappelli (left) and Django Reinhardt (center) with the Quintette du Hot Club de France.

Reinhardt. Reinhardt was a guitar phenomenon, all the more amazing since he had been burned in a fire and was unable to use two of the fingers on his left hand. In Woody Allen's 1999 movie, *Sweet and Lowdown,* the main character is a 1930s American jazz guitarist who is haunted by the fact that Reinhardt will always be the better guitarist.

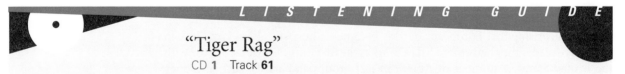

L I S T E N I N G   G U I D E

"Tiger Rag"
CD **1**   Track **61**

Django Reinhardt et le Quintette du Hot Club de France avec Stéphane Grappelli: "Tiger Rag" (Nick LaRocca).
Ultraphone AP-1423. Paris, December 1934. Stéphane Grappelli, violin; Django Reinhardt, Roger Chaput,
Joseph Reinhardt, guitars; Louis Vola, bass.

This performance of "Tiger Rag" by the Quintette du Hot Club de France provides interesting points of comparison with the original ODJB of CD 1, Track 57. In contrast to the exciting but earthy playing of the ODJB, Reinhardt and Grappelli display deft, fleet virtuosity. It is remarkable how thoroughly both soloists absorbed the jazz idiom, although as Europeans they did not participate in the U.S. jazz scene. This strings-only performance (without customary horns, piano, or drums) provides a remarkable textural contrast to the standard New Orleans ensemble of the ODJB "Tiger Rag."

A strain: 8 bars, repeated

0:00   As in the ODJB introduction, the piece begins right at the A strain for the opening eight-bar section. Grappelli has the principal melody, with Reinhardt harmonizing the dexterous melodic line in a lower register. Note how much faster the performance is compared with the ODJB's. Such virtuosity will also be evident in the Tatum performance (CD 1, Track 62).

0:06   Repeat of the eight-bar A strain.

B strain: 8 bars

0:12   The second strain does not quite feature the stop time chorus we heard with the ODJB because the bass continues to walk. Nevertheless, the effect of the stop time is similar because the ensemble accents the measures' downbeats strongly.

A strain: 8 bars

0:18   Repeat of the A section.

C strain: 24 bars, as C1 (16) and C2 (8)

0:24   As compared with the ODJB performance, the group shortens the second half of the C strain. For the C strain's first half, Grappelli's melodic line contains the piece's first blue notes. The first half of the strain also features brilliant instrumental breaks throughout, the first two for Reinhardt, the third for bassist Vola. Grappelli's double-stops (two notes at a time) at 0:31 are exciting and add a new textural element.

0:37   For the second half of the strain (truncated to eight bars), the music finishes with a conclusive cadence.

D strain (32 bars), 1st chorus

0:43   An interesting question for the D strain is: Will we miss the trombone glissandos leading to the "Hold That Tiger!" figure? The strain begins with a Reinhardt solo. His bluesy bending and held-out notes provide an effective contrast to the busy virtuosity of the C strain. After returning to faster notes, Reinhardt ends the first half of the strain with a break (0:54)

0:56   Second half of the D strain. After a melodic figure that arpeggiates a seventh chord, Reinhardt holds a note by using a tremolo (0:59), an effect created by rapidly moving the pick up and down on the string.

D strain (32 bars), 2nd chorus

1:09   For the second chorus, Grappelli solos. His break at 1:20 features a brilliant arpeggio on a diminished-seventh chord.

1:22   The second half of Grappelli's solo features a nice change to triplets at 1:29.

D strain (32 bars), 3rd chorus

1:34   A stop time bass solo for the first half, with the guitars providing downbeat accents every two bars. A loud tremolo in the guitars sets up the second half of the D strain.

1:48   The second half of the D strain. Here the band phrases together in a passage planned to prepare the **out-chorus**. Loud guitar accents usher in the final chorus (1:59).

D strain (32 bars), 4th (out-) chorus

2:00   For the out-chorus, the band picks up the intensity under Grappelli's exciting final solo. Grappelli's break at 2:12 signifies the end of the first half.

2:13   The second half of the out-chorus. At its conclusion, a descending chromatic chord progression broadens into the final chord.

The Harlem Renaissance

By the end of the 1920s, New York—already the media and entertainment capital of the country—had become the leading center of jazz, a position it still occupies today. If bands or artists were to have a national presence, they needed to gain acceptance and promotion in New York. The major figures of New Orleans—Louis Armstrong, King Oliver, Jelly Roll Morton—eventually came to the Big Apple. Bix Beiderbecke spent his last productive years in the city with Paul Whiteman's band, and many of the Chicagoans earned their reputation in Manhattan. New York had become the center of the music publishing industry, which was concentrated in the district known as Tin Pan Alley.

Tin Pan Alley pioneered mass marketing and aggressive sales techniques in the popular music industry, techniques that still define the business today. The district eventually consolidated on West Twenty-Eighth Street in Manhattan. As part of their sales strategy, Tin Pan Alley promoters actively plugged songs by hiring pianists to play, sing, and hawk the latest tunes at the publishers' offices. Customers would wander down the street, in and out of the publishing offices, in search of the sheet music for songs that caught their ears. In the days before air conditioning, publishing companies kept the windows and doors open during the warm months—the sounds of all the song pluggers playing simultaneously led to a street cacophony that recalled the banging of tin pans.

Many musicians—from George Gershwin to Fletcher Henderson—got their start as song pluggers playing and singing the constant stream of newly written popular songs that flowed from Tin Pan Alley. New York had become the heart of the nation's recording industry, and jazz musicians such as cornetist Red Nichols and guitarist Eddie Lang earned much of their living from playing in studios.

From 1917, when the Original Dixieland Jazz Band performed at New York's Reisenweber's Restaurant, to 1931, when Duke Ellington gave his last performance at Harlem's Cotton Club, jazz had matured. The ODJB's success in New York owed much to its onstage antics and comical barnyard effects, and in the public's eye jazz was synonymous with novelty and slapstick. Duke Ellington described this public perception of jazz in his early years:

> When I began my work, jazz was a stunt, something different. Not everybody cared for jazz and those that did felt it wasn't the real thing unless they were given a shock sensation of loudness or unpredictability along with the music.[22]

Published in 1932 in New York, this sheet music aptly captures the energy and high style of the Harlem Renaissance that attracted so many to its nightlife. Patrons, black and white, came to listen and dance to the great jazz bands.

Throughout the 1920s, Ellington and many others helped change this perception. Although the music continued to develop as entertainment, particularly as dance music, players improved technically. Jazz earned a seal of approval from important musicians in Europe. European composers—including Maurice Ravel, Darius Milhaud, Ernst Krenek, and Arthur Honegger—incorporated jazz elements into their orchestral concert works. Promoters and practitioners, both in Europe and in the United States, began to present jazz as serious and sophisticated entertainment rather than as the comical stepchild of vaudeville.

In New York's African-American community, the growing acceptance of jazz paralleled the rise of the *Harlem Renaissance.*[23] Harlem in the 1920s became the central locale for black artists, writers, and musicians and the engine of a self-confident black artistic consciousness. The primary shapers of the Harlem Renaissance "aspired to high culture as opposed to that of the common man, which they hoped to mine for novels, plays, and symphonies."[24] For example, writers Langston Hughes and Zora Neal Hurston, painter Aaron Douglas, and composer William Grant Still gravitated to Harlem as the primary center of African-American culture.

A period of outstanding artistic activity among African Americans—roughly 1921 to 1929—is referred to as the ***Harlem Renaissance***. The movement was centered in Harlem in New York City.

As pianist Eubie Blake pointed out, music was central to the Harlem Renaissance.[25] Historians often date the beginning of the Harlem Renaissance from Noble Sissle and Eubie Blake's show *Shuffle Along,* which opened in 1921 and ran for 504 performances. Other shows quickly followed, including Maceo Pinkard's *Liza* (1922) and James P. Johnson's *Runnin' Wild* (1923). Black musical theater on Broadway flourished during the 1920s—from two to five productions were initiated each year.

For many of the key figures of the Harlem Renaissance, the concert stage was the appropriate place for musical performance. Singers Marian Anderson and Paul Robeson performed spirituals in concert; the National Association of Negro Musicians initiated concerts and recitals. As early as 1918 Will Marion Cook took his Southern Syncopated Orchestra, which included Sidney Bechet, to play concert venues in England; and during the twenties and thirties Cook became a pivotal figure in establishing recital performances for African-American performers and composers. Black classical composers sought to incorporate African-American music into larger concert forms. William Grant Still stated that his role was "to elevate Negro musical idioms to a position of dignity and effectiveness in the field of symphonic and operatic music."[26] Such values exercised a powerful impact on many Harlem jazz players, particularly James

Noble Sissle appears on the cover of his composition published in London in 1929. Noble Sissle and Eubie Blake wrote the first all-black Broadway musical, *Shuffle Along,* a huge success of 1921.

P. Johnson and Duke Ellington, who themselves later merged jazz into concert music and classical forms.

Harlem and jazz were inextricably bound. Harlem-based jazz musicians Duke Ellington and Fletcher Henderson became the two primary black bandleaders, developing their bands through nightly performances at all-white nightclubs. White musicians such as Artie Shaw, Benny Goodman, and Paul Whiteman frequented these clubs, and classical composers such as Darius Milhaud and Aaron Copland heard the bands and listened closely.

In addition to nightclub performances, *rent parties* allowed many Harlem jazz pianists to develop their technique. These were "funky, down-home affairs," writes Samuel Floyd:

A **rent party** was an informal gathering held to raise money for rent or groceries. At these parties, musicians often gathered and performed, sometimes in competition with one another.

> As far as creativity is concerned, such affairs served as the proving ground for the pianists. Dominating this creative world were James P. Johnson, Willie "The Lion" Smith, Thomas "Fats" Waller, Luckey Roberts, and Duke Ellington. It was in this world that these and other musicians honed their artistic tools and worked out their ideas for presentation in the world of show business.[27]

The Harlem Renaissance and the coinciding rise of jazz in New York City during the 1920s contributed to the spirit of excitement and creativity that changed jazz from a curiosity to a phenomenon. Many musicians helped secure jazz as a music of cultural and artistic significance. Among them was a group of pianists known as the "Harlem Stride" school.

Harlem Stride Piano

Around World War I, New York became the center of a type of piano playing that developed out of ragtime but took on techniques that led to a high degree of virtuosity. This early jazz style, called *stride piano*, evolved at the same time that the musical developments in New Orleans and Chicago did. It embodies the transition of jazz from ragtime; stride energized ragtime with greater flash, speed, incorporation of blues elements, and sometimes improvisational variations that were planned. The development of ragtime into stride parallels the hectic pace of U.S. life during and after World War I, with stride's energy mimicking the speed of the assembly line, the automobile, the telephone, and the airplane.

Stride piano is a school of jazz piano playing derived from ragtime. With greater speed and virtuosity than ragtime, stride combines a left-hand accompaniment of alternating bass notes and chords (march bass) with a tugging right hand that seems to pull at the left-hand rhythm to impart swing.

Fundamentally, stride playing described the left hand "striding" up and down the keyboard, with a bass note or octave played on the first and third beats of the 4/4 measure, alternating with a midrange chord on the second and fourth beats. Various stride players cultivated their own flashy techniques and trademarks as well. At rent parties in Harlem, at the Jungles Casino on West Sixty-Second Street, in the piano competitions known as "cutting contests," pianists James P. Johnson, Luckey Roberts, Willie "The Lion" Smith, and Richard "Abba Labba" McLean emerged as the best players in the highly competitive New York world. Scholars sometimes call this stride style the eastern school to distinguish it from midwestern styles, but regional influences overlap so that we cannot always distinguish them. In any event, while centered in Harlem, stride piano boasted fine players working throughout the Northeast and as far south as Washington, D.C.

Piano Rolls

Piano rolls were cylinders of rolled paper punched with holes. When fed through a properly equipped ***player piano***, the holes activated hammers that played the piano automatically. Many of the great pianists of the teens and twenties recorded piano rolls, including James P. Johnson, Eubie Blake, Fats Waller, and George Gershwin. The rolls, however, could not reproduce a performer's dynamics and phrasing adequately, and tempo depended on how fast the roll was fed through the piano. Hence, the "recordings" of piano rolls are not accurate guides to players' styles. In the past several years, the use of electronic technology has vastly improved the performance of piano rolls, and remarkably lifelike versions of piano-roll performances by George Gershwin, for example, are now available.

Harlem stride linked ragtime to swing by featuring elements of both; its melodies floated effortlessly between angular ragtime rhythms and smooth swing. Even the music of later Harlem pianists, such as Fats Waller, continued to exhibit connections to ragtime in both melodic style and left-hand rhythm. Stride bass formed the basis for many solo jazz piano styles.

The stride pianists took their repertory from reworkings of popular show tunes and traditional ragtime pieces, as well as classical compositions played in a ragtime style. In addition, several prominent stride pianists began composing their own works.

EUBIE BLAKE

Eubie Blake (1883–1983), who began his career playing piano in Baltimore's bars and brothels, recorded in 1917 a version of his brilliant "Charleston Rag" on a piano roll. (A recording of the piece, issued as "Sounds of Africa," followed in 1921.) Blake later claimed that he wrote the work, which was extremely forward looking, in 1899. If so, it would be evidence of a jazz style emerging on the East Coast around the same time as New Orleans jazz.

Blake was an important pianist and composer who, with lyricist Noble Sissle, wrote the most successful black musical of the 1920s, *Shuffle Along* (1921). The same year that Blake recorded his piano roll of "Charleston Rag" (1917), James P. Johnson issued piano rolls of his compositions "Caprice Rag" and "Stop It." Johnson would take the ragtime-stride style to a new level. (See the box "Piano Rolls" above for more on this technology.)

JAMES P. JOHNSON

James P. Johnson was born in 1894 in New Brunswick, New Jersey, and raised in Jersey City and New York. Though essentially a stride and popular composer-pianist, he had a strong classical background and always remained interested in concert music.

Known as the "father of stride piano," Johnson developed his style from playing dance music at clubs in the Jungles, the black section of New York's Hell's Kitchen in the West Sixties. At the Jungles Casino, he played for transplanted southern workers,

James Johnson (CD 1, Track 56).

many of them black merchant seamen from Savannah and Charleston; those from the Georgia Sea Islands were called "Gullahs" and "Geechies." These patrons demanded the country dances they had heard growing up in the South, and this provided the origin for one of Johnson's most famous compositions, "Charleston":

> The Gullahs would start out early in the evening dancing two-steps, waltzes, schottisches; but as the night wore on and the liquor began to work, they would start improvising their own steps and that was when they wanted us to get-in-the-alley, real lowdown. Those big Charleston, South Carolina, bruisers would grab a girl from the bar and stomp-it-down as the piano player swung into the gut-bucketiest music he could.[28]

Johnson wrote "Charleston" for the Broadway musical *Runnin' Wild*. His playing and compositions became celebrated for the way they combined ragtime with elements of blues and jazz. Johnson's most famous stride composition was "Carolina Shout," which appeared on piano rolls twice in the teens. Johnson first recorded it to disc in 1921. "Carolina Shout" served as a test piece for players attempting virtuosic stride; in fact, the young Duke Ellington claimed to learn the style by slowing down the player-piano mechanism of "Carolina Shout" and fitting his fingers to the rising and falling keys.

Johnson did more than just play brilliant solo piano; he also recorded with blues singers Bessie Smith and Ethel Waters, and he composed *Runnin' Wild,* his first Broadway musical, in 1923. A true child of the Harlem Renaissance, he began composing large-scale concert works that placed elements of jazz and African-American music in classical forms and models. For example, *Yamekraw* (1927) was written for piano and orchestra and premiered at Carnegie Hall with Fats Waller as the soloist. Johnson suffered several strokes in the 1940s but continued to play and record up to a final recording with Sidney Bechet in 1950. A stroke in 1951 left him unable to play, and he died in 1955.

FATS WALLER

James P. Johnson's student, Thomas "Fats" Waller (1904–1943), went on to even greater fame and renown than Johnson himself. Although Waller became better known as a humorous entertainer, his virtuosity on the piano was unparalleled. Before meeting Johnson, Waller at age fifteen had been the organist at Harlem's Lincoln Theatre. Under Johnson's tutelage he began to excel as a stride pianist. With the help of his mentor, he established himself in the New York musical world and began to record piano rolls in 1922.

Like Johnson, Waller was a fine songwriter who wrote such classics as "Squeeze Me," "Honeysuckle Rose," "Black and Blue," and "Ain't Misbehavin.'" Also like Johnson,

Waller composed for the Broadway stage, working with lyricist Andy Razaf on the 1928 musical *Keep Shufflin'* as well as *Hot Chocolates* (1929), which had Louis Armstrong as a singer and soloist.

Waller was the first important jazz musician to record on the pipe organ, an instrument not especially disposed to the sharp attacks of jazz phrasing. Despite his unparalleled keyboard prowess, Waller ultimately succeeded in the public eye as a popular singer and entertainer: His witty asides often called attention to the emptiness of the disposable pop songs he was increasingly called on to play.

Nevertheless, Waller's solo piano recordings are among the high points of stride piano. The piano works written and recorded between 1929 and 1934—"Handful of Keys," "Smashing Thirds," "Numb Fumblin'," "Valentine Stomp," "Viper's Drag," "Alligator Crawl," and "Clothes Line Ballet"—keep alive many of Johnson's techniques while projecting an eloquent swing regardless of tempo. Much of his fluency derived from his large hands: Pianist George Shearing compared shaking hands with Waller to "grabbing a bunch of bananas."[29]

The next pianist to command attention in the stride tradition was the incomparable Art Tatum.

ART TATUM

Art Tatum was certainly one of the most prodigious virtuosos in jazz history. Blind in one eye and visually impaired in the other, Tatum was trained in the classics in his native Toledo, Ohio, where he was born in 1909. He learned to read music in Braille. He forged a piano style marked with dazzling runs, lightning-fast arpeggios, and an impeccable stride technique derived from Fats Waller. Tatum's repertory drew primarily on popular songs such as "Tea for Two" and "Willow Weep for Me." While retaining the melody of the tune, he would recast the harmonic structure, substituting more-advanced chromatic harmonies for the original chords. As a solo pianist playing with trios, quartets, and larger bands, Tatum made more than 600 recordings that testify to his unerring technique and creative fluency.

Tatum elevated the technique of jazz piano to new heights of excellence—beyond what anyone had thought possible. Although his basic touch was light, his sense of rhythm was extraordinarily secure and provided a swinging foundation to his work that pianists everywhere envied. Moreover, his imaginative treatment of popular melodies and his sense of chordal enrichment influenced and inspired the newly emerging bebop scene of the early 1940s.

Tatum won the admiration of jazz musicians and the public alike for his renditions of light classical pieces in a virtuoso format and at unbelievably fast tempos. His arrangements frequently made use of *rubato* (rhythmically flexible) introductions that moved into up-tempo interpretations based on the rhythms of stride and swing. The arrangements and instrumentation of his trio, which included bassist Slam Stewart and guitarist Tiny Grimes, provided the inspiration for later jazz piano trios. Tatum influenced not only swing-era pianists

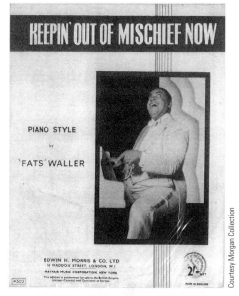

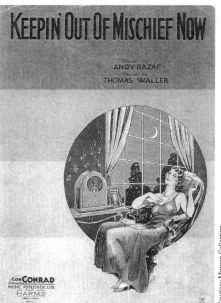

By the 1930s, jazz had become a mainstream entertainment and a gradually integrating force in U.S. culture. Although jazz was performed by black and white artists to black and white audiences, white acceptance of the work of black composers was gradual in the United States. Notice that for the successful Fats Waller composition, "Keepin' Out Of Mischief Now," the cover of the British edition (top) carried a picture of Fats Waller, but the U.S. edition (bottom) did not.

Virtuoso pianist Art Tatum in a publicity still from the 1940s.

such as Duke Ellington and Teddy Wilson but also saxophonists Coleman Hawkins and Charlie Parker. In fact, Tatum's virtuosity may very well have been the decisive influence on Parker's emerging bebop style.

Tatum's musical personality had two sides—the popular virtuoso and the after-hours pianist. Listeners often remarked that his best playing took place during sessions that sometimes lasted all night long. Tatum expanded the vocabulary of stride and swing piano in four significant ways:

▶ Timing of chords: Most stride and swing pianists played octaves, single notes, or perhaps tenths on the first and third beats and three-note or four-note chords on the second and fourth beats, but Tatum sometimes played richly voiced, full chords on all four beats.

▶ Runs: While many stride and swing pianists used embellished runs to connect melodic phrases, Tatum used these runs more consistently and elaborately.

▶ Rapidity: Swing and stride pianists always featured impressive dexterity and speed, but Tatum's playing was the most rapid.

▶ Harmony: While jazz piano had been slowly developing more-sophisticated harmonies, including extended chords and nondiatonic progressions, Tatum was the most harmonically advanced of any of his contemporaries.

L I S T E N I N G G U I D E

"Tiger Rag"
CD **1** Track **62**

Art Tatum: "Tiger Rag" (Nick LaRocca). Brunswick B13164-A. New York, March 21, 1933. Art Tatum, piano.

Our study of "Tiger Rag" continues with another justly famed performance. Art Tatum recorded this piece on his first recording session in March 1933. His virtuosity is astounding. This recording established Tatum's supremacy in the highly competitive world of New York solo piano. While Tatum's performance can be considered an example of stride piano, its incredibly fast tempo, similar to what we heard on the Quintette du Hot Club de France recording, invites a variety of left-hand textures. Tatum incorporates a striding left hand from time to time but sustains this texture only toward the end of the performance.

Introduction

0:00 The introduction is played freely ("out of time"). Tatum's harmonies are reminiscent of Impressionist composers Debussy and Ravel. This is an introduction that works as a contrast to what follows, but Tatum, as will become clear, does not abandon this material completely.

A strain (8 + 8)

0:14 Tatum's statement of the A strain hints at the original melody. A calm left-hand part largely alternates the tonic and dominant notes of the key.

0:20 On the repeat of the eight-bar A strain, Tatum is already embellishing the melody with added runs in the right hand. Note that the entire 16-bar A strain is played in only ten seconds!

B strain (8 bars)

0:25 The second strain—the bridge between the repeated eight-bar A strain and its return—offers a change of texture. Just as the original ODJB recording featured stop time in this section, Tatum imitates this procedure with stop time punctuations in his left hand. The right hand, meanwhile, creates an arching melody that first runs up the keyboard, then back down to complete the strain.

Courtesy Morgan Collection

A strain (8 bars)

0:30   Repeat of the A section with the original left-hand texture.

C strain (24 bars, as 16 + 8)

0:35   As we have seen, the music changes key to the subdominant (E♭ major) at the C strain. The original ODJB recording featured breaks. Again, Tatum follows tradition with breaks that are blistering descending runs in the right hand.

0:40   For the first time in the piece, we hear a conventional stride texture, as the left hand drives the rhythm home after the conclusion of the breaks (right-hand runs). There is yet another break (0:44) for an upward run to conclude the first half of the C strain.

0:4   Tatum abridges the second half of the C strain to eight bars. He accomplishes this by moving more quickly to the concluding chord progression of the C strain. He also returns to the more conventional stride texture to create a contrast with the texture of the D strain.

D strain (32 bars), 1st chorus

0:50   In the famous D strain, Tatum deconstructs the melody: The "Hold That Tiger!" tune is reduced to a syncopated chordal punctuation over continuous running eighth notes in the left hand. The strain normally divides into 16 + 16, and the first time through the strain, Tatum maintains the form.

1:01   In the second half of the D strain, however, Tatum deviates by returning to the impressionistic chordal material that we heard in the introduction. The effect is to create a marvelous contrast in color to the straightforward tonic-dominant harmonies that characterize the piece as a whole.

D strain (32 bars), 2nd chorus

1:12   After the deviation from the piece's harmonies at the end of the first performance of the D strain, the return to tempo and a driving left-hand stride rhythm create terrific swing in Tatum's second D strain. The continuous eighth notes that we heard in the left hand of the first D strain are converted to a right-hand line of similar texture.

1:23   Tatum blurs the form of the D strain here by beginning a complex right-hand run two measures before the beginning of the D strain's second half. The accented note in the left hand is the actual point where the second half of the strain begins. The end of the chorus features another return of the impressionistic harmonies leading to a sustained dominant.

D strain (31 bars), 3rd chorus

1:33   For the D strain, third time, Tatum changes the texture yet again. Here the right hand repeats a syncopated rhythm on high chords while the left hand walks in octaves. The end of the first half features a break (1:42).

1:44   For the second half of the D strain (third time), Tatum returns to a stride texture as he builds the excitement still further. As he moves into the fourth strain without changing the texture, Tatum truncates the form by a bar; this has the effect of adding yet more urgency and drive to the concluding fourth chorus.

D strain (32 bars), 4th (out-) chorus

1:54   For the out-chorus, Tatum repeats brilliant descending runs in his right hand over the driving left-hand stride texture. A break at measure 15 (2:03) creates a smooth flow into the second half of the out-chorus.

2:04   The second half of the out-chorus begins with the break begun two bars earlier. Tatum builds strongly into the ending of the piece, in which a descending run brings the fireworks to an unexpectedly quiet but effective conclusion.

In the 1950s, record producer Norman Granz produced a voluminous number of Tatum's recordings that advanced the pianist's career. Sadly, though, Tatum died in 1956, probably because of the effects of alcoholism. Still, we are lucky that his art was documented with exceptionable thoroughness, and it has inspired jazz pianists ever since.

Many pianists from the heyday of stride piano kept the tradition alive well past the twenties and thirties. In addition to Johnson, Waller, and Tatum, Willie "The Lion" Smith and Luckey Roberts continued to perpetuate the Harlem solo piano style. Eubie Blake, already discussed as an important predecessor to Johnson and Waller as both pianist and composer, enjoyed a comeback in 1969 at the age of eighty-six. Stride piano was the developmental core in the playing of such pianists as Duke Ellington, Earl Hines, Teddy Wilson, and Count Basie, although these players quickly departed from a pure stride style. Still, later pianists—Johnny Guarnieri, Ralph Sutton, Dick Wellstood, and Dave McKenna—studied and kept alive the Harlem piano tradition.

Paul Whiteman and his band, who had appeared in the 1930 Universal film *King of Jazz,* featured another dance fad called "Crazy Walk" in 1933; it did not endure.

Whiteman and Gershwin

The elevation of jazz's status during the 1920s—and its increased popular appeal—owed a particular debt to the energies of several white musicians and composers. Paul Whiteman became the most successful American bandleader during this period, in part by incorporating jazz elements within an orchestral format. Whiteman's recordings of "Whispering" and "Japanese Sandman" from 1920, the year he came to New York, sold more than a million copies. He referred to his music as "symphonic syncopation" and devised lush, colorful, and complicated arrangements, often more suitable for listening than for dancing. Whiteman's renown led to his label, "King of Jazz," and in 1930 he appeared in a film by that name.

As he put it, Whiteman was attempting "to make a lady out of jazz" when he took jazz out of the nightclub and into the concert hall. His most celebrated concert took place in New York's Aeolian Hall on February 12, 1924. Entitled "An Experiment in Modern Music," the concert's grand finale featured the premiere of George Gershwin's *Rhapsody in Blue,* which Whiteman had commissioned. The composer appeared as the piano soloist. With its opening chromatic slide for clarinet, its use of blue notes, and its syncopated rhythms, *Rhapsody in Blue* placed on the concert stage the devices and rhetoric of jazz that Gershwin had enthusiastically absorbed from black Harlem musicians.

Whiteman had commissioned *Rhapsody in Blue* after hearing Gershwin's earlier jazz-influenced work, the one-act opera *Blue Monday.* Gershwin was an important composer of popular song and musical theater prior to *Rhapsody in Blue.* After its success, however, he turned more of his energy to jazz-based concert works and became increasingly preoccupied with the integration of jazz and classical music. He subsequently composed several important concert works with jazz elements, including *Concerto in F* (1925). The second of his *Preludes for Piano* (1926) and the orchestral work *An American in Paris* (1928) employ the 12-bar blues structure. Gershwin's most ambitious work was his folk opera *Porgy and Bess* (1935), based on a drama about black Americans and infused with elements of jazz and the blues. It is arguably the best twentieth-century American opera written. Because of the general popularity of his tunes, their syncopated melodies, and their numerous performances by jazz musicians, Gershwin has been called "The Jazz Composer."

Beginnings of the Big Bands

Aside from our glance at the Quintette du Hot Club de France and stride piano, we have so far concentrated on the New Orleans and Chicago traditions in which groups tended to be roughly five to seven players. In such groups, the front line combination of cornet, trombone, and clarinet featured one instrument per function: cornet (or trumpet) with the lead, trombone with a lower counterpoint or countermelody, and clarinet with an upper obbligato.

The big band featured a *section* of instruments for each instrument in the New Orleans–style band: a section of trumpets, a section of trombones, and a section of reeds (as saxophones or clarinets). In general, the use of sections required either written arrangements or *head arrangements* worked out in rehearsal because it was difficult to be completely spontaneous with a larger number of players.

A ***head arrangement*** is a musical plan and form worked up verbally by the players in rehearsal or on the bandstand.

The evolution of the early big band is a matter of some controversy in jazz history. Who was the first bandleader to use a saxophone section? Recent scholarship suggests that the Art Hickman band, a San Francisco–based group, may have been the first to use two saxophones as a "proto-reed section" in 1919.[30] Bands led by Paul Whiteman and Fletcher Henderson continued to pioneer band division into four sections (trumpets, trombones, reeds, and rhythm), but the early history of the big band remains murky. If the actual course of innovation remains unclear, it is likely that the major New York–based groups, such as the Whiteman and Henderson ensembles, solidified the use of big-band sectional formulas and textures for the 1930s.

FLETCHER HENDERSON

Fletcher Henderson arrived in New York in 1920. The twenty-two-year-old came from Atlanta, where he had received a degree in chemistry from Atlanta University. He worked as a song plugger for the Pace-Handy Music Company, one of the first and most successful black publishing companies, and recorded, as pianist, with dozens of blues singers, including Bessie Smith, Ma Rainey, and Ethel Waters.

In the meantime, Henderson had formed his own band and played at the Club Alabam for half a year before moving in 1924 to the Roseland Ballroom at Broadway and Fifty-First Street. Shortly after the band opened at Roseland, Louis Armstrong left Chicago to join Henderson as third trumpet and the featured hot soloist. Armstrong's technique, sound, and rhythmic sense revolutionized the Henderson band's playing. The group's somewhat stiff *staccato* rhythms loosened into Armstrong's more swinging, propulsive, and smooth style, which affected the work of the soloists as well as that of the entire ensemble.

Staccato is the technique of playing short notes with distinct spaces between them. The opposite of staccato is ***legato***.

A ***stock arrangement*** or ***stock*** was an arrangement created and sold by a publishing company to bandleaders. In some cases, stock arrangements were generic and unimaginative; other times the arrangements were quite effective. Bands performed stock arrangements to keep up with the latest hit songs. They would either play them as given or modify them to work with their band's individual style.

In addition, arranger Don Redman began to create many of the techniques that would be used by bands for years to follow. In some cases, Redman altered preexisting *stock arrangements* to improve them. Redman's arrangements and modifications not only heightened the distinction between improvised and written sections but also made skillful use of the contrast between brasses and reeds. The high point of Redman's work for Henderson during this period was his arrangement of "Copenhagen." Working from a stock arrangement, Redman transformed the original into a highly effective tour de force that seemed to summarize the collective developments in jazz while predicting its future direction.

In 1927, however, Don Redman left to become the arranger for McKinney's Cotton Pickers. Henderson then began arranging for his group, turning out excellent ***charts*** that highlighted the band's capabilities. The band also hosted an arsenal of top-notch soloists, including saxophonist Coleman Hawkins, trumpeter Rex Stewart, and trombonist Jimmy Harrison. Alto saxophonist Benny Carter began contributing arrangements in 1930. Carter would go on to become one of the finest arrangers in jazz as well as a premier saxophone stylist (see Chapter 3).

Ultimately, Henderson could not sustain his band. He lost many of his players to other groups and, because of his poor management skills, was often unable to pay those who remained. Many band members were heavy drinkers, which contributed to a general decline in quality; they were, in Duke Ellington's words, "probably one of the partyingest bands that ever was."[31] Financial difficulties forced Henderson to sell his arrangements. In 1934 Benny Goodman bought many of them; ironically, Goodman, as a successful white bandleader, brought Henderson's music to more

Fletcher Henderson with his band in New York, 1924. Left to right: Howard Scott, Coleman Hawkins, Louis Armstrong, Charlie Dixon, Henderson, Kaiser Marshall, Buster Bailey, Elmer Chambers, Charlie Green, Bob Escudero, Don Redman. (Except for Henderson and Bailey, the band includes different personnel on CD 1, Track 64.) Coleman Hawkins went on to form his own groups (CD 1, Track 71).

Courtesy Frank Driggs Collection

people than Henderson himself ever had. Henderson became the staff arranger for Goodman between 1939 and 1941 but returned to lead his own bands until his death in 1950.

Historically, Henderson's band of the 1920s and early thirties formed a crucial link to the succeeding swing era. With its careful chemistry of ensemble passages and solo playing, the group played a fundamental role in the development of the big band. Moreover, Henderson's ensemble writing was often written to sound like the hot solo improvisations it surrounded, bringing about a swinging style of ensemble playing. This would soon become the signature sound of the big bands as they jumped to unprecedented popularity in the 1930s. We shall return to Henderson in the next chapter to explore one of the band's swing-style compositions.

DUKE ELLINGTON'S EARLY CAREER

When Duke Ellington originally put together a big band in New York, he modeled it on Henderson's successful group.[32] Although Henderson's band was much better known during the 1920s, Ellington's unique combination of musicianship, compositional skill, professional savvy, and aristocratic persona eventually made him perhaps the most celebrated bandleader and composer in the history of jazz.

Born in Washington, D.C., on April 29, 1899, Edward Kennedy Ellington began studying piano at the age of seven. As a teenager, he developed an interest in stride piano and began to perform publicly. During this period, he earned the nickname "Duke" for his aristocratic deportment and tasteful dressing. After high school, Ellington formed his own band in Washington, the Duke's Serenaders.

Ellington first moved to New York in 1923 to play with Wilbur Sweatman's vaudeville act. Gigs were scarce at first. Ellington remained briefly before returning to Washington, but later that year he moved permanently to New York with his Washington band—Sonny Greer on drums, Otto Hardwick on saxophone, Elmer Snowden on banjo, and Arthur Whetsol on trumpet. Their band, the Washingtonians, became regular performers at the Hollywood Cafe. Though Snowden initially led the band, Ellington replaced him as leader early in 1924, and the Hollywood Cafe changed its name to the more down-home Kentucky Club.

During their earliest days, the Washingtonians represented a typical downtown dance band that was probably more sweet than hot. However, one change in the band's personnel had far-reaching consequences—the addition of cornetist Bubber Miley. Not only was Miley a hot player, but his use of the plunger mute and the straight mute also created a "growling" style of

Courtesy Morgan Collection

In Duke Ellington (CD 1, Track 68), the black performer's progression from minstrel buffoon to serious artist became complete—as we see here in a publicity photograph of the elegant Ellington at about age 30.

Bubber Miley and Joe "Tricky Sam" Nanton

Bubber Miley (1903–1932) was the cornerstone of Duke Ellington's early band. Miley's mute playing, which incorporated both the straight and cup varieties, owed a debt to King Oliver as well as to the New York–based cornetist Johnny Dunn. The growling sound formed the basis of Ellington's "jungle effects," a key feature of the band's Cotton Club performances that was adopted by subsequent Ellington trumpeters and trombonists. Ellington historian Mark Tucker suggests that "Miley's power comes not from volume or speed but from his subtle coloring of individual notes and his ability to create

and sustain a mood. . . . Miley was a different kind of hot trumpeter from the brilliant and rhythmically daring Armstrong."*

In the second half of the 1920s, trombone players cultivated a solo approach over the polyphonic role they had played earlier. With the Ellington band, Joe "Tricky Sam" Nanton (1904–1946) adapted Miley's plunger-and-growl technique to the trombone. (Listen to Track 24 of CD 1 for an example of plunger-and-growl technique on the trombone.)

* Mark Tucker, *Ellington: The Early Years* (Urbana: University of Illinois Press, 1991), 148.

playing that entirely altered the sound of the band. Miley became the featured soloist of the band. "Our band changed its character when Bubber came in," Ellington acknowledged. "He used to growl all night long, playing gutbucket on his horn. That was when we decided to forget all about the sweet music."[33]

The "growling" style of brass playing was not restricted to the cornet: As the group gradually expanded to a ten-piece band during its four-year tenure at the Kentucky Club, trombonists Charles Irvis and, later, Joe "Tricky Sam" Nanton cultivated the "gutbucket" sound on their instruments. (See the box "Bubber Miley and Joe 'Tricky Sam' Nanton" above for more on these players.)

Throughout his career, Ellington melded his players' individual sounds with the color of the entire band. Each musician contributed to the group's distinctive timbre, enhanced by Ellington's own stride-based piano style. Many of the band's compositions were clearly collaborative efforts.

Under the management of Irving Mills, Ellington and the band enjoyed increasing prestige. Mills began touting Ellington as the leader of the "foremost dance band in America."[34] Mills's hyperbole soon proved true. After the band moved from the Kentucky Club to Harlem's Cotton Club in 1927, Ellington quickly became one of the leading national jazz figures. At the Cotton Club the band played music for dancing, vocalists, and elaborate floor shows to a well-heeled after-theater crowd. With a ride from Broadway to Harlem, patrons could feel the slightly risky thrill of enjoying black entertainment in a black neighborhood while remaining part of an all-white audience. The club's jungle decor enhanced the exotic atmosphere, and the band exploited the brass section's growl techniques to create the jungle sound in such compositions as "East St. Louis Toodle-Oo," "The Mooche," "Jungle Nights in Harlem," and "Echoes of the Jungle."

The band's four years at the Cotton Club served as "a prolonged workshop period."[35] Nightly performances for thirty-eight months allowed Ellington the freedom to develop the band's musical identity, to highlight the individual players, and—most important—to experiment with unusual instrumental combinations and colors. Ellington began to create larger extended compositions. In later years, his extended compositions took the form of *suites,* works that are collections of smaller movements.

In the heady atmosphere of the Harlem Renaissance, Ellington's manager Mills sought to portray Ellington not merely as a bandleader and songwriter but as "a great musician who was making a lasting contribution to American music."[36] Ellington's work was taking on elements of "mood" or "character" pieces, many with African-American themes. As Ellington noted,

> Our aim as a dance orchestra is not so much to reproduce "hot" or "jazz" music as to describe emotions, moods, and activities which have a wide range, leading from the very gay to the somber. . . . Every one of my song titles is taken principally from the life of Harlem. . . . [I look] to the everyday life and customs of the Negro to supply my inspiration.[37]

Ellington's big band was an expression of his artistic vision. He composed works that drew on the individual skills of his musicians. Band members felt that they were given an opportunity to express their own talents while playing Ellington's unique music. Unlike other bands, members often worked with Ellington for years, sometimes decades, enabling them to absorb his style as he continued to develop. As we shall see in the next chapter, as composer, spokesperson, and bandleader, Ellington would be a central force in the ongoing evolution of jazz as a serious art form.

> A musical form of the classical European tradition, the **suite** most often denotes a piece containing several sections, each with distinctive melodies and moods. The sections may or may not be related thematically. Composers often extract the most popular or most effective sections from extended works such as opera or ballets to create a suite for concert performance.

LISTENING GUIDE

East St. Louis Toodle-Oo"

CD **1**   Track **63**

Duke Ellington and His Orchestra: "East St. Louis Toodle-Oo" (Ellington, Miley). New York, December 19, 1927. Victor 21703. Duke Ellington, leader, piano, and arrangement; James "Bubber" Miley, Louis Metcalf, trumpets; Joe Nanton, trombone; Otto Hardwick, Harry Carney, Rudy Jackson, saxophones and clarinets; Fred Guy, banjo; Wellman Braud, bass; Sonny Greer, drums.

"East St. Louis Toodle-Oo" is a fine example of the Ellington band's style in the late 1920s. The somewhat mournful quality of the piece can be attributed in part to the string bass which, when bowed, imparts an eerie somberness to the dark chord voicings of the band. Given the underrecorded presence of the drums, the beat is often audible only in the banjo strumming the backbeats and in the occasional chords of the piano flavoring the more lightly scored sections.

Introduction

0:00   The piece begins with an eight-bar introduction consisting of richly voiced chords in the saxophones, piano, and bass, an Ellington trademark. These chords form the background for Bubber Miley's following trumpet solo. The lowest saxophone, the baritone, is played somewhat louder than the others and imparts an earthiness to the chords.

AABA—Trumpet solo

0:14   The trumpet solo by Bubber Miley captures the jungle sounds for which he and the band as a whole were famous. Miley's use of mute creates a growling effect that is a main component of the jungle sound. His ability to bend notes is an especially memorable feature of the piece. Saxophone chords accompany the A sections.

0:58   In the B section a muted trombone takes over the accompaniment.

CC—Baritone saxophone solo

1:13   In this next section, baritone saxophonist Harry Carney contrasts the somber mood with an almost jaunty solo in the major mode. Carney's solo divides into two C sections with a break in the middle. The second C section has a two-bar extension at the end.

CC—Trombone solo

1:45   "Tricky Sam" Nanton's trombone solo, although identical in form to Carney's baritone saxophone solo, features the muted growling sounds first heard with trumpeter Miley (at 0:14–1:13).

AA—Clarinet solo

2:18   A return of the thick opening chords forms the background for the clarinet solo, which begins with growling in the lower register. Later in the solo the upper register is explored as well, without a loss of intensity or mood.

CC—Ensemble

2:47   After the clarinet solo, the first ensemble passage of the arrangement follows, built on the harmony and form of the baritone saxophone solo. As in that solo, this section is in two parts, with a break between.

Return of A section

3:18   Rounding off the arrangement, Miley returns with an eight-bar reprise of the A section, accompanied by the saxophones and trombones.

In contrast to many other arrangers of the time, Ellington is more inclined to employ mixed instrumental groupings. For this reason, his scoring is often harder to identify on first hearing and his textures differ from those of most other ensembles. Moreover, "East St. Louis Toodle-Oo" is conceived as a jazz composition, not an arrangement of a popular tune.

Ellington continually strived for distinctive timbres and a unique overall sound for his band. A tone we might call "brooding," as heard in "East St. Louis Toodle-Oo," is created by: atypical use of bowed string bass; solos that feature growling, jungle sounds; dark, muted timbres; thick chord voicings; and interplay of major and minor keys.

Ellington frequently sought unusual formats for his compositions. In arranging an AABA song for a band, it is often difficult to vary the basic "*head*-solos-head" pattern creatively and still fashion a workable, uncontrived arrangement. Ellington circumvented this problem by both composing and arranging the material. In so doing, Ellington not only composed great popular songs such as "In My Solitude," "Sophisticated Lady," and "Mood Indigo" but also penned more-extended works such as "East St. Louis Toodle-Oo" and later very lengthy works such as "Black, Brown, and Beige," "Liberian Suite," and the "Sacred Concerts." Particularly in the extended works, the arrangement was conceived as an intrinsic part of the composition. Given the brilliance and originality of his work, there is little doubt that Ellington was one of the foremost arranger-composers in twentieth-century American music.

Questions and Topics for Discussion

1. How did ragtime and the blues each contribute to the formation of early jazz?

2. How did recording influence the early history of jazz?

3. What are the key stylistic components of the early New Orleans jazz ensemble as typified by King Oliver's Creole Jazz Band? Discuss instrumentation, repertory, and the role of each instrument within the ensemble.

4. How did Louis Armstrong revolutionize the role of the soloist in jazz? What are key aspects of his style?

5. How does Bix Beiderbecke's style compare with Armstrong's?

6. What leaders and arrangers contributed to the foundations of the big-band style in the 1920s? What were some of the stylistic features of 1920s big-band writing?

Key Terms

Break 49
Chart 82
Chicago jazz 51
Creoles of Color 48
Dixieland 50
Harlem Renaissance 73
Head 86
Head arrangement 81
Hot bands 52
Inside playing 69
Legato 81
Mute 56
New Orleans jazz 50
Out-chorus 71
Outside playing 69
Piano rolls 75
Player piano 75
Plunger 60
Rent party 74
Scat singing 60
Speakeasy 52
Staccato 81
Stock arrangement (stock) 82
Stride piano 74
Suite 85
Sweet bands 32
Tag 55
Tailgate trombone 64
Terminal vibrato 61
Vibrato 47

3

THE SWING ERA

FROM ROUGHLY 1935 TO 1945, *swing* dominated the popular music of the United States, the only time that any type of jazz achieved such mainstream success. Adoring fans idolized the top players and made the most successful bandleaders rich. The big-band era had arrived.

This chapter presents the *big bands* in the context of their time along with some of the major swing soloists. Andy Kirk's Twelve Clouds of Joy was an important *territory band* from Kansas City that featured Mary Lou Williams, a excellent pianist and arranger who carved out a major career in an era unreceptive to women as jazz musicians. After examining the growth of the territory bands, we shall turn to three of the most influential big bands: the Count Basie Orchestra from Kansas City and the Benny Goodman and Duke Ellington bands from New York. Complementing Mary Lou Williams, we shall also examine a well-known women's big band, the International Sweethearts of Rhythm.

Of all the big bands, Goodman achieved the greatest mainstream success, although Basie and Ellington probably contributed the most significant elements to the big-band style. All three musicians enjoyed long and influential careers that extended beyond the swing era.

Overview: A Decade of Swing

Swing music was a phenomenon. Between 1935 and 1945, it became the popular music of a generation. Speaking for the generation who came of age between the beginning of the Great Depression and the end of World War II, James Lincoln Collier remembers the following:

> Swing was theirs alone. Dancing to swing was central to their courtship style. Young people danced—at first the fox-trot, then the so-called jitterbug dances which arose in the mid- to late-1930s—in huge, often elaborate dance palaces, in hotel restaurants and ballrooms, in high school gyms and, perhaps most of all, in living rooms to swing music from radios and record players. By means of the new "portable" radios their music went with them everywhere: on woodland picnics, to beaches, summer houses, skating ponds, big city parks. These people not only danced to swing, they ate to it, drank to it, necked to it, talked to it, and frequently just listened to it. It was everywhere.[1]

As Ivie Anderson sang in Duke Ellington's band, "It Don't Mean a Thing (If It Ain't Got That Swing)." In the early 1930s when the song was released, however, *swing* was only an insider's term. Duke Ellington even had to explain in 1933 that his orchestra and a few others "exploited a style known as 'swing' which is Harlem for rhythm."[2] Within a few years, though, the term—and the music—dominated popular culture.

As the 1930s progressed, more people had access to the music. Radios, increasingly more affordable, broadcast the big bands from ballrooms and hotels in the major cities. In 1930 only one-third of U.S. households had radios; by 1935 two-thirds of all homes had them. Similarly, the number of jukeboxes jumped from 25,000 in 1933 to 300,000 in 1939. The dramatic growth of the record and radio industries changed popular music forever. People no longer had to sing or play an instrument to enjoy music whenever they wished. Furthermore, musical success came from the numbers of records sold, not just prestigious live engagements.

It is impossible to sort out all the reasons why both white and black audiences demanded to hear, more than any other style, the hot jazz music of the 1920s pioneered by black bands. At the beginning of the 1930s, Duke Ellington and Fletcher Henderson, with their enlarged bands, were becoming the primary interpreters of swing music; many of the white bands, such as the Guy Lombardo band, played in a sentimental, sweet style. We should

The advent of radio spread the sounds of jazz around the country. This advertisement for the Philco radio appeared in 1936 on the back of *Etude Magazine*. Notice the prices—from $20 to $600.

not carry this divided view of white and black bands too far, though. The repertory of the black bands was never exclusively hot jazz: Some of their arrangements qualified as sweet music, and Ellington's Cotton Club revues and Jimmie Lunceford's shows always included novelty and show numbers. By the same token, some white bands of the early 1930s used elements of jazz: In particular, the Casa Loma Orchestra, popular on college campuses, was another of the most important bands in establishing big-band swing. It mixed raucous up-tempo works with sentimental waltzes. Thus, while the black bands featured more hot music than the white bands did, all the bands widely varied their repertories—it was necessary in order to survive.

By the middle of the decade, Benny Goodman became known as the "King of Swing" after rising to dizzying heights of success playing many of Fletcher Henderson's arrangements. Goodman's success was contagious. By the end of the 1930s, there were more than 200 name bands, each with star soloists. Often the prominent soloists, having begun their careers in other bands, went on to lead their own groups. Clarinetist Goodman, trumpeters Harry James and Bunny Berrigan, trombonists Jack Teagarden and Tommy Dorsey, drummer Gene Krupa, and pianists Duke Ellington and Count Basie all formed their own bands. Each had a distinctive sound:

> You could hear all types of swing bands: the hard-driving swing of Benny Goodman, the relaxed swing of Jimmie Lunceford, the forceful dixieland of Bob Crosby, the simple, riff-filled swing of Count Basie, the highly developed swing of Duke Ellington, and the very commercial swing of Glenn Miller.[3]

When we listen today to the music that the swing bands played in their heyday, we would not consider much of it to be jazz. Continuing a trend from the 1920s, bands often avoided outright improvisation. Some bands worked out the solo (or improvisational) sections in advance and played them identically night after night—often because listeners expected the same improvisations they heard on the recordings. Many of the bands continued to churn out sentimental ballads along with up-tempo swing. And almost all of the bands had singers—invariably called "girl" singers and "boy" singers, whatever their age—and vocal music constituted a sizeable portion of any band's song list. Many of the singers who later became famous on their own began their careers singing with swing bands: For example, Frank Sinatra got his start with the bands of Harry James and Tommy Dorsey, and Peggy Lee with Benny Goodman.

The swing boom continued unabated through the early 1940s but began to decline during World War II. Gasoline rationing and the shortage of tires made trips difficult to schedule or prohibitively expensive for bands that needed to travel extensively for live performances. Many of the singers who began with the bands gained more success on their own. The decline of nightlife made it more expensive to spotlight the bands. At the end of 1946, eight of the most famous groups disbanded either temporarily or permanently—including those of Benny Goodman, Jack Teagarden, Harry James, Woody Herman, Tommy Dorsey, and Benny Carter—and the swing boom came to an end.

Beyond the societal upheavals that hastened the end of the swing era, swing itself was largely exhausted as a jazz style—the public wanted something new. While it lasted, swing defined a golden age of jazz, a time when great musicians and first-rate bands produced outstanding music and brought jazz its greatest popular acclaim.

The Big Band in the Swing Era

INSTRUMENTATION, TECHNIQUE, AND ARRANGEMENT

The dance orchestra and large jazz ensemble became all but synonymous during the swing era. The lindy hop—also called the jitterbug—was a frenetic and virtuosic dance that required an up-tempo, hot-jazz sound. As discussed earlier, the big band evolved for the most part from the dance orchestra, but during the 1920s the hot rhythm and improvisation of Dixieland jazz players gradually transformed these orchestras. We have seen how bandleader Fletcher Henderson and his talented arranger, Don Redman, began to develop the big-band style. Other popular bands, such as the relatively mainstream Jean Goldkette and Paul Whiteman orchestras, incorporated jazz improvisation and spread the influence of large bands. These groups, along with the band of Art Hickman, spurred the development of the big band into an ensemble using four instrumental divisions. The four divisions, or *sections*, of instruments in a typical big band are:

> A *section* of a big band is a group of related instruments; three trumpets and three trombones might form the brass section.

- ▶ Trumpets (listen to Tracks 12–15 of CD 1 ♫ for an example)

- ▶ Trombones (with trumpets and trombones grouped together as the "brass") (Tracks 22–25 of CD 1 ♫)

- ▶ Woodwinds, usually called "reeds" (saxophones and related instruments) (Tracks 16–21 of CD 1 ♫)

- ▶ The rhythm section, frequently consisting of piano, guitar, bass, and drums (Tracks 26–43 of CD 1 ♫)

The demands on the musicians playing in a big band differed significantly from those placed on small-group players. The extensive library, or book, of arrangements that all big bands developed required that the musicians be skilled in reading parts. Playing with a big-band section required that musicians blend with similar

Big-Band Terms

A band's *library* or *book* is its collection of arrangements or pieces. Arrangements are often called *charts*. These are usually songs but may also include larger-scale works. A library is necessary for big bands, but smaller groups may also have one.

Musicians with good *intonation* are said to be playing "in tune." That is, the players know how to make small adjustments in the pitch of their instruments as they play so that they match the pitches of the other players in the section.

Balance refers to the ability of a section to blend. In a well-balanced section,

none of the players will be too soft or too loud relative to the others.

An often-heard term for each part in a section is *chair*, as in first trumpet chair, first trombone chair, and so on.

The player who usually takes the melody or top part in a section is called the *lead player* of the section. That is, the lead player occupies the first chair of the section. Within a given section, the lead player will usually be slightly louder than the other players in a correct balance.

A band depends in particular on the

lead chair or first trumpet player of the trumpet section. The *lead trumpet* must be a dominating player, capable of precision, power, and control of the high register.

The *jazz chair* of a section may be a player hired especially for improvisational fluency. For example, Bix Beiderbecke occupied the jazz trumpet chair in the Paul Whiteman band, as did Bubber Miley in the Ellington band.

A player who is not a lead player or a featured soloist is usually called a *sideman*.

instruments, that is, play together with precision and constant attention to intonation and balance. (See the box "Big-Band Terms" on page 91.)

Big-band arrangements formed the basis of the swing-era repertory. The most creative arrangers of the period—including Don Redman, Duke Ellington, Fletcher Henderson, Eddie Sauter, Sy Oliver, and Benny Carter—successfully and creatively balanced written ensemble sections with sections for improvised solos that showed off the star players in the bands. These arrangers skillfully used the band's various resources—for example, by setting off the brass section from the reed section or writing a brass or reed accompaniment behind the soloist.

One characteristic technique that arrangers used involved *antiphony*, particularly the antiphonal alternation of different sections of the band. An example of this occurs in Fletcher Henderson's celebrated 1935 arrangement of Jelly Roll Morton's "King Porter Stomp" (see Music Example 3-1).[4] Notice how the arranger gives the figure to

Antiphony is the trading of melodic figures between two different sections of the band; it is a more formal musical term for *call-and-response* (see the Introduction). Antiphony implies an equal division of the musical forces rather than an answering response to a leading call. Listen to Track 47 of CD 1 🎧: The trumpet and saxophone, by trading twos, engage in a form of antiphony.

Music Example 3-1
From the Fletcher Henderson arrangement of "King Porter Stomp."

the brass in the pickup and measures 2 and 4 and to the reeds in measures 1, 3, and 5. This typical passing back and forth of the figure between brass and reeds continues the use of the call-and-response patterns we first saw applied to vocal music. Henderson's "Down South Camp Meeting" also illustrates antiphony (see the Listening Guide below).

Henderson created an especially fine composition and arrangement in "Down South Camp Meeting," which, like "King Porter Stomp," later became a huge hit for Benny Goodman.

L I S T E N I N G   G U I D E

"Down South Camp Meeting"
CD **1** Track **64**

Fletcher Henderson and His Orchestra: "Down South Camp Meeting" (Henderson). Decca 213. New York, September 12, 1934. Fletcher Henderson, arrangement, piano, leader; Henry Allen, Irving Randolph, Russell Smith, trumpets; Keg Johnson, Claude Jones, trombones; Buster Bailey, clarinet; Hilton Jefferson, Russell Procope, clarinet, alto saxophone; Ben Webster, tenor saxophone; Lawrence Lucie, guitar; Elmer James, bass; Walter Johnson, drums.

In "Down South Camp Meeting," which predates the more famous versions by Goodman, we can hear many of the swing-style techniques discussed in this chapter. Note that there is little solo improvisation in the arrangement—only one 24-bar solo by trumpeter Henry Allen. The focus instead is on the composition and arrangement.

Introduction—4 bars

0:00   The introduction features a syncopated figure played by the entire ensemble; this sets up section A.

A section—8 bars as 4 + 4

0:05   The saxophone section has the syncopated melody, sustained notes that are attacked just before the beat. The use of blue notes contributes a hot, blues-tinged quality typical of up-tempo swing pieces. In the fourth bar of each four-bar unit, the brass answer antiphonally.

B section—8 bars as 4 + 4

0:14   In the contrasting B section, brass and saxophones reverse roles: The brass take the lead, while the saxophones answer.

A section—8 bars as 4 + 4

0:23   The A section returns with minor embellishments to the principal melody.

ABA trumpet solo as 8 + 8 + 8

0:32   The ABA framework just presented serves as background for a Henry Allen trumpet solo. The saxophones sustain chords as an accompaniment.

0:42   Allen alludes to the original melodic idea of the B section in the B section of his solo.

0:52   Return to A section of the solo.

Transition—8 bars

1:01   In this transitional and modulating section, hear the antiphonal saxophone and trumpet solos. Saxophones and trombones accompany with sustained chords, which crescendo (grow louder) as they are held.

C section—CCDC as 8 + 8 + 4 + 8

1:10   The C section is analogous to the trio in the older ragtime-, march-influenced jazz of the 1920s. The saxophones have the melody for the most part. The C section (first eight bars) features a swinging tune that uses blue notes.

1:29   The bridge of this C section, D, is only four bars and is syncopated to provide a contrast to the relative rhythmic regularity of the C section's main theme, which contains many on-the-beat and accented quarter notes.

1:33   The return of the C section's main theme is modified, creating a more conclusive ending to the section.

C section repeated—CCDC as 8 + 8 + 4 + 8

1:43   The brass take the melody for the first two C sections. There are some modifications and embellishments to the C theme, which we first heard in the saxophones.

2:02   The saxophones take the bridging D theme, which is also modified from its first presentation. These small changes indicate the care Henderson took to enhance the effectiveness of the arrangement.

2:06   Return to C section.

Transition—4 bars

2:15   An antiphonal transitional section sets up the following section, a second "trio." Note the call-and-response between the brass and reeds (with lead clarinet).

E section—8 bars, played 4 times

2:19   A new timbre complements a new melody and key: The melody is in the saxophones, but with a clarinet lead in a fairly low register. The first note of the lead clarinet is a blue note. Thus, Henderson continues the idea of featuring blue notes as key elements of his themes. The section is played four times.

2:39 and **2:48**   The third and fourth times, the reeds play an octave higher. The brass answer the short phrases in the reeds antiphonally.

Tag—1 bar

2:56   A short tag consisting of rising chords—syncopated off the beat—extends the E section by a bar.

One of the many reasons big bands enjoyed such popularity was their focus on the hit songs of the day. The bands developed a symbiotic relationship with the publishers of Tin Pan Alley and would vie to be the first to perform and record the best new songs. Similarly, the publishers would try to interest the most popular bands in their latest efforts. The result was a steady stream of hit songs that the public enjoyed and their favorite bands personalized. For an extremely popular song, different groups would compete with arrangements that varied from quite similar to distinctive.

During the course of writing a chart, arrangers often took liberties with the melodic and rhythmic structure of the original song and reworked it into swing style. They frequently syncopated melodies to give them the rhythmic character of an improvised jazz solo. This swing-style melody made the transition from written sections to improvised-solo sections more seamless.

Territory bands and the groups in and around Kansas City favored the *head arrangement* (discussed in Chapter 2), which was fashioned by ear during rehearsal or performance. Band members worked out their own parts or suggested parts to each other. These arrangements were often simple and riff-oriented, lacking the variety of textures available to arrangers working with printed scores.

THE CHANGING ROLE OF THE RHYTHM SECTION

The rhythm section largely generated the hard-driving swing that propelled the ensemble and improvised sections of the bands. In the big-band era, expectations of the rhythm section—piano, guitar, bass, and drums—changed. Responding to innovations in the design of instruments and changes in musical taste, these instruments performed differently during the swing era than before. During the 1920s either the tuba or the string bass provided the rhythmic underpinning for the band, but the bass gradually superseded the tuba. In addition, the bass or tuba player was expected to play either on beats 1 and 3 or on all four beats of the measure. By the mid- to late-1930s, however, the bass player often played consistently on all four beats, creating the *walking bass* sound. The four-beat walking bass then freed the pianist from a timekeeping role. Pianists could play fewer notes and were able to accompany soloists by playing syncopated chordal figures.

In performing a ***walking bass***, the bassist articulates all four beats in a 4/4 bar. The bass lines often follow simple scale patterns, avoiding too many disruptive leaps between notes. The walking bass is common in jazz, heard in all styles since becoming firmly established during the swing era. Listen to Track 43 on CD 1 to hear a walking bass.

The drummer's role changed considerably after the hi-hat became a part of the drummer's set. The hi-hat, introduced in 1927, consisted of two face-to-face cymbals that the drummer controlled with a foot pedal. The pedal closed the cymbals with a "chick" sound. (Listen to Track 31 on CD 1 to hear this sound; Track 32 shows a swing beat played on the hi-hat.) Instead of keeping the pulse in the bass drum, swing drummers such as Walter Johnson of Fletcher Henderson's band and Jo Jones of Count Basie's band used the hi-hat to create a more subtle propulsion that could drive an entire big band. Soon other drummers learned to keep the pulse on the hi-hat. Often the drummer would close the pedal on beats 2 and 4, slightly accenting these beats in relation to the first and third beats. In addition, by the mid- to late-1930s, many drummers used the bass drum on all four beats, as exemplified by Gene Krupa's work with Benny Goodman, especially on what Goodman called his up-tempo "killer-diller" numbers.

By the end of the twenties, the guitar gradually replaced the banjo in the rhythm section. Eddie Lang (1902–1933) was an important player who helped create this change. A Philadelphia-born guitarist, he contributed to the important Beiderbecke-Trumbauer recordings and recorded with Red Nichols, Jean Goldkette, and Paul Whiteman, as well as with violinist Joe Venuti.

As the swing era evolved, guitarists began to play four chords to the measure, giving a slight accent to the second and fourth beats. The introduction in 1936 of the electric guitar allowed the guitarist to be heard in a large group. The electric guitar also enabled the performer to take on an improvisational role in a large ensemble rather than merely providing accompaniment. (The various sounds of the acoustic guitar and electric guitar can be heard on Tracks 36–42 on CD 1.)

Territory Bands

The rise of swing took place gradually over time and across the country. While New York bands of the late 1920s and early 1930s were developing the swing style, many midwestern and southwestern territory bands were contributing to its evolution as well. From St. Louis to Denver, between Texas and Nebraska, in towns such as Omaha,

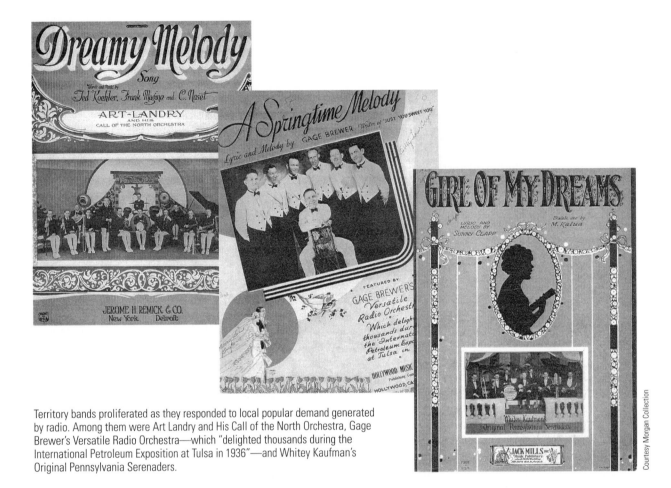

Territory bands proliferated as they responded to local popular demand generated by radio. Among them were Art Landry and His Call of the North Orchestra, Gage Brewer's Versatile Radio Orchestra—which "delighted thousands during the International Petroleum Exposition at Tulsa in 1936"—and Whitey Kaufman's Original Pennsylvania Serenaders.

Oklahoma City, and Salina, territory bands abounded. Centering themselves on a regional capital, they toured their regions and played dance halls and theaters for one-night or multiweek engagements. Many of the bands covered a lot of territory:

> Jumps of 800 or 1,000 miles between engagements were not uncommon, and, among the less affluent orchestras, these trips were made by passenger car, with perhaps a truck carrying the instruments and arrangements, if any. Accounts of panic trips, with twelve musicians crammed into a single automobile, and a man or two hanging onto the running board or fender, are encountered in interviews dealing with the Depression years.[5]

Many of the territory-band members were not music readers. Players and soloists relied on head arrangements and their own improvisational skills. The territory bands had rivalries, some friendly and some not, and legendary "battles of the bands" in dance halls show a fierce competitive spirit that helped improve the bands' sounds. Most important, many of the significant players of the swing era—Coleman Hawkins, Ben Webster, Herschel Evans, Lester Young, Buster Smith, and Count Basie—received their earliest training in these bands.

KANSAS CITY

As William Saunders recalled in discussing the Kansas City scene in the late 1920s:

> We listened. We didn't have radios or television to interrupt us. . . . That developed the Kansas City style because you would hear in a cluster and the style just developed between your ideas coming in here from Texas and Oklahoma and possibly Nebraska and Colorado, and there's a fusion of all those ideas together, and over a period of years and a period of sessions it became obvious as the Kansas City style.[6]

In all the Midwest, only Kansas City seemed immune to the Depression. Music flourished. In 1935 there were more than three hundred Kansas City clubs with live music. Jam sessions took place nightly; musicians spoke of leaving a session and returning several hours later to find the band still jamming on the same tune. Like the gunfighters of the old West—or stride pianists at the rent parties of New York—the local Kansas City musicians issued challenges to well-known players who were passing through town. Listeners could go to the Sunset Club and hear blues singer Big Joe Turner and pianist Pete Johnson, Count Basie's band at the Reno Club, and the arrangements of pianist Mary Lou Williams with Andy Kirk's Twelve Clouds of Joy.

In part, corruption in city government protected Kansas City from the Depression. Between 1926 and 1939, city alderman Tom Pendergast and his machine dominated the city; Pendergast made certain that gambling, liquor, and prostitution were readily available. Although Pendergast himself had no interest in music, his practices allowed nightlife and live music to flourish.

Kansas City bands had several features that set them apart from the bands of the urban Northeast. In contrast to the complex arrangements of the eastern bands, Kansas City bands tended to feature head arrangements. The 12-bar blues was a staple of their repertory. Kansas City players developed riff compositions based on simple melodic ideas, and horn players often spontaneously composed riffs to play behind other soloists.

One Kansas City band that achieved national recognition was Andy Kirk's Twelve Clouds of Joy. Like most of the bands of the swing era, they played both hot and sweet jazz. Led by Kirk, who played bass saxophone and tuba, the band featured pianist Mary Lou Williams, an accomplished musician who created many of their arrangements.

MARY LOU WILLIAMS AND THE CLOUDS OF JOY

Mary Lou Williams (1910–1981) was a remarkably fine pianist and composer, a superb musician who emerged from the swing era with a unique career. She remains not only one of the most important women in jazz history, but one of the very few women of her time able to develop a notable career in jazz at all. Prominent as

The remarkable career of pianist, composer, and arranger Mary Lou Williams (CD 1, Track 65) spanned five decades.

both a pianist and an arranger-composer, she was the person primarily responsible for the sound of the Andy Kirk band and its hits in the 1930s. Although she left the band in 1942, she continued to provide excellent arrangements for the major band leaders of the era: Duke Ellington, Benny Goodman, Earl Hines, and Tommy Dorsey.

In addition to creating musical arrangements, Williams built a strong career in composition. The New York Philharmonic performed part of her *Zodiac Suite* in 1946. Though her work reflects mostly the late 1920s and the swing era, Williams befriended many of the jazz modernists in the 1940s and absorbed aspects of their style. She continued to develop as both composer and pianist, eventually writing bebop-style arrangements for the Dizzy Gillespie band. In the 1950s, her strong religious interests led her to compose many sacred works. She remained active through the 1970s, eventually teaching at Duke University.

L I S T E N I N G   G U I D E

"Mary's Idea"
CD **1** Track **65**

Andy Kirk and His Twelve Clouds of Joy: "Mary's Idea" (Williams). Decca 2326. New York, December 6, 1938. Andy Kirk, director; Harry Lawson, Clarence Trice, Earl Thomson, trumpets; Ted Donnelly, Henry Wells, trombone; John Harrington, clarinet, alto and baritone saxophones; John Williams, alto and baritone saxophones; Earl Miller, alto saxophone; Dick Wilson, tenor saxophone; Mary Lou Williams, arrangement, piano; Ted Robinson, guitar; Booker Collins, bass; Ben Thigpen, drums.

"Mary's Idea" is just one of the many superb charts Mary Lou Williams wrote for the Andy Kirk band. In them, she deftly combines a solid understanding of swing-era conventions with sufficient experimental curiosity to produce works of uncommon interest and effectiveness.

Introduction—4 bars

0:00   The four-bar introduction consists of a *vamping* figure (a repeating passage often used as an introduction) in the saxophones, doubled by the bass and the piano. The drummer provides a clear example of a swing beat on the hi-hat cymbals; you can hear the foot pedal closing the cymbals on the second and fourth beats of each bar.

A section—8 bars, repeated

0:06   The brass enter with a theme in counter-point to the saxophone vamp. Note how well the different sections combine in counterpoint.

The trumpet melody is almost entirely off the beat, while the saxophone vamp mixes on- and off-beat notes.

0:15   The saxophones answer the brass in the last two bars of the A section (first time).

B section—Bridge, 8 bars

0:29 The saxophones take over the lead for the first four bars of the bridge.

0:35 The last four bars are a trombone solo, which provides further textural contrast and variety.

A section—8 bars

0:41 The A section returns with brass lead and saxophone vamp. The music is modified in both brass and reeds to create a more definitive cadence.

AA—16 bars as 8 + 8, trumpet solo

0:51 An improvised trumpet solo over the A-section material.

1:01 The saxophones answer at the end of the first eight bars.

1:13 The entire band answers at the end of the second eight bars.

BA—16 bars as 8 + 8, piano solo

1:15 Williams takes over the solo at the B-section bridge and continues on to the final A section. Her spare melodic style contrasts the busy virtuosity typical of the 1920s stride stylists. Nevertheless, you can detect a remnant of the stride left hand, which occasionally follows the march-bass pattern. Her right-hand melody is elegant, with occasional blues licks fitted in.

1:32 She finishes her solo with syncopated, virtuosic runs.

1:36 In the last two bars of the section, the saxophones usher in the clarinet solo.

C section—14 bars as 8 + 6, clarinet solo

1:38 The clarinet solos over a new harmonic progression. The combination of muted brass and clarinet is refined and quite attractive. The final two bars are elided into a break that develops into an interlude.

Interlude—5 bars

1:59 The complex syncopation of the interlude imposes a 3/4 rhythmic pattern on the 4/4 bars. The section ultimately can be measured as five 4/4 bars, but this is clear only after the next section, a climax, has begun. This is one of Williams's fine experimental twists.

AA—16 bars as 8 + 8, climactic development

2:06 The climax features extensive syncopation over the final four bars of the eight-bar unit. There is again the implication of a 3/4 pattern imposed on the 4/4 meter. On the whole, the section develops material from the opening A section.

2:18 These eight bars, a wonderful and experimental development of the opening idea, repeat.

B section—8 bars

2:29 A trombone solo for the first four bars of the B section provides a satisfying release from the dislocating syncopation of the preceding section.

2:35 The whole band enters for the second half, leading to the last A section statement.

A section—6 bars

2:40 A reprise of the A section as first heard. The "missing" two bars that would complete an eight-bar section are elided into the coda to become its beginning.

Coda—8 bars

2:49 The opening vamp begins the **coda** (a concluding passage) and continues for four bars.

2:55 The last four bars transform the opening material into a final cadence.

The young Count Basie (CD 1, Track 66) on a one-cent publicity postcard from Music Corporation of America.

Courtesy Morgan Collection

A **lick** (also called a **formula**) is a worked-out melodic idea that fits a common chord progression. Most improvisers develop formulas for up-tempo pieces because the rapid tempo does not allow time for total spontaneity.

Count Basie

Bill "Count" Basie was born in Red Bank, New Jersey, in 1904. He learned many of his piano skills by hearing Fats Waller play piano and organ in Harlem and early on made his living touring the Theatre Owners Booking Association (TOBA), the largest black vaudeville circuit. In 1927, while touring in Kansas City, the show he was with broke up and left Basie stranded. He remained in town and worked with the Blue Devils and the Bennie Moten band. By 1932 Moten's band included many of the finest players in Kansas City. Among their recordings, "Prince of Wails" is an especially interesting virtuoso number that showcases Basie and his connection to Fats Waller and stride style. Moten's death in 1935 left one of the most important bands in Kansas City without a leader, and the job fell to Basie.

Basie's band gained a national reputation as an outfit capable of playing swing with equal measures of drive and relaxation. Additionally, it was remarkably long-lived; Basie managed to keep his group together until his death in 1984, and it continued to perform under different leaders afterward. Led by Basie's nearly imperceptible cues and nods at the piano, the band played with incredible rhythmic drive and exuberance. The band's book was based on blues and riff compositions—a legacy of their origin as a territory band. Basie became famous for his understated solos, a few well-placed chords or a simple repeated *lick* that propelled the band. Like a finely calibrated machine, the band's infectious swing drove such compositions as "Jumpin' at the Woodside" and Basie's signature song, "One O'Clock Jump."

The band's break came when record producer John Hammond heard the band broadcast from the Reno Club. Hammond went to Kansas City in 1936 and was overwhelmed. He later wrote:

> Basie became almost a religion with me and I started writing about the band in *Down Beat* and *Melody Maker*. . . . (M)y first night at the Reno in May, 1936, still stands out as the most exciting musical experience I can remember. The Basie band seemed to have all the virtues of a small combo, with inspired soloists, complete relaxation, plus the drive and dynamics of a disciplined large orchestra.[7]

Much of the band's appeal came from the exuberant drive of the rhythm section. The combination of Basie on piano, Walter Page on bass, Jo Jones on drums, and Freddie Green on guitar drove the band brilliantly, at all tempos and levels of volume and energy. Despite his roots in Harlem stride piano, Basie developed a freer, less cluttered, more up-to-date accompaniment style. Page's walking bass and Freddie Green's regular guitar strumming worked with Jo Jones's timekeeping on the hi-hat and stated all four beats to the measure. Pianist Teddy Wilson wrote:

> The Basie rhythm section was a completely new sound at the time. Musicians took a great deal of notice of it. . . . Jo Jones was playing with open cymbals, not choking them like other drummers, plus a very light bass drum and his particular use of the sock [hi-hat] cymbal. . . . [Walter Page] created quite a stir among the bass players with his use of the G string—the high string on the bass violin—in a 4/4 rhythm, playing very high notes with . . . sparkling crisp chime-like notes from Basie's piano.[8]

Unfettered by the more complicated arrangements of the urban Northeast bands, the band's top-flight soloists had ample freedom. Lester Young's light tenor sound provided a wonderfully cool pastel contrast to the red-hot swing of the band in recordings such as "Lester Leaps In" and "Roseland Shuffle." Herschel Evans, Basie's other tenor player, provided a foil to Young's airy sound.

LISTENING GUIDE

"Shoe Shine Boy"
CD **1** Track **66**

Jones-Smith Incorporated: "Shoe Shine Boy" (Cahn-Chaplin). Vocalion 3441. Chicago, November 9, 1936. Carl Smith, trumpet; Lester Young, tenor saxophone; Count Basie, piano, leader; Walter Page, bass; Jo Jones, drums.

Basie's small-group ensemble recorded "Shoe Shine Boy" under the name Jones-Smith Incorporated because of record company agreements. It is one of the most famous examples of Kansas City small-group jazz in the swing era.

Introduction—8 bars, repeated

0:00   Basie developed a trademark of opening his tunes with a swing vamp of four or eight bars. Here the eight-bar idea, repeated, serves as an introduction to his own piano solo. Basie's Shoe Shine vamp is shown here.

Although the striding bass is evident in the left hand, it is not really an example of stride piano because the right-hand figuration incorporates a light swing riff, which is not a characteristic of stride. This open, lighter sound is more typical of swing-era piano styles, which sometimes kept the striding left hand but featured airier right-hand playing. The sometimes-striding left hand became known as "swing bass."

0:07   Repeat.

AABA—Basie piano solo, 1 chorus

0:14   Basie presents the overall form of the piece, a 32-bar structure, which is a close variant of the chord progression known as "rhythm changes." The lightness of Basie's touch and ideas is reminiscent of Mary Lou Williams's solo in "Mary's Idea." Jones enters with a swing beat on the hi-hat.

0:22   Basie's second A section states the main idea of the original melody, which is never given in its entirety in the performance.

0:29   B section.

0:37   Return to A section.

AABA, repeated—Young tenor solo, 2 choruses

0:44   Young's two-chorus tenor solo was one of the most famous of the swing era.

0:59   In the B section of this chorus, Young and drummer Jo Jones play "kicks" together (by accenting and holding a note) every two bars.

1:15   Second chorus.

AABA—Smith trumpet solo, 1 chorus

1:45   Trumpeter Carl Smith plays one chorus with his trumpet muted. This third consecutive improvised solo shows that the performance is not projecting a complex arrangement but instead is simulating a jam-session atmosphere with loose, freewheeling solos and ideas. Smith begins in the high register with a syncopated lick that emphasizes blue notes.

1:53   The second time through the A section provides contrast by avoiding emphasis of these notes.

2:01–   The repeated-note ideas heard here were foreshadowed earlier in the solo.
2:03

AA—2-bar breaks

2:16   The band alternates two-bar solo breaks in this order: Basie piano, Young tenor saxophone, Smith trumpet, Basie piano, Young tenor, Smith trumpet, Basie piano, Young tenor. Note that because *three* players each take two bars, the music is unevenly distributed through the 16-bar AA. The use of alternating solo breaks here is called *trading twos.* More common than trading twos is *trading fours,* with each soloist getting four bars of improvisation. *Trading eights* is also sometimes heard. The technique of trading solos is often used to create climaxes in performance.

B section—Drum solo

2:32   An eight-bar Jo Jones drum solo. Basie articulates the chord changes to provide a sense of the bridge harmony through the drum solo.

A section—Whole ensemble

2:40   An exciting ***out-chorus*** with the whole ensemble improvising. Smith provides a lead riff reminiscent of the beginning of his solo; Young complements with a countermelody.

Coda—10 bars

2:47   To wrap up the performance, a coda features four two-bar breaks by (in order) Basie, Young, Jones, and Page, and then the whole ensemble in a two-bar cadence.

Jo Jones: Modernizing the Drums

Jo Jones modernized drumming techniques by transferring the timekeeping role from the bass and snare drums to the cymbals, particularly the hi-hat. His feel for time helped popularize the four-beats-to-the-bar orientation of most of the swing bands; he was also well known for his work with brushes.

Born in Chicago in 1911, Jones grew up in Alabama. He worked as a tap dancer in carnival shows before joining Walter Page's Blue Devils in Oklahoma City in the late 1920s. Eventually he made his way to Kansas City, where he joined Basie in 1934. After leaving Basie, he continued to work in swing-style groups. He died in 1985.

A prime example of small-group swing style, "Shoe Shine Boy" highlights some of the features that made the Basie band unique:

▶ Emphasis on up-tempo jazz and improvisation instead of sweet dance music

▶ Fine balance between ensemble tightness and uninhibited swinging solos

▶ First-rate personnel, including some of the finest improvisers of the day

▶ Relaxed, understated atmosphere that provides the soloists with the opportunity to develop ideas against a relatively free backdrop

Basie continued to record and tour with his group throughout his long career—including visits to Europe and Japan. His health began to deteriorate in the 1970s when he suffered a heart attack, but he continued to perform. In the early 1980s, he began working with Albert Murray on his autobiography, *Good Morning Blues,* which was published in 1985. After Basie's death, his band continued to tour and perform under the leadership of other players.

Basie's legacy is undiminished. Ironically, his piano style is so familiar that other pianists cannot appropriate it without sounding clichéd. Still, he continues to inspire; fans will always revere Basie's music for its joy, its swing, and its exemplary balance between freewheeling improvisation and classic arranging. As Basie himself put it at eighty years old, "The main thing for me is the music. That's what excites me. That's what keeps me going. The music and people having a good time listening to it. People dancing or just patting their feet."[9]

SAXOPHONIST LESTER YOUNG

Lester Young was one of the two most important tenor saxophone stylists of the swing era. (The other, Coleman Hawkins, we discuss later in this chapter.) Billie Holiday claimed to have given him the nickname "Pres" (or "Prez"), short for *president.* "His way of hearing music was the way of the blues—and of telling a story in music."[10]

Young, who in the mid-1930s leaped to prominence as a featured soloist with the Count Basie Band, located his influences in white saxophonists Jimmy Dorsey and Frankie Trumbauer. Young cultivated their lighter sound that featured less vibrato than other styles. Reputedly, Young even carried a copy of Trumbauer and Beiderbecke's recording "Singin' the Blues" (see Chapter 2) in his saxophone case. In addition, Young was attracted to Trumbauer's ability to develop an improvisation in a logical and unhurried sequence of events. As Young put it:

> I had to make a decision between Frankie Trumbauer and Jimmy Dorsey—y'dig: I wasn't sure which way I wanted to go, y'dig. . . . The only people that was tellin' stories that I liked to hear were them. . . . Ever hear him [Trumbauer] play "Singin' the Blues"? That tricked me right there, that's where I went.[11]

Born in 1909 outside New Orleans in Woodville, Mississippi, Young moved at age eleven to Minneapolis with his father. Young's father formed a minstrel-type band with which Young toured the Midwest, playing carnivals in the Dakotas, Kansas, and Nebraska. A versatile musician, Young played the violin, drums, and alto saxophone before making the tenor his primary instrument. In 1933 he settled in Kansas City.

Young made his earliest recordings in 1936 with Basie. His solos on "Oh, Lady Be Good" and "Shoe Shine Boy" made an immediate and lasting impact. In his discussion of Young's style, jazz historian Lewis Porter has pointed out many of Young's melodic formulas, which reappear in numerous solos.[12] In addition, Porter shows Young's ability to logically develop a solo through repeated reference to particular melodic ideas, as can be heard in Young's solo on "Shoe Shine Boy." This solo shows the following characteristics, all of which influenced the next generation of jazz saxophonists:

▶ Bluesy melodies with rhythmic variety in contrast to eighth-note swing lines

▶ Light, airy tone

▶ Use of space between phrases

▶ Irregular phrase lengths

▶ Melodic connections based on *motivic* contrast, *voice leading*, and use of formula

▶ Concentration on the midrange of the instrument

▶ Cool expression

▶ A preference for blues scales and harmonies

Young remained with Basie until 1940. Playing both tenor and clarinet, he also recorded with Billie Holiday, a singer with whom he developed a close bond. In 1944, Young won first place in the *Down Beat* poll for tenor saxophonists. Unfortunately, Young was also inducted into the army that same year, an experience that proved hellish for the thirty-five-year-old tenor player. Arrested for drug use and court-martialed, he spent much of the following year in detention barracks.

A ***motive*** or ***motivic material*** is a short melodic fragment used as the basis for improvisation or development.

Voice leading is a means of making logical melodic and harmonic sequences within an improvised solo. ***Step connection***, a key element in voice leading, is the principal means of stringing together the melodic and harmonic elements. The steps are often based on the scale determined by the key of the piece.

Lester Young (CD 1, Track 66), 1939. Notice the tilt of Young's head and the angle at which he holds his saxophone.

Courtesy Frank Driggs Collection

After returning to civilian life, Young could not recapture the consistency of his great swing playing, although he made several fine recordings—for example, "These Foolish Things" in 1945. Still, he continued to win numerous polls during the forties, and in Leonard Feather's jazz musician poll in 1956, Young won the category of "Greatest Tenor Saxophone Ever." Exacerbated by chronic drinking, Young's health had begun to deteriorate. He died in March 1959, only a few months before the death of his close friend Billie Holiday.

Young's controlled style of playing affected a generation of musicians. Saxophonists who acknowledged a debt to Young included many of the next generation. Among them was Charlie Parker, who adapted the flexibility and blues of Young's melodic lines to greater virtuosity and decisively influenced the emerging bebop language of the early 1940s (discussed in the next chapter). Young's embrace of understated, lyrical improvisation overturned the dominance of such virtuosos as Louis Armstrong and Coleman Hawkins. In the words of Gunther Schuller, Young's legacy was the launching of "a completely new aesthetic of jazz—for all instruments, not just the tenor saxophone. The essence of his heritage is that he proposed a totally new alternative to the language, grammar, and vocabulary of jazz."[13]

Benny Goodman: King of Swing

For many people, the name Benny Goodman is synonymous with swing. His record sales and performances helped usher in the swing craze of the 1930s; for more than a decade, the "King of Swing" enjoyed incredible heights of popularity. Members of his band became near cult figures. With his flashy playing and ever-present grin, Gene Krupa, Goodman's drummer, was a popular idol; trumpeter Harry James was one of the best-known brass players of the period; pianist Teddy Wilson became one of the era's most emulated pianists; and Lionel Hampton helped to popularize the vibraphone as a jazz instrument.

Although Goodman's dance band was a big band, Goodman also developed the idea of a "band within a band" that featured a small group—first a trio, then a quartet—for performances that incorporated more improvisation than the big band did. Although interracial bands had recorded prior to Goodman's band, Goodman's small group—with black musicians Teddy Wilson and Lionel Hampton—was the first important interracial band to perform live concerts.

Goodman was born on May 30, 1909, to an extremely poor immigrant family in Chicago. Coming of age in the early 1920s, Goodman associated with a group of inner-city musicians from the gritty and mostly poor immigrant sections of the city. Goodman began learning the clarinet at age ten when he played with a boy's band at a local synagogue. A child prodigy, Goodman gave his first public performance in 1921.

Benny Goodman (CD 1, Track 67), the "King of Swing," on the cover of one of his hit songs from 1938.

Race Relations in Early Jazz

As in other important institutions—baseball most prominently—the story of racial relations in jazz mirrors the troubles of American society more generally. In Chapter 1, we noted that race was a complex factor in U.S. music at least as far back as the minstrel era of the early nineteenth century. Both black and white minstrel troupes, in characteristic blackface, performed throughout the nineteenth century at a time when integrated groups would have been unthinkable. As vaudeville supplanted minstrelsy in the later nineteenth century, the passage of strict segregation laws continued to bar mixed-race bands from appearing in public. Indeed, the black-and-tan clubs in the 1920s show that even audiences remained largely segregated through the first decades of the twentieth century. More typically, Ellington's clientele at the Cotton Club in the later 1920s was white, for example. For bands to have been publically integrated in the 1920s would have been impossible.

Once recordings became a factor in U.S. music, however, the situation changed slightly, and it is possible that mixed-race recording set a precedent for integrated ensembles to perform live. Because it was impossible for a record buyer to know the race of the performers on a record, there were instances of blacks and whites "passing" for each other on early jazz recordings. The most celebrated early integrated recordings in jazz found the Creole Jelly Roll Morton sitting in with the white New Orleans Rhythm Kings on July 17, 1923, for Gennett Records in Richmond, Indiana.

In the later 1920s, mixed-race recordings became slightly more common. One particularly important session, which featured the upcoming stars black pianist Fats Waller and white trombonist Jack Teagarden, took place on September 30, 1929. The resulting cuts were issued as Fats Waller and His Buddies.

Once Benny Goodman determined that he would appear in public with black pianist Teddy Wilson, it was clear that the success of their joint appearances greatly depended on Wilson's calm, professional demeanor. In those days of outright racism, Wilson could have endangered his life if he confronted any audience members who taunted him. About a year after Goodman hired Wilson, he also took on black vibraphonist Lionel Hampton (1908–2002). Wilson is remarkably understated in his description of the menacing situation he and Hampton found themselves in: "So it is to Benny Goodman that the credit must go to for hiring me, a Negro, against the advice of his booking agents. By doing so he in fact took a gamble on his career. . . . Of course there were incidents, and I know Benny had to put his foot down many times on this issue when it came to bookings, often without either Lionel or I knowing. Goodman always insisted that the agent should take the band in its entirety or not at all, and we played all the jobs."*

Hiring Wilson and Hampton resembled the later integration of baseball in 1947, when Brooklyn Dodgers owner Branch Rickey signed Jackie Robinson. In a famous story, Rickey began lecturing Robinson on the importance of ignoring the screaming fans, abusive teammates, etc. At last, Robinson erupted, "Mr. Rickey, do you want a ballplayer who's afraid to fight back?" Rickey replied, "I want a player with guts enough not to fight back."[†]

---

* Teddy Wilson with Arie Ligthart and Humphrey van Loo, *Teddy Wilson Talks Jazz* (London and New York: Cassell, 1996), p. 46.

† Benjamin G. Rader, *Baseball: A History of America's Game*, 2nd ed. (Urbana and Chicago: University of Illinois Press, 2002), p. 156.

In 1925 Goodman joined Ben Pollack's band, an important group in the mid-1920s, and in 1928 made his way to New York. He was not only an excellent sight-reader but also a strong, hot improviser, and he developed a busy career playing in studio recordings, radio broadcasts, and pit bands on Broadway.

In 1934 Goodman formed his own big band featuring vocalist Helen Ward. The radio series "Let's Dance" hired them as the hot band, allowing Goodman to purchase top-flight arrangements. For example, Fletcher Henderson provided the charts for "Sometimes I'm Happy," Jelly Roll Morton's "King Porter Stomp," and "Down South Camp Meeting." Edgar Sampson, the arranger for Chick Webb's band, contributed "Don't Be That Way" and "Stompin' at the Savoy."

While he was getting his big band off the ground, Goodman jammed with pianist Teddy Wilson at a private party; this led to a recording session with Wilson and drummer Gene Krupa. In addition to these three highly individual musical personalities, the lack of a bass pegged the sound of the group. Wilson's swing-bass left hand coupled with Krupa's drumming provided the group's rhythmic backbone. The Goodman trio (and later quartet) recordings were among the key small-group recordings of the 1930s.

A hardworking musician and perfectionist, Goodman maintained exacting standards for the band. His extensive rehearsals required, as Goodman stated, "good musicians, work on intonation, a blend of tone, and uniform phrasing."[14] During his career, he earned a reputation as an unyielding taskmaster. He became infamous for what musicians called "the Goodman ray"—a hostile glare so unnerving that it drove some of his musicians to quit the band. Nevertheless, the rigorous musicianship he required of the band helped Goodman rise to the top of the competitive music business.

When the "Let's Dance" show ended in May 1935, Goodman took his band on the road heading west. The group's reception was decidedly lukewarm in many towns, particularly in Denver, Colorado, but the group had a triumphant performance at the Palomar Ballroom in Los Angeles on August 21. According to Goodman, the band began by playing their more conservative and commercial arrangements to a listless and unresponsive crowd. Once the group launched into their hot repertory, though, the audience came alive. As Goodman told it:

> To our complete amazement, half of the crowd stopped dancing and came surging around the stand. It was the first experience we had with that kind of attention, and it certainly was a kick. That was the moment that decided things for me. After traveling three thousand miles, we finally found people who were up on what we were trying to do, prepared to take our music the way we wanted to play it. That first big roar from the crowd was one of the sweetest sounds I ever heard in my life—and from that time on the night kept getting bigger and bigger, as we played about every good number in our book.[15]

Goodman soon realized that the difference in time zones between California and New York helped account for his overwhelming success. On his radio broadcasts from the East Coast, Goodman reserved his hot numbers until later in the evening, and these exciting swing arrangements reached California during prime time and thrilled younger listeners.

In the years following the success of the Palomar Ballroom performance, Goodman's fame reached phenomenal heights. Goodman's celebrated Carnegie Hall performance in 1938 brought together his big band, his small group, and guest stars from Duke Ellington's and Count Basie's bands. This concert contained one of Goodman's most famous numbers, "Sing, Sing, Sing," an extended composition that featured Gene Krupa in a series of drum solos and included a duet with Goodman on clarinet and Krupa on tom-toms.

Goodman hired only the strongest players and improvisers, and at one time or another his band featured many of the important players of the swing era, including trumpeter Bunny Berrigan as well as pianists Jess Stacy and Mel Powell, who also contributed arrangements. At the request of John Hammond, Goodman took on guitarist Charlie Christian in 1939. During Christian's all-too-brief career (discussed later in this chapter), he was one of the leading improvisers of the period and revolutionized jazz guitar playing.

Gene Krupa: Drums with Drive

Gene Krupa (1909–1973) was originally from Chicago. After he performed with numerous bands, his reputation in the New York studio scene led to an opportunity to join Benny Goodman in late 1934. Krupa became one of Goodman's most important sidemen and possibly the most idolized. Inevitably, he broke from Goodman in 1938 to form his own band, which was among the most popular of the early forties. Later in the decade, Krupa worked with his own groups, performed with Tommy Dorsey, and found time for occasional reunions with Goodman. After breaking up his band in 1951, he performed with the Jazz at the Philharmonic tours. In 1954 he founded a percussion school in New York with drummer Cozy Cole.

Gene Krupa was probably the most well-known drummer of the swing era, though his contributions to technique did not equal those of such pioneers as Jo Jones and Kenny Clarke. While famous for his showmanship, he was often criticized for being heavy-handed and unswinging, with a tendency toward crowd-pleasing antics. Ultimately, however, Krupa's legacy is positive—within his limitations, he worked with Goodman to create a band unequaled in its appeal, a band that derived its energy from Krupa's drive and power.

In the early 1940s, Eddie Sauter wrote arrangements for the Goodman group, earning it the nickname the "Sauter band" for some of the most ambitious jazz arrangements of the era, such as "Benny Rides Again" and "Clarinet à la King." After 1942, when Sauter left, Goodman tried to stave off the downturn in swing-band popularity by returning to a simpler style, but to no avail. Semiretirement followed in 1946 while he considered what to do next.

The bebop revolution—a modern jazz development of the early 1940s discussed in the next chapter—intrigued Goodman. Despite occasional negative comments, he decided to experiment with the style. When his fans did not respond positively, Goodman ended his flirtation with bebop in 1949. For the remainder of his long life, Goodman led small groups ensconced in swing and, occasionally, big bands assembled for specific events.

There is no question that Goodman set jazz clarinet style for the 1930s. It has been said that his perfect conception of swing on the clarinet made him a difficult act for others to follow. After Goodman, the clarinet declined as an instrument of modern jazz; only in recent years has its popularity begun to recover. That Goodman was the consummate swing stylist was perhaps best shown by his difficulties adapting to bebop.

Goodman continued to perform until his death in 1986. He undertook several overseas tours, playing in the Far East and South America, and appeared as a highly regarded "exhibit" at the United States pavilion of the Brussels World's Fair in 1958. During the height of the cold war in 1962, he traveled to the Soviet Union. With his classical training, he maintained a remarkably high degree of commitment to musicianship and clarinet technique, and he frequently performed classical works as well as jazz. For example, he recorded and performed works by Mozart, Debussy, and Stravinsky and also commissioned works by classical contemporary composers Béla Bartók, Aaron Copland, and Paul Hindemith.

"Avalon"

CD **1** Track **67**

The Benny Goodman Quartet: "Avalon" (Jolson-Rose). Victor 25644. July 30, 1937, Hollywood, California.
Benny Goodman, clarinet; Lionel Hampton, vibraphone; Teddy Wilson, piano; Gene Krupa, drums.

The Benny Goodman Quartet was created by adding vibraphonist Lionel Hampton to the preexisting Goodman trio. Featured with the Goodman big band, the quartet was one of the acclaimed small jazz groups of the 1930s. Their recording of "Avalon" is typical of the impeccable and stylish swing performances associated with Goodman throughout his career.

Introduction—4 bars, vibraphone solo

0:00   Count "Avalon" in a moderate two beats or a fast four beats to the bar. Hampton begins with an up-tempo solo that ushers in the main melody. His melodic line outlines the principal chords of the key, the tonic and dominant (I and V7), with the dominant chord slightly modified.

Head AA'BC chorus—32 bars, Goodman lead

0:04   Main presentation of the melody. Rather than an AABA form with a well-defined bridge, "Avalon" has a more irregular form, although still comprising the conventional thirty-two bars. Examining it in eight-bar blocks reveals something like an AA'BC form, with each main phrase occupying eight bars. The A and A' sections have the same harmonic structure, four bars of V7 to four bars of I.

0:19   The B section (bridge) features a change of harmony.

0:27   The C section begins on the tonic, unlike the A and A' sections. All four sections develop the opening thematic idea, which begins in half notes after a quarter-note pickup.

1 AA'BC chorus—Wilson piano solo

0:35   Wilson plays his solo in the classic piano swing style he epitomized. You can hear occasional march-bass motions in the left hand, but rendered now as the lighter swing bass we heard from Count Basie in "Shoe Shine Boy." Here, Wilson's right hand develops light swing figuration.

0:51   A particularly nice harmonic moment comes at the beginning of the B section. Rather than follow the chord progression of the original tune, Wilson modifies the harmony imaginatively. At the end of Wilson's solo, a drum fill by Krupa introduces Goodman's clarinet solo.

1 AA'BC chorus—Goodman clarinet solo

1:06   Goodman's style epitomized swing for clarinet, much as Wilson's style did for piano. Of all the jazz clarinet styles, none has ever achieved the popularity of Goodman's easygoing, swinging melodiousness. Goodman's style features a suave, songlike sweetness, a wonderful sense of timing, and an underlying structure marked by melodic and rhythmic accessibility. Goodman's fine solo on "Avalon" reflects the simplicity of Goodman's ideas and his unhurried, sure sense of direction at every moment, a manner that recalls Bix Beiderbecke's style. The exquisitely timed spaces between the phrases ensure that a cool overall tone and a sense of effortlessness finely balance Goodman's virtuosity. For Goodman's solo, both Wilson and Hampton add accompanying chords.

1 AA'BC chorus—Hampton vibraphone solo

1:39   Hampton begins his solo with an arpeggio-like reference to the original melody. This textural idea is repeated at the top of the A' section, but with emphasis on the tonic note even though it does not fit the dominant (V7) harmony. Wilson, meanwhile, accompanies with a light swing bass in both hands: bass note in the left (on beats 1 and 3) with chord in the right (on beats 2 and 4).

Out-chorus AA—Arranged ensemble

2:10   The climax of the performance arrives as an ingenious arranged-ensemble figure. Goodman and Hampton play a syncopated chromatic scale in descending minor triads that creates a cross-rhythm with the underlying swing bass as maintained by Wilson. The figure lasts four bars, with Krupa accenting the descending scale. The second four bars of the A section (on the E♭ tonic) feature a call-and-response figure on G♭–F–E♭.

2:18   The whole eight-bar unit then repeats.

Out-chorus B—Goodman clarinet solo

2:26   For the B section, Goodman improvises a lead line, while Hampton improvises a countermelody. Note the increased intensity and energy as the band drives to the conclusion of the piece.

Out-chorus C—8 bars, return to the arranged ensemble

2:35   For the final eight bars, the band returns to syncopated, descending minor triads. This time, instead of continuing through four bars, the band extends the figure through the entire eight bars of the section to create an unexpected, highly satisfying conclusion.

Goodman's solo in "Avalon" demonstrates several characteristics of Goodman's playing:

▶ Supple melody characterized by few large leaps within a phrase

▶ Frequent arpeggiation (moving through chords one note at a time, up and down) and use of scale fragments

▶ Basic eighth-note rhythm

▶ Limited space between phrases

▶ Lyrical tone

▶ Use of the entire range of the instrument

▶ Avoidance of blues effects

▶ Cool expression occasionally contrasted by fast vibrato

▶ Slightly irregular phrase lengths

▶ Note choices that emphasize the notes of the chord (inside playing)

Ellington After the Cotton Club

Duke Ellington may have been dismayed during the mid-1930s when the commercial success of such leaders as Benny Goodman eclipsed the popularity of his own band. But Ellington's perseverance paid off. When he died in 1974, it was as one of the world's preeminent jazz artists. The recipient of numerous musical and international honors, Ellington served for many as the most important figure in the history of jazz.

Ellington's artistry was wide-ranging. Known for a prodigious output of music, his command of arranging and orchestration detail, and his expansive musical creativity, Ellington established his excellence while crisscrossing the globe under a hectic and seemingly incessant touring schedule. As the title to one laudatory biography concluded, Ellington was "beyond category."[16] Still, we can identify four areas of compositional interest:

▶ Popular songs such as "Satin Doll" and "Don't Get Around Much Anymore"

▶ Big-band arrangements

▶ Compositions featuring particular members of the band

▶ Extended concert works

After leaving the Cotton Club, Ellington began to tour widely. The band traveled to Europe in 1932, playing to enthusiastic crowds and attracting critical attention in the British press. Moreover, during the 1930s, he became increasingly successful as a composer writing in the American popular song tradition—usually 32-bar AABA compositions. Among the most famous were "Sophisticated Lady," "In a Sentimental Mood," and "Prelude to a Kiss."

Following the death of his mother, to whom he was extremely close, Ellington in 1937 wrote the extended "Reminiscing in Tempo," his most ambitious work to date. Thirteen minutes long, the piece covered four record sides. Critical reaction to the composition was more negative than positive, but Ellington had shown growth as a composer. Another extended work from 1937 was "Crescendo in Blue" and "Diminuendo in Blue," companion pieces occupying both sides of a 78-rpm record. Again, these longer works, rooted in the blues form and tradition, use little improvisation.

BUILDING ON THE BAND

Because Ellington was determined to build on the strengths of individual band members, much of the band's distinctive character came from its players. Indeed, during the 1930s Ellington's compositions sometimes grew out of whole-band collaborations—works that were composed "almost by unanimous inspiration while the orchestra was gathered together for a practice session. New ideas are merged at each meeting, and each man contributes to the offerings of the other."[17] This tendency to borrow ideas from his sidemen led to an infamous reproach to Ellington by trombonist Lawrence Brown: "I don't consider you a composer. You are a compiler."[18] Brown was going too far of course, but the remark reveals the tensions that can develop in a band when creativity among all the players is constantly encouraged.

As part of his desire to work closely with his band, Ellington wrote with particular players in mind. A number of his compositions feature individual musicians showing off their strengths. For example, Ellington displayed Cootie Williams's multifaceted trumpet playing in the celebrated "Concerto for Cootie," the first theme of which became "Do Nothin' Till You Hear From Me," a hit song in 1943. "Clarinet Lament," based on the harmonic progression of the standard song "Basin Street Blues," exhibited the playing of Ellington's New Orleans–born clarinetist Barney Bigard. For trumpeter Rex Stewart, who left Fletcher Henderson to play with Ellington from 1934 to 1943,

Ellington wrote "Boy Meets Horn." And with his trombonist from San Juan, Puerto Rico—Juan Tizol—Ellington co-composed the exotic Latin-tinged song "Caravan." Ellington's work provided the perfect vehicle for his players; commentators noted that his sidemen often faltered in their playing and careers once they left the band.

Johnny Hodges (1907–1970), Ellington's alto saxophonist, became a stalwart of the band. Along with Benny Carter, he was one of the best alto saxophone players of the swing era. Except for a brief departure between 1951 and 1955, Hodges remained in the Ellington band for four decades. Nicknamed "Jeep" and "Rabbit," Hodges was considered the leading soloist of the Ellington band in the mid-1930s, and he became its highest-paid member. Hodges's ballad performances were said to be aphrodisiacal: The wife of one of the Ellington musicians reputedly warned, "Don't leave me alone around Johnny. When I hear him play, I just want to open up the bedroom door."[19]

CHANGES FOR THE BETTER

Toward the end of the 1930s, Ellington made several radical changes. He broke with Irving Mills, who had been his manager and business partner for more than a decade. He also left Columbia Records and by 1940 was recording for RCA Victor. On the heels of a successful tour of Europe in 1939, Ellington took on several new players and entered what was one of the most intensely fertile periods of his career.

With the addition of tenor saxophonist Ben Webster, Ellington's saxophone section increased to five players. Webster was a big-toned, breathy player from Kansas City who had played with Benny Moten and Andy Kirk in the early 1930s and had played an integral role in the Kansas City scene. "Cottontail," a Webster feature with Ellington, offers an electrifying display of his solo ability. Along with Coleman Hawkins and Lester Young, Webster was one of the most important tenor saxophone stylists of the swing era.

Ellington also added Jimmy Blanton on bass in 1939. The virtuosity of this twenty-year-old from Chattanooga, Tennessee, revolutionized jazz bass playing. Creating a driving sense of swing while walking the bass, Blanton was the first bass player to become a proficient soloist in his own right. In his first studio outing with the full band, Ellington featured Blanton in opening and closing solos on "Jack the Bear."

Finally, Ellington took on a diminutive pianist born in Dayton, Ohio. Initially hired as second pianist and assistant arranger, Billy Strayhorn (1915–1967) developed a remarkably close musical relationship with Ellington that lasted nearly three decades. Strayhorn quickly began contributing compositions for the band, including one of the group's theme songs, "Take the 'A' Train." Strayhorn's musical collaborations with Ellington were so intertwined that scholars have only recently begun to untangle where Ellington's contributions left off and Strayhorn's began. Strayhorn had studied the elements of Ellington's style that contributed to what Strayhorn called the "Ellington effect." He described it this way:

> Each member of the band is to him a distinctive tone color and set of emotions, which he mixes with others equally distinctive to produce a third thing, which I like to call the Ellington effect. Sometimes this mixing happens on paper and frequently right on the bandstand. I have often seen him exchange parts in the middle of a piece because the man and the part weren't the same character.[20]

THE 1940s AND BEYOND

The forties were a mixed time for Ellington and the band. Relatively ignored in the polls during the 1930s, the group now began to achieve national prominence, winning the *Esquire* poll in 1945 and taking the *Down Beat* polls in 1942, 1944, 1946, and 1948. Ellington began to receive handsome royalties for many of his compositions, such as "Don't Get Around Much Anymore," "I'm Beginning to See the Light," and "Do Nothin' Till You Hear From Me." The years also witnessed, however, an increased turnover in players. Sidemen in Ellington's band were beginning to attract offers from competing bands; other players were lost to the wartime draft.

In 1943 Ellington began an annual series of concerts at Carnegie Hall. In addition to featuring his songs and hits, Ellington composed and premiered large-scale concert works. These were often based on themes of African-American culture and history. The first concert on January 23, 1943, included a performance of his *Black, Brown, and Beige: A Tone Parallel to the History of the Negro in America.* This was an ambitious three-movement tone poem that traced the history of African Americans through the story of an African named Boola who is brought to the United States as a slave. In many of the works that followed *Black, Brown, and Beige*—such as "New World a-Comin'," "Liberian Suite," and "Deep South Suite"—we see how Ellington inherited the Harlem Renaissance tradition as he celebrated the history and achievements of African Americans in a concert venue.

By the 1950s, the heyday of the swing era was long gone, and it was becoming increasingly difficult for Ellington to keep his band together. For a while, times for the band were difficult, but in July 1956 its fortunes miraculously reversed themselves. On stage at the Newport Jazz Festival, during a performance of "Diminuendo and Crescendo in Blue," the tenor saxophonist Paul Gonsalves played twenty-seven electrifying choruses. The response of the crowd was overwhelming: Listeners danced in the aisles, stood on chairs, and cheered. Ellington was in vogue again. With characteristic irony he noted, "I was born in 1956 at the Newport Festival."[21]

The band continued to perform widely, undertaking a State Department–sponsored tour of India and the Middle East. At the end of the decade, Ellington wrote the score for the 1959 Otto Preminger film *Anatomy of a Murder;* the sound track won three Grammy awards. He and Strayhorn continued to turn out larger musical suites, notably "Such Sweet Thunder," inspired by Shakespeare and written for the Shakespeare Festival in Stratford, Canada; and "The Queen's Suite," in honor of Queen Elizabeth II.

Though usually modest about his own piano-playing abilities, Ellington showcased his playing in several small-group recordings in the early 1960s. He cut an album with John Coltrane and recorded *Money Jungle* with

A Hollywood-style musical with music from the big bands, *Reveille with Beverly* (1943) is a low-budget film with fine music and big-name stars. Here, the Ellington band performs Strayhorn's "Take the 'A' Train."

© Bettmann/CORBIS

Charles Mingus and Max Roach in 1962. Much of Ellington's final work involved religious compositions. For example, San Francisco's Grace Cathedral commissioned him to write a work. His *Concert of Sacred Music*, which incorporated segments of some of his earlier pieces such as *Black, Brown, and Beige* and "New World a-Comin'," premiered in 1965. Ellington performed his *Second Sacred Concert* two years later and the third and most introspective of his sacred concerts in 1973, the year before his death.

Ellington's influence and legacy continue to be profound. He had the administrative ability to run a large band for decades. As a pianist, he recorded solos, worked with his large band, and found time to record small-group work. Dozens of his compositions have kept their status as standards of jazz literature, and their melodic and harmonic structure still attract jazz musicians. As an orchestrator, Ellington created instrumental effects that were dazzling, eerie, and masterly. As a composer of larger works, Ellington elevated the perception of jazz to a music worthy of the concert stage. Some consider him to be the greatest American composer in any category.

L I S T E N I N G   G U I D E

"Sepia Panorama"
CD **1**   Track **68**

Duke Ellington and His Famous Orchestra: "Sepia Panorama" (Ellington). Victor 26731. New York, July 24, 1940. Wallace Jones, Cootie Williams, trumpets; Rex Stewart, cornet; Joe Nanton, Lawrence Brown, trombones; Juan Tizol, valve trombone; Barney Bigard, clarinet, tenor saxophone; Johnny Hodges, alto saxophone; Ben Webster, tenor saxophone; Harry Carney, baritone saxophone, clarinet; Duke Ellington, arrangement, piano, leader; Fred Guy, guitar; Jimmy Blanton, bass; Sonny Greer, drums.

Exhibiting an arch-form structure, "Sepia Panorama" is an imaginative composition typical of Ellington's three-minute recordings during the late 1930s and early 1940s. The arch form of "Sepia Panaorama" can be summarized as ABC–D1D2–CBA–tag. Ellington contrasts dramatic and quiet sections, thus projecting a full "panorama" of expressive devices.

This piece also shows how Jimmy Blanton developed a greater role for the bass: Rather than simply keeping time, he plays prominent solo passages that show off his dexterous technique. Among other innovations, Blanton developed a facility in the higher register of the instrument, which until then had been relatively neglected. The higher register is particularly useful for projecting the melody, which was important for solos before routine amplification of the instrument in the latter half of the 1960s.

Section A—12-bar blues

0:00   The first 12-bar blues section has an interestingly varied structure. In the first five bars, the whole band presents a theme with a dramatic rising figure.

0:11   An unaccompanied Blanton bass solo answers in measures 6–8.

0:17   In measures 9–10, the saxophones answer Blanton with a syncopated figure emphasizing a blue note.

0:22   Blanton completes the form with an unaccompanied solo in measures 11–12.

Section B—8 bars, repeated

0:26   The second section contrasts the first with an eight-bar structure. The first four bars are a trombone solo with saxophone chord accompaniment. These chords are typical of Ellington's intriguing harmonies.

0:34   In the second four bars, the saxophones accompany answering figures in a solo muted trumpet.

0:44   The section repeats.

Section C—8 bars

1:02   The whole band with open and aggressive brass accompanies a solo baritone saxophone in a call-and-response format. This more dramatic section recalls section A.

Section D1—12-bar blues

1:19   A duet of Blanton on bass and Ellington on piano. The quieter mood (first heard in section B) returns. Ellington remains in the high register and uses a combination of blues licks.

1:25   Blanton, rather than just walking in time, creates a duet of equal voices with melodic passages, often with eighth-note triplets.

Section D2—12-bar blues

1:45   Ben Webster tenor solo. Webster was one of the premier saxophonists of the swing era. With a sensuous tone and beguiling vibrato, he begins gently and builds his solo to the reprise of section C.

Section C—8 bars

2:12   Reprise of section C.

Section B—8 bars

2:29   Reprise of section B.

Section A—12-bar blues

2:47   Reprise of section A.

Tag—2 bars

3:13   The whole band plays a final tag. Ellington finishes with a final low F on the piano, held to ring out.

Jimmy Blanton: Bassist as Soloist

Jimmy Blanton revolutionized bass playing during his brief tenure with the Duke Ellington band. Born in 1918, he was from a musical family (his mother was a pianist) and was raised in Chattanooga, Tennessee. Although he attended Tennessee State College briefly, his musical interests and ambitions eventually led him to St. Louis in the late 1930s. Here Duke Ellington discovered Blanton in 1939 and hired him for his orchestra.

Blanton's performances with the Ellington orchestra were exceptional. He recorded numerous pieces in which his virtuosity and ability to carry a solo changed the perceived role of bass players in ensembles. One of the most famous of his pieces was "Jack the Bear." Before Blanton, it was rare to give a solo to a bass player; after Blanton, it became common as bandleaders grew to expect more from their bassists than routine timekeeping.

Sadly, Blanton's playing began to decline in 1941. He was diagnosed with tuberculosis and died in 1942.

Influential Big Bands of the Swing Era

The Basie, Goodman, and Ellington bands were perhaps the most important of the big-band era, but numerous other groups, both black and white, contributed to the excitement and verve of swing. Among them were the bands of Cab Calloway, Jimmie Lunceford, Chick Webb, Benny Carter, Gene Krupa, Charlie Barnet, Harry James, Boyd Rayburn, Bob Crosby, Tommy and Jimmy Dorsey, Glenn Miller, and Artie Shaw, as well as the Casa Loma Orchestra and McKinney's Cotton Pickers. Many soloists in the big bands became famous in their own right, and audiences idolized them. Their performing styles formed the roots of jazz music to come. Some big-band performers left their original bands to lead their own groups—a few successfully, but many less so. Some players, such as Coleman Hawkins, worked largely as "singles"—stars who performed at clubs throughout the country and worked with local rhythm sections.

During the 1930s, the hub of the music industry remained in New York, as it had in the 1920s. The record industry was centered there, and radio stations widely broadcast the big bands as they played in popular ballrooms and dance halls. The more successful bands alternated extended performances in the hotels and dance halls of Harlem and midtown Manhattan with engagements on the road.

The draft during World War II was one of the factors propelling the rise of women's big bands—groups that helped reduce the stigma of women as jazz musicians. Probably the best-known was the International Sweethearts of Rhythm.

Bandleader Glenn Miller's appearance (1939) reflects the careful polish that went into his music and made it so popular to a wide audience.

IN THE MOOD

Words by
ANDY RAZAF

Music by
JOE GARLAND

Introduced by
GLENN MILLER

Courtesy Morgan Collection

World War II and the "All-Girl" Bands

The focus of jazz history is usually on male musicians. However, there have been significant contributions by women musicians. Jazz histories typically mention important and innovative female pianists and singers, such as Lil Hardin, Mary Lou Williams, Bessie Smith, Billie Holiday, Ella Fitzgerald, and Sarah Vaughan. Yet many jazz histories ignore female musicians who were respected in their day but who played instruments more associated with men: these include trumpet players Valaida Snow and Dolly Jones, trombonist Melba Liston, saxophonist Vi Redd, and drummer Paula Hampton.

Recently, however, historians and scholars have attempted to describe women's participation in jazz to a greater degree. Sherrie Tucker's *Swing Shift: "All-Girl" Bands of the 1940s** highlights the role of women musicians during World

---

* Sherrie Tucker, *Swing Shift: "All-Girl" Bands of the 1940s* (Durham, NC: Duke University Press, 2000).

War II. Using oral histories and interviews, Tucker details a number of the all-women bands (invariably called "all-girl" bands in the press) that sprang up prior to and during the war years, including the International Sweethearts of Rhythm, the Prairie View Co-Eds, and the Darlings of Rhythm.

One reason for the increased visibility of these bands was that the number of male bands dwindled, since many of those players had been drafted into the army. Thus, the female musician became the counterpart to "Rosie the Riveter," the figure who symbolized women working in the factories to support the war effort while the men were fighting overseas. However, many female jazz bands existed before the war, and many of their musicians had established careers as early as the 1920s and 1930s. In fact, some of the most popular female groups, such as the bands of Ina Ray Hutton and Rita Rio, broke up even before America entered the war.

Tucker shows that the visibility of these all-women bands during the war years often led to heated debates in the jazz press as to whether women could—or should—play jazz.

The groups encountered not only gender discrimination but also racial discrimination. Traveling and performing in the South led to many difficult circumstances for the all-women bands. During this time of the Jim Crow segregationist laws, it was illegal in the South for blacks and whites to eat, work, or travel together. Whites and blacks had to use separate bathrooms and water fountains. Some all-women groups like the International Sweethearts of Rhythm were primarily African-American but often had one or two white musicians with the band, who then had to try to pass as black by using dark makeup to avoid being arrested. The group members talked about outwitting the police when traveling through the South. In one incident, one of the members remembered the police discovering several white musicians on the bandstand. The group was asked to follow the police in their car to the station. When the musicians discovered they were driving by the hotel at which they were staying, they quickly dropped off the white musicians and continued on to the station without them. The police, unable to make any arrests since there were now no white musicians present, had to let the musicians go.

The all-women band—in this case, Ina Ray Hutton and Her Melodears—was still a novelty in 1934, when this song was published.

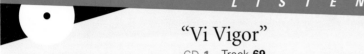

LISTENING GUIDE

"Vi Vigor"
CD **1** Track **69**

International Sweethearts of Rhythm: "Vi Vigor" (Maurice King). New York, October 14, 1946.
Victor 40-0146-A. Rae Lee Jones, leader; Anna Mae Winburn, conductor; Johnnie Mae "Tex" Stansbery,
Ernestine "Tiny" Davis, Nora Lee McGhee, Floye Dreyer, trumpets; Julia Travick, Helen Jones, Ima Belle Byrd,
trombones; Violet Burnside, Colleen Murray, Myrtle Young, Willie Mae Lee, Jacqueline Dexter, saxophones;
Jackie King, piano; Carlene Ray, guitar; Edna Smith, bass; Pauline Braddy, drums.

Violet Burnside (1915–1964) was a featured soloist with the International Sweethearts of Rhythm. She joined the band in 1943 after working with various "all-girl" groups, including the Dixie Rhythm Girls and the Harlem Play-Girls. In 1949 she formed her own group, again working with all-female personnel. In the 1950s she led bands mostly in the Washington, D.C., area, where she settled.

"Vi Vigor" is a swinging showcase for Burnside that is based on rhythm changes. While the scoring is in the big-band tradition, the phrasing shows hints of bebop, which in 1946 was continuing to grow in popularity.

Introduction—4 bars
0:00   The full band in an introduction with syncopation that is influenced by bebop. The aggressive trumpet lead line gives way to the trombone section, in which the three players enter one note at a time on a held chord.

Head—32-bar rhythm changes
0:04   First A. The first four-bar phrase is played by the saxophones; the brass take over the lead for the second four bars while the saxophones play a countermelody.

0:12   Repeat of the A section. A modification at the end of the section allows the saxophones to complete the section with the lead line.

0:20   The B section features Burnside. Note how she fits her phrases between the aggressive entrances of the brass. This kind of "getting in the way" of the soloist is another feature of the recording that is characteristic of the aggressive feel of bebop.

0:28   The third A section is rather like the second, but Burnside closes the section with a brief melodic solo.

Interlude—8 bars
0:36   Interlude by the full band to set up the Burnside chorus.

Burnside solo 1st chorus—32-bar rhythm changes
0:44   Burnside solo, first A. For this section, the brass phrases quietly in full chords. We get to hear more of Burnside by this point; her style, like that of many tenor players in the era, recalls Lester Young and Ben Webster, but is uniquely hers at the same time.

0:52   Second A. The texture from the first A section continues.

1:00   In the bridge, the brass provide stabbing chords on the downbeat of every other measure.

1:08   Third A. The sustained chords from the first A sections return.

Burnside solo 2nd chorus—32-bar rhythm changes
1:16   First A. The texture simplifies to just the rhythm section accompanying Burnside. She turns to the lower register at this point, not having to worry about being heard.

1:24   Second A with continuing accompaniment by the rhythm section only. Burnside returns to using the full register of the horn.

1:32 In the bridge, the full band returns to back Burnside for the first half. The second half of the bridge uses the simpler texture.

1:40 Third A. Again, the simpler texture with rhythm section only.

Burnside solo 3rd chorus—32-bar rhythm changes

1:48 First A, added countermelody in trombones and saxophones. Here Burnside builds a passionate statement over the trombones with blue notes.

1:56 In the second A, the trombones and saxophones continue their counterline, but Burnside moves to the middle register.

2:04 Bridge, just the rhythm section.

2:12 Third A, the counterline returns.

Burnside solo out-chorus with band—32-bar rhythm changes

2:20 The band returns behind intense playing by Burnside shouting in the upper register with prominent blue notes.

2:27 Second A. The busy textures continue, with Burnside moving to blueslike phrases in the middle register.

2:35 Bridge. The background texture is lightened somewhat here, with Burnside continuing the intensity.

2:43 For the final out-chorus A section, Burnside provides a wonderfully passionate counterpoint to the band. The piece ends with a cadencing phrase for Burnside answered by a full chord in the band.

The saxophone section of the International Sweethearts of Rhythm in 1944. *Clockwise from lower left:* Grace Bayron (tenor), Helen Saine (alto), Rosalind "Roz" Cron (lead alto), Violet Burnside (tenor), and Willie Mae Wong (baritone).

Swing-Era Stylists

Here we examine a selection of some of the most celebrated swing-era players, composer/arrangers, and vocalists not discussed previously. All contributed greatly to the sound we call "swing." Following is a list of these artists with their instrument:

▶ Saxophone: Coleman Hawkins

▶ Trumpet: Roy Eldridge

▶ Trombone: Jack Teagarden

▶ Piano: Earl Hines and Teddy Wilson

▶ Guitar: Charlie Christian

▶ Composing/arranging: Benny Carter

▶ Singing: Billie Holiday and Ella Fitzgerald

COLEMAN HAWKINS: ELEVATING THE SAXOPHONE

During the late teens and early 1920s, the front line of clarinet, trombone, and cornet dominated New Orleans– and Chicago-style jazz, relegating the saxophone to be used as a novelty vaudeville instrument. As the 1920s wore on and the big-band sound evolved, the saxophone grew more and more popular until it became an important reed voice. By the 1930s, Coleman Hawkins, a powerful soloist on the saxophone, had made it a serious improvisational instrument.

Coleman Hawkins, known as "Bean" or "Hawk," was the player most responsible for elevating the tenor saxophone to prominence as a jazz voice. Born in St. Joseph, Missouri, in 1904, Hawkins began playing tenor saxophone at age nine. Three years later he was working professionally for school dances. By 1921 he was living in Kansas City and playing in the Twelfth Street Theater orchestra, where vocalist Mamie Smith heard him and invited him to tour with her group, the Jazz Hounds.

Hawkins's first recordings, with Mamie Smith, date from 1922, but he first attracted national attention during his ten-year association with the Fletcher Henderson Orchestra in New York from 1924 to 1934. His earliest recorded solos with the Henderson Orchestra, on such compositions as "Dicty Blues," had a strong sound but used dated, novelty devices such as slap-tonguing, which produces a rather humorous effect on the instrument. Hawkins's style quickly became more authoritative and more legato, particularly after Louis Armstrong's year in Henderson's orchestra exerted its influence. Hawkins's solo in "The Stampede," for example, used call-and-response patterns that may owe a debt to Armstrong.

Hawkins's burgeoning solo style demonstrated a hard propulsive attack, a wide vibrato, and technical virtuosity. Drawing on his skill at the piano, Hawkins developed an improvisational saxophone style rooted in harmonic conception. In contrast to earlier solo styles that tended to paraphrase the original melody of a composition, Hawkins created solos with *arpeggiating figures* that often followed the chord progression. In addition, Hawkins's sophisticated harmonic knowledge made him fluent in chord substitution, which allowed him to replace the given harmonies of a composition for added effect in his improvisations.

An ***arpeggiated figure*** is a melodic fragment based on the notes of the chord harmony and played in succession. Listen to Track 2 on CD 1 to hear various arpeggios.

Copyright © Bettmann/CORBIS

Saxophonist Coleman Hawkins (CD 1, Track 70) in the 1940s. A competitive player always interested in cutting-edge developments, Hawkins performed with many of the younger musicians who were innovating bebop in the early 1940s.

After spending five years in Europe, Hawkins returned to the United States in 1939. His recording of "Body and Soul" from that year is an acknowledged masterpiece. The record solidified Hawkins's standing as the undisputed master of tenor saxophone; for example, in *Down Beat* magazine that year, the general public elected him "Best Tenor Saxophonist."

A dominating force in the 1930s, Hawkins influenced practically all other saxophonists. His contemporaries—Ben Webster, Chu Berry, and Herschel Evans—acknowledged allegiance to Hawkins; later tenor players such as John Coltrane rediscovered his works. In his relentless quest for virtuosity on the instrument, Hawkins constantly sought new modes of expression. In an unusual step, he recorded unaccompanied saxophone solos on his "Hawk Variations" (1945) and "Picasso" (1948). His willingness to absorb and adapt to new styles was evident in his performances with new generations of musicians: Dizzy Gillespie and Thelonious Monk in the 1940s and Max Roach in the 1960s. Hawkins continued to record and perform prolifically until his death in 1969.

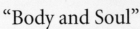

"Body and Soul"

CD 1 Track 70

Coleman Hawkins and His Orchestra: "Body and Soul" (Green, Heyman, Sauer, Eyton). New York, October 11, 1939. Victor 20-2539. Coleman Hawkins, leader and tenor saxophone; Tommy Lindsay, Joe Guy, trumpets; Earl Hardy, trombone; Jackie Fields, Eustis Moore, alto saxophones; Gene Rodgers, piano; William Oscar Smith, bass; Arthur Herbert, drums.

The mature style of Coleman Hawkins can be heard on "Body and Soul," one of the most well-known recordings of a jazz ballad. Its romantic, understated eloquence remains unimpeded throughout, even by the forceful phrases in the last part of the second chorus. In the recording, Hawkins departs frequently from the tune's melody. Instead, his "vertical" style of improvisation, based on his ability to outline the chordal harmonies, is in evidence throughout the solo.

Introduction

0:00   The piece begins with a four-bar piano introduction in tempo. The pianist plays a chord at the beginning of each measure, followed by a brief melodic idea.

1st chorus—AABA

0:09   Hawkins plays the first A section, both stating the melody and improvising around it. Hawkins's gentle lyricism is enhanced by his use of vibrato at the ends of phrases.

0:30   Hawkins departs further from the melody of the composition by including more improvisation during this second A section.

0:51   In the B section Hawkins starts to use a wider range, using both higher and lower notes than previously.

1:11   The final phrase of the B section carries over into the return of the A section, somewhat masking the sectional division.

2nd chorus—AABA

1:31   Listen for Hawkins's ability to repeat and develop melodic ideas based on rhythm and shape. During the A sections of the second chorus, the horns play a slow-moving background behind Hawkins.

2:12   Return of B section.

2:32   In the final A section, Hawkins's tone gets increasingly louder and edgier, setting up an effective climax to the performance. The highest note of the solo occurs at 2:38.

2:50   Hawkins plays a short unaccompanied passage before the final chord is played.

In "Body and Soul," we glimpse Hawkins's mature style. Many other players emulated his techniques, as heard in this solo. These techniques include the following:

▶ Sensitive, smoothly articulated melodies

▶ Complex melodic connections based on motivic development and voice leading

▶ Rich, sensuous tone

▶ Loose, free phrasing over the beat, with irregular phrase lengths that remain "vertical," that is, tied to the prevailing harmony

▶ Emotional expression

▶ Large variety of note values

▶ Use of the entire range of the instrument

ROY ELDRIDGE: FROM ARMSTRONG TO GILLESPIE

Because the trumpet, as part of the big band, was a major voice in jazz during the swing era, it may be misleading to select one soloist as dominating stylistically. For one thing, Louis Armstrong continued to be the most famous personality in jazz and a major swing-era stylist as well, despite his pioneering work in the 1920s. But if Armstrong's overwhelming presence is discounted, no swing-era player is more significant than Roy Eldridge.

Although Eldridge was hailed as the successor to Louis Armstrong, as well as the predecessor to Dizzy Gillespie, Eldridge evaded Armstrong's influence until he heard the older trumpeter live in 1932. After 1932 Armstrong exerted a strong influence on swing-style improvisation, but Eldridge would move beyond him through forward-looking melodic and rhythmic innovations. For example, he fully exploited the three-octave range in the trumpet, and his solos exhibited a fiery vigor and an ability to handle breakneck tempos. His keen awareness of harmony and his instrumental dexterity significantly influenced the pioneers of the subsequent bebop era, especially Dizzy Gillespie.

Born in Pittsburgh in 1911, Eldridge came to New York in 1930. His first recorded solos are from 1935 with the Teddy Hill Band, and he later spent a year as lead trumpeter with the Fletcher Henderson Orchestra. Eldridge's stature as the leading trumpet soloist of the swing era led to offers from numerous successful white bands, and in 1941 he joined Gene Krupa's band as a featured soloist and occasionally as singer. Eldridge played ballads and up-tempo numbers equally well, and his performance on Krupa's "Rocking Chair" contains one of his most famous solos.

Flamboyant high-note playing, which comprised more crowd-pleasing antics than successful musical statements, characterized some of Eldridge's work from the 1940s. As a trumpet virtuoso, Eldridge thrived in the competitive world of the jam session. While touring Europe with the Benny Goodman band in 1950, Eldridge left to spend a year in Paris. Until he suffered a stroke in 1980, Eldridge led his own groups and performed with Benny Carter, Johnny Hodges, and Coleman Hawkins. He died in 1989.

JACK TEAGARDEN: TROMBONE STYLES

Jack Teagarden (1905–1964) seemingly spanned all periods and styles with his warm, friendly, blues-oriented approach to the trombone. Although he eschewed the rough technique of the early New Orleans players, he became prominently associated with the New Orleans revival of the 1940s, performing often with Louis Armstrong and the fine swing-Dixieland trumpeter Bobby Hackett. His singing was always as relaxed and appealing as his playing. Teagarden based his technique on 1930s swing trombone technique, but he imbued it with a unique personality and feeling for the blues that even avant-garde players respected.

EARL HINES: FLUID AND LINEAR PIANO

Earl Hines established himself as a major talent on piano by performing superbly on the Louis Armstrong Hot Five recordings in the late 1920s. He was the musician most responsible for developing a linear, fluid concept of jazz piano; as historians have often remarked, he applied the style of Armstrong's trumpet playing to the keyboard. The dramatic change of style that Hines initiated in the mid-1920s can be appreciated by comparing the earlier Armstrong records with pianist Lil Hardin with the later Hot Five selections with Hines. The graceful, easygoing sense of forward movement he contributed to the band predicted the swing style of the 1930s, even while other sidemen remained entrenched in the New Orleans sound.

Born in Duquesne, Pennsylvania, in 1903, Hines was raised in a musical family. He studied classical piano and played his first gigs in his hometown, which was near Pittsburgh. In 1923 his musical travels brought him to Chicago, where he played with the Carroll Dickerson band and met Armstrong. He performed with the trumpeter for several years but decided to continue with his own groups after Armstrong headed off to New York with the Carroll Dickerson band.

Hines's solo piano recordings from the later 1920s—"Blues in Thirds," "I Ain't Got Nobody," and "57 Varieties"—show his superb stride-based piano technique as well as his unparalleled rhythmic creativity. With some earlier experience directing bands, Hines now put together his own group for the Grand Terrace Ballroom in Chicago. The band eventually grew into a twelve-piece group. Increased celebrity came to Hines when his band began radio broadcasts around 1932.

Earl Hines conducting his orchestra during a 1940 session.

Courtesy Frank Driggs Collection

Hines's solo approach featured clean, swinging lines with much linear emphasis and rhythmic surprise; furthermore, his use of octave tremolos strongly recalled the terminal vibrato of Louis Armstrong's trumpet style. Hines's stunning technique elevated the piano to the level of a lead voice that filled the same role as that of other solo improvisers. He was a phenomenal technician whose ability to provide consistently inventive improvisations never diminished. He was indeed one of the finest jazz pianists of all time.

TEDDY WILSON: ELEGANT ENSEMBLE PIANO

Teddy Wilson was probably the most imitated of the swing-era pianists. Earl Hines excelled in both solo piano work and group playing, but Wilson, despite many fine solo efforts, was principally a group pianist. Wilson came to national attention as the pianist in Benny Goodman's trio and quartet from 1936 to 1939. His crystalline touch and refined elegance showed an almost classical restraint. Benny Goodman remarked, "My pleasure in playing with Teddy Wilson equalled the pleasure I got out of playing Mozart, and that's saying something."[22]

Born in Austin, Texas, in 1912, Wilson grew up in Alabama, where he studied classical piano and music theory. He learned jazz piano by memorizing works such as Fats Waller's "Handful of Keys" note for note. Wilson eventually forged his own style out of the influences of Earl Hines, Waller, and Art Tatum, but his playing avoided the flamboyance of his mentors.

Courtesy Morgan Collection

Pianist Teddy Wilson (CD 1, Track 67) on the cover of "Goodnight Sweetheart," published in London in 1931. Wilson was probably the most influential swing pianist.

Through the intercession of John Hammond, Wilson joined Benny Carter's band and moved to New York in 1933. Wilson's earliest recording, dating from 1932, is with Carter's group. Hammond's advocacy of Wilson laid the groundwork for some of Wilson's most significant musical achievements in the 1930s. For instance, Hammond introduced Wilson to Billie Holiday and set up the famous Brunswick recording series that led to Wilson and Holiday's recording numerous sides together. Between 1935 and 1939, Wilson played and wrote these seven-piece arrangements for Holiday and brought together in the recording studio such luminaries as Benny Goodman, Ben Webster, Roy Eldridge, Johnny Hodges, and Lester Young. Much later, Wilson remembered those sessions:

> People have often asked me how I ever managed to get together such a collection of star musicians to accompany Billie Holiday on those records. . . . They were all big names and it was natural to think it must have cost a fortune to get them together. . . .
> I can only explain the mystery by saying that it was only in those sessions that those artists could only play with a group which was at their own level. In their own bands they were the number one soloist, but at my recording sessions they themselves were one of seven top soloists. . . .
> So the Teddy Wilson small group sessions were the only chance these men had to play with their peers instead of being the best in the whole band. The result was that nobody really cared about the money they were getting; they were more interested in the excitement of playing with seven men who were all as good as they were.[23]

Hammond also introduced Wilson to Benny Goodman, who was impressed with Wilson's suave pianism. Although Wilson's right-hand work was rooted in Hines's "trumpet" style of improvisation, Wilson's solos were more restrained than Hines's flights of fancy. At their best, Wilson's small-group recordings with Goodman's trio and quartet had a "chamber music" quality of improvisation, a balanced conversation among musical peers. This quality can best be heard in Goodman's 1935 landmark recordings of "After You've Gone" and "Body and Soul," as well as on the Goodman quartet version of "Moonglow," recorded the following year, and "Avalon," which was discussed earlier.

After leaving Goodman in 1939, Wilson briefly attempted to lead his own band. In his later career, Wilson continued to perform, fronting his own small groups and performing with Goodman in reunion concerts, touring Russia with him in 1962, and appearing with him at Carnegie Hall twenty years later. He taught jazz piano at Juilliard beginning in 1950 and performed well into the 1980s. Acclaimed as one of the world's great jazz pianists, he died in 1986.

CHARLIE CHRISTIAN: SHIFT TO ELECTRIC GUITAR

Charlie Christian's legendary career was meteoric and brief. John Hammond, hearing of the guitarist from Oklahoma City, arranged an audition for Christian with Benny Goodman in 1939. Goodman hired him immediately. As a member of Goodman's Sextet, Christian recorded outstanding solos on "Flying Home," "Seven Come Eleven," "Stardust," and "Air Mail Special." In 1941 he was taking part in the ground-breaking jam sessions at Minton's in Harlem and playing nightly sessions with the future architects of the bebop movement, including Dizzy Gillespie and Thelonious Monk (see Chapter 4). By March 1942 he was dead of tuberculosis at the age of twenty-five.

Born in 1916, Charlie Christian was the first major player to feature electric guitar in jazz ensembles—in fact, Christian played a fundamental role in the shift to the electric guitar, an instrument available only after 1936. Although the arched-top acoustic guitar was suitable in the studio, where microphones could be strategically placed, it was frequently drowned out in live performance. In the era of the big band, amplification soon became necessary.

With his swinging eighth-note lines, Christian developed an improvisational style with a fluidity akin to that of a horn player. Christian thus made his mark not as a rhythm guitarist, in the manner of Freddie Green's four-to-the-bar style of propelling the Basie band, but as a complete soloist. Although his recordings span a mere two years, they show him to be one of the most fertile improvisers of the era, a revolutionary profoundly influencing a generation of guitarists. In light of the recordings made toward the end of his life with players of the upcoming bebop movement, it is interesting to speculate on whether Christian would have developed into one of the preeminent voices of the newer bebop idiom.

Christian's solos are remarkably elegant, as definitive of swing as Lester Young's or Benny Goodman's. Christian's guitar tone, with slight variations, became the established jazz guitar timbre for more than two decades.

Christian was perfectly poised between swing and bebop. A relaxed sense of swing, perfect voice-leading control, subtle motivic manipulation, variety of phrase length, and imaginative harmonies characterized his style. With his exemplary command of swing improvisation, Charlie Christian was one of the greatest guitar players in jazz history.

BENNY CARTER: COMPOSER AND ARRANGER

Still performing, arranging, composing, and even touring until the turn of the twenty-first century, after eight decades in the music business, Benny Carter personifies the history of jazz. Although an elegant alto saxophone stylist who also recorded impressively on the trumpet and other instruments, Carter was most noted for his superb arrangements. It was perhaps Carter's misfortune to be so multitalented that he is difficult to categorize.

Born in 1907 and raised in New York, Carter worked with several local teachers but primarily taught himself. He performed with Earl Hines in the mid-1920s and with Fletcher Henderson from 1930 to 1931. He wrote important arrangements for Henderson, including "Keep a Song in Your Soul" (1930). After a stint as the music director of McKinney's Cotton Pickers, he started his own band in New York in 1932—a band that helped influence the newly emerging swing style. He worked in London as a staff arranger for the British Broadcasting Corporation (BBC) from 1936 to 1938 and returned to New York to form a new orchestra at the Savoy ballroom in 1939.

As the swing era began to wane, Carter saw his future in writing for Hollywood. He moved to Los Angeles in 1942, led some bands, and grew more involved in the studios, which eventually led to uncredited work on the movie *Stormy Weather* (1943). From 1946 on, he was associated with the Jazz at the Philharmonic tours; in the 1950s and 1960s, he concentrated on arranging and scoring, and in the 1970s he resumed active performing. He died in 2003.

Carter was probably one of the two leading alto saxophone stylists of swing, the other being Johnny Hodges of the Duke Ellington band. As an arranger, he helped innovate swing style and was especially well known for his writing for saxophones. Also a songwriter, Carter composed numerous popular tunes, including the standard "When Lights Are Low."

BILLIE HOLIDAY: TRAGIC SINGER

Billie Holiday was the touchstone of jazz singing. From Louis Armstrong's model, Holiday cultivated a free sense of rhythm and phrasing, much like an instrumental soloist, and she had an uncanny ability to inhabit and project the lyric of a composition. Despite an untrained voice, "Lady Day," as Lester Young named her, had an unerring sense of pitch. She was perhaps best known for her performances of slow, poignant ballads, frequently of unrequited love; these songs came to mirror her own complex and tragic life, marred by both failed romances and, ultimately, drug addiction.

Holiday was born in Philadelphia in 1915, but the details of her early life remain murky. We do know that her mother moved to New York and left the young child with family in Baltimore. She may have been abused; by her own accounts, Holiday was raped as a child and compelled to work as a prostitute during her early teens.

Billie Holiday (CD 1, Track 71) and Lionel Hampton (CD 1, Track 67) perform together at Esquire's Fourth Annual All-American Jazz Concert held at the Metropolitan Opera House in New York City in 1944.

To be with her mother, she moved to New York in 1928 and began working small clubs as a singer in the early thirties. In 1933, John Hammond heard her sing and arranged for her to record with Benny Goodman.

At the peak of her vocal powers in the 1930s and 1940s, Holiday usually performed with small jazz groups. Her studio recordings with the Teddy Wilson Orchestra from 1935 to 1942 are treasures of the swing era, featuring such soloists as Chu Berry, Lester Young, Benny Goodman, and Roy Eldridge (see the earlier discussion of Teddy Wilson in this chapter). These recordings show the uncanny musical rapport Holiday had with tenor saxophonist Lester Young, who often weaves his melodic lines around Holiday's vocals in the same relaxed, behind-the-beat manner. Holiday worked with Basie's big band in 1937. Her performances with Artie Shaw in 1938 number among the first instances of a black singer working with a white band.

LISTENING GUIDE

"Body and Soul"
CD **1**   Track **71**

Billie Holiday and Her Orchestra: "Body and Soul" (Green, Heyman, Sauer, Eyton). New York, February 29, 1940. Vocalion 5481. Billie Holiday, vocal and leader; Roy Eldridge, trumpet; Jimmy Powell, Carl Frye, alto saxophones; Kermit Scott, tenor saxophone; Sonny White, piano; Lawrence Lucie, guitar; John Williams, bass; Harold "Doc" West, drums.

Holiday interprets the classic "Body and Soul" beautifully, with elegant phrasing and heartfelt emotion. The song itself, since its introduction in 1930, has become one of the most enduring of jazz ballads. A particularly nice feature of this recording is the presence of Roy Eldridge, one of the great trumpeters of the swing era.

Introduction

0:00   The piece begins with a four-bar piano introduction featuring Eldridge. The saxophones hold chords as a "cushion" behind the trumpet soloist.

1st chorus—AABA

0:11   Holiday is faithful to the melody but often "back phrases"—that is, she delays her entrances a bit behind the beat to convey a conversational, intimate performance of the tune. The saxophones continue to hold chords as a background.

0:35   The second A section. The same background texture continues.

0:58   In the B section, we can hear Eldridge, muted, added to the saxophone chords.

1:21   The last A section returns to the background texture of saxophone chords without trumpet.

2nd chorus—ABA

1:45   Roy Eldridge trumpet solo, muted. The repeat of the A section is omitted, probably to fit the performance into three minutes (necessary because records could not exceed much more than three minutes due to the limitations of recording technology). Eldridge begins by quoting the melody but, in contrast to Holiday, does not continue with a literal statement; he instead develops an original solo line. The saxophones continue with chords in the background.

2:08   Holiday returns for the bridge. Again, saxophone chords provide the backup.

2:32   In the final A section, Eldridge joins the saxophone section in providing backup chords for Holiday. The tempo slows at the end of the piece for a more conclusive ending.

Holiday's popular appeal increased. While appearing at New York's Cafe Society in 1939, she recorded "Strange Fruit," a song about lynching in the South. This brave and unusual step for a jazz performer won her critical acclaim as her signature song. (Holiday sometimes claimed to have written the song, but in fact a white male composer, Lewis Allen, wrote it.) She began to focus on dark ballads, exemplified by her own "God Bless the Child." Audiences took these works as autobiographical, reflecting her two failed marriages, arrests, incarceration, and drug addiction.

Increasingly, Holiday's arrests and failing health during the 1950s sidelined her career. Although drug abuse ravaged her vocal range and timbre, she could still sing with tortured expression. Her version of the blues song "Fine and Mellow" from the 1957 television show "Sound of Jazz" shows how much she could express with so few notes still available in her range. She died in 1959, only a few months after the death of Lester Young.

Few jazz singers escaped Holiday's influence and her interpretive style. As she herself described it:

> I don't think I'm singing. I feel like I am playing a horn. I try to improvise like Les Young, like Louis Armstrong, or someone else I admire. What comes out is what I feel. I hate straight singing. I have to change a tune to my own way of doing it. That's all I know.[24]

ELLA FITZGERALD: SIXTY YEARS OF SONG

The career of Ella Fitzgerald spanned six decades. Her supreme vocal dexterity, large pitch range, dramatic dynamic contrasts, use of melodic ornaments, and—above all—scat singing made her name synonymous with jazz singing. From the time of her earliest recordings with Chick Webb in the 1930s, her ability to straddle jazz and popular styles made her one of the most beloved performers in jazz.

Fitzgerald was born in Virginia in 1917, but in early childhood she moved to New York. As a teenager, she overcame her basically shy nature by entering local talent contests with dreams of becoming a dancer. It soon became clear that dancing was not her strength, but she had tremendous talent as a singer. Chick Webb hired her to work in his band soon after she appeared in a singing contest at the Apollo Theater in 1934. Their recordings of such songs as "A-tisket, A-tasket" and "Undecided" catapulted Fitzgerald to fame.

Fitzgerald led Webb's band for several years following his death in 1939, but later she pursued a solo career. She preferred the backing of a small group, often a quartet or trio, that for four years included her onetime husband, bassist Ray Brown. Some critics find her strongest work to be the "songbooks" recorded with Verve Records between 1956 and 1961, each interpreting the repertory of a particular American popular song composer or songwriting team, including Cole Porter, Rodgers and Hart, Duke Ellington, George and Ira Gershwin, and Harold Arlen.

Fitzgerald's performances on the songbooks treat the melodies in relatively unadorned fashion, but her improvisational skill was unparalleled. Her scat singing showed an improvisational ability equaling the best instrumental soloists. Her ballad singing has sometimes been criticized for a lack of gravity, but her technique and inventiveness have made her a jazz virtuoso.

Blessed with a long career, Fitzgerald continued to work through the latter part of the twentieth century. Her health compromised by diabetes, she began to have difficulty with her eyesight in the 1970s. She also had heart surgery in 1986, but did not stop performing until the early 1990s. She died in 1996.

Pictured on a small-format wartime edition of the "Cow Cow Boogie" published in Belgium (for 7.5 Belgian francs), an exuberant Ella Fitzgerald showcases the Universal picture *Ride 'Em, Cow-Boy.*

Courtesy Morgan Collection

Summary of the Features of Swing

The following tables summarize the swing-era features, most of which have been discussed in this chapter.

Features of Swing on Piano

RIGHT-HAND TEXTURE

▶ Single-note improvisation much like swing-style, melodic improvisation on other instruments

▶ Less syncopated than ragtime with less pivoting around fixed notes

▶ Looser, greater use of long eighth-note lines

▶ Brilliant runs between phrases

▶ Less aggressive interlock of left hand and right hand (as heard in stride style)

LEFT-HAND TEXTURE

▶ Stride-derived practice of bass as swing bass, but bass notes often in tenths

▶ Use of walking tenths and occasional cross-hand textures

▶ Light, accompanying chords often emphasizing the piano's midrange

HARMONY

▶ Mostly diatonic (based on the chords of the major scale)

▶ Sixth and seventh chords predominating in left hand, with ninth chords occurring from time to time

Features of Swing Improvisation in Ensembles

TIMBRE

▶ More refined and polished than New Orleans/Dixieland

▶ Less use of vibrato

▶ Smoother, lighter saxophone tone

▶ More-brilliant trumpet tone

▶ Less use of specific instrumental effects

▶ Instrumental ranges extended upward

▶ Softer attacks and more legato playing

▶ Somewhat less use of blue-note effects

PHRASING

▶ In two-bar or four-bar units, but more varied in later swing styles (ballad playing featured more-irregular phrasing)

▶ Not much space between phrases

RHYTHM

▶ More swinging, although less syncopation than in Dixieland

▶ Up-tempo reliance on eighth-note lines

▶ Ballads that feature a greater variety of rhythmic values

THEMATIC CONTINUITY

▶ Less reliance on motive and song embellishment in up-tempo solos, more reliance on voice leading

▶ In ballads, motivic relationships more prominent

CHORD-TO-SCALE RELATIONS

▶ Inside playing

▶ In later swing, more experimentation with extended chord tones within melodic lines

LARGE-SCALE COHERENCE

▶ Voice leading and song paraphrase more often than motivic structure

▶ Gestural balance

FORM AND STRUCTURE

▶ AABA, ABAC, or blues forms

▶ Tempos ranging from slow to very fast

▶ Improvisations structured by voice leading and motivic relationships

Questions and Topics for Discussion

1. What were some of the important big bands of the swing era besides Ellington, Basie, and Goodman?

2. How did Lester Young's style on tenor saxophone differ from that of Coleman Hawkins?

3. How did swing-era piano style differ from the stride style of the 1920s? Did some pianists retain elements of stride? Who? How did they?

4. How did Kansas City provide a foundation for swing? Cite specific bands and aspects of their styles. Among the important bands associated with Kansas City were territory bands. What were they, and how did they function?

5. In what ways was Benny Goodman's nickname, "King of Swing," appropriate? In what ways was it inappropriate?

Key Terms

Antiphony 92
Arpeggiated figure 120
Balance 91
Big band 88
Chair 91
Chart 91
Coda 99
Head arrangement 94
Intonation 91
Jazz chair 91
Lead player 91
Lead trumpet 91
Library (book) 91
Lick (formula) 100
Motive (motivic material) 104
Out-chorus 102
Section 91
Sideman 91
Step connection 104
Swing 88
Territory band 88
Vamp 98
Voice leading 104
Walking bass 95

4 THE BEBOP ERA

WE THINK of the "modern jazz" era as beginning with bebop in the mid-1940s. But what makes bebop "modern," distinguishing it from the preceding swing era? This chapter explores bebop's most significant characteristics:

- ■ General aesthetics grounded in improvisation—that is, in individual solos, not in melody, popular song, and arrangement
- ■ The emergence of bebop compositions with melodies—"heads"—that stylistically complement the improvisations
- ■ Smaller groups rather than big bands
- ■ Musical venues in jazz clubs rather than large dance halls
- ■ De-emphasis on commercial or popular success
- ■ De-emphasis on dancing:
    - ▶ Tempos that are considerably faster or slower than in swing
    - ▶ Rhythmic pulse that is less obviously articulated than in swing
- ■ Rise in black consciousness resulting from a new perception of African Americans' contributions to jazz

Many of these points provided the cultural context of jazz for the remainder of the twentieth century. Besides defining a more modern sensibility, these characteristics helped transform jazz from popular entertainment into an art form in many of its substyles. Before exploring the characteristics of bebop further, we shall look at the origins of bebop in the 1940s.

Revolution Versus Evolution

The emergence of *bebop* in the 1940s irrevocably altered the jazz landscape. In contrast to the well-polished big bands of the swing era—many of them incredibly successful—some jazz musicians began gravitating toward smaller groups. Initially they developed their musical ideas in impromptu jam sessions, especially in such after-hours Harlem clubs as Monroe's Uptown House and Minton's Playhouse. By the end of World War II, these cutting-edge musicians had moved downtown to appear at the nightclubs on West Fifty-Second Street. Dozens of clubs—such as the Three Deuces, the Onyx, the Downbeat, the Famous Door, the Spotlite, Kelly's Stables, and the Hickory House—opened their doors on what became known as "The Street." They called the new music *rebop* (eventually to fall into disuse), bebop, or just bop.

Many of the architects of bebop—such as Charlie "Yardbird" or "Bird" Parker, John Birks "Dizzy" Gillespie, and Kenny Clarke—began their careers playing in big bands, but bebop represented a radical rejection of the musical conventions of the swing era. Instead of elaborate dance halls, bebop players performed in bars and nightclubs. Some of its players seemed indifferent to commercial success as entertainers—they played for listening rather than dancing. Rather than the slick show-business theatrics of the big bands, bebop bands aimed to capture the informal spirit of the jam session. Its groups often comprised only five or six musicians—two or three horn players and a rhythm section of piano, bass, and drums. While the big-band arrangers of the swing era carefully inserted improvised solos within longer written arrangements, the smaller bebop bands avoided elaborate charts and emphasized, above all, virtuosic improvisational skill.

Many older musicians were perplexed by these new sounds. Bandleader Cab Calloway is said to have derided trumpeter Dizzy Gillespie's playing as "Chinese music." In 1948 trumpeter Louis Armstrong dismissed bebop as an annoying novelty performed by overly competitive musicians. He said:

> All they want to do is show you up, and any old way will do as long as it's different from the way you played it before. So you get all them weird chords which don't mean nothing, and first people get curious about it just because it's new, but soon they get tired of it because it's really no good and you got no melody to remember and no beat to dance to.[1]

Drummer Dave Tough, a "Chicagoan" in the 1920s who later became an important drummer during the swing era, reacted with less hostility but was clearly confused by the new music. After first hearing Dizzy Gillespie and Oscar Pettiford's band on Fifty-Second Street, he noted:

> As we walked in, see, these cats snatched up their horns and blew crazy stuff. One would stop all of a sudden and another would start for no reason at all. We never could tell when a solo was supposed to begin or end. Then they all quit at once and walked off the stand. It scared us.[2]

Reactions such as these were not uncommon in the music world, but the fans of traditional jazz were the most disappointed: The music they loved was being called passé, old-fashioned, and—the worst insult of all—unhip. As expected, many champions bemoaned the demise of classic jazz and argued that bebop abandoned jazz music's most treasured principles. Modernists called these listeners *moldy figs*. Arguments between the two sides enlivened much jazz discourse in the late 1940s.

Bebop (bop) is a nervous, energetic style of jazz that developed in the 1940s. The terms probably developed from the nonsense syllables used by scat singers to re-create the characteristic melodic phrases of the new style.

Moldy figs was a term used by younger musicians and fans in the 1940s to describe older jazz fans who clung to the music of the 1920s and 1930s and derided the newer bebop style.

Bebop began in the early 1940s as "insider's" music—music for musicians. Despite the efforts of the moldy figs, bebop would become the dominant jazz style by the end of the decade. Among other factors, a wartime tax on dance halls triggered the decline of the big bands. Small jazz clubs, such as the ones found on Fifty-Second Street, boomed. Younger players, who had fewer outlets for musical employment than the stars of the big bands, joined small groups and experimented with the new musical language.

Bohemianism added an attractive element to the music. Performers and their *hipster* audiences often took on the affectations and inside slang of beboppers. Some of these affectations—such as Dizzy Gillespie's beret, goatee, and horn-rimmed glasses—were benign; others—such as Charlie Parker's heroin addiction—were not.

With bebop, jazz ceased to be a strongly commercial music. Some musicians, such as Dizzy Gillespie, felt that bebop should try to adapt to dancing. Many of its devotees, however, interpreted the music as a political statement, a rejection of all things conformist and mainstream. This view included a reaction against American racism and segregation. Many players felt that Louis Armstrong and other older musicians conformed to racial stereotypes of black entertainers. Bebop was meant to challenge and defy these stereotypes. Indeed, political activism among some black musicians can be traced to the nonconformity of the beboppers. As institutional segregation came under attack in the 1950s and 1960s, black musicians often used their music as a public statement of their political beliefs. Thus the conventions of

The word *hipster* was used to describe a young, often white, follower of jazz who affected the dress, speech, and manner of jazz musicians working in the new jazz styles of the late 1940s and early 1950s.

In 1943, the "zoot-suit" riots—named for the stylized clothing of young Chicanos—erupted in Los Angeles and continued for a week as whites, including soldiers and sailors on leave, attacked Hispanics. A future recording supervisor of jazz for Mercury Records, Norman Granz, organized a concert at the Philharmonic Auditorium in Los Angeles to benefit Mexican youths, and an enduring concert series began. Here is the 1949 program for Jazz at the Philharmonic, picturing, among others, Ron Brown on bass and Shelley Manne on drums. Notice the integrated seating, part of an anti-discrimination clause Granz wrote into all his contracts.

bebop laid the foundation for modern jazz, both in musical style and in the convictions of its players.

Despite these dramatic, possibly revolutionary, developments, much of the musical style of bebop evolved naturally from swing style. Players carried over to bebop the following features of earlier jazz:

- Improvisation on the following:
  - ▶ Thirty-two–bar popular songs in AABA or ABAC form
  - ▶ Rhythm changes
  - ▶ The blues
- Improvisation based mostly on eighth-note melodic lines
- Characteristic instrumentation of rhythm section plus horns
- Overall performance formats of head-solos-head

Seen in this light, bebop was a natural next step in the musical development of jazz. This should not be surprising because the musicians who innovated bebop had trained extensively in swing bands. Although many of the revolutionary aspects of bebop were more social than musical, jazz musicians and fans at the time were indeed caught up with what they perceived as the radical newness of its language. In the description of bebop style to follow, we shall emphasize these innovations rather than the older swing elements.

Characteristics of the Bebop Style

The new music that offended or confused older musicians such as Cab Calloway, Louis Armstrong, and Dave Tough differed from earlier jazz in improvisational style, melodic language, and harmonic language. Much of the repertory changed considerably. In typical bebop compositions, the horns played the melody, improvised solos followed, and a reprise of the melody formed the ending. The horns frequently stated the melody in unison or in octaves, creating a starker, leaner sound than the full-voiced chords played by big bands. Bebop groups played at brighter tempos than those of swing bands, but played their ballads much more slowly.

Bebop also departed from swing because the newer style did not support dancing as well as the older style. As we have seen, musicians created the jazz of the 1920s and 1930s for dancing. The musicians of the era speak fondly of the energizing give-and-take between the dancers and the bands. The beboppers, however, disassociated jazz from the jitterbugging crowds of the 1930s in an attempt to win respect for their music as an art form. The radical change in tempo also certainly affected dancing. Further, some argue that the swing era had run its course, making separation of the music from dancing and popular song inevitable. To remain vibrant, jazz needed to evolve. The popular audience, of course, wanted danceable, singable music—a void soon to be filled by rock and roll.

The repertory for bop-style bands continued to depend on the 12-bar blues and compositions based on the chords of "I Got Rhythm"—both a legacy of Kansas City style—as well as the 32-bar AABA or ABAC form in standard popular songs. But an important innovation of the repertory was the *recomposition* of these popular songs into a bebop framework. In these recompositions, players abandoned the original melody and composed a new one over the harmonic structure of the original. (See

A ***recomposition*** is a new melody composed to fit the harmonic and formal structure of a previously composed popular song.

A Recomposition: Dizzy Gillespie's "Groovin' High"

Here is a comparison of the original melody of "Whispering" with Gillespie's recomposition "Groovin' High":

The "Whispering" melody, which is primarily diatonic, almost masks its harmonic progression. In "Groovin' High," Gillespie writes a new melody mostly in eighth notes and with more notes than in the original composition—typical of the bebop melodic language. Gillespie's recomposed melody:

▶ Is much more chromatic

▶ Is jagged and angular

▶ Outlines and highlights the harmonic progression through a repeated motive (marked as B)

▶ Has accents that crop up in unexpected places

These are the features of bebop that swing fans sometimes found hard to understand. Gillespie's melody, too, has the typical double-eighth-note figure prevalent in bebop melodies and improvisations (marked as A). This characteristic two-note figure may very well be the source of the word *bebop.*

the box "A Recomposition: Dizzy Gillespie's 'Groovin' High'" above.) For the bebop player, recompositions had two advantages:

▶ The new melody resembled the bebop improvisations that followed and kept the musical language unified.

▶ Performers and record companies did not have to pay song royalties because they did not use the original melodies.

Many of the significant early works of the bebop era were recompositions:

BEBOP-STYLE TUNE (COMPOSER)	ORIGINAL (COMPOSER)
KoKo (Charlie Parker)	**Cherokee** (Ray Noble)
Hot House (Tadd Dameron)	**What Is This Thing Called Love?** (Cole Porter)
Crazeology (Benny Harris)	**I Got Rhythm** (George Gershwin)
Groovin' High (Dizzy Gillespie)	**Whispering** (Rose-Coburn-Schonberger)

Dizzy Gillespie, one of the founders of the new style, acknowledged the obvious differences in bebop from earlier jazz but was keenly aware of how the music evolved logically from swing. When asked to contrast the newer bebop music with the older style, he cited several differences:

> [C]hords. . . . And we stressed different accents in the rhythms. But I'm reluctant to say that anything is *the* difference between our music of the early forties and the music before that, of the thirties. You can get records from the early days and hear guys doing the same things. It just kept changing a little bit more; one guy would play a phrase one way, and another guy would come along and do something else with it. . . . Charlie Parker was very, very melodic; guys could copy his things quite a bit. [Thelonious] Monk was one of the founders of the movement too, but his playing, my playing, and Charlie Parker's playing were altogether different.[3]

The one characteristic that players most frequently singled out as new was the harmony. As saxophonist Illinois Jacquet pointed out, "The major difference in the new music was the chord changes."[4] The harmonies used by the bebop players sometimes emphasized the upper parts of chords such as ninths, elevenths, and thirteenths. These additions to chords, called *tensions,* or *extended chord tones,* would be contributed not only by the accompanying pianist but also sometimes by the soloist. Hearing the emphasis on these extensions, early critics of the music thought the improvisers were playing "wrong notes."

Extended chord tones, sometimes called *tensions*, are notes added to seventh chords to make the harmony richer and more pungent. These tones are usually ninths, elevenths, and thirteenths. Extended chord tones usually resolve to more-stable pitches such as roots, thirds, and fifths.

Music Example 4-1a, the opening of Gillespie's "A Night in Tunisia," shows a prominent use of the seventh, ninth, and thirteenth as arpeggiated chordal extensions. Also prominent in bebop was the so-called flatted fifth, the use of a pitch a tritone away from the root of the chord. The melody of measures 7–8 of "A Night in Tunisia" illustrates the use of the flatted fifth: Here, E♭ is used in conjunction with the A7 chord.

a. Opening

b. Measures 7–8

Music Example 4-1
"A Night in Tunisia."

Reharmonization was another important new aspect of bebop harmony. Bebop players often inserted new chords and chord progressions into a standard composition: This gave soloists more chords to improvise over. Reharmonization was popular at jam sessions in Harlem in the early 1940s. "We'd do that kind of thing in 1942 around Minton's a lot," Dizzy Gillespie recalled. "We'd been doing that kind of thing, Monk and I, but it was never documented because no records were being made at the time."[5] Historians have frequently cited pianist Art Tatum's influence on bebop reharmonization because of his extensive harmonic reworkings of popular songs. (See Tatum's performance of "Tiger Rag" in Chapter 2.)

Reharmonization refers to the bop practice of inserting different chords into the fundamental chord structure of a well-known song to freshen the interpretation and expand harmonic options for the soloist.

The way rhythm players accompanied soloists also changed. In particular, because of the influence of Kenny Clarke, Max Roach, and others, bebop drummers kept time very differently. Whereas many swing-era drummers marked all four beats of a 4/4 measure with the bass drum, bebop drummers such as Clarke switched to the

Dropping bombs is a term describing how bebop drummers used the bass drum for sharp, irregular accents in the rhythmic accompaniment.

ride cymbal to maintain the pulse. They used the bass drum for *dropping bombs*—sharp, irregular accents that were far more disruptive than the accents of the swing drummers. Bebop drummers used the snare drum to punctuate the musical texture with accents or to maintain a kind of irregular "chattering" as an aside to the principal beat on the ride cymbal.

The faster tempos of the bebop players lay behind some of these changes in drumming. Clarke admitted that he was unable to maintain the breakneck speeds and keep his foot playing the bass drum on all four beats, so he switched the timekeeping role to the ride cymbal. Clarke, nicknamed "Klook" or "Klook-mop" in response to his use of unpredictable accents, played a fundamental role in developing this new style of drumming.

The faster tempos also brought about changes in piano playing. Bebop pianists abandoned the left-hand striding style that kept steady time. Instead, the pianist broke up the texture with chords, often syncopated, leaving the timekeeping role to the bass and the drummer's ride cymbal. This type of accompanying came to be called *comping*. During their improvisations, the bebop pianists also played lines like those of horn players with the right hand while the left hand accompanied with short, staccato chords.

Comping refers to the chordal accompaniment provided by pianists or guitarists in jazz bands. This accompaniment is often syncopated. The term *comp* is probably derived from a contraction of the word *accompany* or *complement*.

With the pianist's left hand and the drummer's bass drum no longer projecting the pulse, bands relied on their bassists to keep time, usually by "walking" the bass on each beat of the measure. Following the influence of Ellington's bassist Jimmy Blanton (see Chapter 3), bebop bass players played in a more linear fashion instead of merely playing the root notes of each chord. Blanton also influenced such bassists as Oscar Pettiford and Ray Brown, who became renowned for their ability to improvise solos as well as accompany and keep time.

The Historical Origins of Bebop

Many factors, both musical and social, contributed to the rise of bebop in the 1940s. In this section we look at the people, places, and political forces that helped create this musical phenomenon. Later, we focus on the specific contributions of several key players in bebop's early development.

THE EARLY FORTIES: JAMMING AT MINTON'S AND MONROE'S

The earliest stirrings of bebop took place in informal jam sessions in Harlem. In 1940, Minton's Playhouse on West 118th Street hired drummer Kenny Clarke as a bandleader. For the house band, Clarke hired trumpeter Joe Guy, bassist Nick Fenton, and an eccentric pianist named Thelonious Monk. Musicians would stop by Minton's and sit in after they had completed their gigs. The atmosphere was informal, so they could try out ideas, network, and engage in friendly (or not so friendly) competition with the other players. In other words, the jam sessions helped the players make connections, develop new ideas, and establish a rough pecking order of talent. The club, as trumpeter Miles Davis pointed out, was "the music laboratory for bebop."[6]

The American Federation of Musicians Strike in 1942

Unfortunately, much of the music that marked the transition from swing to bebop in the early 1940s was never documented on studio recordings because the American Federation of Musicians (AFM) called a strike in August 1942. Protesting the lack of payment to musicians for records played on the radio, the union insisted on a recording ban—with the exception of "V-discs" (Victory discs) produced specifically for the armed forces overseas. Decca settled in September 1943, Columbia and Victor held out another year, and eventually the strike ended. These three record companies held the lion's share of the market before the ban, but several smaller labels sprang up shortly afterward and focused their attention on recording the younger players.

Pianist Thelonious Monk composed regularly for the band at Minton's. There, he wrote some of his most enduring compositions, including two haunting ballads, "'Round Midnight" and "Ruby My Dear," which showed the unique harmonic sense that characterized Monk's style. Even when playing standard tunes, Monk often made unusual reharmonizations, especially in introductions. One musician in the audience remembered that Monk "generally started playing strange introductions going off, I thought to outer space, hell knows to where."[7]

Monroe's Uptown House on West 134th Street was another site for jam sessions. Run by pianist Allen Tinney, they normally began at 3:00 A.M. and lasted until morning. As one participant at Monroe's remembered, "The musicians used to go there and battle like dogs, every night, you know, and just playing for nothing and having a good time."[8] Charlie Parker, in town with the Jay McShann band, was so stunned by the level of musical activity at Monroe's that he left the McShann band and remained in New York:

> At Monroe's I heard sessions with a pianist named Allen Tinney; I'd listen to trumpet men like Lips Page, Roy [Eldridge], Dizzy, and Charlie Shavers outblowing each other all night long. And Don Byas was there, playing everything there was to be played. I heard a trumpet man named Vic Coulson playing things I'd never heard. Vic had the regular band at Monroe's, with George Treadwell also on trumpet, and a tenor man named Pritchett. That was the kind of music that caused me to quit McShann and stay in New York.[9]

BIG BANDS IN THE EARLY 1940s

If the uptown Harlem clubs like Minton's and Monroe's functioned as the "laboratories" for bebop, the more commercial format of the big band also provided opportunities for many of the newer players to develop and test their ideas. Particularly significant in the early part of the 1940s were the big bands of Earl Hines and, shortly thereafter, Billy Eckstine. These bands included both Charlie Parker and Dizzy Gillespie, so they were especially notable. Because of the record ban, however, most of their music went unrecorded. (See the box "The American Federation of Musicians Strike in 1942" on page 141.)

In 1942 Hines recruited Gillespie on trumpet and Parker on tenor saxophone (there was no opening for an alto saxophone player). Outside of Harlem jam sessions, this was the first time Parker and Gillespie had worked together on the bandstand. The band also featured two outstanding singers who would develop major careers, Sarah Vaughan and Billy Eckstine.

Sarah Vaughan (1924–1990) became a preeminent jazz singer, possibly the greatest to develop in the bebop era. Her leap to the limelight came during the heyday of bop, when she sang with both the Earl Hines and the Billy Eckstine big bands in the early 1940s. There, her associations with Parker and Gillespie established her reputation and refined her ability to sing with the looseness and unexpected vocal twists and turns of the newer style. She seems to have concentrated more on jazz singing than did Ella Fitzgerald, who, after leaving the Chick Webb band, became firmly entrenched in a more pop-jazz style. Vaughan also maintained a close connection to the other jazz musicians of her generation.

Billy Eckstine (1914–1993) was a suave baritone vocalist who also played trumpet and valve trombone. In the early 1940s he had a hit with the Hines band in the slightly bawdy blues song "Jelly, Jelly." Persuaded to form his own band, Eckstine left Hines and hired Gillespie as musical director. Gillespie convinced many of the most forward-looking of Hines's musicians to join Eckstine's band, including Parker, pianist John Malachi, and eventually drummer Art Blakey.

The Eckstine band of 1944 has frequently been called the "first bebop big band," but the group did not achieve significant commercial success. Although they played at dance halls in the South, the band's bop-oriented compositions—many written and arranged by Gillespie—kept most people off the dance floor. Parker soon left the band, never having recorded with Eckstine, and Gillespie remained only a short time afterward. Eckstine, long one of the principal singers in jazz, would continue with a distinguished career as a jazz vocalist.

JAZZ MOVES TO FIFTY-SECOND STREET

Around the middle of the 1940s, the clubs of West Fifty-Second Street became the primary venue for bebop bands. "The Street" comprised two blocks between Fifth Avenue and Broadway. The jazz clubs were tiny, crowded, and often poorly lit—far removed from the elaborate dance halls played by the big bands. In fact, there was no dance floor, merely tables for listening and an area where listeners were not required to buy drinks. During the war an immense concentration of jazz players developed in the city. For the cost of a cover charge, a listener could stroll down The Street and stop in to hear Sidney Bechet, Art Tatum, Coleman Hawkins, or Fats Waller anytime between 9:00 P.M. and 3:00 A.M. Gradually, the newer bebop bands worked their way into Fifty-Second Street.

As Dizzy Gillespie remembered it, the birth of the bebop era came after he left the Eckstine band in 1944. With bassist Oscar Pettiford, Gillespie formed a band to play at the Onyx Club, one of several acts on the bill. Gillespie and Pettiford hired Max Roach on drums and George Wallington on piano; both had been in the house band at Monroe's Uptown House. Gillespie tried to contact Charlie Parker, who had returned to Kansas City after leaving Eckstine, but Parker never received the telegram. When tenor saxophonist Don Byas, a fine player with a big sound reminiscent of Coleman Hawkins, began sitting in with the group, they eventually invited him to join them. With the horns playing in unison, the group's repertory was new and startling:

> In the Onyx Club, we played a lot of original tunes that didn't have titles. We just wrote an introduction and a first chorus. I'd say, "Dee-da-pa-da-n-de-bop. . . ." and we'd go on into it. People, when they'd wanna ask for one of those numbers and didn't know the name, would ask for bebop. And the press picked it up and started calling it bebop. The first time the term *bebop* appeared in print was while we played at the Onyx Club.[10]

The group itself did not record, but much of the band—Gillespie, Pettiford, Roach, and Byas—assembled in the studio in early 1944 under the auspices of Coleman Hawkins for a series of historic recordings. Hawkins, some twenty years into his career, was attempting to stay in the musical vanguard by hiring the more visible young players on the scene. According to many, this attempt resulted in the first bebop recordings. Although half of the six tunes were ballads for Hawkins, the rest were in the newer style: Gillespie's "Woody n' You," Budd Johnson's "Bu-Dee-Daht," and a blues piece called "Disorder at the Border." In these recordings, bebop had an embryonic sound: The ponderous big band, the rhythm section, and many of the solos still seemed weighted down by the conventions of swing. Only Gillespie's energetic start-and-stop solos hinted at the music to come—the music fundamentally indebted to the innovations of Gillespie and Charlie Parker.

The Architects of Bebop

Numerous musicians contributed to the formation of bebop, but none were more significant than Charlie Parker and Dizzy Gillespie. Kenny Clarke, whose role in modifying drum styles also greatly affected bebop, was discussed earlier. Among pianists, the preeminent contributors included Thelonious Monk and Bud Powell.

CHARLIE PARKER

Charlie Parker was probably the greatest, most consistently brilliant jazz saxophonist of all time. Parker's influence on jazz history rivals that of Louis Armstrong: Both generated a major jazz style while radically increasing the level of technical proficiency on their instruments. Parker's improvisations left a mark on almost every subsequent jazz musician.

Born in Kansas City on August 29, 1920, Parker first played baritone and alto horns in his school bands, but turned to the alto saxophone in 1933. Within two years, he left school to play full-time with a local bandleader known as Lawrence "88" Keyes.

Parker's talent was not immediately apparent. Bassist Gene Ramey described Parker as the "saddest thing in the Keyes band."[11] In the cutthroat world of the Kansas

Charlie Parker (CD 2, Track 1), pictured on the cover of a Gil Fuller transcription of bebop themes, including "Oop Bop Sh-Bam" and "Ray's Idea."

City jam session, Parker learned about competition the hard way. In a radio interview, Parker recalled his first jam session:

> I'd learned how to play the first eight bars of "[Up a] Lazy River," and I knew the complete tune to "Honeysuckle Rose." I didn't never stop to think about there was other keys or nothin' like that. [Laughter] So I took my horn out to this joint where the guys—a bunch of guys I had seen around were—and the first thing they started playing was "Body and Soul," long beat [implied double time] you know, like this. [*Demonstrates.*] . . . So I go to playin' my "Honeysuckle Rose" and [unintelligible], I mean, ain't no form of conglomeration [unintelligible]. They laughed me right off the bandstand.[12]

But Parker was diligent. Known for carrying his horn in a paper bag, the teenager learned a few Lester Young solos note-for-note while studying basic harmony with some of the local guitarists. He joined the band of Buster Smith, a saxophonist who was an early influence on Parker. Then in 1938 he joined the band of Jay McShann, a pianist based in Kansas City but originally from Oklahoma.

In early 1939, Parker moved to New York for the first time, playing sessions at Monroe's Uptown House and washing dishes at Jimmy's Chicken Shack to hear pianist Art Tatum, who often performed there. Undoubtedly, Tatum's sophisticated harmonic sense influenced Parker; further, Tatum's effortless virtuosity and streams of high-speed runs quite likely helped to determine the mature Parker style. In a famous anecdote, Parker credited a guitarist named Biddy Fleet with teaching him more-advanced harmonies: Playing "Cherokee," which would become one of his signature tunes, Parker realized that he could emphasize the higher chordal extensions—ninths, elevenths, or thirteenths. These too became a feature of his mature style.

In 1940 Parker returned to Kansas City and the McShann band to become one of its musical directors. An amateur recording, probably from 1940, is the first we have of Parker. This recording preserved a solo practice session on "Honeysuckle Rose" followed by "Body and Soul"—significant choices given the story of Parker's first jam session.

Parker cut his first professional recordings informally at a radio station in Wichita, Kansas, on November 30 and December 2, 1940, with the McShann band. In 1941 and 1942, still with the McShann band, Parker made his first studio recordings, including "Swingmatism," "Hootie Blues," "Sepian Bounce," and "The Jumpin' Blues." "Hootie Blues" featured Parker's first important solo—his first statement as a new saxophone stylist.

Parker and the McShann band returned to New York in late 1941 or early 1942 to play at the Savoy. At that time he immersed himself in the New York scene, frequently attending the after-hours sessions at Minton's and Monroe's. He shared the stand with trumpeters Roy Eldridge, Dizzy Gillespie, and Charlie Shavers, as well as saxophonist Don Byas. Drummer Kenny Clarke, who in 1941 considered himself among the newer innovators, was stunned by Parker's playing:

> Bird was playing stuff we'd never heard before. He was into figures I thought I'd invented for drums. He was twice as fast as Lester Young and into harmony Lester hadn't touched. Bird was running the same way we were, but he was way out ahead of us. I don't think he was aware of the changes he had created. It was his way of playing jazz, part of his own experience.[13]

After stints with the Hines and Eckstine big bands, Parker settled in New York and rapidly became an underground hero. His jams with the band of guitarist Tiny Grimes became especially significant. On September 15, 1944, Grimes invited Parker to cut four sides with the band, including Parker's own composition "Red Cross." In the two takes of "Red Cross" we hear Parker's first recorded solos with rhythm changes. More generally, as Parker's first small-group records featuring him as soloist, we hear the early crystallization of Parker's bebop playing. (Listen to Track 10 of CD 1 🅟 to hear an example of rhythm changes.)

Although the Grimes band was more of a swing than a bop group, Parker plays his solos superbly, presenting several of his trademarks:

▶ A lean, edgy tone

▶ Use of blues inflections

▶ Double-time sixteenth-note runs

▶ Bebop-style licks that were to become the mainstay of the new style

After the Grimes recordings of late 1944, Parker began to work with small groups as his bebop style matured. Most significantly, he teamed up with Dizzy Gillespie, and their musical relationship began to flourish. By May 1945 the two were fronting a band at the Three Deuces on Fifty-Second Street, where they remained until July. The group recorded several tunes that became mainstays of the bebop era, including "Groovin' High," "Dizzy Atmosphere," "All the Things You Are," and "Salt Peanuts."

L I S T E N I N G   G U I D E

"Salt Peanuts"
CD **2** Track **1**

Dizzy Gillespie and His All Stars: "Salt Peanuts" (Gillespie). New York, May 11, 1945. Guild 1003.
Dizzy Gillespie, trumpet and vocal; Charlie Parker, alto saxophone; Al Haig, piano;
Curley Russell, bass; Sidney Catlett, drums.

"Salt Peanuts" may be the best-known bebop tune, perhaps because its humorous motivic idea is unforgettable. The tune is an audience-pleaser, less often adopted for performance by Parker, who generally refused to play up to his listeners. Yet there are instances of Parker performing—and *singing*— "Salt Peanuts" in live versions! This classic recording, an early instance of Parker and Gillespie together on record, has a remarkably complex layout for an early bebop tune. Compare it with the modern version by Steve Coleman (CD 2, Track 18).

Introduction—16 bars as 8 + 8

0:00   Introduction, part 1. A driving drum solo sets a very bright tempo—typical for a tune in bebop style.

0:06   The rest of the ensemble enters. The last two bars feature a break for pianist Haig playing the "Salt Peanuts" (SP) octave motive.

1st chorus head—32-bar AABA

0:12   The head consists of two licks, the second of which is the SP motive. Parker and Gillespie divide the SP motive, with Parker on the lower note and Gillespie on the upper.

0:19   Repeat of the A.

0:26   The bridge features Parker and Gillespie in octaves. There are alterations in the harmonies, which themselves are based on rhythm changes. Some of the melodic leaps are diminished fifths (called "tritones" or "flat fives" by jazz musicians), a popular interval in bebop melodies.

0:32   The third A section completes the first chorus.

Interlude: A—8 bars

0:39   A composed line for Parker and Gillespie on the A-section changes.

2nd chorus head—32-bar AABA

0:45   Parker takes the first lick of the tune himself, while Gillespie sings the SP motive.

0:52   Repeat of the A.

0:58   Parker solos on the bridge.

1:05   The third A section completes the two-chorus presentation of the head, with Parker on the tune's first lick and Gillespie singing the SP motive.

Interlude—16 bars as 8 + 8

1:11   The rhythm section plays alone for the first eight bars.

1:18   Parker and Gillespie rejoin the band for the second section of the interlude, which features prominent tritones. Pianist Al Haig takes the last two bars as a solo break.

3rd chorus—32-bar AABA piano solo

1:24   Haig solos on a full chorus. Haig's left hand is relatively inactive, while the right hand concentrates on "running the changes," as is typical in up-tempo bebop.

4th chorus—32-bar AABA alto saxophone solo

1:50   Parker's solo is virtuosic and features the edgy tone for which he was well known.

Interlude—8 bars

2:16   An interlude to set up Gillespie's entrance and solo break in the last two bars.

5th chorus—32-bar AABA trumpet solo

2:23   The first two bars of Gillespie's solo continue the break from the interlude. His use of extreme high notes is typical of his style, as is the fleet dexterity of the entire improvisation.

Drum solo

2:50   Catlett's drum solo maintains the time, leading into the introduction, part 1.

Introduction—As coda

3:09   The second part of the introduction repeats with the band singing the final SP motive.

From "Salt Peanuts" we can summarize these characteristic features of Parker's up-tempo style:

▶ Disjointed, irregularly accented melodic lines, mostly comprising eighth-notes with occasional arpeggiations

▶ Little space between phrases

▶ Melodic connections based on extremely subtle motivic interrelations and voice leading

▶ A commanding, insistent tone quality

▶ Use of melodic chord extensions

▶ Intense, powerful expression

▶ Frequent blues inflections

▶ Concentration on middle and upper range of instrument

▶ Scale-chord relationships generated from the use of altered and extended chord harmonies

Gillespie's style echoes Parker's, and bop melodic playing in general, in its use of the following elements:

▶ Angular melodic lines made up largely of eighth notes

▶ Less rhythmic variety because of the eighth-note emphasis

▶ Phrases of irregular length

▶ Long phrases that may complete a section or more of a chorus

▶ The use of extended and chromatic extended chord tones

▶ A lack of vibrato in up-tempo playing

▶ Emotional though virtuosic playing

▶ An emphasis on the middle and high range of the instrument

▶ Melodic continuity based on voice leading and large-scale phrasing

▶ The de-emphasis of motive structure, at least in up-tempo playing

▶ Few blues inflections in up-tempo playing

▶ Adventurous chord-scale associations

On November 26, 1945, Parker supervised his first session as a leader. These recordings for Savoy Records included some of his most important performances as well as the original compositions "Billie's Bounce," "KoKo," "Now's the Time," and "Thriving on a Riff." "KoKo" also featured Dizzy Gillespie on trumpet, but a nervous, nineteen-year-old trumpeter from St. Louis named Miles Davis played the other cuts.

In December 1945 Parker and Gillespie traveled with a band led by Gillespie to the West Coast for an engagement in Hollywood. The gig, at a club called Billy Berg's, was not successful. Gillespie and the band returned to New York within a few months, while Parker stayed on. Reputedly, he pawned his plane ticket to support his heroin habit. His addiction, which he had developed when he was a teenager, caused Parker intense physical and emotional problems. While still in California, Parker entered Camarillo State Hospital in July 1946 and remained there for six months. Following his release and several performances and recordings, Parker returned to New York in April 1947.

The following four years proved to be the most intensely fertile period of Parker's career. He formed his most long-lived working quintet with trumpeter Miles Davis, pianist Duke Jordan, bassist Tommy Potter, and drummer Max Roach, a group that remained together for a year and a half. The band recorded many Parker compositions that became jazz standards.

As he gained wider public acceptance and acclaim, Parker undertook several new and interesting projects. He made two European tours, playing Paris in 1949 and Sweden the following year. He recorded in many different settings, including "South of the Border" sessions with Machito's Afro-Cuban band. Most significant was the unusual step of recording with string accompaniment, in which Parker

The original caption for this photo read: "The show at the new Birdland Restaurant, which opened on Broadway, December 15 [1949], offers music to suit just about every taste. Entertaining at their specialties are (left to right) trumpeter Max Kaminsky, Dixieland style; saxophonist Lester Young, swing; [Oran] "Hot Lips" Page, famed for sweet swing; Charlie Parker on the alto sax, representing bop; and pianist Lennie Tristano, exponent of a new style called 'music of the future.' It marked the first time that these noted musicians, representing completely different schools of modern music, were gathered on the same stage."

fulfilled a long-held ambition. In *Bird with Strings* Parker played standards in a subdued mood. His recording of "Just Friends" became a classic; it was not only Parker's best-selling record but reputedly Parker's favorite of his recorded solos.

One of Parker's most significant devices, not new to jazz but one that he developed extensively, was his tendency to quote other music in his solos. The quotations ranged from classical themes to well-known pop tunes, jazz heads, and children's songs. For example, in a solo on "Salt Peanuts" performed in Paris in 1949, Parker quoted the beginning of Igor Stravinsky's *The Rite of Spring,* a famous classical work that had premiered in Paris in 1913. At the other extreme, in a solo on "Just Friends" recorded in 1950, Parker quoted "Pop Goes the Weasel." Both of these performances were live; Parker tended to quote more often in live settings than in studio recordings. Perhaps Parker chose the live venue because he realized that the joke implied in a quotation would quickly become stale on repeated listening. Of note is the unequaled ingenuity with which Parker wove his quotations into the flow of his solos. Parker's freewheeling quotations greatly influenced later generations of players.

Parker spent his final years in a downward slide both physically and mentally. He suffered from ulcers, became overweight, and drank heavily. When one of his daughters, Pree, died of pneumonia, Parker became severely depressed. In 1954 he twice attempted suicide and voluntarily committed himself to Bellevue Hospital in New York. Parker last performed at a club named for him, Birdland. The performance was disastrous, a visible airing of his feud with pianist Bud Powell. A week later, on March 12, 1955, he died at the apartment of the Baroness Pannonica de Koenigswarter, a jazz patron who had befriended the saxophonist. His body was so ravaged by years of substance abuse that the examining doctor listed Parker's age as fifty-three. He was only thirty-four.

DIZZY GILLESPIE

Along with Charlie Parker, John Birks "Dizzy" Gillespie played a crucial role in promoting the new bebop style in the 1940s. "Bird might have been the spirit of the bebop movement," said Miles Davis, "but Dizzy was its 'head and its hands,' the one who kept it all together."[14] Despite Gillespie's reputation for clowning around—which early on earned him the nickname "Dizzy"—he was dedicated to his craft as a musician. He made a point of working out experimental harmonies and chord progressions at the piano, often enthusiastically teaching and coaching the other players. Gillespie clearly rejected the stereotype of the untutored, "natural" jazz musician. As he told *Time* magazine in 1949,

> Nowadays we try to work out different rhythms and things that they didn't think about when Louis Armstrong blew. In his day all he did was play strictly from the soul—just strictly from the heart. You got to go forward and progress. We study.[15]

Although his style had originally been influenced by trumpeter Roy Eldridge, Gillespie soon developed an improvisational technique that was much more free-wheeling. With his impressive command of the upper register of the trumpet, he punctuated his solos with wild leaps into the "stratosphere." He could play much faster than previous trumpeters, with sinuous chromatic lines in dramatic contrast to the diatonically based solos of swing.

As a composer and an arranger, Gillespie was prolific. Many of his bebop heads became jazz standards in their own right, such as "Groovin' High," "Woody n' You," "Salt Peanuts," and "A Night in Tunisia" (see the earlier Music Example 4-1). Written while Gillespie was a member of the Hines band during the early 1940s and originally titled "Interlude," "A Night in Tunisia" was perhaps his most famous piece. Although unusual in its exoticism, it showed many of the hallmarks of the nascent bebop style. The use of the Latin-tinged rhythm in the opening section reflected Gillespie's interest in Afro-Cuban music.

Gillespie was born in Cheraw, South Carolina, on October 21, 1917. Years later, he moved with his family to Philadelphia and began working his way up in the swing-band pecking order until finally joining Cab Calloway in 1939. He was summarily dismissed by Calloway in 1941 after the leader mistakenly accused Gillespie of hurling a spitball at Calloway during a performance.

Like Parker, Gillespie frequently participated in the after-hours sessions at Minton's and had been a member of the big bands of Earl Hines and Billy Eckstine. Gillespie soon began to achieve success as an arranger, contributing numbers to the bands of Boyd Raeburn and Woody Herman. After winning the New Star Award in the *Esquire* magazine Jazz Poll in 1944, Gillespie formed the band with bassist Oscar Pettiford that performed at the Onyx Club on Fifty-Second Street. (See the box "Jazz Moves to Fifty-Second Street" on page 142.) It was the recordings and performances with Charlie Parker, however, that thrust Gillespie squarely into the front line of the bebop movement. The 1945 performances and recordings of the two principal talents of bebop culminated in the disastrous West Coast trip at the end of the year (discussed earlier).

After his split with Parker, Gillespie returned to the large-group format and, from 1946, led his own big band with increasing commercial success through 1950. On many of their recordings we hear the successful translation of bebop from small group to big band, including the exciting "Things to Come," a prophetically titled piece written and arranged by Gillespie and Gil Fuller.

In addition to embracing bebop, Gillespie's big band became well known for its blend of jazz with Afro-Cuban elements. Gillespie had been interested in Afro-Cuban music since the early 1940s, when he befriended Latin trumpeter Mario Bauza (1911–1993). At the time, both were performing with the Cab Calloway orchestra. When Gillespie formed his own big band, he decided to highlight the Afro-Cuban connection through both appropriate arrangements and fiery conga drummer Chano Pozo (1915–1948), whose playing generated considerable excitement. (Gillespie featured him in a famous Carnegie Hall concert in 1947.) The result merged jazz and Afro-Cuban style into a hybrid known as *cubop*. The best-known of the Gillespie band's cubop pieces were "Manteca" and "Cubana Be, Cubana Bop," the latter by George Russell. Gillespie felt that Afro-Cuban music complemented and expanded the rhythmic resources of jazz, so he adopted it as an important part of his work. (See the box "Latin Jazz" on the next page.)

Dizzy Gillespie (CD 2, Tracks 1 and 2) on the cover of "Lop-Pow" published in 1948 and billed as "Be-Bop (The New Jazz)."

Latin Jazz

Latin music has had a continuous influence on jazz throughout the twentieth century. For example, it is quite possible that Latin rhythms helped furnish the characteristic syncopation of New Orleans hot melody in the teens. Moreover, many of the important early New Orleans musicians had Latin roots from a variety of countries. Latin rhythms also appear in ragtime—in particular the habañera rhythm, which can be heard in Scott Joplin's "Solace—A Mexican Serenade" from 1909. The habañera rhythm was probably the most common Latin ingredient heard in jazz until the 1940s. In the habañera and other Latin rhythms, the beat is divided into two even halves, contrasting with the "swung" eighth notes more typical of swing.

The habañera beat appears in what is undoubtedly the most important blues tune in classic jazz, W. C. Handy's "St. Louis Blues." Handy, in his autobiography *Father of the Blues,* recalls that around 1910 he saw the effect on the dancers of the Latin-tinged tune "Maori" by Will Tyer. At that moment, he made the decision to try to incorporate the habañera rhythm into his works. That same beat crops up with one of the more famous techniques associated with Jelly Roll Morton: His so-called *Spanish tinge* is also based on the habañera beat. This rhythm can be heard on Morton's recordings of "Mamanita" and "New Orleans Joys."

Meanwhile, Latin dances in the U.S. supplemented the exploding number of ballroom dance fads through the teens, twenties, and thirties. Well-known Latin bandleaders such as Desi Arnaz and Xavier Cugat promoted the tango, rumba, and other Latin dances, many of which became highly popular with the public. Among the important percussion instruments that set the style and pace for these dances was the *claves,* essentially two thick wooden sticks that, when struck together, produce the characteristic "click" of the Latin percussion sound. The impulse of the clave

William P. Gottlieb/Ira and Leonore S. Gershwin Fund Collection, Music Division, Library of Congress.

Machito, an important innovator in blending Afro-Cuban music with bebop, plays the maracas; the young woman is playing the claves.

beat is syncopated over the duple meter of the underlying beat and is one of the characteristic sounds of much Latin rhythm.

Most of the Latin influence in early jazz can be traced to Mexico and South America, although there is a decisive Caribbean influence as well. In the latter 1920s, there began a major immigration of Cubans to New York City. Their music, which was distinguished from earlier Latin music, was called Afro-Cuban and was often more aggressive in its rhythmic power, possibly because of its closer connection to African roots. As an addition to the claves among the Latin percussion, the conga drum was popularized by Afro-Cuban musicians. Their music grew in popularity through the 1940s. Among the influential promoters of the Afro-Cuban sound was Machito, a Cuban vocalist who came to New York in 1937 and teamed up with trumpeter Mario Bauza, who had played with numerous jazz big bands. Machito called his group "The Afro-Cubans" and often worked with well-known jazz performers as soloists.

Since cubop of the 1940s, Latin music has continued to have a major presence

in jazz. For many decades, the best-known Latin musician with jazz associations was percussionist and bandleader Tito Puente (1923–2000), a New York native raised in Spanish Harlem. Puente's first big break in the music business—when he was all of thirteen years of age—was becoming Machito's drummer.

Separate contributions came from Brazil. The "samba," a fast syncopated dance, was introduced in the United States in the 1930s and 1940s. During the 1960s, a blend of jazz harmonies with softened, sultry melodies and textures, known as *bossa nova,* became extremely popular. Many Brazilian musicians became well known in jazz circles through the bossa nova fad as it developed through the 1960s. Jazz musicians such as tenor saxophonist Stan Getz did much to popularize the samba and bossa nova. The most important composer of bossa nova tunes was Antonio Carlos Jobim (1927–1994), who wrote "Desafinado," "The Girl from Ipanema," and many other hits. On Track 16 of CD 2, we hear Brazilian pianist Eliane Elias playing one of his best-known songs, "One Note Samba."

"Manteca"

CD **2** Track **2**

Dizzy Gillespie and His Orchestra, with Chano Pozo: "Manteca" (Chano Pozo, Dizzy Gillespie, Gil Fuller).
New York, December 30, 1947. Victor 20-3023-A. Dizzy Gillespie, trumpet, leader; Dave Burns,
Elmon Wright Jr., Benny Bailey, trumpets; William Shepperd, Ted Kelly, trombones; John Brown,
Howard Johnson, alto saxophones; Joe Gayles, George "Bick Nick" Nicholas, tenor saxophones; Cecil Payne,
baritone saxophone; John Lewis, piano; Al McKibbon, bass; Kenny Clarke, drums; Chano Pozo, conga.

Introduction

0:00   In much Afro-Cuban music, the groove, projected by the rhythm section, is an essential part of the composition. In the introduction to "Manteca," we hear a groove that builds through the addition of instruments and leads to a solo statement by Gillespie. After the bass and conga beginning, we hear the baritone saxophone entering at 0:08, the rest of the brass at 0:16, and finally Gillespie at 0:19. The acculumulated forces culminate in chords for the full band at 0:31 with a "fall-off" on the last chord, leaving just the bass, drums, and conga.

Head—40-bar AABA

0:37   The groove, continuing from the introduction, leads into the head. Here, there is a pick-up figure in the saxophones that is answered by the full brass in a call-and-response pattern. The eight-bar A section builds into its pattern, repeated intensely in measures 7–8 (0:46).

0:48   Repeat of the eight-bar A section.

0:59   The bridge is unusual in being sixteen bars instead of the customary eight. For the first eight bars, we hear lush saxophone chords that provide a fine contrast to the A section. For the second eight bars (1:11), Gillespie solos over the chordal cushion provided by the saxophones.

1:21   Return of the eight-bar A section.

Interlude

1:33   The groove of the introduction returns and leads to entries of intense brass figures. These figures culminate in a restatement of the basic AABA form of the tune, but with the AA as a tenor solo.

Tenor saxophone solo—AA, 16 bars

1:47   The groove provides a background for the first eight bars of the tenor solo.

1:58   The second eight bars of the tenor solo use the rhythm section alone as accompaniment.

Bridge—B section, 16 bars

2:08   The bridge returns scored for full band.

2:18   Gillespie returns to solo with the second half of the bridge. He is accompanied by chords in the saxophones in addition to the rhythm section.

Head—A section, 8 bars

2:30   The call-and-response figure that characterizes the head returns.

Introduction—As coda

2:42   The groove established in the introduction returns, but now grows quieter until a sudden surge in the drums ends the piece.

Compared with Charlie Parker, Gillespie presented a more commercial side to bebop. He insisted that the music be entertaining and lamented its separation from dancing. To the mainstream audience, his stage persona—which included hipster posturing with goatee, glasses, and beret—became at least as well known as his music. However, his many innovations and tireless championing of the music made Gillespie a significant founder and fundamental contributor to the development of bebop. He continued to perform bebop-based jazz with groups both large and small for decades to come as one of the great personalities and elder statesmen of the jazz scene. He died on January 6, 1993.

BUD POWELL

Earl "Bud" Powell (1924–1966), generally considered the finest of the bop pianists, transferred Parker's and Gillespie's bebop technique to piano. He gained acclaim for playing up-tempo lines at blistering speed and exercised a profound influence on a generation of pianists. He best codified the "right-hand" bop piano style in which sparse, sharply articulated chords in the left hand punctuated and rhythmically set off linear improvisations in the right. But he was also an immensely capable player in the more two-handed style derived from Art Tatum and the classic stride masters.

Courtesy Morgan Collection

The influential pianist Bud Powell.

A New Yorker, Powell began gigging around town when he was a teenager. He soon began to participate at Minton's, where house pianist Thelonious Monk took an early interest in his development. He began to work with trumpeter Cootie Williams in 1944 and became a mainstay on Fifty-Second Street.

Around this time, during a racial incident, Powell was beaten by a policeman and received wounds to his head. Afterward, he began showing signs of erratic behavior and mental instability and was institutionalized five times between 1945 and 1955. "Bud was always—ever since I've known him—he was a little on the border line," recalled tenor saxophonist Dexter Gordon. "Because he'd go off into things—expressions, telltale things that would let you know he was off."[16] Despite his often moody and withdrawn behavior, Powell's playing astounded his contemporaries.

Powell's performances are well documented by recordings. In January 1947, Powell made his first recording as a leader, with Curley Russell on bass and Max Roach on drums. Powell's trio recordings of 1949, with bassist Ray Brown, showed him to be not only a stunning pianist but also a gifted composer. Powell's work during the 1950s was less even. He recorded for Blue Note, Verve, and Victor, but his mental problems, often made worse by drinking, interfered with his playing. He recaptured some of his fiery spirit in a famous concert recorded at Massey Hall, Toronto, on May 15, 1953, in which he performed with Charlie Parker, Dizzy Gillespie, Max Roach, and bassist Charles Mingus—a recording justly acclaimed as reuniting Parker and Gillespie in a "summit meeting" of the top talents in bebop. Unfortunately, Powell continued to suffer health problems and was eventually diagnosed with tuberculosis in 1963. He died in 1966.

The quintessential bebop pianist, Powell made a direct impact on the piano styles of Al Haig, Barry Harris, Hank Jones, Tommy Flanagan, and Sonny Clark. Indeed, no pianist who followed Powell could escape his influence. His right-hand-dominated style became the prime technique for nearly all jazz pianists and made Powell the father of modern jazz piano.

THELONIOUS MONK

Thelonious Sphere Monk was an original. Avoiding the virtuosic flamboyance of Art Tatum and the up-tempo facility of Bud Powell, Monk instead created a piano style that struck many of his contemporaries as either erratic and awkward or just plain odd. But all of Monk's peers considered him one of the prime movers of bebop. "Monk's contribution to the new style of music was mostly harmonic," Dizzy Gillespie said, "and also spiritual."[17]

Although Monk's technique was rooted in the Harlem stride tradition, his solos avoided the energy and virtuosity of the older school. His playing was lean and spare, making abundant use of silence around the notes. A noted characteristic of his playing used clusters and "crushed notes"—a dissonant group of pitches out of which Monk would release all but one or two notes.

Much of Monk's early influence on bebop came from his practice of reharmonizing popular standards, in which he displayed the wit and quirkiness that would come to be associated with his style. As Miles Davis put it, "Monk had a great sense of humor, musically speaking. He was a real innovative musician whose music was ahead of his time. . . . [He] taught me more about music composition than anyone else on 52nd Street."[18]

As house pianist at Minton's during the early 1940s, Monk was positioned to have his pieces performed frequently by the up-and-coming bebop players. Curiously, however, they rarely asked Monk to record with them.

Finally signed by Blue Note records in the later 1940s, Monk recorded pieces that highlighted his strengths as a composer. His poignant ballads "'Round Midnight," "Ruby My Dear," and "Monk's Mood" featured a rich harmonic vocabulary. Some of his melodies, such as those in his blues pieces "Straight, No Chaser" and "Criss Cross," seemed to shift the beat around by using motives repeated in different parts of the measure.

Thelonious Monk (CD 2, Track 3) performing at the Beehive Club, Chicago, 1955.

Monk's distinctive approach to jazz dramatically foreshadowed the minimalism and abstract objectivity that were to become fashionable features of modernist art from the 1950s on. Monk's performances draw us into a conscious awareness of each note and ask us to judge it, to place it in its context, and to enjoy its unique occurrence at that particular moment. In his decision to revamp traditional jazz piano values, Monk addressed the problem of how to imbue each pitch—out of the few pitches available—with special significance and still create good music. Hence, Monk did not rely on dazzling the listener with flashy, previously worked-out licks.

"Four in One"
CD **2** Track **3**

Thelonious Monk Quintet: "Four in One" (Monk). Blue Note 1589. New York, July 23, 1951. Monk, piano;
Sahib Shihab, alto saxophone; Milt Jackson, vibraphone; Al McKibbon, bass; Art Blakey, drums.

"Four in One" is a characteristic Monk composition. This piece also shows off to excellent advantage
Monk's idiosyncratic piano playing in a group setting.

Introduction—8 bars

0:00 Piano solo. Blakey taps the hi-hat lightly on the second and fourth beats of each bar.
The third and fourth bars contain syncopated runs based on the whole-tone scale, a scale
used frequently by Monk.

AABA head—1st 2 A sections

0:12 The entire band plays the melody first in unison and then moves quickly to notes occasionally
harmonized with other intervals. The third and fourth bars use syncopated and repeated whole-
tone runs.

0:20 The eight-bar A section ends humorously with a "bebop" rhythmic figure.

0:24 The A section repeats.

AABA head—B section (bridge)

0:37 The eight-bar bridge begins with the vibraphone and alto saxophone on the melody.
The second four-bar group turns to
Monk-style humorous "wrong-note"
chords for measures 6–7. The downbeat
chord of measure 6 is especially sharp:

AABA head—Final A section

0:49 Repeat of the A section.

Monk piano solo—1 AABA chorus

1:02 As the solo begins, Monk refers to the head's melodic motives.

1:34 At the downbeat of the sixth bar of the bridge, Monk repeats the sharply dissonant chord from
the B section of the head. He ends the bridge with a paraphrase of the head, which continues
during the first two bars of the last A section.

1:41 During the whole-tone sequence of measures 3–4 of the last A, Monk develops an alternate
higher-register whole-tone syncopation. The solo is remarkable in its imaginative references to
the head.

Shihab alto solo—1st half of chorus (AA)

1:51 Shihab has a Parker-like quality in his tone, lines, and bebop phrasing.

2:04 At the start of the second A, he refers directly to the melody.

Jackson vibraphone solo—2nd half of chorus (BA)

2:15 Entering at the bridge of the tune, Jackson continues the pattern of clear melodic references.
His final A section is freer.

| 2:17–2:26 | Monk's accompaniment ranges in the B section from single notes in octaves to dense chords. |
| 2:27–2:35 | Monk then moves on to a leaner accompanimental sound in the final A section. |

Reprise of the head

| 2:39 | The head repeats almost exactly. As a brief coda, Monk plays a witty "bebop" cutoff in measure 7 of the last A. |

Monk's trademarks, heard in such pieces as "Four in One," include the following:

▶ Unusual rhythmic irregularities in the melodic line

▶ Use of the *whole-tone scale*

▶ A conventional large-scale form (AABA with eight-bar sections) that, because of its predictability, sets off the more personal, stylistic elements

▶ From time to time, intriguing harmonies that break the conventional "rules" of jazz harmony

▶ A whimsical effect created by the contrast between Monk's personal idioms and bebop norms

A *whole-tone scale* is a scale with whole steps only and thus no dominant, making it impossible to form major or minor triads. A whole-tone scale starts on a note and proceeds up or down by whole step only. There are only two whole-tone scales: C–D–E–F#–G#–B♭ and D♭–E♭–F–G–A–B. Notice that they share no notes.

In the latter part of the 1950s, Monk gained visibility and praise from his masterly album *Brilliant Corners* and his celebrated 1957 engagement at the Five Spot in New York with saxophonist John Coltrane. In 1959, at New York's Town Hall, he appeared in a concert that featured his compositions with a big band. By 1964, his visibility and reputation had increased so much that *Time* magazine pictured him on its cover. Interestingly, his solo piano recording from that same year, *Solo Monk,* revealed Monk's indebtedness to the Harlem stride school.

Although Monk continued to perform and record into the mid-1970s, he spent his last years living in seclusion at the home of his patron, Baroness Pannonica de Koenigswarter. He died in 1982.

Slightly outside the mainstream bop tradition, Monk's playing nevertheless enormously influenced several generations of pianists, including Randy Weston, Andrew Hill, and Chick Corea. Some aspects of Monk's style prefigure the "free jazz" that burst on the scene in the late 1950s (See Chapter 6). Although Monk was relatively neglected during his lifetime, his performing legacy is secure and many of his compositions have become jazz standards.

Bebop-Era Melodic Features

TIMBRE

▶ Tougher, edgier sound than swing, often raspy
▶ Little use of vibrato except on ballads
▶ Little use of instrumental effects
▶ Strong attacks combined with legato lines
▶ Little use of blue-note effects on up-tempo pieces
▶ Instrumental ranges extended upward, especially for brass

PHRASING

▶ Highly irregular, perhaps to offset symmetrical AABA forms
▶ Little space between phrases

RHYTHM

▶ Great reliance on eighth-note lines in up-tempo pieces
▶ Ballads featuring more rhythmic variety

THEMATIC CONTINUITY

▶ Voice leading almost exclusively in up-tempo pieces
▶ Motivic relationships less obvious, except on ballads

CHORD-SCALE RELATIONS

▶ Inside, but based on more-complex scales that include extended chord tones

LARGE-SCALE COHERENCE

▶ Voice leading
▶ Occasional reliance on use of climax followed by relaxation
▶ Balance of gesture

Key Terms

Bebop (bop) **135**

Comping **140**

Dropping bombs **140**

Extended chord tones (tensions) **139**

Hipster **136**

Moldy figs **135**

Recomposition **137**

Reharmonization **139**

Whole-tone scale **157**

Questions and Topics for Discussion

1. What are some of the differences between bebop and swing? What are some of their similarities? In what ways are the differences revolutionary or evolutionary?

2. How was Charlie Parker the consummate bebop musician? Refer to aspects of his life and music.

3. How did the lives of Dizzy Gillespie and Thelonious Monk differ from Charlie Parker's life? Refer to big bands, compositions, attitudes toward music, and personal history.

4. How did the repertory of bebop change from that of swing? What aspects of the repertory stayed the same?

5. Is it appropriate to regard bebop as the beginning of "modern jazz"? Cite both musical and sociological factors in arguing your case.

THE FIFTIES AND NEW JAZZ SUBSTYLES

5

THE CONTROVERSIES surrounding bebop in the 1940s led to a profoundly different jazz environment in the 1950s. No longer was it possible to speak of "jazz" and expect everyone to understand the meaning. It became necessary to indicate the *kind* of jazz, because the music now included a variety of substyles, the most important being hard bop and cool. *Hard bop* developed from bebop, whereas *cool* developed, in part, as a reaction against bebop. In addition, Dixieland continued to flourish everywhere, thanks to a revival in the early 1940s. Finally, popular performers such as Ella Fitzgerald and Frank Sinatra, who had roots in the swing bands of the 1930s or early 1940s, retained many of the elements of swing from the big-band era.

It is difficult to track general trends in such a complex jazz world. However, there was one point of view that musicians in the vanguard shared at the time—modernism. According to this view, jazz must develop, even progress. This was not an entirely new idea. As far back as the 1930s, jazz musicians thought of themselves as technically and artistically more advanced than the "rough" and "naive" early players. But in the 1950s many musicians, propelled by the changes of the late 1940s, came to consider jazz one of the fine arts, a category that embraced the principle of progressive development and mandated change. If jazz was to remain *art,* the artist and the music had to move forward in a constant, conscious evolution. Thus the advancing of jazz, as we shall see, became an important goal for many of its players and writers.

Hard bop drew on the speed, intensity, and power of behop and sometimes married bop to gospel and blues-influenced music.

Cool jazz was a reaction to bebop. It embraced the values of increased compositional complexity, slower tempos, and at times less emotional involvement.

Courtesy Morgan Collection

Encouraged by advertisements such as this one featuring Hopalong Cassidy on a 1950 Motorola television, mainstream America grew entranced with the new medium.

Counterpoint is the use of simultaneously sounding musical lines. Music that has counterpoint is often called *polyphonic* (see the Introduction).

Jazz and the New Substyles

The decade of the 1950s witnessed a flowering of jazz styles as the music splintered in several directions. We shall examine two general trends and one or two subgenres of each:

- Cool jazz
  - ▶ Third-stream music
  - ▶ Modal jazz
- Hard bop
  - ▶ Funky or soul jazz

As with all categories, these are not hard-and-fast distinctions. For example, some third-stream music is not cool. And in the 1960s, modal jazz is often linked more closely with hard bop than with cool jazz.

The cool jazz style, which was associated with the West Coast, rejected some of the significant features of bebop and pursued different aesthetic principles. Miles Davis, Gerry Mulligan, Chet Baker, Dave Brubeck, the Modern Jazz Quartet, and others emphasized the following characteristics:

- ▶ Restraint
- ▶ Lyricism
- ▶ Musical space
- ▶ *Counterpoint*
- ▶ Quieter dynamic range

In contrast to the breathtaking pace of some of the bebop players, many cool players concentrated on relaxed tempos. Many tenor saxophonists emulated Lester Young's light sound along with his relaxation, control, and wit. Composers Charles Mingus, George Russell, Gunther Schuller, J. J. Johnson, and Pete Rugolo frequently focused on larger, ambitious works such as suites and multimovement compositions. Cool jazz groups took different sizes, although after Miles Davis's nine-piece group made its highly influential recordings for Capitol Records in 1949 and 1950, several eight- to ten-piece groups arose. Note that the players did not always embrace the term *cool jazz* because it implied a lack of passion and emotional depth.

Although cool jazz was undoubtedly a new direction for the music, many players were committed to perpetuating bebop. These players forged a style that came to be known as hard bop. Interestingly, many of them came to New York from the urban centers of Detroit and Philadelphia. The hard bop groups varied in size, but their instrumentation often kept the standard bebop quintet of a rhythm section with piano, bass, drums, and two horns, typically a tenor saxophone and a trumpet. Many of these groups favored 32-bar compositions and a straight-ahead improvisation full of intensity, speed, and volume.

Technological Advances in the 1950s

The decade of the 1950s profited from two technological advances in recording. By the end of the 1940s, magnetic-tape recording had replaced the more limited and cumbersome metal discs. Tape recording offered several advantages:

▶ *Performance editing* (splicing together different parts to create a performance with fewer errors)

▶ *Overdubbing* (adding new parts to a previously recorded performance)

▶ Longer performance times, which encouraged the creation of longer compositions specifically for listening

▶ Live recording, when tape machines became more portable

Overdubbing or multitracking is a recording studio technique that was generally available by the 1950s. Recording tape has several parallel "tracks" that enable musicians to record additional performance parts at later times. The added part is called an *overdub*. By wearing headphones, the players follow and "play to" the previously recorded tracks. In current recording studios, computer-controlled equipment and digital technology permit virtually unlimited overdubbing and editing of recorded parts.

Along with tape recording, the *long-playing disc (LP)* contributed greatly to the evolution of jazz. LPs first became commercially available when Columbia released its 33⅓ rpm recordings in 1948. LPs were made with polyvinyl chloride (hence the nickname "vinyl" for records), which allowed more than twice the number of grooves on each side of the record than the 78 rpm did. The new "microgroove" records thus allowed more playing time per side—up to twenty-five minutes (versus the previous three or four). LPs and magnetic tape freed musicians to record in longer segments and to approximate live performances more closely than ever before.

In addition, the repertory of hard bop groups often included music that wedded the traditions of bebop to simpler, earthier blues, creating a style sometimes known as *funky jazz, gospel jazz,* or, in the 1960s, *soul jazz.* Strongly influenced by currents in black popular music, funky/soul jazz took much of its inspiration from gospel music, blues, and rhythm and blues, as in the music of gospel singer Mahalia Jackson and blues singer/pianist Ray Charles. Leaning toward the popular-music side of jazz, funky/soul jazz used a bluesy harmonic style; catchy, earthy melodies; and often the call-and-response formulas of black churches.

Funky jazz or *soul jazz* represented an equal wedding of rhythm and blues or gospel styles with the traditional jazz ensemble and was in many ways an outgrowth of hard bop.

New jazz venues—concerts especially—arose during the 1950s. Annual jazz festivals sprang up and allowed the music to reach large audiences. The first international jazz festival opened in Nice, France, in 1948; in the United States, the famous Newport Jazz Festival, directed by George Wein, began in Newport, Rhode Island, in 1954. In addition to jazz festivals, students on college campuses in the 1950s sponsored jazz concerts that helped such groups as the Dave Brubeck Quartet and the Modern Jazz Quartet gain visibility and popularity. Finally, jazz received a boost from the new recording technology, which allowed artists to record at length. (See the box "Technological Advances in the 1950s" above.)

Cool Stylists

Many artists contributed to the cool jazz style. One of the most influential was Miles Davis, with his groundbreaking pieces later collected as the album *Birth of the Cool.* Other artists and groups who played major roles include Gerry Mulligan, Chet Baker, the Modern Jazz Quartet, Dave Brubeck, and Stan Getz.

The young Miles Davis (CD 2, Tracks 4 and 8) signed this Fontana publicity postcard for a fan in Belgium.

Gerry Mulligan (CD 2, Track 4) in a publicity photograph.

MILES DAVIS AND BIRTH OF THE COOL

A series of influential recordings for Capitol Records in 1949–1950, later released as *Birth of the Cool,* helped set the tone of jazz for the decade to come. Through three studio sessions, trumpeter Miles Davis led a nine-piece group in startling arrangements that represented a drastic shift for Davis. Since coming to New York in 1944, he had been recording and performing consistently with bebop players, particularly Charlie Parker. In contrast to the freewheeling, loose, intense improvisations of Parker's quintet, the *Birth of the Cool* sessions exhibited careful arranging, musical restraint, and lyricism.

Davis capitalized on the cool elements of his style, which had begun to emerge in his earlier recordings: He focused his trumpet in the middle register, played with less virtuosic bravura, and used more "space," or rests between phrases. Given his natural inclination toward the cool, Davis admired the arrangements Gil Evans had created for the Claude Thornhill band. He decided to emulate Thornhill's sound with fewer instruments. The result was his nonet, which had three rhythm players (on piano, bass, and drums) and six horns. The horns were grouped in pairs of high and low ranges: trumpet/trombone, French horn/tuba, and alto saxophone/baritone saxophone. Significantly, there was no tenor saxophone, an unusual omission for a medium-sized band. Even more striking was the use of French horn and tuba, instruments more common to the European classical tradition than to jazz but part of Evans's earlier arrangements for Thornhill.

Gil Evans was not the only arranger for the group. Pianist John Lewis, trumpeter Johnny Carisi, and baritone saxophonist Gerry Mulligan all contributed charts and compositions. Aside from Duke Ellington's baritone saxophonist Harry Carney, Mulligan was possibly the most important baritone saxophonist in jazz. During the 1950s, he took the baritone out of the big band and placed it in a small-group setting, working with trumpeter Chet Baker and others. His importance as a composer-arranger is shown in "Jeru" for the *Birth of the Cool* sides.

L I S T E N I N G   G U I D E

"Jeru"
CD **2** Track **4**

Miles Davis and His Orchestra: "Jeru" (Mulligan). Capitol M-11026. New York, January 21, 1949.
Miles Davis, trumpet and leader; Kai Winding, trombone; Junior Collins, French horn; Bill Barber, tuba;
Lee Konitz, alto saxophone; Gerry Mulligan, baritone saxophone, composer-arranger;
Al Haig, piano; Joe Schulman, bass; Max Roach, drums.

Gerry Mulligan's "Jeru" is a fine example of the *Birth of the Cool* recordings. The piece features a complex formal structure that in many ways anticipates third-stream practice.

Head—AA section, 16 bars

0:00   No introduction; the head is in AABA form. The whole band plays and repeats the eight-bar A section.

Head—B section, 12 bars with changing meter

0:21   This bridge is irregular, consisting of twelve bars; meter changes disrupt the regular metrical pulse.

0:30   The baritone saxophone has the lead for the last four bars of the bridge, which return to the 4/4 meter.

Head—A section, 9 bars

0:36   The return of the A section features an extra bar that leads to the Davis trumpet solo.

Davis trumpet solo—AABA, 32 bars

0:48   Davis's 32-bar solo consists of a regular 8 + 8 + 8 + 8 grouping, dropping the irregular groupings heard previously in the head.

AA—Band alternates with Mulligan baritone solo, irregular 18 bars

1:31   When the band reenters, the arrangement features a section that is in stop time and in a 3/4 meter. The meter change produces an odd number of bars.

1:35   Mulligan solos through measures 6–9 in 4/4.

1:41   The format repeats for the second A.

BA—Last part of Mulligan solo, 16 bars

1:51   For the bridge and final A of Mulligan's solo, the form is straightforward: two eight-bar sections.

Out-chorus AABA—Irregular as 8 + 8 + 12, final A extended with coda

2:13   The two A sections from the head are dramatically recomposed for the climactic out-chorus.

2:35   The 12-bar B section is similar to its earlier presentation, with meter changes. The last part of the bridge is also recomposed to be more polyphonic.

2:50   The final A section uses the out-chorus theme but is extended with a coda. The final chord uses a dissonant voicing.

The *Birth of the Cool* recordings had an enormous influence. Their emphasis on subtlety and their balance of composition and improvisation provided an alternative model to bebop. Jazz critic Nat Hentoff described the influence of *Birth of the Cool* as follows:

> These records were comparable in their impact on a new generation of jazz musicians to the Louis Armstrong Hot Five and Hot Seven records of the 1920s, some of the Duke Ellington and Basie records of the Thirties, and the records made by Parker and his associates in the early and middle Forties.[1]

THE MODERN JAZZ QUARTET

Ironically, the group known as one of the leading exponents of cool jazz started out by playing bebop with Dizzy Gillespie. The original members of the Modern Jazz Quartet—pianist John Lewis (1920–2001), drummer Kenny Clarke (1914–1985), bassist Ray Brown (1926–2002), and vibraphonist Milt Jackson (1923–1999)—came together in Gillespie's big band in 1946. After Percy Heath replaced Ray Brown on the bass, they issued their first records as the Modern Jazz Quartet on Prestige Records. Connie Kay became the drummer after Kenny Clarke left the group.

The Modern Jazz Quartet (MJQ) became celebrated for their polished, refined performances. Like many jazz groups of the 1950s, the MJQ attempted to avoid the stigma of the disreputable jazz musician and to bring greater respectability to jazz performances. In formal tuxedos, they performed with the serious demeanor of the classical musician—and filled concert halls.

Milt Jackson and John Lewis were the fire and ice of the band. Jackson, the primary soloist, played an exuberant, swinging, blues-based vibraphone above the

The Modern Jazz Quartet in the mid-1950s. Left to right: Percy Heath, Connie Kay, John Lewis, Milt Jackson.

Courtesy Frank Driggs Collection

subtle accompaniments and countermelodies of pianist Lewis. In a style that often featured single-line counterpoint rather than the chordal punctuation typical of bebop pianists, Lewis's simplicity and restraint on the piano contrasted well with Jackson's ebullience. He consciously attempted to develop extended compositions and forms—to move away from the 32-bar frameworks that were the mainstay of jazz. As Lewis noted in an address in 1958:

> The audience for jazz can be widened if we strengthen our work with structure. If there is more of a reason for what's going on, there'll be more overall sense, and therefore, more interest for the listener. I do not think, however, that the sections in this "structured jazz"—both the improvised and written sections—should take on too much complexity. The total effect must be within the mind's ability to appreciate through the ear.[2]

One of the best examples of Lewis's interest in this "structured jazz" can be heard in his "Django," a tribute to European jazz guitarist Django Reinhardt (Chapter 2). The piece alternates a plaintive 20-bar lament in F minor with a medium-tempo bluesy section. Even more ambitious were collaborations with composer Gunther Schuller, who experimented with merging jazz and European classical music into a "third stream." The MJQ made a recording entitled *Third Stream Music* with the Beaux Arts String Quartet and performed Schuller's *Concertino for Jazz Quartet and Orchestra* with the Stuttgart Symphony.

The MJQ broke up in 1974 because Milt Jackson wanted to pursue a solo career, but it reunited in 1981 to seek concert bookings. They continued to perform together for various tours through the 1990s.

DAVE BRUBECK

One of the most commercially successful jazz musicians of the 1950s and 1960s was pianist and composer Dave Brubeck (b. 1920). Brubeck's quartet, with alto saxophonist Paul Desmond, came together in 1951 and gained visibility through concerts on college campuses. Brubeck also brought academic respectability to jazz by performing and recording at such schools as Oberlin College, Ohio University, and the University of Michigan during a time when the music was considered inappropriate for campus concerts—jazz had long been performed on campus, but usually only at parties. Brubeck's success led to his appearance on the cover of *Time* magazine in 1954. Moreover, he consistently won the *Down Beat* popularity polls throughout the fifties and sixties. However, critics sometimes vilified him for music they considered heavy-handed and unswinging.

The quartet with Paul Desmond was the group that made Brubeck famous. Originally from San Francisco, Desmond (1924–1977) played alto saxophone with a liquid, creamy sound. Consistently inventive and lyrical,

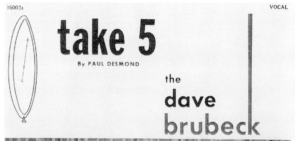

Courtesy Morgan Collection

The cover of the Dave Brubeck classic. Left to right: Paul Desmond, composer, on saxophone; Joe Morello on drums; Eugene Wright on bass; and Dave Brubeck on the piano. Based in California, far from New York's Fifty-Second Street, Brubeck was especially popular on college campuses.

Desmond rarely played a wasted note. In 1959 Desmond penned the group's most famous composition, "Take Five," a catchy, bluesy melody in 5/4, a meter rarely explored in jazz.

By the time "Take Five" was recorded on Brubeck's 1959 album, *Time Out*, Brubeck's famous quartet had taken shape: Brubeck on piano, Desmond on alto, Joe Morello on drums, and Eugene Wright on bass. The group was celebrated for its exploration of unusual meters. Aside from "Take Five," their most well-known piece was Brubeck's "Blue Rondo à la Turk," written in a 9/8 meter subdivided into unusual groupings of 2 + 2 + 2 + 3.

Although Brubeck became well known as a jazz pianist, his principal interest was composition, and he disbanded his group in 1967 to devote more time to composing. He has since written ballets, an oratorio, cantatas, and other music for jazz groups and orchestras, while occasionally performing and recording with jazz groups. In recent years he has intensified his touring schedule and recorded with his sons, keyboardist Darius Brubeck, trombonist and electric bassist Chris Brubeck, and drummer Danny Brubeck.

Used by permission of Edward B. Marks Music Company

The young Stan Getz on the cover of a jazz samba collection.

Bossa nova is a Latin jazz style developed in the late 1950s and early 1960s from Brazilian rhythms. Of all the jazz players with bossa nova hits, Stan Getz was the most prominent.

STAN GETZ

Like Desmond, many of the cool saxophonists avoided the influence of Charlie Parker. Instead, they looked back to tenor saxophonist Lester "Prez" Young for a lighter, airier sound and a more relaxed approach. As tenor saxophonist Stan Getz (1927–1991) suggested in his aptly named composition, they sought "Prezervation." Of Young's disciples on tenor saxophone, Getz won the most praise. Born in Philadelphia, he made his first recording at age sixteen with Jack Teagarden and subsequently played with Stan Kenton, Benny Goodman, and Woody Herman.

Getz was certainly capable of playing virtuosic bebop—his 1949 recording of "Crazy Chords" traveled through the blues in all twelve keys at a hair-raising tempo—but he had a distinctive tone that shone beautifully in ballads. His sound was breathy and relaxed, with evident vibrato, yet surprisingly strong and centered. Although problems with drug addiction led him to live in Scandinavia for much of the late 1950s, he returned to the United States in 1961 and embarked on several projects. His 1961 album, *Focus*, featured daring string arrangements by Eddie Sauter that overtly merged jazz with elements of classical music. Several of his recordings combined Brazilian rhythms with jazz, resulting in *bossa nova*. The most famous of these was "The Girl from Ipanema," sung by Brazilian vocalist Astrud Gilberto. This became a hit that brought Getz much commercial popularity. His landmark record, *Jazz Samba* (1962), contributed significantly to the bossa nova craze and catapulted his name into public consciousness. Rarely did another post-1950s mainstream jazz musician, with the possible exception of Cannonball Adderley, achieve Getz's commercial success.

Jazz on the West Coast

The musical aesthetic of cool jazz, a deliberate alternative to bebop, became a touchstone for many bands and performers of the 1950s. This was particularly true for players on the West Coast. Shelly Manne, a highly visible drummer at the time, acknowledged the importance of Miles Davis and described some of the important characteristics of the West Coast music scene during the 1950s:

> I think the main influence on West Coast Jazz, if one record could be an influence, was the album Miles Davis made called *Birth of the Cool*. That *kind* of writing and playing was closer to what we were trying to do, closer to the way a lot of us felt, out on the west coast. . . . It had a lot to do not only with just improvisation and swing. It was the main character of the music we liked—the chance for the composer to be challenged too. To write some new kind of material for jazz musicians where the solos and the improvisation became part of the whole and you couldn't tell where the writing ended and the improvisation began.[3]

The term *West Coast jazz* has often been used interchangeably with *cool jazz,* although they are not necessarily synonymous. Not all cool jazz players lived in California, and not all West Coast players played cool jazz. Nevertheless, several jazz players in and around Los Angeles were considered important figures. Many of them had been affiliated with the postwar bands of Woody Herman and of Stan Kenton and had settled in California. They earned their living performing in the studio music industry and at jazz clubs such as the Lighthouse and the Haig.

West Coast jazz embodied many of the principles of cool jazz as performed by a group of players centered in California.

The big band of pianist Stan Kenton was, for some, "the starting point for West Coast jazz."[4] Kenton's band earned immense popularity during the late 1940s as well as intense condemnation from critics who considered it unswinging, bombastic, and pretentious. "Let's face it," shrilled one critic, "this is the loudest band ever."[5] In trying to avoid any of the old associations of jazz with dance music, Kenton (1911–1979) championed what he called "progressive jazz," named after his 1949 twenty-piece band. Kenton envisioned concert works, and he and staff arrangers Pete Rugolo, Bill Holman, and Bill Russo wrote arrangements with such titles as "Artistry in Rhythm," "Artistry in Bolero," "Fantasy," and "Opus in Pastels."

Although Kenton's arrangements often emphasized improvisation less than written compositional structures, his band included significant soloists strongly associated with jazz on the West Coast—for example, Lee Konitz, Art Pepper, Stan Getz, Zoot Sims, and Bud Shank. Alto and baritone saxophonist Art Pepper (1925–1982) was the leading soloist of the Kenton band between 1946 and 1951. One of the "hotter" players of the cool West Coast style, he played with an intense, fiery passion. Pepper's career suffered from his drug addiction and incarceration, which he chronicled in painful detail in his autobiography *Straight Life*.

The West Coast cool players and bands that emerged during the decade emphasized written arrangements, compositional structures, restrained dynamics, and unusual instrumentation. Miles Davis's *Birth of the Cool* nonet—with a single representative of each instrument rather than big-band sections—became the model for many octets, nonets, and tentets that arose in California during the decade. As in *Birth of the Cool,* much West Coast cool jazz emphasized subdued dynamics, with the drummer providing an understated accompaniment. Shelly Manne (1920–1984), a drummer working with his own groups and in a trio with pianist André Previn (b. 1929), was known for his elegant and supportive brush work.

Another West Coast drummer with an even more subdued approach was Chico Hamilton (b. 1921), who played quietly not only when accompanying soloists but also when performing his delicate and subtle drum solos. Hamilton's group exhibited another trait of several groups on the West Coast: the use of unusual combinations of instruments. Hamilton's quintet included a guitarist, a bass player, a drummer, a cellist, and a saxophonist who doubled on flute. At the time, cello and flute were rarely encountered in jazz. In the 1960s, Hamilton changed his style and became a more driving player.

Perhaps the most unusual instrumental combinations were recorded by saxophonist Jimmy Giuffre (b. 1921), who had replaced Zoot Sims in the Woody Herman saxophone section. This saxophone section, nicknamed "The Four Brothers," comprised an unusual choir of three tenors plus baritone (rather than the more traditional combination of alto, two tenors, and baritone saxophone). Giuffre's "Four Brothers" became a hit for the Herman band. Giuffre began his career as a cool tenor saxophonist in the Lester Young tradition, but he was a restless experimenter. On his 1956 album, *The Jimmy Giuffre Clarinet,* he featured a work for solo clarinet; a work for clarinet and celesta; a work for flute, alto flute, bass flute, clarinet, and drums (with Shelly Manne playing drums with his fingers); and an arrangement of the well-known standard "My Funny Valentine" for clarinet, oboe, bassoon, English horn, and bass.

Third-Stream Music

Many of the features associated with West Coast jazz were not confined to California. The emphasis on compositional structures and counterpoint, the understated role of the rhythm section, and the inclusion of instruments more typical of European classical music than jazz (such as the French horn or cello) were part of an aesthetic that suggested a new synthesis. To composer and jazz historian Gunther Schuller, who had himself played French horn in the *Birth of the Cool* sessions, this fusion seemed part of an inevitable trend. In a 1957 lecture at Brandeis University, Schuller labeled this trend *third-stream music,* representing the merging of the two streams of jazz and classical music into a third stream.

Third-stream music blends jazz with European concert music. In many instances, third-stream composers create concert works that allow for improvisation within larger-scale structures influenced by both jazz and concert music.

Certainly, the blend of jazz and the concert tradition was not new, as can be seen in works ranging from Scott Joplin's ragtime opera *Treemonisha* to George Gershwin's *Rhapsody in Blue* and Duke Ellington's *Black, Brown, and Beige.* But Schuller's term *third stream* captured a renewed interest in the synthesis that the changing artistic consciousness of the musicians themselves had sparked during the decade.

Gunther Schuller (b. 1925) also composed third-stream works that united complex compositions and improvisation. One of his most notable was *Concertino for Jazz Quartet and Orchestra,* which was performed by the Modern Jazz Quartet. Schuller's "Transformation" explored a conflict between the classical and the jazz elements. The soloist on "Transformation" was pianist Bill Evans, who also recorded some memorable works with composer George Russell (b. 1923). Russell featured Evans on *Concerto for Billy the Kid,* inspired by the classical concerto, which normally pits the soloist against the ensemble. As early as 1949 Russell explored the combination of jazz and classical music with his "A Bird in Igor's Yard," the title wittily acknowledging both Charlie "Yardbird" Parker and Igor Stravinsky.

Third-stream music has never provided a full-blown direction for jazz artists, and some have argued that it is tangential to jazz. Nevertheless, the works of the 1950s reflect an earnest desire to investigate different and extended forms. From its genesis in ragtime and the blues, jazz had evolved rapidly, particularly in the sphere of instrumental technique, harmony, and rhythm. Yet jazz forms had remained relatively static. Much early jazz was limited to the 16-bar sections of ragtime (derived from the march) and the 12-bar blues; later, players often confined themselves to 12-bar blues and 32-bar song forms. Those composers writing third-stream music offered jazz challenging new ideas in the one realm—the formal—that had so far remained unchanged.

Piano Stylists

In Chapter 4 we explored pianist Bud Powell's astounding single-line improvisations and sparse left-hand accompaniments, which greatly influenced the bebop pianists of the day. Other pianists, however, developed alternative styles. The quintet of blind pianist George Shearing (b. 1919) was known for its distinctive sound resulting from Shearing's *locked-hands* or *block-chord style* (see Music Example 5-1). Earlier, Milt Buckner, the pianist for Lionel Hampton, had used this method of rendering melodies. In Shearing's quintet, the vibraphone doubled the upper note of the piano while the guitar doubled the pianist's lower note, providing an elegant and sophisticated sound. With its five notes contained within the octave, locked-hands style emulated big-band writing for saxophone sections.

Music Example 5.1
Locked-hands style.

Locked-hands style is a mode of performance in which the pianist plays a four-note chord in the right hand and doubles the top note with the left hand an octave below. The hands move together in a "locked" rhythmic pattern as they follow the same rhythm. This style is also called *block-chord* or *full-chord style*. (Listen to Track 9 on CD 1 for an example of locked-hands style.)

Shearing's somewhat commercial ensemble sound was immensely popular. His most famous composition was the hit "Lullaby of Birdland," written in 1952 and titled after the New York jazz club named after Charlie Parker. He was also trained as a classical pianist.

Erroll Garner (1921–1977), on the other hand, had no formal musical education, was completely self-taught, and did not read music. Originally from Pittsburgh, Garner was a mainstay on Fifty-Second Street in the mid-1940s and even recorded with Charlie Parker on the West Coast in 1947. Still, he stood apart from the mainstream bebop tradition.

Garner cultivated a highly distinctive solo piano style in which the left hand kept a quarter-note pulse, playing four chords to the bar. His insistent style often pushed or anticipated a bar's downbeat with the preceding upbeat. Against the left hand, Garner's right hand often played full chords that dragged "behind" the beat. He often led off compositions by playing extended, involved, and often witty introductions. In ballads such as his famous "Misty" (also recorded by singer Johnny Mathis), he made use of full, thick chords, creating a dense, orchestral texture. Garner's 1955 trio recording *Concert by the Sea* became one of the best-selling jazz records of the 1950s.

Erroll Garner on the cover of his 1956 composition "Dreamy." His most famous composition is the jazz-pop ballad "Misty."

Pianist Oscar Peterson's prodigious technique made him particularly suited to inherit the mantle of virtuoso Art Tatum. Encouraged and mentored by Tatum himself, Peterson concentrated on fast boplike lines and blues lines in an energetic style. He recorded with countless players throughout his career—Ben Webster, Lester Young, Dizzy Gillespie, Stan Getz, Ella Fitzgerald, and Milt Jackson among them—and his own piano trio was extremely successful during the 1950s and 1960s.

Peterson grew up in Montreal, where he was born in 1925 and where jazz concert promoter Norman Granz heard him play and brought him to the United States. After an important appearance in 1949 at Carnegie Hall, Peterson toured with Granz's Jazz at the Philharmonic series. He then formed his own trio with piano, bass, and guitar, an instrumentation popularized by Nat King Cole and Art Tatum. With bassist Ray Brown and guitarist Herb Ellis, Peterson wowed audiences and critics, playing blues and sophisticated, complex arrangements of standards such as "Love for Sale" and "Swinging on a Star." In 1959 drummer Ed Thigpen replaced guitarist Ellis and remained in the group for six years.

In his later years, Peterson's playing was sometimes more dazzling than creative, although some of his solo piano recordings, such as *Tracks*, showed Peterson at his most harmonically advanced and exploratory. One of the most popular jazz musicians of our time, Peterson has continued to perform and record, despite suffering a stroke.

Vocalists

The 1950s was an important time for vocalists as well as instrumentalists. With its intrinsic focus on melody, singing provided a respite from the hectic instrumental pyrotechnics of bebop. During the 1940s, many popular singers established themselves with solo careers as heirs to the big bands. These singers' careers flourished into the 1950s and beyond.

In general, four main characteristics identify jazz singing:

In **back phrasing**, the singer delays phrases of the song relative to their normal rhythmic placement as written. Occurring most often in ballads, it generally conveys a loose feeling, as if the singer were delivering the song spontaneously.

▶ Loose phrasing, often becoming *back phrasing*

▶ Use of blue notes and occasional blues inflections

▶ Free melodic embellishment

▶ A repertory of songs preferred by jazz musicians

Of the four main characteristics of jazz singing, the first is by far the most important. Back phrasing has influenced the performance of all American popular music, including rock. Although many jazz singers are talented at scat singing, this technique does not necessarily occur in the best jazz singing. For example, Billie Holiday—the standard against which all jazz singing is measured—was not a scat singer.

JOE WILLIAMS

One of the most important jazz singers was Joe Williams (1918–1999). Although his career had already begun, he achieved major success in the 1950s. Virtually no other singer has so successfully bridged jazz and blues.

After working with Coleman Hawkins and others, Williams attracted attention as a replacement for Jimmy Rushing in the Count Basie band of the 1950s. He left Basie in 1961 to pursue a solo career, at the same time enlarging and enriching his style. His big, rich, smooth tone established a virtual genre of its own in jazz singing. Williams's lengthy solo career led to a Grammy Award in 1984 for best jazz vocalist, and his recording career continued up to 1995 with his final album, *Feel the Spirit*.

VOCALESE: EDDIE JEFFERSON AND LAMBERT, HENDRICKS, AND ROSS

In contrast to the career of Joe Williams, Eddie Jefferson (1918–1979) just lately has been recognized as an important jazz vocalist, an original artist who established an alternative singing style strongly dissociated from the Billie Holiday–Ella Fitzgerald mainstream. Jefferson was interested not only in improvising vocally but also in composing lyrics to fit existing instrumental solos, a technique called *vocalese*. To provide a change of pace from these carefully worked-out settings, Jefferson also mixed scat singing into his performances.

Vocalese is the technique of setting lyrics to existing jazz solos. Eddie Jefferson was probably the most important pioneer of this technique, although the practice can be traced to the late 1920s.

Jefferson's performance strength lay in his tremendous vocal agility. His flexible falsetto never seemed to strain or bury the lyric. Unlike the regular four-bar phrases usually found in popular songs, the jazz solos he set usually featured complex phrasing. Despite the difficulty of setting lyrics to freely wandering instrumental lines, Jefferson often found felicitous solutions that incorporated intriguing rhyme schemes.

The jazz vocal group began in the 1950s and continues to attract artists today. Vocal ensembles were certainly not new; after all, Bing Crosby and his Rhythm Boys were an important feature of the Paul Whiteman Orchestra in the 1920s. Featured groups, such as the popular Boswell Sisters and the Andrews Sisters, who sang in harmony with band backups, continued through the swing era. But the 1950s witnessed a different kind of vocal ensemble, one allied more with the jazz tradition than with rendering popular songs in close harmony. In the latter half of the decade, a pioneering vocal group broke onto the scene. This trio—Dave Lambert, Jon Hendricks, and Annie Ross—mixed three distinct styles:

▶ Imitation of big-band textures and arrangements

▶ Vocalese

▶ Traditional scat

This extremely inventive group provided much inspiration for such contemporary singing ensembles as the Manhattan Transfer and the New York Voices.

FRANK SINATRA

No survey of vocalists in the 1950s can ignore the overwhelming importance of Frank Sinatra (1915–1998), whose active career lasted well into the 1990s. Although a popular icon, he has rightfully been included in the ranks of the jazz singers for his exceptionally free phrasing, his swinging big-band recordings, his identification with outstanding songs, and his ability to convey the meaning and emotional content of a lyric. Given these attributes, his domination of the pop-vocal market for five decades, and the respect many jazz musicians have given him, Sinatra's importance remains indisputable. We place him in this chapter because he established many of the essential attributes of his persona during the 1950s.

In some ways Sinatra belied the image of the cool 1950s. He projected a macho image—the girl-chasing, booze-loving tough guy who hobnobbed not only with the elite Kennedy family but also with gangsters. Nonetheless, much of Sinatra's work from the 1950s and 1960s captured the essence of jazz singing: loose phrasing, direct expression, and the ability to make a song his own.

Along with most of the singers discussed in this section, Sinatra had his roots in the big-band era. In the 1940s, he achieved teen idol status, bringing screaming fans to their feet much in the way that Elvis Presley would do in the 1950s and the Beatles in the 1960s.

Frank Sinatra's career spanned more than 50 years, beginning with his earliest hits in the 1940s with the Tommy Dorsey Orchestra. Notice that the publisher of "Paper Doll" hoped to capitalize on the hit recording by the Mills Brothers. Soon nothing more than a picture of Frank Sinatra on the cover could help sell a song. By the end of his life, his signature song had become "My Way," published in 1969.

Hard Bop and Funky/Soul Jazz

For some players and listeners, cool jazz was overly cerebral and devoid of energy and emotion. The airy counterpoint of Gerry Mulligan and the Chet Baker Quartet, the smoky atmosphere of Sinatra with strings, the compositional experiments of the Dave Brubeck Quartet, and the concert hall settings of the tuxedo-clad Modern Jazz Quartet all seemed to abandon the elemental fire and passionate core of the jazz tradition. The compositional sophistication of many of the West Coast players and third-stream composers too frequently seemed to be an attempt to align with the European classical tradition—a pretentious striving for the cachet of "high art."

In contrast, the hard bop players continued to extend the bebop tradition with its emphasis on improvisation, 32-bar formal structures, and straight-ahead swinging. The bands of Art Blakey and the Jazz Messengers, Horace Silver, Charles Mingus, the Clifford Brown–Max Roach Quintet, and Miles Davis were representative of the driving hard bop bands. Further, some of the compositions of these bands made use of the simpler, earthier style known as funky (or soul) jazz.

ART BLAKEY AND THE JAZZ MESSENGERS

Drummer Art Blakey, born in Pittsburgh in 1919, recorded the album *Hard Bop*, which gave its name to the 1950s resurgence of forceful, swinging jazz. Blakey became one of the leading exponents of the hard bop tradition. Never cool, Blakey's drumming was aggressive, strong, and loud. His group, the Jazz Messengers, remained active from the 1950s until Blakey's death in 1990.

Blakey began his career with Fletcher Henderson and pianist Mary Lou Williams, but in the mid-1940s he played drums for the Billy Eckstine band, from where he quickly moved to the center of the growing bebop movement. Blakey organized his first group in 1947, a rehearsal band called the Seventeen Messengers, and later that year recorded with an octet called the Jazz Messengers.

Courtesy Morgan Collection

Art Blakey (CD 2, Track 5) performing with characteristic energy in a publicity shot.

In 1955 he formed another group with pianist Horace Silver that kept the name Jazz Messengers; this was the group that helped propel Blakey to fame. The quintet—with tenor saxophonist Hank Mobley, trumpeter Kenny Dorham, and bassist Doug Watkins—recorded three albums before Silver left the group. Blakey continued to lead the Messengers. With its classic quintet instrumentation (even after the group added a trombone in the early sixties to become a sextet) and its emphasis on aggressive soloing accompanied by Blakey's powerful drumming, it was the quintessential hard bop group. The band's personnel shifted over time, and Blakey staffed the group with young players, many of whom—such as trumpeters Donald Byrd, Freddie Hubbard, Lee Morgan, and Chuck Mangione; saxophonists Johnny Griffin, Jackie McLean, and Wayne Shorter; and pianists Cedar Walton, Bobby Timmons, and Keith Jarrett—would go on to develop successful careers of their own.

Blakey gave ample room to his players as both soloists and composers. Some of them contributed jazz compositions that would become standards of the jazz repertory. In the late 1950s Blakey's pianist Bobby Timmons composed several tunes representative of funky/soul jazz. His "Moanin'" made use of call-and-response formulas and the "Amen" harmonic *church cadence* (also known as a *plagal cadence*). Tenor saxophonist Bennie Golson contributed "Whisper Not," a minor-key work that employed stop time. Golson's "I Remember Clifford" was a plaintive and posthumous tribute to trumpeter Clifford Brown, who played with Blakey in 1954.

Dizzy Gillespie called Blakey "The Fire" of jazz drumming. Blakey, who had visited Africa in the late 1940s, derived some of his techniques from African practices—using an elbow on the tom-tom to alter its pitch or playing on the side of the drum. His impact on jazz drumming was tremendous, and many of his techniques came to identify his style: the precise clicking of the hi-hat on the second and fourth beats of the measure, the tom-tom roll, and Blakey's *shuffle* pattern, sometimes even called the "Blakey Shuffle."

A *plagal cadence*, sometimes called a *church cadence* or an *Amen cadence*, contains the harmonic progression IV–I (instead of the more common progression V–I). It is often used at the ends of hymns with the concluding Amen. Plagal cadences were featured frequently in funky/soul jazz.

A *shuffle* is the 4/4 rhythmic pattern shown here. The drummer usually plays a shuffle on the ride cymbal accompanied by a walking bass:

L I S T E N I N G   G U I D E

"Moanin'" (excerpt)
CD **2** Track **5**

Art Blakey and the Jazz Messengers: "Moanin'" (Timmons), from *Moanin'*. Blue Note Reissue CDP 7 46516 2. New York, October 30, 1958. Lee Morgan, trumpet; Benny Golson, tenor saxophone; Bobby Timmons, composer, piano; Jymie Merritt, bass; Art Blakey, drums.

"Moanin'" is a fine example of gospel jazz. The melody features a written-out call-and-response that can be heard as an "Amen" or "Yes, Lord." (In Lambert, Hendricks, and Ross's arrangement, the "Yes, Lord" was sung.) With its expressive blues inflections and considerable passion, Morgan's solo is especially memorable. This excerpt fades after Golson's tenor saxophone solo.

Head—1st A section, 8 bars after 3-beat pickup

0:00   Pianist Timmons states the head with no introduction. The band answers with the two-note "Amen" (or "Yes, Lord") motive:

Head—2nd A section, 8 bars

0:15   For this second time through the A section, the trumpet and the tenor state the call. The pianist, drums, and bass take over the response.

Head—Bridge, 8 bars

0:31   The bridge goes into straight time with the trumpet and the tenor on the melody—a perfect example of a *release,* an older term for the B section. The straight time and elegant chord progression of the bridge unleashes the tension built up in the repetitive A section.

Head—Final A section, 8 bars

0:44   The pianist returns with the call while the rest of the band, led by the trumpet and the tenor, take the response.

Morgan trumpet solo—2 choruses

1:00   Morgan's solo begins with half-valve inflections and catchy funky riffs. The half-valve inflections are the almost "squeaky," "bent" sounds that are produced by depressing the trumpet's valves partway. Blakey's drumming keeps a constant back beat, emphasizing beats two and four.

1:15   In the second A section of the first chorus, Morgan incorporates "double-tonguing," a technique that allows him to repeat the same note rapidly. The double-tonguing idea returns twice.

2:55   Double-tonguing wraps up the solo.

Golson tenor solo—2 choruses

3:04   Golson picks up the end of Morgan's solo to launch his own and begins simply with variants of phrases strung together quite logically.

4:03   The beginning of his second chorus displays a move to the higher register that signals greater activity to come. The solo in fact becomes quite modernist in its second chorus: The bluesy runs and the use of the high register sometimes seem to run outside the chord changes in ways that sound like the work of John Coltrane.

HORACE SILVER

Pianist Horace Silver left the Jazz Messengers in 1956 to lead his own quintet. Silver, who was one of the most imaginative of the major funky jazz players of the 1950s, became one of its most important and prolific composers as well. Although Silver was born in Norwalk, Connecticut, in 1928, his family was from the former Portuguese colony of Cape Verde, off the coast of northern Africa. As a child, he was exposed to Cape Verdean folk music by his father, who encouraged Silver to adopt the idiom to jazz. Although bebop pianist Bud Powell influenced him early on, Silver's piano playing by comparison became less technical, more economical, more tuneful, and bluesier. In reacting against the bop players, Silver learned to play with fewer notes, emphasizing instead a few funky figures and favoring tremolos and crushed notes separated by generous space.

Many of Silver's compositions were infectious and catchy, such as his "Song for My Father," a Latin-tinged work dominated by a simple tonic-and-fifth bass motive. Silver wrote numerous blues compositions: His "Opus de Funk" and "Señor Blues," for example, were recorded by dozens of other artists. In summary, Silver helped solidify the hard bop and funky tradition, codifying its instrumentation and providing some of its most memorable compositions.

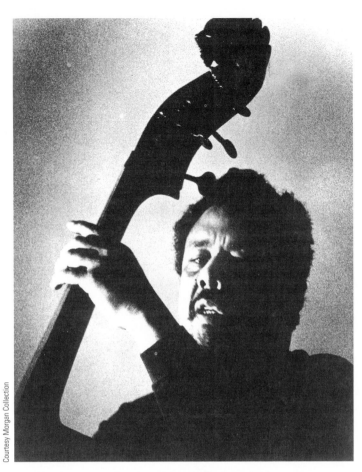

Courtesy Morgan Collection

Bassist Charles Mingus (CD 2, Track 6) in a publicity still from the 1960s.

CHARLES MINGUS

Bassist and composer Charles Mingus attained legendary status for both his uncompromising view of the jazz tradition and his innovative approach to the art form. As a bassist, he developed a flawless technique, extending the accomplishments of Duke Ellington's bassist, Jimmy Blanton. As a composer, Mingus became increasingly visible and important throughout the 1950s and 1960s. He wrote works that encompassed numerous influences, especially the music of Ellington and the soulful expressiveness of the black church.

The scope of Mingus's music was enormous, embracing the whole of jazz—from historical references to the New Orleans tradition to a forward-looking use of collective improvisation that provided an important precedent for free jazz. Much of Mingus's work paid homage to gospel music and the blues, but it also included inventive instrumentation, tempo changes, and stop time. Although he began composing and arranging conventionally—writing a careful score with worked-out parts—his later techniques of dictating from the keyboard recalled the head-arrangement procedures of early jazz and its spirit of collective improvisation.

Originally from Arizona, where he was born in 1922, Mingus was raised in the Watts section of Los Angeles, where he paid his dues as a bass player and sideman with both swing and bop groups, working with Louis Armstrong, clarinetist Barney Bigard, and vibraphonist Lionel Hampton.

Mingus founded his own workshop in 1955, putting together a group to feature his compositions. The group numbered from four to eleven players. Dissatisfied with printed musical notation, Mingus dictated from the piano the parts and lines he wanted his sidemen to play. Considering his "workshop" to be just that, he sometimes shouted instructions to his players on the bandstand or interrupted compositions in midstream to correct one of his musicians or castigate the audience. He made reference to New Orleans pianist Jelly Roll Morton in "Jelly Roll Soul" and to gospel music in "Wednesday Night Prayer Meeting" and "Better Git It in Your Soul"; he paid tribute to Charlie Parker in "Bird Calls" and to Lester Young in "Goodbye Pork Pie Hat." "Fables of Faubus"—a denunciation of Arkansas Governor Orville Faubus, who attempted to ignore desegregation—was formally inventive. Mingus's most ambitious composition was "The Black Saint and the Sinner Lady," a complex four-movement work recorded in 1963.

L I S T E N I N G   G U I D E

"Hora Decubitus"
CD **2**   Track **6**

Charles Mingus and His Orchestra: "Hora Decubitus" (Mingus), from *Mingus, Mingus, Mingus, Mingus,
Mingus*. Impulse AS-9234-2. New York, September 20, 1963. Charles Mingus: bass, director;
Eddie Preston, Richard Williams, trumpets; Britt Woodman, trombone; Don Butterfield, tuba; Eric Dolphy,
Dick Haffer, Booker Ervin, Jerome Richardson, woodwinds; Jaki Byard, piano; Walter Perkins, drums.

"Hora Decubitus" is a hybrid work, adroitly straddling traditional and free jazz. Throughout the
performance, Mingus maintains control of the ensemble through forceful, interesting bass lines.

   The following analysis shows that the fundamental idea of the piece is a mixture of various lines
in counterpoint. These are introduced gradually, slowly building a complex group sound. (This group
sound anticipates some of the stylistic attributes of free jazz described more fully in Chapter 6.)

Introduction—Mingus solo bass, 12 bars

0:00   Alternating octaves here reveal Mingus's strength and sense of forward momentum. Mingus sets
the tempo, harmony, and mood for the blues choruses that follow.

Head—Chorus 1

0:12   A rifflike blues tune played on the baritone saxophone. Although the rhythmic and melodic
character of the tune is traditional, it borders on **atonality**.

Head—Chorus 2

0:24   The baritone continues to play the theme, joined now by the other saxophones, sometimes
playing in unison but occasionally splitting into different parts.

Head—Chorus 3

0:37   A trombone is added, playing a counter-riff that often seems to clash with the saxophones,
who meanwhile repeat their second chorus.

Head—Chorus 4

0:50   An alto saxophone separates from the reed section to add still another part, while the trombone
and remaining saxophones repeat what they had played in the preceding chorus.

Head—Chorus 5 (final chorus of head)

1:02   A trumpet player joins the others with still another riff in counterpoint with the ongoing parts.
This set of contrasting and competing lines remains traditional in its blues-riff orientation as well
as in the marvelous cacophony of everyone playing together.

Ervin tenor saxophone solo—4 choruses

1:15   At first reminiscent of gospel jazz, Ervin's solo finishes with the fleet, atonal runs that are
somewhat more typical of free jazz. As accompaniment, the orchestra enters from time to
time with background figures derived from the opening riffs of the head.

1:51   On Ervin's last chorus, Mingus pushes the beat so forcefully that he seems almost ahead
of the pulse.

Dolphy alto saxophone solo—4 choruses

2:03   After beginning with the more "outside" melodic lines of free jazz, Dolphy returns to a more
typical blues line, though many of his pitches still purposely avoid the chord changes.

2:40   Mingus briefly quotes his opening introductory statement in the middle of Dolphy's solo as if
trying to forge together the disparate sections of the work. The other instruments freely enter
with riffs and sharp punctuations as if to comment on Dolphy's solo.

Williams trumpet solo—4 choruses

2:56   A few bebop licks can still be heard from time to time. The passionate cries Williams injects into the solo are both expressive and appropriate.

Return of the head—3 choruses

3:40   Some of the opening riffs are heard but are exchanged here, that is, played by different groups of instruments. The alto saxophones "lay out" (don't play) during the second chorus. During the third chorus, the ensemble plays the main riff tune in unison, which lends a feeling of finality to the performance.

Tag

4:16   Here are two chords that may be heard as echoing the "Amen" cadence heard in church music. On the first of these chords, the instruments freely interpolate runs and fills in the manner of a cadenza. The second chord is not so heavily scored, and as it dies out Mingus plays the last few notes himself, thus recalling his solo introduction.

Mingus wrote about his career in a highly creative and sometimes fanciful autobiography, *Beneath the Underdog* (1971). After his death in 1979, his family found portions of a score for a two-hour work entitled "Epitaph." Gunther Schuller completed the partial score and recorded it in 1989.

Charles Mingus was one of the very few bassists in jazz to contribute directly to the formation of a jazz substyle and a new way of thinking about music. Today the Mingus Dynasty is a renowned jazz ensemble. Under the direction of his widow, Sue, the group continues to explore the dimensions of Mingus's original and challenging music.

CLIFFORD BROWN–MAX ROACH QUINTET

Many of the trumpeters of the 1950s followed Miles Davis and Chet Baker by cultivating a lyrical, restrained style in the medium range of the instrument. Others, though, kept alive the bebop tradition of Dizzy Gillespie and Fats Navarro. Clifford Brown was perhaps the finest trumpet player of the 1950s, perpetuating the running

Max Roach and Modern Drumming

Max Roach (b. 1924) was one of the leading innovative drummers of the bebop generation, performing and recording with Gillespie and Charlie Parker in the 1940s. He became a member of Parker's longest-lived quintet and was also heard on Miles Davis's *Birth of the Cool*. With other bebop drummers such as Kenny Clarke, Roach was instrumental in transferring the pulse from the bass drum and hi-hat to the ride cymbal. He developed a conversational style of accompanying improvisers, creating a dialogue with the soloists and accenting with the bass and snare drums. Roach's technique provided a foundation for modern jazz drumming. By giving separate roles to each hand and foot, Roach's style helped establish what came to be called "coordinated independence."

Trumpeter Clifford Brown
(CD 2, Track 7).

Photo by John Krantz. Courtesy Morgan Collection.

eighth-note style of Gillespie but with a personal, intimate sound that was arguably warmer than the older player's style. Brown's playing emphasized clean technique, a vast variety of articulations, and a satisfying, logical progression in his solos that usually avoided the gratuitous, showy high notes of Gillespie. Brown had a slightly percussive attack and negotiated impossibly fast tempos with ease.

Brown won the *Down Beat* "New Star" award in 1954. However, his career ended two years later—one of the great tragedies in jazz. As a result, Brown's recorded output is relatively small, although it establishes him as one of the greatest of all trumpet players. Originally from Wilmington, Delaware, where he was born in 1930, he worked mostly around Philadelphia and New York. In 1953 he toured Europe with Lionel Hampton's band, making several records there.

Brown's most important legacy was his participation in the Clifford Brown–Max Roach Quintet with drummer Max Roach. (See the box "Max Roach and Modern Drumming" at left.) Roach and Brown formed their cooperative quintet in 1954. The band, along with Brown on trumpet and Roach on drums, included bassist George Morrow, pianist Richie Powell (the brother of bebop pianist Bud Powell), and saxophonist Harold Land. (Sonny Rollins replaced Land in 1955.) The group was one of the most brilliant in jazz, lasting until Brown's death in 1956 in an automobile accident that also killed pianist Richie Powell.

A publicity photograph of Dizzy Gillespie (CD 2, Tracks 1 and 2) and Max Roach (CD 2, Tracks 4 and 7) in the 1960s.

Photo by Carol Friedman. Courtesy Morgan Collection.

L I S T E N I N G   G U I D E

"Powell's Prances"

CD **2**   Track **7**

Clifford Brown–Max Roach Quintet: "Powell's Prances" (Powell). EmArcy 36070. New York, January 4, 1956.
Clifford Brown, trumpet; Sonny Rollins, tenor saxophone; Richie Powell, piano, composer-arranger;
George Morrow, bass; Max Roach, drums.

"Powell's Prances" is a fine example of the Brown–Roach quintet. This up-tempo, swinging number with an unusual structure typifies the sound of the band. The bluesy piece is a minor mode composition in the tradition of earlier bop works such as Bud Powell's "Tempus Fugit."

Head—24 bars as ABA

0:00   After a short drum-fill introduction, the head begins with an up-tempo, driving sound. The trumpet and the tenor play the melody in octaves. The unusual form of the head is ABA, with each section having eight bars. The middle eight bars are in stop time.

Brown trumpet solo—2 choruses

0:22   The variety of Brown's articulations is evident in the solo. The clarity of each note derives from Brown's ability to tongue at a rapid tempo. Brown begins his second chorus by emphasizing and repeating a single note.

Rollins tenor saxophone solo—2 choruses

1:00   Rollins contrasts his solo with Brown's by including passages of longer note values. Listen to how he develops a motivic idea in the second chorus, bridging the end of the first A section and the beginning of the B section. His solo closes with a blues-based idea.

Powell piano solo—2 choruses

1:38   Powell's solo concentrates on developing simple blues-like riffs in the piano's midrange. It moves out of the range only briefly for a short contrast.

Roach drum solo—2 choruses

2:15   Roach begins his solo by echoing and developing the rhythm played by Powell at the end of his solo. Roach maintains the energy and drive of the preceding solos. Notice that he avoids playing the cymbals during his solo, concentrating instead on the snare drum, bass drum, and tom-toms.

Reprise of the 24-bar head as ABC

2:48   After the solos, the head returns but is not literally restated. A new section (C) replaces the final A section, with the piano and horns playing a unison passage that almost sounds like an exercise.

Coda

3:08   The C section of the head has introduced a coda consisting of a dramatic series of out-of-time chords prolonged over drum fills. These unusually dissonant chords provide a dramatic conclusion to the piece.

SONNY ROLLINS

A star with the Brown–Roach quintet, Sonny Rollins was one of the leading tenor saxophonists of the 1950s. Rollins's playing boasted rhythmic imagination, harmonic ingenuity, and a strong, muscular sound. He achieved his big, dramatic tone by infusing the traditional, full-throated eloquence of Coleman Hawkins with the edgy raspiness sometimes heard in Charlie Parker.

Rollins was born in 1930 in New York and raised in the same neighborhood that produced Coleman Hawkins, Bud Powell, and Thelonious Monk. Rollins was a teenager while bebop was taking hold as the dominant jazz style.

During the 1950s, Rollins recorded and performed with many significant players and groups. He formed an association with Miles Davis that continued throughout the decade and brought Rollins to the forefront not only as an exceptional improviser but also as a composer. To a Davis recording session for Prestige in 1954, Rollins contributed three compositions that were to become jazz standards: "Oleo," based on rhythm changes; "Doxy"; and "Airegin," a minor-key romp whose title was a thinly disguised tribute to Nigeria. Rollins's sense of humor resonated throughout his playing and his occasionally idiosyncratic choice of repertory, such as his 1957 album *Way out West,* which boasted "I'm an Old Cowhand" and "Wagon Wheels" in a pianoless trio of saxophone, bass, and drums.

Rollins was passionately committed to his musical growth. Highly self-critical, he took three extended sabbaticals during which he stopped performing in public. The first of these, which began in November 1954, ended a year later when he joined the Clifford Brown–Max Roach Quintet, where he remained until 1957. During his tenure with the quintet, Rollins earned prestige for his technical proficiency and the fertility of his musical ideas.

Rollins's style includes the following characteristics:

▶ A wide variety of melodies, from bop lines to floating phrases slightly reminiscent of cool jazz

▶ Melodic connections based on voice leading and motivic development, some of which are quite subtle

▶ Varied melodic rhythms

▶ Highly irregular phrase lengths, from single notes to long bop phrases

▶ Rich tone with occasional raspiness

▶ Use of space between phrases

▶ Use of the entire range of the instrument

▶ Full range of emotional expression

▶ Mostly "inside" playing, with chord-scale relationships based on the bop practice of using extended chords and altered scales

During the latter half of the 1950s, Rollins continued to record as a leader. His tune "Valse Hot" was one of the first bebop compositions in 3/4 meter. In 1956 Rollins recorded *Saxophone Colossus*—a quartet recording hailed by critics as a milestone. It included the sunny calypso tune "St. Thomas," the first of several compositions in that vein by Rollins.

The ever self-critical Rollins took another sabbatical between 1959 and 1961. During his self-imposed retirement, his late-night practice sessions on the Williamsburg Bridge over New York's East River became legendary. When he returned to performing, he made reference to his nocturnal habit in an album titled *The Bridge,* which included guitarist Jim Hall.

In the early 1960s, Rollins continued to expand musically with projects that encompassed both old and new. For the latter, Rollins attempted to come to grips with the free jazz movement of Ornette Coleman. Yet he also recorded with his idol Coleman Hawkins on an album entitled *Sonny Meets Hawk.* Picking up on a practice Hawkins had embraced in the 1940s, Rollins experimented with performing unaccompanied saxophone solos.

Several years after Rollins provided the sound track to the 1965 Michael Caine movie *Alfie,* Rollins took yet another sabbatical; upon his return he concentrated on playing in a slightly more commercial vein. Influenced by jazz trends in the late 1960s and early 1970s, he brought the electric piano into his groups and began emphasizing rock and funk rhythms and often doubled on soprano saxophone. Currently, Rollins remains one of the most honored players in jazz, appearing in prestigious venues throughout the world, both as a guest and with his own groups.

Miles Davis in the 1950s

Earlier in this chapter, we explored Miles Davis's seminal contributions to cool jazz. But there was much more to his career; in fact, Miles Davis became one of the most profoundly influential figures in the history of jazz. Lasting more than four decades, his career was marked by an uncanny ability to explore and develop new styles. Davis was consistently on the cutting edge of musical developments:

- ▶ Bebop in the late 1940s
- ▶ Cool jazz in the early 1950s
- ▶ Hard bop in the mid-1950s
- ▶ Modal jazz the later 1950s and 1960s
- ▶ Jazz-rock fusion in the 1970s
- ▶ MIDI sequencing and sampling in the 1980s

Never content with relying on earlier successful formulas, Davis hired the best young players, who continued to challenge him. As one of his former sidemen noted, Davis was a "star-maker": Many of the most important jazz performers in the later twentieth century at one time had played in his band.

Though nurtured on bebop, Davis did not follow Dizzy Gillespie in developing fireworks in the trumpet's higher register. His playing was usually lyrical and spare, though still impassioned despite often being centered in the middle range of the instrument. He cited trumpeter Freddie Webster as an early influence; Webster played in an unfussy style without much vibrato.

Davis was born in Hilton, Illinois (near St. Louis), on May 25, 1926, and began playing professionally as a teenager. A pivotal event occurred when he was eighteen. The Billy Eckstine band, with Charlie Parker, Dizzy Gillespie, and Sarah Vaughan, came to town, and Davis was asked to sit in. In his autobiography, Davis wrote,

"[Hearing the band] changed my life. I decided right then and there that I had to leave St. Louis and live in New York City where all these bad musicians were."[6] For the remainder of his life, Davis claimed that he was always attempting to recapture the awesome musical experience of that St. Louis performance.

Davis arrived in New York in fall 1944, ostensibly to study at the Juilliard School of Music, but he was more interested in pursuing bebop opportunities with Charlie Parker. The following year, at age nineteen, Davis achieved his first remarkable success: He recorded for Savoy as part of Parker's first session as a leader. That session, on November 26, 1945, was in fact Davis's second recording session; though brilliant for Parker, this recording was not entirely successful for the young trumpeter. Davis's playing on "Billie's Bounce" and "Now's the Time" revealed him to be almost out of his depth with the group. Because Davis was unable to perform the virtuosic "KoKo" with Parker, Dizzy Gillespie played the cut.

Davis continued to improve and develop his own voice. Critics began to speak of Davis as representing a new generation of trumpeters with a warmer, softer, mellower sound than Gillespie's. He performed with Parker through 1949, becoming a member of his working quintet. He contributed compositions such as "Donna Lee" (though the tune is attributed to Parker) and hired Parker to play tenor saxophone for his own Savoy session as leader.

Despite Davis's long association with Parker, the alto saxophonist was unpredictable and often difficult to work with. On December 23, 1948, Davis's irritation with what he considered Parker's lack of professionalism came to a head. Davis stormed off the bandstand of the Royal Roost, claiming, "Bird makes you feel about one foot high."[7] No longer part of the Davis quintet, Parker struck out on his own.

While working on the *Birth of the Cool* sessions, Davis traveled to Paris to perform at the Festival de Jazz in 1949, which earned him increased visibility and critical attention. When he returned to the States, Davis, like many other jazz players of his generation, succumbed to heroin addiction. Although he won the *Metronome* Critics Poll each year between 1951 and 1953, some of Davis's performances for Prestige Records suffered from technical problems that can probably be traced to his addiction. Some writers even began to consider his best work behind him.

Fortunately, Davis overcame his addiction in 1954 and in the same year recorded several brilliant performances. Hailed for his early involvement in cool jazz on the *Birth of the Cool* sessions, Davis now returned to his bebop roots, providing some of the finest hard bop music of the decade. Davis discussed the difference:

> *Birth of the Cool* had . . . mainly come out of what Duke Ellington and Billy Strayhorn had already done; it just made the music "whiter," so that white people could digest it better. And then the other records I made, like "Walkin'" and "Blue 'n' Boogie"—which the critics called hard bop—had only gone back to the blues and some of the things that Bird and Dizzy had done. It was great music, well played and everything, but the musical ideas and concepts had mostly been already done; it just had a little more space in it.[8]

Davis continued to record other jazz classics in 1954. On Christmas Eve, Davis assembled pianist Thelonious Monk and vibraphonist Milt Jackson and recorded six sides, including two takes each of Jackson's "Bags' Groove" and Gershwin's "The Man I Love." The session was notorious: Monk was reputedly furious over Davis's request that Monk not play behind Davis's solos. Davis's playing showed a mastery of timing and a depth in his economical style.

A *harmon mute* is a hollow metal mute that, when placed in the bell of the trumpet, gives the sound a distant, brooding quality. Miles Davis's adoption of the harmon mute from 1954 onward helped popularize its use.

The 1954 recordings helped revive Davis's career, as did his performance on Thelonious Monk's "'Round Midnight" at the Newport Jazz Festival the following year. In this piece he enraptured the audience with a wistful solo in which he used a *harmon mute* (listen to Track 14 on CD 1). Davis was becoming a hot commodity. Signing with Columbia Records, he put together a quintet that featured some rising stars: tenor saxophonist John Coltrane, pianist Red Garland, bassist Paul Chambers, and drummer Philly Joe Jones. The group combined poignant ballads, often performed with Davis on muted trumpet, along with fiercely intense swing. Ever interested in the use of space and openness in his music, Davis asked pianist Garland to listen and learn from Chicago pianist Ahmad Jamal, whose strategic use of silence Davis admired.

In addition to his rise in popularity, Davis found notoriety. Critics and audiences noted his prickly personality, his unwillingness to announce compositions, and his disappearance from the bandstand when other soloists were playing. Yet this almost surly behavior helped Davis become a cult figure, noted for his mystique. He was also laconic and temperamental. In a flash of anger in 1956, he raised his voice too soon after a throat operation, thereby permanently reducing his voice to a whisper.

In 1958 alto saxophonist Julian "Cannonball" Adderley joined the band, making it a sextet. The two saxophonists, Coltrane and Adderley, had markedly different styles: Coltrane's playing was rigorous, technical, and exploratory; Adderley's

What Is Modal Jazz?

Modal jazz loosely describes a body of music that originated in the late 1950s and 1960s. Miles Davis's recordings on *Kind of Blue,* Davis's earlier 1958 composition "Milestones," and the music of John Coltrane's classic quartet (1960–1964) are important points of departure for modal jazz.

Modal jazz gets its name from the idea that modes (particular scales) provide improvisers with the appropriate pitches to use in their solos over individual chords. In the liner notes to *Kind of Blue,* pianist Bill Evans indicates that each chord is associated with a particular scale. These scales are the modes, including the Ionian, Dorian, Phrygian, Lydian, Mixolydian, Aeolian, and Locrian.

The term *modal jazz* often leads to confusion, however, because many of the qualities attributed to modal jazz do not necessarily have to do with the use of modes. In fact, as critics of the term point out, improvisers do not always restrict themselves to the pitches of the mode in their solos.* In addition, the term often refers to a composition or accompaniment that makes use of one or more of the following techniques:

▶ Slow-moving harmonic rhythm, in which a single chord may last for four, eight, sixteen, or more measures

▶ Use of *pedal points* (focal bass pitches over which the harmonies may shift)

▶ Absence or suppression of standard functional harmonic patterns

▶ Chords or melodies that make use of the interval of a perfect fourth

As this list suggests, many of the features associated with modal jazz concern composition and accompaniment rather than improvisation. Accounts of modal jazz, however, often do not distinguish among these three related yet distinct ideas. After Miles Davis and John Coltrane, such performers as Herbie Hancock, Wayne Shorter, and McCoy Tyner were considered important exponents of modal jazz.

---

* See Barry Kernfeld, "Adderley, Coltrane, and Davis at the Twilight of Bebop: The Search for Melodic Coherence" (Ph.D. diss., Cornell University, 1981).

was traditional, rooted in bebop and the blues. The sextet's recording *Milestones* began to show a new musical direction for Davis, particularly on the title tune. Coltrane commented:

> I found Miles in the midst of another stage of his musical development. There was one time in his past that he devoted to multichorded structures. He was interested in chords for their own sake. But now it seemed that he was moving in the opposite direction to the use of fewer and fewer chord changes in songs.[9]

Coltrane was referring to a move to modal jazz. Instead of the complex chord progressions of bebop and hard bop, Davis's compositions incorporated fewer chords. Significantly, the improvisations over these chords were often based on a single scale. (See the box "What Is Modal Jazz?" on the facing page.) The decisive shift toward modal jazz was evident in Davis's 1959 recording *Kind of Blue,* an album universally acclaimed as one of the most significant in the history of jazz. All the elements of Davis's mature style—his deep lyricism, economy, and searching—crystallized on this record. The introspective nature of much of the record was inspired by Davis's pianist, Bill Evans—a lyrical player who brought an impressionistic transparency to the music.

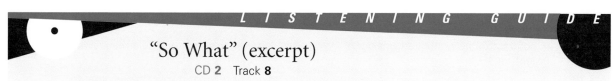

L I S T E N I N G   G U I D E

"So What" (excerpt)
CD **2**   Track **8**

Miles Davis Sextet: "So What" (Davis). New York, March 2, 1959. Columbia CS 1355.
Miles Davis, trumpet, leader; John Coltrane, tenor saxophone; Julian "Cannonball" Adderley, alto saxophone;
Bill Evans, piano; Paul Chambers, bass; Jimmy Cobb, drums.

Arguably, Miles Davis reached the apex of his improvisational ability in the 1950s and 1960s with a stream of brilliant albums and solos. Among his many fine small groups, a classic sextet was established in the 1950s with John Coltrane, alto saxophone player Julian "Cannonball" Adderley, and pianist Bill Evans. *Kind of Blue,* which contains the classic recording of "So What," is one of this sextet's finest albums and remains one of the best-selling jazz albums of all time. Miles Davis's trumpet solo on "So What" is masterly, combining elements of cool jazz with the emerging modal style.

   Although "So What" is a normal 32-bar AABA composition, each of the eight-bar A sections is based on a single chord and scale (or *mode*), while the eight-bar B section transposes the original chord and scale up a half-step. The slow-moving harmony (one chord per eight measures) and the use of a single scale over that chord are important characteristics of modal jazz. The excerpt here contains the Miles Davis trumpet solo and the John Coltrane tenor saxophone solo.

Introduction

0:00   "So What" begins out of tempo with the bass and the piano laying down a moody introduction. The left hand of the piano doubles the melodic line played by the bassist.

Head—AABA

0:32   For the first A section, the bass plays the melody and the piano answers with the two-chord ("So What") figure. The two instruments establish a call-and-response idea, with the drums playing softly on the cymbals.

0:47   At the return of the A section, the alto and tenor saxophones and the trumpet join the piano on the two-chord answering figure, while the drummer continues keeping time on the cymbal.

1:02   The B section repeats the A section, but now played a half-step higher. Again the bass plays the melody for the call while the piano and horns provide the response.

1:16   Return of A section.

Davis solo—2 choruses (AABA)

1:31   A cymbal crash announces the change to a walking bass and the two-chorus trumpet solo. Davis's solo begins with his characteristically lyrical and wistful sound that relies on the use of space between phrases.

1:46   At the second A section, Evans's comping creates a dialogue with the trumpet solo.

2:00   During the B section, Evans's comping relies on dense chords beneath the trumpet solo.

2:14   Again, Davis uses a significant amount of space between his melodic ideas in this final A section of his first chorus.

2:28   Chorus 2. During this first A section of Davis's second chorus, bassist Paul Chambers continues to keep time, but plays only a few different notes. This gives a static quality to the pulse of this section that contrasts with the following A section.

2:43   Chambers now returns to a walking bass beneath the solo, effectively setting up a feeling of release during this second A section. Davis uses "bent" notes in this section, an effect achieved by pushing the trumpet valves only halfway down.

2:56   B section.

3:10   Davis concludes his solo with some lyrical ideas focused in the midrange of the horn.

Coltrane solo—2 choruses (AABA)

3:25   In contrast to the restrained lyricism of Davis's solo, the tenor saxophone solo maintains an urgent tone.

3:39   In this second A section, Coltrane starts to rely on faster notes that display his celebrated technical ability on the instrument. Here Evans's comping is unusual: He plays quick, short notes in the right hand while playing longer-held chords in the left hand.

3:52   In the B section, Coltrane uses faster notes and the upper register of the instrument more frequently.

4:06   In the final A section of this second chorus, Coltrane repeats and develops a single melodic idea.

4:20   Chorus 2. Coltrane continues to develop single melodic ideas in each section. As in Davis's solo, bassist Paul Chambers uses only a few different notes, setting up a feeling of stasis that will be released in the following section.

4:34   Chambers returns to a walking bass in this second A section.

5:01   Listen for Coltrane's combination of faster notes combined with the use of longer-held tones at the ends of phrases in this final A section of his solo.

Evans wrote the liner notes to the album: "Miles conceived these settings only hours before the recording dates and arrived with sketches that indicated to the group what was to be played."[10] Many of the tunes on *Kind of Blue,* such as "So What," "Flamenco Sketches," "Blue in Green," and "All Blues," have become jazz standards.

Although Davis has undergone various style changes throughout his career, the following list summarizes his cool/early modern playing:

▶ Sensitive melodic lines with frequent blues inflections

▶ Irregular phrase length

▶ Wide range of note values

▶ Use of space between phrases

▶ Concentration on the midrange of the trumpet

▶ Full but reticent tone (especially obvious in his playing with the harmon mute)

▶ Melodic connections based on motives and large-scale gestures

▶ Sensitive yet cool expression

▶ Little reliance on previously composed licks

▶ "Inside" playing, using conservative chord-scale associations

During the late 1950s, Davis also revived his collaboration with arranger Gil Evans, with whom he had worked in the *Birth of the Cool* sessions a decade before. The pair turned out three recordings, noted for their lush instrumentation beneath Davis's searing sound. Davis also began to use a flugelhorn, which is like a trumpet but with a larger bore and a much mellower timbre (see the photo on page 8). The first of these collaborations, the album *Miles Ahead,* featured Davis as soloist with a nineteen-piece orchestra. More remarkable was their 1958 recording of *Porgy and Bess,* in which Davis put his definitive stamp on Gershwin's compositions, such as "Summertime." The concerto ideal—soloist with accompanying orchestra—reached its culmination in *Sketches of Spain,* which actually featured an arrangement of a guitar concerto, the *Concierto de Aranjuez* by Joaquin Rodrigo.

By the end of the 1950s, Davis had established himself as one of the leading figures in jazz, exploring new directions for improvised ensemble music. We shall return to his seminal band in our discussion of the music of the 1960s in the following chapter.

Cool and Hard Bop Melodic Styles

QUALITY	COOL	HARD BOP
Timbre	▶ Softer, smoother, more relaxed ▶ Midrange of instruments emphasized ▶ Almost no use of blue-note effects ▶ Soft attacks and legato	▶ Beboplike, hard-edged, brittle, insistent ▶ Use of upper registers ▶ Blue-note effects, blues riffs ▶ Wide variety of attacks and articulations
Phrasing	▶ Irregular, like bebop ▶ Much use of space between phrases	▶ Slightly more regular than bebop phrasing ▶ Return to two- and four-bar units in funky/soul jazz
Rhythm	▶ Much greater variety than bop in up-tempo and medium-tempo pieces	▶ More syncopated ▶ Trend toward simpler blues patterns ▶ More variety than bebop
Thematic continuity	▶ Balanced between motivic and voice leading	▶ Motives sometimes emphasized over voice leading
Chord-scale relations	▶ Inside, often with extended chord tones heard in bop	▶ Inside, often based on blues scale
Large-scale coherence	▶ Motivic structure and voice leading ▶ Balance of gesture	▶ Motivic, especially in funky/soul jazz, use of climax-release, and gestural balance

Key Terms

Questions and Topics for Discussion

1. What new jazz substyles developed in the 1950s? Which performers were associated with which substyle?

2. How was cool jazz distinguished from bebop? Was the separation always distinct?

3. Why is cool jazz sometimes called West Coast jazz?

4. What aspects of the jazz tradition were modified or experimented on by third-stream musicians? Who were some of the important third-stream musicians?

5. Who were the principal hard bop musicians? How did their music differ from cool jazz and third-stream music?

6. How did Miles Davis transcend some of the standard 1950s substyle boundaries?

THE SIXTIES

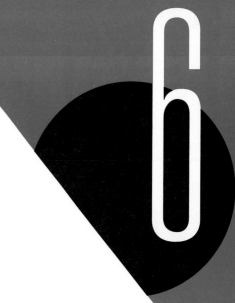

6

WE CAN THINK OF THE 1960s as differentiated by the activities of the vanguard musicians, known as the "avant-garde," and the more mainstream musicians, although as usual there is much overlap. We begin with an investigation of the avant-garde, then pick up the story of Miles Davis, which ended Chapter 5, as exemplary of the more mainstream 1960s players.

The 1960s Avant-Garde

The stylistic innovations in jazz during the 1950s led directly to the formation of a controversial avant-garde in the 1960s. Heated debates arose, recalling the vitriolic exchanges between the beboppers and the moldy figs during the 1940s. The principal issue in the 1960s (as in the 1940s) was disagreement between innovators and populists: Innovators felt that the music must progress, while populists thought that the music should attract and please a mass audience. Even today these controversies remain far from settled. In many respects these issues mirror the general tension in the West between popular and fine art. What ultimately validates an art form? Acceptance by a large audience (the popular) or the originality resulting from cutting-edge experimentation (the avant-garde)?

Given that this issue had been around a while, what made the 1960s *free jazz* of the *avant-garde* (also called the *New Thing*) so controversial? The principal reason was that the avant-gardists radically rejected aspects of the jazz tradition that many

Free jazz, the *avant-garde*, and the *New Thing* are terms used to describe the 1960s jazz substyle that overturned many of the traditional elements of jazz.

189

players and listeners considered fundamental. Improvisation still remained, but other elements were drastically altered—changes that made the music seem incoherent to some. These changes included the following:

▶ *Absence of a steady pulse or meter.* The 4/4 swing feel, often considered essential to the jazz tradition, was frequently abandoned.

▶ *Absence of a predetermined harmonic structure.* For the avant-garde soloists, improvisations did not have to be bound by an underlying harmonic progression. Many groups did away with the instruments that normally provided harmonic support, such as the piano or guitar.

▶ *Altered role for rhythm-section instruments.* Avant-garde bassists and drummers no longer performed their typical timekeeping roles but instead often participated in collective improvisation.

▶ *Freer formal structures.* Before the 1960s, musical structures were based on smaller groupings of four, eight, and sixteen measures, helping listeners orient themselves within the form. The avant-garde players eschewed this regularity in composing and improvising.

▶ *Use of atypical or extended sounds.* The avant-garde soloists cultivated new timbres and sounds. Percussion became more prominent; saxophonists and trumpeters explored the highest registers and incorporated shrieks and wailing.

Voices of Discontent

In part as a result of blacks' frustrations in their attempt to gain equality with whites, much social and racial turbulence erupted in the 1960s. Black separatism became an important force in the African-American community, as many intellectuals sought to distance themselves from what they considered to be the unyielding white power structure. These efforts were often accompanied by conscious attempts to incorporate Afrocentrism into art and everyday life: African names and clothing as well as Afro hairstyles became more common.

Despite the Supreme Court rulings of the 1950s and the 1964 Civil Rights Act, the 1960s did not see the expected improvement in the relationship between the races. In fact, the separation of whites and blacks increased through the growth of the black ghettos in U.S. inner cities during this time. The ghettos were created largely by "white flight" to the suburbs, which left blacks in decaying city centers without jobs or opportunity. Long frustrated at the ingrained racism of white society, black people grew angry at the crime, housing conditions, poverty, and lack of opportunity in the inner city. This anger fueled militancy on the part of many. The phrase "Black power" was coined by activist Stokely Carmichael in response to the intransigence of white society. At the same time, the Black Panther Party was formed to promote a

volatile mix of race, sex, and Maoist revolution [that] coalesced in a new violent cultural figure—a photogenic caricature of black masculinity, which the New Left loved for its seditious outrageousness and "authenticity" and which would haunt the public's understanding of young black males for the next 30 years.*

Given such tension, small events could trigger major explosions. Eventually, rioting erupted in such important urban centers as Newark, New Jersey; the Watts section of Los Angeles; and Detroit.

Musicians aroused by political concerns also became involved in the general turbulence of the black population. Early on, in the 1940s and 1950s, jazz musicians focused on the importance of black contributions to music. In the 1960s, LeRoi Jones—who later changed his name to Amiri Baraka—made an influential contribution to American social history by writing *Blues People* (1963). In this book,

---

* Charles Johnson, "A Soul's Jagged Arc," *New York Times Magazine*, January 3, 1999, 16.

Avant-Garde Jazz and Black Activism

As the avant-garde jazz movement expanded during the 1960s, it became intimately connected to and nurtured by black nationalism and militant protest. As pointed out earlier, an increase in black ethnic pride has paralleled the history of jazz. This increase was rooted in the Harlem Renaissance and before that in the writings of W. E. B. Du Bois and others. Du Bois's concept of the "talented tenth"—the elite of the black population, whose achievements could inspire and "uplift" blacks as a whole—helped spur the growth of a black intelligentsia. The Harlem Renaissance was an early realization of Du Bois's vision (see Chapter 2). Later, the bebop musicians of the 1940s upheld the importance of black achievement when they

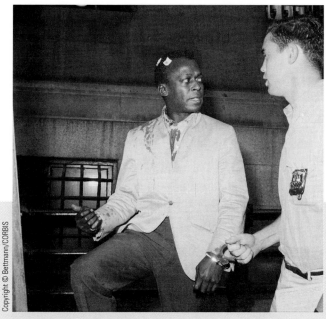

Copyright © Bettmann/CORBIS

The original New York City newspaper caption read: "Noted jazz trumpeter Miles Davis (left) is led into court for arraignment here, August 26th [1959]. Davis, thirty-two, was arrested for felonious assault and disorderly conduct after allegedly grappling with a policeman outside the Birdland Jazz Emporium on Broadway. Police said that Davis suffered a head laceration when a detective hit him with a blackjack. The trouble reportedly happened when patrolman Gerald Kilduff ordered the trumpeter to clear the sidewalk. Police said that Davis refused to move and that the jazz musician wrested a nightstick from the patrolman when Kilduff took Davis by the arm to lead him to the police station."

he claimed that jazz and American popular music in general was essentially black. Baraka argued that the blues defined blacks as Americans—that is, it made them American Negroes rather than displaced Africans working in a new land. The blues, once matured, later defined jazz:

> When Negroes began to master more and more "European" instruments and began to think musically in terms of their timbres, as opposed to, or in conjunction with, the voice, blues began to change, and the era of jazz was at hand.[†]

[†] LeRoi Jones, *Blues People* (New York: William Morrow, 1963), 70.

In the 1960s, then, the onset of black militancy and separatism espoused by Malcolm X and the Black Panthers was paralleled by angry claims that although jazz was a form of black music, its economic rewards flowed to whites, its imitators. These views were forcefully argued in 1970 by Frank Kofsky in *Black Nationalism and the Revolution in Music,* in which he stated:

> Whites can learn to play jazz... but for most whites... this new accomplishment will ordinarily come later in life than if they had been raised in the traditions of the ethnic group that they now seek to emulate; and in most cases the "second language" thus acquired will always be a touch more stiff and stilted for the "outsider" than for the "insider."[‡]

Kofsky also claimed:

> The number of white musicians who have made a permanent contribution to the tradition of jazz... is astonishingly small. More than likely, one could count them on one's fingers. ... It is probably safe to state that there have been more black innovators of consequence on any *two* instruments we might choose at random—trumpet and trombone, say—than there have been whites on all instruments put together.[**]

Kofsky also proclaimed his view of the essential economic injustice of jazz. He quoted tenor saxophonist Archie Shepp at length, including Shepp's succinct summary of their views: "You own the music and we make it."[††]

[‡] Frank Kofsky, *Black Nationalism and the Revolution in Music* (New York: Pathfinder Press, 1970), 17.

[**] Ibid., 19.

[††] Ibid., 26.

I HAVE A DREAM

DR. MARTIN LUTHER KING

★ ★ ★ APPEARING AT THE ★ ★ ★

SOUTHERN BAPTIST CHURCH
APRIL 4th - 1968
MEMPHIS, TENNESSEE

Courtesy Morgan Collection

The fight for civil rights was the hallmark of the 1950s and 1960s. Dr. Martin Luther King Jr. (1929–1968) was at the forefront of nonviolent protest against segregation. This poster advertises his last speech, given at a rally in support of striking garbage collectors; later that evening James Earl Ray shot and killed King as he stood on his motel balcony.

worked to separate themselves from what they perceived as the subservience of older black entertainers to the white mainstream.

In the 1950s, growing activism among blacks, including the brilliant legal tactics of Thurgood Marshall, led to important court victories in which societal barriers to equality were overturned. For example, the Supreme Court decision in *Brown v. Board of Education* struck a major blow against segregation in the South. Further protests against segregation, including the "Freedom" demonstrations of the early 1960s, eventually led to the passage of the Civil Rights Act of 1964, which officially outlawed discrimination. Leaders such as Martin Luther King Jr., were instrumental in these efforts. Unfortunately, the legal end to segregation and discrimination did not lead to acceptance of blacks into the dominant society. Black militancy in the 1960s was a direct result of these developments.

This revolution in black activism anticipated a wider rebellion within middle-class society as well. Inspired by the Beat movement of the 1950s, many young people in the following decade rebelled against what they considered unthinking conformity and social duty. This rebellion took special aim at the war in Vietnam, which many people, young and old, considered pointless and unwinnable. The smaller but more visible group called "flower children" embraced the hippie lifestyle and derided their parents' sexual timidity as "uptight." "Do your own thing" became a catchphrase.

The 1960s have rightly been considered pivotal in the history of U.S. society and of the West as a whole. The civil rights movement and racial rebellion formed only one part of a general cultural upheaval. The decade witnessed increasing activism among feminists, whose roots reached back to the women's suffrage movement in the nineteenth century, but whose demands now included equal access to jobs and careers and equal pay for equal work. The so-called sexual revolution together with the birth control pill challenged conventional sexual mores, leading to growing sexual activity among unmarried adults and increasingly graphic depictions of sex in novels, movies, and television. This was paralleled by a dramatic upturn in violence and explicit language in virtually all media. The "Stonewall Rebellion," rioting incited by a 1969 police raid on a gay bar in New York, galvanized political activism for gay rights and led to a growing acceptance of what were called "alternative lifestyles." The increasing popularity of rock music and political activism by leading rock stars provided a focal point for social protest and the antiwar movement. This era of unprecedented social rebellion was reflected in jazz, in particular by musical substyles that were as uncompromising as the attitudes of its foremost musicians.

ARCHIE SHEPP

Archie Shepp (b. 1937) was one of the most vocal and articulate of the avant-garde musicians championing the cause of blacks. His album *Fire Music* (1965) featured the piece "Malcolm, Malcolm, *Semper* Malcolm," a tribute to black leader Malcolm X. Shepp studied dramatic literature at Goddard College, where he earned his bachelor of arts in 1959. Originally an alto player, he switched to tenor through the inspiration of John Coltrane, with whom he eventually performed. He also worked with Cecil Taylor, Bill Dixon, Roswell Rudd, and others.

Shepp thought that free jazz ought to be a political medium. His calls for justice for blacks have not wavered through the years. In 1999 he pointed out that Jewish survivors of the Holocaust were seeking monetary compensation: "What if our people asked for compensation for all the years of slave labour?"[1]

Shepp performed on Coltrane's important free jazz album, *Ascension* (1965). In addition to *Fire Music,* Shepp recorded several other significant albums in the 1960s, including *Four for Trane* (1964). Eloquent in his defense of black nationalist principles, Shepp became an educator, teaching at the State University of New York at Buffalo and the University of Massachusetts at Amherst.

ALBERT AYLER

Another important contributor to the scene, Albert Ayler (1936–1970), brought a fiercely independent style and an abundance of avant-garde techniques to the tenor saxophone. Like Shepp, Ayler worked with Cecil Taylor. *Ghosts* and *Spiritual Unity* (both 1964) were two of his most important albums. His works encompassed shrieks, cries, wails, *multiphonics,* and other techniques that can be summed up as a sound-oriented approach to the instrument rather than anything one could notate easily. Unfortunately, the jazz world would lose this innovator all too soon. In 1970 Ayler disappeared for almost three weeks before his body was found in New York's East River. The circumstances surrounding his death are sketchy, but the official verdict was death by drowning.

Ayler's "Ghosts" followed the first wave of the avant-garde jazz recordings by artists Ornette Coleman and Cecil Taylor. Many avant-garde tenor saxophonists of the 1960s, such as Ayler and Pharoah Sanders, drew much of their initial inspiration from John Coltrane. For his part, Coltrane keenly supported these players, even helping both Ayler and Sanders obtain contracts from Impulse Records.

"Ghosts" is from Ayler's most productive period: He recorded four albums during 1964. Ayler uses the entire range of the tenor saxophone during his solo. Gary Peacock is on bass, and Sunny Murray is on drums. There is no piano, which is typical of many free jazz recordings of the 1960s.

Multiphonics is a technique of producing more than one note at a time on a wind instrument. Using nonstandard fingering and appropriate embouchure, the player splits the air stream into two or more parts, thus producing a multinote "chordal" effect. The technique is difficult to control, may be strident, and is generally associated with avant-garde playing.

L I S T E N I N G   G U I D E

"Ghosts: First Variation" (excerpt)

CD **2**   Track **9**

Albert Ayler Trio: "Ghosts: First Variation" (Ayler), from *Spiritual Unity*. ESP 1002. New York, July 10, 1964.
Albert Ayler, tenor saxophone; Gary Peacock, bass; Sunny Murray, drums.

Like many of the avant-garde recordings, the improvisation in "Ghosts" makes listening particularly challenging. What is unusual, however, is the simplicity of its melody. Drawn to this simplicity, Ayler recorded at least five different versions of "Ghosts." "I'd like to play something—like the beginning of 'Ghosts'—that people can hum," he acknowledged. "And I want to play songs that I used to sing when I was real small. Folk melodies that all people would understand."[2]

The group follows the traditional "melody-solos-melody" format, but following the statement of the melody, members engage in free collective improvisation. The players abandon a regular pulse, an underlying tonal center or harmonic progression, and a predetermined formal structure.

Ayler plays extremely freely, developing a repertory of extended tenor saxophone techniques, over-blowing notes and distorting pitches. During the head, Peacock provides bass notes that imply a conventional harmonic progression. Murray's earlier work with Cecil Taylor contributes to the "arhythmic" approach to the drums heard here. Murray often played with a stripped-down drum set, using only cymbal, snare drum, and bass drum. In the excerpt here, we fade during the Ayler solo.

8-bar intro

0:00   Ayler plays an introductory melody alone, using both fixed and indeterminate pitches.

Melody—Three 8-bar phrases

0:11   Bass and drums enter, accompanying Ayler beneath the melody. This melody is very lyrical, similar to Sonny Rollins's tuneful calypso melody "St. Thomas."

0:21   Two folklike eight-bar ideas closely related to the melody appear, setting up a clear tonal center.

Ayler tenor saxophone solo

0:44   In the first twenty seconds of the solo, Ayler vaguely recalls the melody: The pitches are often indeterminate, but the phrasing seems to echo the starting and stopping places of the melody. Careful listening reveals the use of some of the motives from the melody.

BLACK ACTIVISM AND THE AVANT-GARDE TODAY

The struggle for equality and recognition of black achievement continues today, as it probably will for some time. Among the influential younger musicians who have sought greater black recognition and advocated multiculturalism is clarinetist Don Byron (b. 1958). He has gained a reputation for combining jazz with Jewish klezmer music in addition to other crossover experimentation. Recently, he confronted racial stereotypes with his album *Nu Blaxploitation* (1998). Byron leads a band called Existential Dred, a name that neatly evokes contemporary angst, the *Dred Scott* Supreme Court decision of 1857, and Byron's own dreadlocks hairstyle. His album *Music for Six Musicians* (1995) featured a piece called "Shelby Steele Would Be Mowing Your Lawn." (Steele is a black scholar who has written against affirmative action programs.)

Photograph copyright © 1955 by Lehman Hamilton. Courtesy Morgan Collection.

Dizzy Gillespie (CD 2, Tracks 1 and 2), shown here with Adam Clayton Powell. For many years Powell represented New York's Harlem in Congress, where he was especially effective in helping create the "Great Society" programs that attempted to generate economic and social opportunities for blacks and the poor.

Although social statement remains an important form of the black avant-garde, its message seems less urgent thirty years later. Nonetheless, the black nationalist movement continues to focus attention on the essential black contribution to jazz. Some feel, however, that this focus has gone too far, that a kind of reverse racism has resulted, with white contributions to the music undervalued and fine white players overlooked. For example, the argument of the essential blackness of jazz has been countered recently by Gene Lee's *Cats of Any Color* (1995) and Richard Sudhalter's *Lost Chords: White Musicians and Their Contributions to Jazz, 1915–1945* (1999). These books argue that jazz is an American music whose innovators have been largely black but to which whites have contributed significantly and that without whites and their input, jazz would not be the rich music it is.

In any case, the jazz avant-garde of the 1960s pioneered forceful political statements that heightened awareness of and emphasis on the African heritage of jazz. The general atmosphere of the 1960s, both in the black community and in society more generally, provided a sympathetic backdrop for musical revolution.

ORNETTE COLEMAN AND FREE JAZZ

With the arrival of alto saxophonist Ornette Coleman on the New York scene in 1959, avant-garde jazz received its strongest initial boost. In fact, "free jazz" received its name from the 1960 Coleman album of the same name. A cover painting by abstract expressionist Jackson Pollock reinforced its avant-garde statement. Coleman, who played a plastic alto saxophone, polarized the jazz community in New York in the late 1950s: Some hailed him as a genius while others denounced him as a charlatan.

Courtesy Morgan Collection

With his pianoless quartet in the late 1950s, Ornette Coleman (CD 2, Track 10) was one of the key figures of early avant-garde jazz.

Coleman's music was controversial. His quartet—with trumpeter Don Cherry, bassist Charlie Haden, and drummer Billy Higgins (replaced by Ed Blackwell in 1960)—had no chordal instruments such as the piano. While some listeners dismissed his music as a radical rejection of the jazz tradition, those who praised him considered his music a logical extension of historical practice. Among Coleman's earliest champions was pianist John Lewis of the Modern Jazz Quartet, who had heard Coleman's group in California:

> I've never heard anything like Ornette Coleman and Don Cherry before. Ornette is, in a sense, an extension of Charlie Parker—the first I've heard. This is the real need . . . to extend the basic ideas of Bird until they're not playing an imitation but actually something new.[3]

As his album titles *Change of the Century* and *The Shape of Jazz to Come* suggested, Coleman's music was new. The improvised solos were not necessarily tied to traditional harmonic progressions but instead were based on loose and shifting tonal centers. Without any harmonic accompaniment, the soloists could move freely to different harmonic areas, although Haden's bass lines sometimes retained the pieces' original forms.

Coleman was an astonishingly prolific composer whose tuneful, sometimes cheerful compositions were written to be interpreted freely. Coleman noted:

> I don't tell the members of the group what to do. I want them to play what they hear in the piece themselves. I let everyone express himself just as he wants to. The musicians have complete freedom, and so, of course, our final results depend entirely on the musicianship, emotional make-up, and taste of the individual members.[4]

Coleman was born in Fort Worth, Texas, in 1930 and began his career performing in rhythm-and-blues (R&B) bands in the mid-1940s. Joining the R&B band of

Ornette Coleman's Chamber and Orchestral Compositions

While in England, Coleman premiered a chamber music work, *Sounds and Forms for Wind Quintet*, that showed his ability to create extended compositional structures. His interest in contemporary concert music and the third stream were earlier revealed by an appearance on Gunther Schuller's album *Jazz Abstractions* in 1960; Coleman was the alto saxophone soloist in "Abstractions," a serial work by Schuller for alto, string quartet, two double basses, guitar, and percussion.

Continuing in a third-stream vein, Coleman in 1967 wrote *Sounds and Forms for Wind Quintet*, performing trumpet interludes between all of the ten movements. This work helped Coleman win the prestigious Guggenheim Award for composition; he was the first jazz composer to be so honored.

Several years later, in 1971, Coleman completed a large-scale work for orchestra entitled *Skies of America*, with movements that included "Foreigner in a Free Land" and "The Men Who Live in the White House." This work was revived at Lincoln Center by the New York Philharmonic in 1997.

Pee Wee Crayton, Coleman traveled to Los Angeles, where he settled in 1954 after being fired by Crayton. He then worked for a while as an elevator operator—a job that allowed him to read and study music theory while parked on the tenth floor.

In 1958 Coleman signed with Contemporary Records and recorded two albums for the label. The forms for Coleman's early compositions were frequently conventional, following the structure of the 12-bar blues and the 32-bar AABA song form. Although Coleman's albums for Contemporary were less radical than his work to come, they show how his music was beginning to evolve toward complete freedom from syntactic constraints.

After signing with Atlantic Records in 1959, Coleman recorded *The Shape of Jazz to Come* and *Change of the Century* with his own quartet, comprising Cherry, Haden, and Higgins. Coleman's approach to the alto saxophone was unique: He emulated the human voice, using bent pitches and unusual intonation. "There are some intervals," he stated, "that carry that human quality if you play them in the right pitch. You can reach into the human sound of a voice on your horn if you're actually hearing and trying to express the warmth of a human voice."[5] Coleman's unusual intonation and motivic playing was often embedded in a relatively simple rhythmic language, creating, as one writer put it, "a touch of folksong naiveté."[6]

These features summarize Coleman's style:

▶ Fragmented, angular melodies instead of the long, spun-out eighth-note phrases of bebop

▶ Melodic connections based on motivic structure and large-scale gestures and more abstract relations among sets of pitches

▶ Little if any use of conventional harmony and voice leading (a means of making logical melodic and harmonic sequences within an improvised solo), but solos that often establish loose, shifting tonal centers

▶ Variety of melodic rhythm but avoidance of even-note phrases

▶ Nasal, insistent tone

▶ Rhythm loosely connected to background pulse

▶ Concentration on the middle and upper ranges of the instrument

▶ Passionate expression

▶ Deviations from standard intonation

As tightly controlled as Coleman's playing was, his pitch structure and rhythmic fluidity created an impression of spontaneous expression. Coleman combined a sensuous, linear approach to the instrument with a strikingly original sound, created in part by his unique, well-controlled intonation. All in all, Coleman succeeded in allying passionate expression to rigorous linear structure; his playing was emotional, powerful, and thoroughly individual.

Pianist John Lewis of the Modern Jazz Quartet was an ardent early supporter of Coleman, arranging for him and Don Cherry to attend the Lenox Jazz School in Massachusetts in 1959. Shortly after, Coleman and his group came to New York for their legendary gig at the Five Spot. Despite the acclaim of Lewis and other famous musical figures such as Gunther Schuller and Leonard Bernstein, the group experienced derision by some older, established players. For example, trumpeter Roy Eldridge claimed, "He's putting everybody on. They start with a nice lead-off figure, but then they go off into outer space. They disregard the chords and they play odd numbers of bars. I can't follow them."[7]

In December 1960, Coleman took the unprecedented step of bringing together eight players (two quartets) in a composition titled *Free Jazz*. Coleman had expanded his quartet—Cherry, Haden, and Blackwell—with Higgins, bassist Scott LaFaro, and bass clarinetist Eric Dolphy. The group recorded two takes, lasting thirty-six minutes, combining solo and collective improvisation with prearranged ensemble passages.

In some ways, *Free Jazz* profoundly influenced the emerging jazz avant-garde. It suggested new sets of relationships among improvisers and allowed the rhythm section to jettison routine timekeeping. Both the use of collective improvisation based on freely improvised motives and the abandonment of cycling harmonic-metric forms redefined the possibilities of group interaction.

During the early 1970s, Coleman worked sporadically, sometimes insisting on fees for records and appearances that were too large for a jazz musician of his celebrity and audience appeal. He preferred to remain underemployed and underrecorded rather than sacrifice his artistic principles.

Coleman regained the jazz limelight during the mid-1970s, combining his free style with funk rhythms. Coleman formed the group Prime Time to incorporate these changes in his style and in his interests—this time, however, with electric instruments. Prime Time began as a quintet, with two electric guitarists and an electric bassist; it was later expanded to a sextet, with the addition of a second drummer. The group featured an interesting amalgam of rhythm and blues, free jazz, and occasional non-Western influences.

Coleman achieved a wider degree of recognition after touring and recording with fusion guitarist Pat Metheny between 1985 and 1986. In 1987 Coleman recorded *In All Languages,* in which his original 1959 quartet including Don Cherry, Charlie Haden, and Billy Higgins was juxtaposed with his Prime Time electric ensemble. It provides a remarkable summary of Coleman's distinguished career.

In 1997 Lincoln Center presented an entire evening dedicated to Coleman—*Civilization: A Harmolodic Celebration*—that featured performances of his group, Prime Time, and reunited Coleman with Charlie Haden and Billy Higgins. (**Harmolodics** is a term coined by Coleman to refer to his theories of improvisation.) Among the other guests were rock musician Lou Reed and progressive artist Laurie Anderson. (See the box "Ornette Coleman's Chamber and Orchestral Compositions" on page 196.)

"Street Woman"

CD **2** Track **10**

Ornette Coleman: "Street Woman" (Coleman), from *Science Fiction*. Original issue Columbia KC31061.
Reissued on Sony SRCS 9372. New York, September 9–13, 1971. Don Cherry, pocket trumpet;
Ornette Coleman, alto saxophone; Charlie Haden, bass; Billy Higgins, drums.

"Street Woman" shows the joyful, up-tempo sound of Coleman's best-known quartet. Like so many of Coleman's pieces, "Street Woman" projects a basic tonal center (in this case, G), although it avoids standard chord progressions. The motivic tightness of the melody is remarkable: After the opening three figures present their abrupt flourishes, the remainder of the melody releases the built-up tension with descending three-note ideas.

Head—1st time through

0:00   The head is stated once. The melody of "Street Woman" uses a number of different melodic figures. Haden's bass accompaniment consists largely of rapid alternations between single-pitch octaves. He follows the horns through the figures of the melody, while his bass line imparts a sense of harmonic movement to the head without detailing specific chords.

Head—2nd time through

0:15   The principal melody is repeated in virtually the same manner.

Coleman alto saxophone solo

0:31   Coleman's solo begins with a flourish and works with pitches from the G major scale.

1:28
and   Coleman returns to the high-pitch G in a passionate statement several times toward the
1:56   end of his solo. Haden gradually assumes a walking bass as accompaniment, although he will return to octaves at times.

Haden bass solo

2:07   Haden works with the idea of keeping one pitch constant and moving the other.

2:46   Later he moves into a freer statement that ushers in Cherry's pocket trumpet solo.

Cherry pocket trumpet solo

3:11   Cherry presents ideas that strongly recall the figures of the head. His solo begins energetically, with a flurry of notes. Haden returns to the octave idea of the head.

3:35   Cherry's lines become more lyrical and tonal, emphasizing G minor.

Head—Return

4:07   The head is played twice, as it was heard at the beginning of the performance.

Coda

4:41   The opening melodic figure is repeated three times with a follow-up high G.

By the 1990s, Coleman was accepted as one of the elder representatives of the jazz avant-garde. He was inducted into the French Order of Arts and Letters in 1997 and was elected to the American Academy of Arts and Letters the same year.

John Coltrane

In the twelve years from 1955, when he joined Miles Davis's Quintet, to his death in 1967, John Coltrane, initially an obscure and often-criticized tenor player, became the leading saxophonist of his generation and one of the most important jazz artists of the 1960s. His influence was profound. He was consistently devoted to his craft, to technical proficiency, to musical exploration, and to endless practicing and studying. His album titles, such as *A Love Supreme* and *Om*, revealed the connection of his music to his religious beliefs and spiritual quest. Fans and listeners heard his extended solos as reaching for the ineffable. Particularly with his quartet of 1960–1965, Coltrane became the symbol of the improvising musician as exploratory seeker. Even in his later, successful years, Coltrane remained uncompromising in his musical ideals and overall goals.

Courtesy Morgan Collection

The career of John Coltrane (CD 2, Track 11) was marked by a restless search for musical growth and the transcendental.

OVERVIEW OF COLTRANE'S CAREER

Although Coltrane underwent many changes and transformations in his sound and style, his career encompasses three general periods:

▶ 1955–1960: Hard bop and "sheets of sound"

▶ 1960–1965: Classic quartet and modal compositions

▶ 1965–1967: Avant-garde

In the first period, he and Sonny Rollins competed to be the premier tenor saxophonist in jazz. At that time Coltrane was often described as a hard bop player with an edgy sound. Jazz critic Ira Gitler coined the phrase *sheets of sound* to describe his rapid-fire execution, irregular groupings of notes, unusual phrasing, and technique of inserting several harmonies over a single chord.

Coltrane launched his second period by bringing together his well-known and long-lived quartet, which included McCoy Tyner on piano, Jimmy Garrison on bass, and Elvin Jones on drums. The repertory of the quartet emphasized modal composition, often with particular attention to minor modes such as the Dorian. (See the box "What Is Modal Jazz?" in Chapter 5.) The group's extended improvisations, such as in their performance of "My Favorite Things," featured fewer and slower-moving harmonies. The quartet's modal approach reached its zenith in the December 10, 1964, recording *A Love Supreme*, a four-movement suite (listen to CD 2, Track 11, to hear one of these movements).

Sheets of sound, an expression coined by jazz critic Ira Gitler, describes a method of playing that features extremely fast notes with irregular phrase groupings. Sometimes, unusual harmonies are introduced over the given chord change. This method originated with John Coltrane.

Coltrane's third and final period spanned the last two years of his life, when he became increasingly involved in the jazz avant-garde. His album *Ascension,* which used several young, radical musicians, provided a significant document of the free jazz movement.

EARLY YEARS

Born in Hamlet, North Carolina, on September 23, 1926, and raised in High Point, North Carolina, Coltrane played alto horn, clarinet, and then, as a teenager, the alto saxophone. After moving to Philadelphia, he studied at several local music schools, then joined the U.S. Navy band and was stationed in Hawaii between 1945 and 1946. The following year, while on tour in California, Coltrane met Charlie Parker, recently released from Camarillo State Hospital.

In 1948 Coltrane joined the band of Eddie "Cleanhead" Vinson. It was at that time that Coltrane took up the tenor saxophone, which opened up a range of possibilities:

> When I bought a tenor to go with Eddie Vinson's band, a wider area of listening opened up for me. I found I was able to be more varied in my musical interests. On alto, Bird had been my whole influence, but on tenor I found there was no one man whose ideas were so dominant as Charlie's were on alto. Therefore, I drew from all the men I heard during this period. I have listened to about all the good tenor men, beginning with Lester [Young], and believe me, I've picked up something from them all, including several who have never recorded. The reason I like Lester so was that I could feel that line, that simplicity. . . . There were a lot of things that [Coleman] Hawkins was doing that I knew I'd have to learn somewhere along the line. I felt the same way about Ben Webster. . . . The first time I heard Hawk, I was fascinated by his arpeggios and the way he played. I got a copy of his "Body and Soul" and listened real hard to what he was doing.[8]

This quotation reveals Coltrane's ability to absorb a huge array of influences. Throughout his career, he remained profoundly interested in the musical developments of his colleagues and was extremely supportive of many younger musicians. In addition to his appetite for music, unfortunately, Coltrane displayed an inclination toward substance abuse. He began using heroin in the late 1940s, and he frequently drank and ate obsessively. He remained addicted to heroin for nearly ten years.

After taking on a staggering variety of gigs as a sideman, Coltrane in 1954 joined the band of one of his earliest idols, alto saxophonist Johnny Hodges. Coltrane appreciated Hodges's musical sincerity and confidence and noted that "I liked every tune in the book."[9] Unfortunately, Coltrane developed problems with drugs and alcohol, causing him to leave the band and return to Philadelphia to recuperate. Although he had already accumulated numerous professional experiences, his most significant ones were yet to come.

HARD BOP WITH MILES DAVIS

Flush with success from his 1955 appearance at the Newport Jazz Festival, Miles Davis formed a working quintet that year, hiring Coltrane on tenor. Although Davis had

Publicity photo by Frank Lindner. Courtesy Morgan Collection.

Saxophonist Sonny Rollins (CD 2, Track 7) preceded Coltrane in the Miles Davis Quintet. Jazz writers and analysts singled out Rollins's musically inventive and thematically coherent solos.

been using tenor saxophonist Sonny Rollins, Rollins had moved to Chicago, taking the first of his extended sabbaticals from performing. Davis's drummer, Philly Joe Jones, and pianist Red Garland—both Philadelphians—persuaded Davis to hire Coltrane, who was then working with organist Jimmy Smith.

"When Coltrane joined Miles Davis's quintet in 1955," writes Thomas Owens, "he formed a musical alliance that would have a great impact on the evolution of jazz."[10] Coltrane's years with Davis were indeed formative. Although critics were initially hostile to Coltrane's aggressive technique and steely tone, his virtuosity was dazzling. Despite his technical advances, Coltrane's drug habit, along with that of Philly Joe Jones, was causing problems on the bandstand. Miles Davis's biographer, Jack Chambers, recounts the story of Coltrane's falling asleep on stage during an entire set. Present was a record executive intent on signing him to a major record label; after seeing his condition, he left without talking to Coltrane.[11]

The year 1957 was pivotal in Coltrane's career. Davis, exasperated by his behavior, fired him. Shaken, Coltrane managed to get off heroin and quit drinking alcohol. During the spring and summer he worked with pianist Thelonious Monk; later that fall, the two teamed up for a famous engagement at New York's Five Spot. Monk gave Coltrane further freedom to experiment, with extended solos often backed by only bass and drums. In Coltrane's words, Monk was "a musical architect of the highest order. . . . I felt I learned from him in every way—through the senses, theoretically, technically."[12] Coltrane also claimed that Monk was the first to show him how to produce two or three notes simultaneously on the tenor saxophone.

Around this time, Coltrane also recorded his first album as a leader. On the LP *Coltrane,* he showed a depth of tone and emotion in the slower, more sensitive solos. Other Coltrane improvisations showed a turn to the long, sixteenth-note phrases and patterns that were to become a distinctive part of his style. Some of Coltrane's hard bop compositions, such as "Moment's Notice" from his 1957 recording *Blue Train,* contained unusual and quick-moving harmonic twists.

As his technique and approach to the instrument continued to evolve, Coltrane rejoined Davis in 1958. Gitler's phrase *sheets of sound* was an apt description for Coltrane's torrid scalar passages. In addition, Coltrane made conscious use of unusual and irregular phrasing. Similarly, Coltrane was candid about harmonic experimentation, sometimes superimposing extra chords on the tunes' basic changes. His solo in "Straight, No Chaser" (from Miles Davis's *Milestones*), for example, contained unusual harmonic substitutions.

Davis's modal music supplied the ideal repertory for Coltrane's experiments in harmonic superimposition. In the spring of 1959, the same period he recorded *Kind of Blue* with Davis, Coltrane took his own group into the studio and recorded one of his most famous works, "Giant Steps." This imaginative tune used the harmonic patterns of hard bop, but reworked them into a large-scale format with fast key changes linked by major thirds. In this tour de force, Coltrane showed his mastery of bebop harmonies and unusual progressions in a driving, up-tempo format.

COLTRANE'S CLASSIC QUARTET

In 1960 Coltrane took the decisive step of leaving the Davis sextet and forming his own quartet, which opened at the Jazz Gallery in May. In McCoy Tyner (b. 1938), Coltrane found a pianist in sympathy with his own modal interests. Tyner's sound was based on chords built in fourths, and his solos projected an extremely forceful and clipped staccato touch on improvised lines, which sometimes culminated in thunderous tremolos. Renowned for his powerful touch and almost demonic energy, Tyner has remained one of the most popular pianists in jazz. In recent years he continues to work with his own groups, including a big band, and has appeared as a special guest both live and on recordings with other major artists.

Pianist McCoy Tyner (CD 2, Track 11), whose powerful playing and modal harmonies were built in fourths, complemented John Coltrane's extended solos.

Like Tyner, Coltrane's drummer, Elvin Jones, was also a fiery, intense player. Born in Pontiac, Michigan, Jones (1927–2004) came from a musical family that included his equally renowned brothers, trumpeter Thad Jones (1923–1986) and pianist Hank Jones (b. 1918). Jones's years with Coltrane brought him fame, not only for his complex polyrhythms but also for sheer physical endurance. In the context of the band's extended improvisations, Jones generated unbelievable energy and drive as both a powerful timekeeper and a complementary voice to Coltrane's own style. The level of energy generated by Jones's playing brought about an increased participation for the drummer relative to the bassist and the pianist. Jones was aware of this role. In discussing his playing with Coltrane, he said:

> I always realize I'm not the soloist, that John is, and I'm merely the support for him. It may sound like a duet or duel at times, but it's still a support I'm lending him, a complementary thing. . . . It's being done in the same context of the earlier style, only this is just another step forward in the relationship between the rhythm section and the soloist. It's much freer—John realizes he has this close support, and, therefore, he can move further ahead; he can venture out as far as he wants without worrying about getting away from everybody and having the feeling he's out in the middle of a lake by himself.[13]

Coltrane's classic quartet was rounded out by bassist Jimmy Garrison (1934–1976), who joined at the end of 1961. Less technically oriented than Tyner and Jones, Garrison was a solid player who often relied on pedal points and fixed patterns in addition to the more customary walking lines when he was accompanying soloists. In his own solos, Garrison featured unusual bass techniques, sometimes strumming the bass with three-note chords in a quasi-flamenco style.

Although the quartet became one of the premier groups in jazz, Coltrane personally continued to expand his musical interests and influences by studying the music and scales of Africa, India, and the Mideast. He also took up the soprano saxophone, which provided further inspiration and new paths to explore. Coltrane featured the soprano on some of his best-known performances, including the well-known "My Favorite Things," recorded in 1960.

During 1961 and 1962, Coltrane's quartet was frequently expanded to a quintet, incorporating Eric Dolphy on flute and bass clarinet. Dolphy's influence on Coltrane's group was liberating. Dolphy's extended improvisations on such compositions as "India," based on a modal scale (G Mixolydian), triggered hostility from music critics, some of whom attacked what they perceived as Coltrane's move toward free jazz. *Down Beat* editor John Tynan dismissed the music as "anti-jazz":

> At Hollywood's Renaissance club recently, I listened to a horrifying demonstration of what appears to be a growing anti-jazz trend exemplified by these foremost proponents [Coltrane and Dolphy] of what is termed avant-garde music. I heard a good rhythm section . . . go to waste behind the nihilistic exercises of the two horns. . . . Coltrane and Dolphy seem intent on deliberately destroying [swing]. . . . They seem bent on pursuing an anarchistic course in their music that can but be termed anti-jazz.[14]

Motivic cells are short melodic ideas subject to variation and development. Also called *thematic cells*.

On the other hand, Coltrane's 1964 recording *A Love Supreme* was enormously successful; selling a half-million copies in its first year, it was hailed as a masterpiece. *A Love Supreme* represented the crystallization of the musical ideas Coltrane had developed since he formed his quartet: modal improvisation, extended pedal points, and the *motivic cell* approach to solos. Moved by Coltrane's fervor and intensity, audiences received the recording as a profound, courageous statement of a man seeking musical and spiritual truth. *A Love Supreme* is a suite in four movements: "Acknowledgement," "Resolution," "Pursuance," and "Psalm."

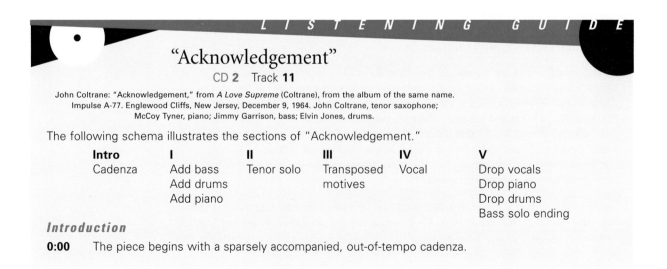

LISTENING GUIDE

"Acknowledgement"
CD **2**   Track **11**

John Coltrane: "Acknowledgement," from *A Love Supreme* (Coltrane), from the album of the same name. Impulse A-77. Englewood Cliffs, New Jersey, December 9, 1964. John Coltrane, tenor saxophone; McCoy Tyner, piano; Jimmy Garrison, bass; Elvin Jones, drums.

The following schema illustrates the sections of "Acknowledgement."

Intro	I	II	III	IV	V
Cadenza	Add bass	Tenor solo	Transposed motives	Vocal	Drop vocals
	Add drums				Drop piano
	Add piano				Drop drums
					Bass solo ending

Introduction

0:00   The piece begins with a sparsely accompanied, out-of-tempo cadenza.

I—Layered background texture

0:32   The bass begins a four-note **ostinato** that establishes the tempo, beat, and modal center. This ostinato provides the thematic material, that is, its motivic cell.

The drummer joins the bass, playing a relatively simple beat that grows more complex and insistent as the piece intensifies.

Tyner on piano follows with chords that reinforce the modal center. The rhythmic backdrop is complete.

II—Tenor saxophone solo

1:04   This solo is an immediate improvisation rather than a head statement. It begins in the prevailing mode (or tonal center), but begins to veer off the mode, which is heard as a point of harmonic stability to which he returns.

1:44   The solo gradually becomes more elaborate and intense as Coltrane varies and explores the numerous rhythms and patterns he can make with the first few notes.

3:52   Here the solo achieves its greatest intensity, highlighting Coltrane's preference for the high notes of the tenor, as if he were reaching for unplayable notes to express the inexpressible.

II continued—Piano and bass

4:14   Coltrane begins to develop a three-note idea here. Tyner and Garrison sometimes follow Coltrane's harmonic excursions, but just as often react freely to them, as if to illuminate rather than track his musical path.

III—Transposed motives

4:56   Coltrane transposes the motive (to all twelve keys) before returning to state it in unison with the bass.

IV—Vocal

6:07   Coltrane and Garrison chant "a love supreme" along with the bass motive in a reprise of the four-note ostinato with added lyric. The transposing-motives section followed by the vocal provides a recapitulation of this minimal but cogent thematic material.

V—Instruments drop out

6:37   In the midst of the vocal section, the motive and the general modal center abruptly drop down (one step to E♭). One by one, the vocals, the piano, and the drums drop out, disassembling the background texture erected at the beginning of the piece, to leave the bass to finish alone.

Each part of *A Love Supreme* is equally compelling. (See the Listening Guide for "Acknowledgement" above.) "Resolution" proceeds with an eight-measure theme over a single harmony. Tyner's piano solo is a powerful statement that demonstrates his ability to create a sense of harmonic evolution over a single modal center. The third movement, "Pursuance," is a 12-bar blues in B♭ minor, played over a blisteringly fast tempo. "Psalm" returns to the out-of-tempo playing of the opening, with Jones doubling on timpani. Coltrane biographer Lewis Porter has shown that the saxophone melody is in fact a wordless recitation to Coltrane's poem included in the liner notes to the album.[15]

The following points summarize Coltrane's mature modal jazz style:

▶ Free melody, usually not formed into square phrases

▶ Melodic connections based on development of motivic cells rather than voice leading, which was more prominent in his bop-oriented work

▶ Widely varying melodic rhythm, from long emotion-charged pitches to fast sheets of sound

▶ Concentration on the upper range and the extreme upper range of the instrument

▶ Passionate expression

▶ Full, rich tone with raspy edge

▶ "Outside" playing, often featuring free chord-scale relationships

A Love Supreme, possibly Coltrane's most popular record, exemplifies his deeply felt spiritual commitment and confirms his intense religious faith.

COLTRANE AND THE AVANT-GARDE

Despite his musical advances and the great success of *A Love Supreme,* Coltrane was still interested in exploring new worlds. He had been supportive of the avant-garde players and took a strong interest in their expansion of musical resources. Among Coltrane's newly developing musical gestures were sounds that imitated human cries, an increased use of multiphonics, and an ability to create a "dialogue" within his solos by alternating different registers of the horn.

Coltrane's 1965 album *Ascension* unveiled a strong move to the jazz avant-garde. This was not completely surprising: The loose modal improvisation in *A Love Supreme* and other albums had foreshadowed Coltrane's evolution into free jazz. In addition to his regular quartet, Coltrane's group on *Ascension* was augmented by a second bassist, two trumpeters, two alto saxophonists, and two other tenor saxophonists. The group recorded two takes of the composition "Ascension." In its use of collective group improvisation, it bore a superficial resemblance to Ornette Coleman's 1960 double quartet recording *Free Jazz,* but *Ascension* was much denser and more dissonant. For example, the work often relied on dense blocks of sound created by the seven horn players, generating what writer Ekkehard Jost called *sound fields.*[16]

Sound fields result when coinciding melodic lines fuse into an indistinguishable web or mass of sound with irregular accentuation within each line.

Coltrane continued to align himself with the avant-garde. Saxophonist Pharoah Sanders joined the group in the fall of 1965, as did a second drummer, Rashied Ali. Unhappy with the group's new directions, both Jones and Tyner left the band by the end of 1965. Coltrane's wife, harpist and pianist Alice Coltrane, replaced Tyner. Among Coltrane's final recordings were *Interstellar Space* (a duet with Rashied Ali) and *Expression.* Coltrane died of liver cancer on July 17, 1967, at age forty.

A case can be made that since the 1950s only Miles Davis has exerted a more powerful influence on jazz than John Coltrane has. Coltrane's intensity, technical skill, spirituality, and continuous search for new sounds remain an inspiration to all jazz musicians. His legendary status was enhanced by his unfortunate early death, probably brought on by the effects of excessive drinking. Uniting non-Western musical models and modal jazz with his original mastery of bebop, John Coltrane created some of the most personal, powerful, and exciting jazz of the 1950s and 1960s.

Cecil Taylor

Because much of the free jazz of the 1960s—such as Ornette Coleman's seminal quartet and the music of Albert Ayler—did not include piano, it is interesting that one of the foremost proponents of free jazz, Cecil Taylor (b. 1929), was a pianist. Taylor's piano style was dissonant and athletic. His power, energy, and unlimited drive produced a fascinating and sometimes foreboding wall of dense sound blocks. Taylor's study of timpani as a youth may have influenced his rhythmic conception because his keyboard concept was as much rhythmic as melodic, with rapid-fire clusters of hands, fists, forearms, and elbows. Throughout his career, Taylor has remained a controversial and fiercely uncompromising figure.

Taylor drew his wide-ranging musical ideas from both jazz and the European concert tradition. Among jazz pianists, he was initially attracted to the dense harmonies of Dave Brubeck and the linear clarity of Lennie Tristano before turning to Duke Ellington, Thelonious Monk, and Horace Silver. He was also inspired by the European composers Igor Stravinsky and Béla Bartók, and much of Taylor's music invoked the aesthetic of the European avant-garde alongside that of traditional jazz.

Only gradually did Taylor reject convention and arrive at his mature style: His recordings prior to 1960 are considerably closer to the jazz mainstream than his later ones are. His first album as a leader was *Jazz Advance,* a trio and quartet recording from December 1955. In other pre-1960 recordings, Taylor's harmonic language was often dissonant, but he also explored standards—Cole Porter's "Love for Sale" and "I Love Paris," for example. As a pianist, he maintained the usual technique of right-hand melody accompanied by left-hand chords.

On his two Candid albums from 1960 and 1961, *Air* and *Lazy Afternoon,* Taylor's performances became decidedly less traditional. He clearly was redefining his overall approach and innovating a new conception of jazz piano. Because of *Air* and *Lazy Afternoon,* Taylor won the *Down Beat* "New Star" award for pianists. Ironically, he was unemployed at the time.

In 1966 Taylor recorded two albums for Blue Note, *Unit Structures* and *Conquistador,* with two bassists and drummer Andrew Cyrille, who worked with Taylor for the decade 1965–1975.

Cecil Taylor's dissonant, athletic pianism was and remains fiercely uncompromising.

Like his predecessor Sunny Murray, Cyrille conformed readily to full-group improvisation while downplaying pulse and meter.

Taylor won increased recognition during the 1970s. He taught at the University of Wisconsin–Madison and at Antioch College in Ohio, where he recorded his solo piano album *Indent*. During the decade he was awarded a Guggenheim Fellowship and an honorary doctorate from the New England Conservatory of Music. His solo piano recording, *Silent Tongues,* won the 1974 *Down Beat* "Jazz Album of the Year" in its international critics poll.

Over the decades, audiences have found Taylor's music difficult or impenetrable. As one writer observed, an initial unprepared encounter with Taylor's music usually causes complete confusion.[17] Nevertheless, even the unprepared respond to the music's intensity and energy.

Chicago: AACM, the Art Ensemble of Chicago, and Anthony Braxton

By the later 1920s, the so-called Second City of Chicago was eclipsed by New York as the country's jazz center. Nevertheless, Chicago's jazz scene has remained active and was especially influential during the 1950s. During the 1960s, Pianist Muhal Richard Abrams became instrumental in creating the Association for the Advancement of Creative Musicians (AACM), a school and cooperative on the South Side that became the center of Chicago's avant-garde jazz scene.

The AACM was an organization that sponsored concerts and performances, and—most important—fostered self-determination for musicians. In allowing musicians to be independent of commercial promoters and agents, it promoted artistic and creative goals. Later, the group also produced radio shows and brought jazz education to inner-city schools.

The liner notes to alto saxophonist Joseph Jarman's recording *As If It Were the Seasons* (1968) described the aims of the organization:

> The Association for the Advancement of Creative Musicians, a non-profit organization chartered by the State of Illinois, was formed . . . when a group of Musicians and Composers in the Chicago area saw an emergent need to expose and showcase original Music which, under the existing establishment (promoters, agents, etc.) was not receiving its just due. A prime direction of our Association has been to provide an atmosphere conducive to serious Music and the performance of new, unrecorded compositions. The Music presented by the various groups in our Association is jazz-oriented.[18]

Along with poetry and social statement, much of the music of the AACM explored timbre, tone color, *nontempered intonation,* collective improvisation, and the use of unusual instruments. It also relied on humor and surprise. Trumpeter Lester Bowie's earliest experiences were with R&B bands and the tent shows of an itinerant carnival troupe, experiences he brought to bear on his work with the AACM. His album *Numbers 1 and 2* used gongs, police sirens, and nonsense syllables sung in falsetto. The AACM players were clearly seeking a release from the conventions of traditional jazz. The notion of freedom became an important theme for these artists. As Bowie noted in the liner notes to *Numbers 1 and 2:*

Nontempered intonation is the use of pitches unrestricted by the "equal-tempered," twelve-note chromatic scale. For example, a nontempered pitch might be a note between D and E♭. Such pitches may also be called **microtones**.

Jazz, at first apart from this struggle for renewal in the western world, has come to face these "freedoms." But there is only one true freedom for us, and that is what this music seeks. The signs of the revolution permeate most of jazz today, and in Chicago there are young musicians who, desiring freedom, are beginning to know how it is created.[19]

Bowie, saxophonists Jarman and Roscoe Mitchell, and bassist Malachi Favors also formed the four principals of the Art Ensemble of Chicago. Pursuing the path begun by the early AACM recordings, the Art Ensemble of Chicago relied heavily not only on free, collective improvisation but also on theater: They incorporated dramatic sketches, poetry, costumes and makeup, dance, pantomime, comedy, and parody in their performances.

Rejecting specialists' roles as performers, the members of the Art Ensemble of Chicago each played several instruments. When they moved to Europe, the group took about 500 instruments with them. On recordings such as *A Jackson in Your House,* the group mixed comical pastiche—mock Dixieland and swing—with sound explorations and free improvisations that were in part a rejection of the showy virtuosity of bebop. The recordings the group made during their eighteen months overseas revealed the varied instruments, many of them percussion, handled by the performers. A list of their instruments compiled by Ekkehard Jost shows this breadth:

▶ Lester Bowie: flugelhorn, trumpet, cowhorn, and bass drum

▶ Roscoe Mitchell: soprano, alto, and bass saxophone, clarinet, flute, cymbals, gongs, conga drums, steel drum, logs, bells, siren, and whistles

▶ Joseph Jarman: soprano, alto, and tenor saxophones, clarinet, oboe, bassoon, flutes, marimba, vibraphone, guitar, conga drums, bells, gongs, whistles, and sirens

▶ Malachi Favors: double bass, Fender bass, banjo, zither, log drum, and other percussion instruments[20]

Whereas the Art Ensemble of Chicago celebrated African elements in their music and theater, the music of another Chicagoan tilted toward European formal organization. Alto saxophonist Anthony Braxton (b. 1945) joined the AACM in 1966. Braxton's earliest influences were cool jazz altoists Paul Desmond and Lee Konitz, but after joining the AACM he began studying Ornette Coleman and John Coltrane, seeking in part to translate Coltrane's raw expressiveness to the alto. He also studied the techniques of avant-garde concert-music composers such as John Cage and Karlheinz Stockhausen.

Along with Leroy Jenkins and Leo Smith, Braxton formed the Creative Construction Company in 1967. The group explored free improvisational methods on Braxton's *Three Compositions,* recorded the following year. In 1968 Braxton made *For Alto,* his first unaccompanied alto saxophone recording.

Braxton later teamed up with the stellar rhythm section of pianist Chick Corea, bassist Dave Holland, and drummer Barry Altschul. The new group, Circle, recorded a concert in Paris for ECM records in February 1971. Braxton's improvisations were masterpieces of free interaction, weaving together multiphonics, unusual sonic and timbral resources, and pointillism. When Corea broke up the group in 1971, Braxton formed his own band, combining the rhythm section of Circle with Kenny Wheeler on trumpet. Braxton's later recordings for Arista records in the 1970s incorporated echoes of bebop, combined notated and improvised music, and brought together free collective improvisation, individual solos, and written ensemble passages.

As a result of his many activities, Braxton became one of the leading figures of the avant-garde. In addition to his jazz work, Braxton has written for band and large orchestra, sometimes with elements of theatricality that recall the early work of the AACM. His compositions often avoid conventional titles and use instead geometric designs, arrangements of numbers and letters, and human and animal figures. Braxton has served as a member of the faculty of Wesleyan University in Middletown, Connecticut, for many years.

Other Avant-Garde Performers

BLACK ARTISTS GROUP AND THE WORLD SAXOPHONE QUARTET

Inspired by artistic independence, self-sufficiency, and many of the ideals of black nationalism—the same goals that helped launch the AACM—other cities formed creative arts organizations that embraced the avant-garde. A particularly successful group of free jazz players in St. Louis formed a cooperative association in 1968, the Black Artists Group (BAG). Like the AACM, the BAG tutored young musicians, sponsored musical and multimedia performances, and received support from government and state grants. Although the BAG folded in 1972, three of its former members—alto saxophonists Oliver Lake and Julius Hemphill and baritone saxophonist Hamiet Bluiett—formed the World Saxophone Quartet (WSQ) in 1976. The fourth member was a Californian, tenor saxophonist David Murray.

The WSQ was unique—a versatile ensemble that turned the absence of a rhythm section to their advantage. Although the players were influenced by the free jazz of Ornette Coleman and Albert Ayler, they also relied heavily on both composed music and traditional styles of improvisation. The four saxophonists produced a remarkable cross-section of twentieth-century music, incorporating elements of bebop, swing, and collective improvisation into an eclectic mix that ranged from the sound of the Ellington saxophone section to that of Stravinsky-style ballet.

A long-lived group, the World Saxophone Quartet has continued to perform in recent years. They are highly effective in concert, with a marked variety of programming and a lighthearted, engaging stage manner. Recent projects of the WSQ have included other musicians, especially drummers and African percussionists.

SUN RA

A unique jazz personality, Sun Ra led a legendary big band called the Myth-Science Solar Arkestra—one among several of its varied, but similar names. Established in the mid-1950s, the Arkestra played "intergalactic music" that painted "pictures of infinity." It also contained numerous musicians loyal to Sun Ra, the music, and its uniquely mystical ambience. With the players and audiences chanting "Space is the Place," the band's performances were transcendental. As his reputation continues to grow, Sun Ra has emerged as one of the most colorful and discussed pioneers of the avant-garde.

Courtesy Morgan Collection

Shown here at an electric keyboard and clad in exotic garb, avant-garde bandleader Sun Ra was one of the few big-band leaders to allow free improvisation.

Sun Ra made wide-ranging contributions to the music. He was one of the first jazz performers to use electric keyboards and synthesizers and was one of the few big-band leaders to encourage extensive free improvisation. The group was especially imaginative with percussion, exploring a large palette of sound colors with timpani, celesta, bells, chimes, and other instruments less often heard in jazz. The emphasis on unusual timbre extended to nonpercussive instruments as well: Sun Ra's saxophonists doubled on such instruments as piccolo, oboe, bassoon, and bass clarinet. As alto saxophonist Marion Brown noted, "Sun Ra plays the piano, but his real instrument is the orchestra."[21]

Sun Ra, however, remained an underground phenomenon, never achieving mainstream success. He was born Herman Blount in Birmingham, Alabama, in 1914 and moved to Chicago in the mid-1940s, working as the arranger-pianist Le Sony'r Ra in a variety theater. Between 1946 and 1947 he played piano for bandleader Fletcher Henderson. He then formed his own band; among his musicians were tenor saxophonist John Gilmore, who became a long-standing associate and who would later influence John Coltrane. The Arkestra's first recordings were from the mid-1950s.

Microtones are pitches between the tempered notes of the chromatic scale, used in nontempered intonation.

The use of *microtonal* melodies and electronic effects enhanced the space-age aura of Sun Ra's music, as did his flowing robes and headdresses. Sun Ra's live performances recalled the "happenings" of the 1960s, complete with the psychedelic paraphernalia. Sun Ra died in 1993.

ERIC DOLPHY

Perhaps no saxophonist has managed the borderline between hard bop and free jazz as convincingly as Eric Dolphy has. In parlance that was new at the time, Dolphy was equally convincing at playing both "inside" and "outside." That is, he could move "outside" the harmonic progressions—with pitches not part of the given chord or mode—then deftly return "inside" to take up the harmonies. Dolphy's album titles, *Outward Bound* and *Out to Lunch,* punned on the notion of "outside" playing.

Dolphy (1928–1964) performed on alto saxophone, flute, and bass clarinet. On alto, Dolphy developed an original sound, characterized by wide intervallic leaps, unusual phrasing that often floated untethered from the beat, and the use of glissandi, smears, and untempered intonation. His influences ranged from Ornette Coleman to African and Indian music. He even attempted, he said, to imitate the music of birds.[22] His flute playing, while original, was more traditional. As his work with John Coltrane on "India" (from *Impressions*) and with Ornette Coleman on *Free Jazz* revealed, Dolphy was also an outstanding virtuoso on bass clarinet, helping generate interest in an instrument fairly new to jazz settings.

Joining the quartet of Chico Hamilton in 1958, Dolphy made his first important musical alliance. He recorded *Gongs East* with Hamilton, a West Coast drummer (discussed in Chapter 5), whose ensemble was notable for including a cellist. After moving to New York in 1959, Dolphy began to work with Charles Mingus; this association lasted until Dolphy's untimely death in 1964. Earlier, we heard Dolphy's alto solo on Mingus's "Hora Decubitis," which bordered on free jazz (CD 2, Track 6).

Dolphy's work on Ornette Coleman's trailblazing *Free Jazz* solidified his reputation as a major presence in the jazz avant-garde; even so, he never abandoned more-traditional settings. Amazingly, on the same day that he recorded *Free Jazz*— December 21, 1960—Dolphy also recorded his own album *Far Cry*. (See the box "Eric Dolphy and Booker Little" on the facing page.)

An invitation to Dolphy to join the John Coltrane Quartet between 1961 and 1962 led to controversy, eliciting the negative label of "anti-jazz" from critics who thought the solos too long, anarchistic, and unswinging. Of course, Coltrane had a more positive view: He insisted that Dolphy's inclusion in the group "had a broadening effect on us. There are a lot of things we try now that we never tried before. . . . We're playing things that are freer than before."[23]

Dolphy was also involved in third-stream and twentieth-century concert music; for example, he performed on Gunther Schuller's 1960 recording *Abstractions*. His interest in the European avant-garde led to a performance of Edgard Varèse's *Density 21.5* for unaccompanied flute at the Ojai Music Festival in California. After touring Europe with Mingus in 1964, Dolphy elected to remain abroad rather than return to the United States. Shortly after, he died in Berlin from a heart attack brought on by diabetes.

Eric Dolphy and Booker Little

Far Cry featured Booker Little, a trumpeter who maintained a close musical relationship with Dolphy until Little's tragic death in 1961 at age twenty-three. A hard bop player from Memphis, Little began his career as a devotee of Clifford Brown. He recorded his first albums with the Max Roach Quintet before he was twenty years old. Little's playing was technically polished, lyrical, and creative.

Dolphy took part in Little's own recording for Candid records, *Out Front*. The two also collaborated on a gig at the Five Spot, which was recorded and released in a series of albums. On the Five Spot recordings, the influence of Dolphy on Little is clear—Little often adopted Dolphy's flurry-of-notes approach.

Although critics often focused on the radical elements in Dolphy's playing, his musical collaborators considered Dolphy's breadth enormous and maintained that he was in complete control of all the musical elements. Pianist Jaki Byard remembered:

Eric's freedom in playing and writing is never chaos. He always makes sense, and those critics who call him disorganized should first have the chords and the overall forms of his tunes written out for them before they make that kind of accusation. Eric is very well organized, but it's not the kind of organization that is immediately apparent to people who are accustomed to more conventional ideas of form.[24]

The 1960s Mainstream

Having discussed some of the avant-garde musicians in the 1960s, we now turn to the evolution of the more mainstream jazz styles and musicians who prospered in the 1960s. Again, we must point out that there was mutual influence between the avant-garde and mainstream, with some artists, like Coltrane, straddling both. No artist had a greater impact on the development of jazz in the 1960s than Miles Davis.

Miles Davis in the Sixties

Miles Davis flowed on a flood tide of activity into the 1960s, garnering immense critical success as his band evolved into one of the most notable groups in jazz. Early in the decade, his group underwent several changes of personnel. Coltrane's departure in 1960 was an enormous loss for Davis, though Davis eventually hired Hank Mobley as a replacement. With Art Blakey and Horace Silver, Mobley (1930–1986) helped found the Jazz Messengers. He performed with Davis from 1961 to 1962, then continued a distinguished career through the 1960s and beyond.

Along with Mobley, Davis used Jamaican pianist Wynton Kelly (1931–1971). Kelly's improvisations displayed a sparkling sense of swing. Although his harmonies were typically less lush and dense than those of Bill Evans, in his ballad playing some Evans-style voicings could be detected beneath Davis's poignant, muted trumpet. These two sides to Kelly—his exuberant, joyful swing and his sophisticated harmonic sense—earned him high praise from Davis, who described his work as "a combination of Red Garland and Bill Evans."[25] Davis also praised Kelly's accompanying ability: His rhythmically subtle and creative comping anticipated and complemented the soloist.

At this time Davis was only in his mid-thirties, but he found himself in the odd position of seeming to be old-fashioned. Ornette Coleman, Cecil Taylor, and Eric Dolphy were stirring up the jazz world with their challenging and controversial innovations. At the same time that Coleman was launching his radical *Free Jazz,* Davis's repertory remained rooted in 32-bar standards, 12-bar blues, and ballads. Davis's rhythm section of Kelly on piano, Jimmy Cobb on drums, and Paul Chambers on bass was a fine, swinging unit, but the group projected a conventional hard bop approach.

This soon changed. In 1963 Davis formed the nucleus of a group that would stay together for the next five years. His most dramatic move was to revitalize his rhythm section by taking on younger players. On piano, he hired twenty-three-year-old Herbie Hancock, who had been recording under his own name as a leader for Blue Note. Ron Carter, an accomplished classical and jazz bassist, left trumpeter Art Farmer to join Davis. Davis's most astonishing choice was an incredibly young drummer from Boston, Tony Williams, who joined the group at age seventeen. Despite his youth, Williams already showed flawless technique, consistent creativity, and fierce drive. Even on their earliest recordings, the new Davis rhythm section was stunning. Hancock, Carter, and Williams interacted at nearly telepathic levels, bringing fresh, free interpretations to Davis's traditional repertory.

Given the group's unparalleled polish and technical aplomb, listeners often missed their high level of creativity. On one of their earliest recordings—Victor Feldman's "Joshua," from *Seven Steps to Heaven*—the rhythm section shifted seamlessly between the 4/4 meter of the A section and the 3/4 meter of the B section. On ballad performances such as "My Funny Valentine" and "Stella By Starlight," the three players rapidly juggled moods and tempos, freely interpreting the harmonic structure to create what sounded like a multimovement suite.

Williams's interest in the jazz avant-garde had a major impact on the group, as Hancock later acknowledged:

> Tony Williams turned me on to different rhythms, overlapping this and that. Tony was really into Paul Bley, Gary Peacock . . . Ornette [Coleman]—like I never paid that much attention to Ornette when he first came out, but Tony got me interested in Ornette and got me to the point where I could get into it.[26]

Although the rhythm section was in place, Davis was unable to settle quickly on a tenor saxophone player. Finally, in the fall of 1964, Davis hired the player he had been after for several years, Wayne Shorter. With this final addition, Davis's group was set. "Getting Wayne made me feel real good," remembered Davis, "because with him I just knew some great music was going to happen. And it did; it happened real soon."[27]

Courtesy Morgan Collection

A Ron Carter publicity shot from CTI Records.

Davis had been trying to lure Shorter into his band since 1960, but Shorter was reluctant to leave Art Blakey's Jazz Messengers. When he finally joined Davis, Shorter began contributing numerous compositions, significantly altering the sound and approach of the group. On tenor, he owed his tone quality and musical ideas in part to Coltrane, although Shorter's melodies were more oblique and filled with space.

With Davis, Shorter, Hancock, Carter, and Williams on board, the group was now stabilized. They tended to emphasize popular standards in live performance and Shorter's compositions in the studio. An outstanding example of their live work is *The Complete Live at the Plugged Nickel,* which, although recorded in December 1965, was not released in the United States until the 1990s. On it we can hear the Davis quintet pushing the envelope on the performance of well-known jazz and popular standards.

Shorter's compositions were also unusual. Avoiding the standard harmonic clichés of the hard bop idiom, he instead explored imaginative melodies, voicings, progressions, and forms. For example, Shorter's composition "Nefertiti" radically reversed the roles of horn soloists and rhythm section: The trumpet and saxophone merely restated the slow-moving 16-bar melody throughout, providing a static obbligato, while the "accompanying instruments"—the piano, bass, and drums—improvised beneath, providing the active role. Although Shorter wrote the majority of compositions for the quintet, all of the members contributed tunes.

Hancock must have been surprised when, at a Davis recording session toward the end of 1967, he was confronted with an unknown instrument:

> I walked into the studio and I didn't see any acoustic piano. I saw this little box sitting there, this little toy, so I said, "Miles, where's the piano?" He said . . . "I want you to play this." . . . So I tested it and I heard this sound—this big mellow sound coming out. . . . I liked it right away.[28]

The instrument was a Fender Rhodes electric piano. Davis's first recording with Fender Rhodes was the 1968 release *Miles in the Sky,* and his continued use of the instrument signaled the onset of an inexorable trend: a gradual shift to rhythms influenced by rock, pop, and soul music. For Davis fans finally acclimated to the innovations of the 1963–1968 quintet, this newer, rock-influenced music was difficult to swallow, but for Davis it was only the beginning. With this move to rock and funk came a shift to electric instruments.

Davis's *In a Silent Way* was even more radical, presenting music that was both harmonically and rhythmically far simpler than Davis's previous work. The riff-oriented album featured three electric keyboardists—Herbie Hancock, Chick Corea, and Josef Zawinul—as well as British guitarist John McLaughlin.

Joe Zawinul (CD 2, Track 14) signed this promotional postcard for a fan in Switzerland.

Courtesy Morgan Collection

In place of the usual recorded performances of individual compositions, *In a Silent Way* was assembled by producer Teo Macero, who edited the studio sessions to create two compositions, each of which took up the entire side of an LP.

In addition to experimentation in the studio, Davis continued to perform live with his quintet. Although Shorter remained, the rhythm section was interested in moving on and gave notice. Hancock was replaced by pianist Chick Corea, Ron Carter by British bassist Dave Holland, and Tony Williams by Jack DeJohnette. At the same time, Davis was increasingly drawn to the popular rock and soul music of James Brown, Jimi Hendrix, and Sly and the Family Stone, as well as Cannonball Adderley's soul jazz hit, "Mercy, Mercy, Mercy."

Davis's next studio recording, *Bitches Brew,* was pivotal. From here on, his music centered on rock-based rhythms and completely abandoned the 4/4 swing feel that had defined his music for twenty-five years. The compositions amalgamated rock and soul influences; a steady, insistent rock or funk beat underscored the freewheeling improvisations by Davis or bass clarinetist Bennie Maupin. Davis also augmented the group's personnel, often including three drummers and a percussionist to create a densely textured and layered rhythmic foundation. The recording sold well, although most of the tracks were long and uncompromising. With *Bitches Brew,* Davis created a significant landmark on the road to the jazz-rock fusion of the 1970s. We shall complete Davis's story in Chapter 7, which is devoted to fusion.

Pianists

As we have seen, several keyboard artists made their mark in the jazz world of the 1960s. Here we look at Bill Evans, Herbie Hancock, Chick Corea, and Keith Jarrett.

BILL EVANS

When Miles Davis's *Kind of Blue* was released in 1959, his listeners were introduced to a young, recently established pianist whose identity at the keyboard was in its own way as individual as Thelonious Monk's. Bill Evans's pianism— his dense, impressionistic voicings, his dreamy, introspective moodiness, his singing lyricism— appeared fresh and original. Despite its apparent uniqueness, Evans's style was rooted in the work of Lennie Tristano, Bud Powell, and Horace Silver,

Pianist Bill Evans (CD 2, Track 12) was a lyrical, poetic player whose improvisations also elasticized the underlying meter.

as suggested by Evans's early recordings. The refined harmonic language of George Shearing also contributed to Evans's stylistic heritage.

Born in 1929, Evans was from Plainfield, New Jersey. As a teenager, he listened to swing and bop, and he occasionally played piano in local bands. Following high school, Evans attended Southeastern Louisiana University with a scholarship for classical piano—an interesting choice of school for a future jazz musician from the Northeast. After Southeastern Louisiana, Evans was drafted, served in the army, then moved to New York in 1956. He attended the Mannes College of Music for a semester and recorded his own albums *New Jazz Conceptions* (1956) and *Everybody Digs Bill Evans* (1958).

Evans joined Miles Davis's sextet in 1958, performing on Davis's *Jazz at the Plaza* and the profoundly influential *Kind of Blue*. As with so many other sidemen, Evans found that his stint with Davis incisively enhanced his visibility and reputation; he was to remain at the forefront of jazz piano for the remainder of his career.

Drastically redefining postbop piano, Evans was praised for the poetic beauty of his playing, which was enhanced by his sensitivity to dynamic shadings. His ballad performances exhibited a rich harmonic vocabulary, often whispered at remarkably soft dynamic levels. On solo piano recordings, Evans brought to the fore sophisticated techniques, frequently reharmonizing the chord progressions with compelling originality. Even Evans's posture at the piano—hunched over the keyboard, listening intently to each and every note—seemed to symbolize his elusive quest for musical transcendence.

Evans generally avoided working with larger groups, preferring the trio format of piano, bass, and drums. Sophisticated listeners heard an unprecedented level of interaction among the members of the group, particularly because of Evans's uncanny ability to develop long, even phrases that stretched across bar lines and avoided emphasized downbeats. To superficial listeners, Evans's style was merely pretty, but beneath the elegant veneer were a sensibility and a formal control that number among the very best in jazz.

Evans preferred sidemen who could interact with him rather than merely provide accompaniment. His bassists were usually virtuoso soloists in their own right who often played in the upper registers of the instrument.

Setting the standard for future groups, Evans's landmark trio was formed in 1959. It consisted of an unusually sensitive and coloristic drummer, Paul Motian, and a superb twenty-three-year-old bassist, Scott LaFaro. Evans's phrases were sometimes separated by dramatic pauses that were themselves punctuated by Motian's drumming and LaFaro's countermelodies. With all the members contributing to the musical conversation, the trio frequently broke up the sense of regular metric flow, a key aspect of Evans's style. He expressed this concern in an interview with pianist Marian McPartland for her radio show, "Piano Jazz":

> As far as the jazz playing goes, I think the rhythmic construction of the thing has evolved quite a bit. Now, I don't know how obvious that would be to the listener, but the displacement of phrases and . . . the way phrases follow one another and their placement against the meter . . . is something that I've worked on rather hard and it's something I believe in.[29]

L I S T E N I N G   G U I D E

"Peri's Scope"

CD **2**   Track **12**

Bill Evans Trio: "Peri's Scope" (Evans), from *Portrait in Jazz*. Riverside RLP-1162.
New York, December 28, 1959. Bill Evans, piano; Scott LaFaro, bass; Paul Motian, drums.

Sophisticated use of meter was a feature not only of Evans's improvisation but also of his compositions. For example, in the head to "Peri's Scope," the melody sometimes contradicts the 4/4 meter, implying a different meter (3/4).

Head—Irregular 24 bars

0:00   The performance begins at the top of the head without introduction.

0:15   Beginning in measure 13, the implied 3/4 rhythm becomes part of the tune, continuing for four 4/4 bars.

0:29   Here there is a two-bar break for Evans to set up his solo.

Evans piano solo—4 choruses

0:31   Evans begins his solo developing a two-note idea before moving to longer lines. Listen for Evans's dynamic shadings during his eighth-note ideas and for the interplay between Evans's left-hand chordal punctuation and Motian's snare drum accents.

2:14–2:37   Evans moves away from single hornlike melodies to chordal textures.

Restatement of head

2:37   Evans's solo flows directly into the restatement of the head. The implied 3/4 meter returns from measures 13–16. The performance ends directly without a coda.

Like many other jazz musicians, Evans wrote numerous compositions, many of which have become jazz standards. He was particularly fond of waltz time (3/4), which was not often heard in traditional jazz performances, and he composed many jazz waltzes, including the popular "Waltz for Debby."

Evans's landmark group came to end, unfortunately, when Scott LaFaro died in a car accident in July 1961. This tragedy dealt Evans a severe musical and personal blow. Although only twenty-five at the time, LaFaro had come close to revolutionizing the role of the bass within the context of the jazz trio. (He had also taken part in the groundbreaking *Free Jazz* sessions with Ornette Coleman.)

Not all of Evans's recordings were with piano trio. For example, his unique 1963 *Conversations with Myself* included solo piano tracks on which Evans overdubbed himself, often in three layers consisting of a bass line, mid-range accompanying chords, and upper solo and melodic lines. Evans's solo piano albums—such as *Alone* (1968) and *Alone (Again)* (1975)—usually emphasized American popular standards, a repertory much beloved by Evans. In particular, Evans liked to interpret slow, dreamy ballads, though occasional faster tempos provided variety.

Evans recorded two duo albums with a remarkably compatible guitarist, Jim Hall (b. 1930), titled *Undercurrent* (1959) and *Intermodulation* (1966). Hall, who achieved recognition through working with both Evans and Sonny Rollins, became one of the premier guitar stylists of the 1960s and still remains at the forefront of jazz guitarists.

Rhythmically and harmonically, Evans profoundly affected the major pianists of the 1960s. Interestingly, many of these pianists—such as Herbie Hancock, Chick Corea, and Keith Jarrett—also worked as sidemen for Miles Davis. From Evans they picked up sophisticated techniques of chord voicings and the manipulation of rhythm and meter. Unfortunately, Evans died at age fifty-one in 1980, succumbing to years of drug and alcohol abuse. Regardless of his early death, Evans was arguably the most influential postbebop pianist of the 1960s.

The sixties witnessed the coming of age of three of the most important jazz pianists of the latter half of the twentieth century. Traces of Bill Evans's approach to the keyboard can be heard in the work of Herbie Hancock, Chick Corea, and Keith Jarrett, but each is also a remarkably innovative player in his own right, with distinct styles as well as varying musical interests.

HERBIE HANCOCK

From 1963 to 1968, Herbie Hancock formed part of Miles Davis's legendary quintet. With performances that were consistently creative, fresh, and versatile, he remained one of the most sought-after pianists for studio recordings throughout the 1960s.

Born in 1940 in Chicago, Hancock was a child prodigy. At age eleven, he performed the first movement of a Mozart piano concerto with the Chicago Symphony Orchestra in a young people's concert. After graduating from Grinnell College, Hancock found himself in demand as a pianist in Chicago. Joining the quintet of trumpeter Donald Byrd, Hancock moved to New York in the early 1960s. On his early Blue Note recordings with Byrd, he assimilated a vast array of styles, from the blues-based approach of funky jazz to the harmonic sophistication and refined lyricism of Bill Evans. He even experimented with classically based compositional principles, which he learned while a music composition major at Grinnell.

Courtesy Morgan Collection

A signed Herbie Hancock (CD 2, Track 13) publicity photograph. Hancock's own Blue Note recordings and his work with the Miles Davis Quintet left many listeners unprepared for his phenomenal success in jazz-rock fusion in the 1970s.

Hancock recorded his first album as a leader for Blue Note in 1962: *Takin' Off*. With its characteristic two horns and rhythm section, *Takin' Off* was a typical hard bop LP, but Hancock's catchy, bluesy composition "Watermelon Man" became a popular hit, making it to the Top 100 of the popular-music charts.

Once he became a member of the Miles Davis Quintet, Hancock continued to record as a leader for Blue Note. By embracing more open-ended improvisations, fewer chord changes, and subtle metric shifts, Hancock moved away from the standard hard bop feel of his first recordings. On *Empyrean Isles,* for example, the most radical composition, "The Egg," incorporated passages of free improvisation.

Hancock's "Dolphin Dance" from *Maiden Voyage* became well known. Its melody grew out of the opening four-note motive, while the complex harmonic progression featured shifting chords over *pedal points* in the bass. Ballads such as "Dolphin Dance"

A ***pedal point*** is a sustained or repeated bass note or drone played to accompany a melody. Harmonies may also shift over pedal points.

Courtesy Morgan Collection

A driving pianist and inventive composer, Chick Corea gradually moved toward electric keyboards during his work with Miles Davis in the late 1960s. His group Return to Forever was one of the celebrated fusion groups of the 1970s.

A *pentatonic scale* is a five-note set that avoids the interval of a tritone and can be arranged as a series of perfect fourths or perfect fifths. The black notes of the keyboard form one such scale.

most fully revealed the connection to Bill Evans in Hancock's style, but his projection of Evans's harmonic palette was enhanced by Hancock's more ambitious textural and tonal sense. Evans responded to his trio but tended to think like a soloist, whereas Hancock seemed to listen to and anticipate his accompaniment more perceptively than Evans did. Evans worked with a sense of absolute stylistic command, whereas Hancock always seemed to be reaching, trying to stretch his harmonic concept to the very limit.

This continual searching perhaps led to Hancock's eventual disillusionment with the modern modal style, which he thought had become too abstract and not responsive enough to the audience. In the early 1970s, he found a release in the repetition, heavy beat, and electronic orientation of jazz-rock funk. Before Hancock's plunge into fusion, however, and before he departed from Davis's touring band, Hancock recorded several important acoustic albums during the 1960s, including *Speak Like a Child* and *The Prisoner*.

Hancock turned exclusively to electric keyboards with his sextet of 1971–1973, playing synthesizer and even featuring a second synthesist. With its electronic sounds, the group seemed to evoke the "space music" of Sun Ra in extended improvisations. Hancock's phenomenal commercial success coincided with his 1973 fusion album *Headhunters* (see Chapter 7).

CHICK COREA

Like Hancock, Chick Corea is a significant composer as well as pianist. A less subtle player than Hancock, Corea developed a steely, percussive touch, particularly on his early recordings, where the influence of John Coltrane's pianist, McCoy Tyner, strongly appeared.

Corea was born in 1938 in Chelsea, Massachusetts. His father was a gigging musician, and he was raised in a musical atmosphere. Corea received early professional experience in the Afro-Cuban bands of Willie Bobo and Mongo Santamaria; not surprisingly, much of his later work reflected Latin and Afro-Cuban music. Corea's first recording as a leader came in 1966, when he made *Tones for Joan's Bones*.

As his playing on Stan Getz's *Sweet Rain* made clear, Corea could be sensitive and lush, but his hard-driving, staccato style was especially influential. Like McCoy Tyner, Corea favored *pentatonic scales* and harmonies based on open fourths. These stylistic attributes came to infuse both his improvisations and his compositions.

In 1968 Corea replaced Herbie Hancock in Miles Davis's group, where he was quickly swept into the jazz-rock experiments of the late 1960s. Despite his initial reluctance to play anything other than acoustic piano with the group, he often performed on the Fender Rhodes electric piano. "At first, Miles kind of pushed the Fender piano in front of me against my will," Corea admitted, "and I resisted. But then I started liking it, especially being able to turn up the volume and combat the drummer."[30]

Two years later, Corea left Davis and returned for a while to acoustic piano. The album *Song of Singing* featured an acoustic trio that strongly reflected the jazz avant-garde. In 1971 Corea augmented his group with the alto/soprano saxophonist Anthony Braxton. The quartet, called Circle, recorded a concert in Paris that was largely given over to free improvisation. The tension between traditional and free playing also arose in Corea's two solo piano albums recorded in the early 1970s, *Piano Improvisations,* volumes 1 and 2.

Corea returned to electric keyboards in the early 1970s and soon became one of the key figures in the jazz fusion movement. We shall resume his story as well in Chapter 7.

KEITH JARRETT AND ECM RECORDS

Like Herbie Hancock and Chick Corea, Keith Jarrett is a significant and innovative pianist whose career began in the 1960s. Although Jarrett made some recordings on electric piano—particularly during his tenure with Miles Davis between 1969 and 1971—he has dedicated himself almost exclusively to the acoustic instrument as the vehicle for his widely heralded, virtuosic performances. Jarrett's playing is eclectic, bringing to the piano not only elements of traditional jazz but also free jazz and traces of classical, folk, and gospel music. Like Hancock and Corea, Jarrett was inspired by the lyricism of Bill Evans, but he also cultivated a freer, open-ended style of playing. Further, Jarrett possesses a *legato,* classically based touch on the piano, a technique that has served him well in widely publicized performances and recordings of works in the European concert tradition.

Legato is the technique of playing notes smoothly in a connected manner. The opposite of legato is *staccato*.

Born in Allentown, Pennsylvania, in 1945, Jarrett began playing at age three; by seven he was already composing and improvising. He moved to Boston after receiving a scholarship from the Berklee College of Music in 1962. Although he attended Berklee only a year, he remained in Boston, playing gigs until moving to New York in 1965. There, he and his wife were nearly penniless until Art Blakey heard him at a jam session. Jarrett joined Blakey's band and recorded the album *Buttercorn Lady* with the group in 1966.

As a member of the Charles Lloyd Quartet between 1966 and 1969, Jarrett received full rein to explore his experimental tendencies and eclectic musical interests. Lloyd (b. 1938) was a West Coast tenor saxophonist whose quartet was astonishingly successful. At the height of the 1960s "flower power" era, his followers consisted of not only jazz fans but also teenagers who thronged to hear the group at rock venues such as the Fillmore Auditorium in San Francisco. Lloyd was something of a guru to the flower children. "I play love vibrations," he insisted in the liner notes to the aptly titled record *Love-In.* "Love, totality—like bringing everyone together in a joyous dance."[31]

Jarrett's performances with Lloyd's quartet dazzled audiences and critics. After leaving Lloyd, Jarrett played electric piano and organ during his eighteen months with Miles Davis, yet he rarely performed on electric instruments after that.

The eclecticism of Jarrett's work grew especially pronounced in the 1970s. Throughout the quartet recordings, Jarrett drew on the whole tradition of piano improvisation, including traditional jazz. For example, a ragtime-inspired solo piano

ECM Records

An important label that issued Jarrett recordings and became one of the most prominent exponents of nonfusion music during the 1970s and 1980s was ECM Records. Founded in Cologne, Germany, in 1969 by Manfred Eicher, ECM released albums by such U.S.-based jazz artists as pianists Keith Jarrett, Paul Bley, and Chick Corea, as well as vibraphonist Gary Burton and guitarist Pat Metheny. Additionally, the label sponsored European jazz players such as Norwegian saxophonist Jan Garbarek and bassist Eberhard Weber.

Some jazz critics and jazz musicians dismissed ECM's music as atmospheric "Euro-jazz"—sterile, moody, cerebral, introspective, and overly refined—a precursor to the New Age music that arose in the 1980s on labels such as Windham Hill. Nevertheless, the ECM label maintained consistently high standards of musicianship and also released recordings best characterized as free jazz. Far from having a single distinctive sound, ECM has represented a wide array of jazz performers and styles.

composition entitled "Pardon My Rags" appeared on *The Mourning of a Star*. Jarrett's 1972 recording *Expectations* included free improvisations and gospel-tinged works, along with pieces for string orchestra and piano.

In contrast to most contemporary jazz pianists, Jarrett explored solo piano performance extensively. By 1973, Jarrett began performing live solo concerts, which generally comprised extended, freely improvised works. Many of these lasted an entire side (or longer) of an LP. (See the box "ECM Records" above.) Jarrett's approach to the keyboard was nearly orgiastic; at times he would stand, grimace, and writhe, and he sometimes sang along with his melodies or moaned between phrases. Jarrett has been taken to task for both his emotional extravagance and his lack of editing. For example, his recording *Sun Bear Concerts* is a ten-record set assembled from five different concerts in Japan.

Some of Jarrett's work in the 1970s was tangential to the jazz mainstream. For example, his album *In the Light* included compositions for string orchestra, brass quintet, and string quartet. Since the 1980s, Jarrett has largely returned to comparatively straight-ahead jazz. His trio with bassist Gary Peacock and drummer Jack DeJohnette has been devoted to recording the standard jazz repertory with chorus structures, chord changes, and regular meter. Though partially incapacitated with chronic fatigue syndrome in the late 1990s, Jarrett continues as a major force in jazz piano.

Funky/Soul Jazz

The *funky jazz* tunes recorded in the 1950s by such groups as Art Blakey's Jazz Messengers and the Horace Silver Quintet were infectious blues-based works steeped in the gospel tradition. As noted in Chapter 5, gospel singing and blues-based music provided two significant influences for funky jazz. During the 1960s, funky jazz continued to attract musicians who preferred more-direct communication with audiences than either cool jazz or free jazz could provide. The term *soul jazz* came about after 1960; it was initially used by Riverside Records to promote the Cannonball Adderley Quintet.

CANNONBALL ADDERLEY

Julian "Cannonball" Adderley (1928–1975) was a superb alto saxophonist from Tampa, Florida. After he moved to New York and appeared in various venues, his growing prominence led to an invitation to join Miles Davis's group in 1957, where he remained until 1959. Adderley was a major factor in the success of Davis's important *Milestones* and *Kind of Blue* albums, in which he helped balance the lyricism of Davis and the emotional intensity of Coltrane. After leaving Davis, Adderley formed his own group with his younger brother, cornetist Nat Adderley (b. 1931).

The Adderley group specialized in both bebop and funky/soul jazz. The latter included such well-known tunes as Nat Adderley's "Work Song," which featured call-and-response between the rhythm section and the horns in imitation of a chain gang. In 1966 Adderley's popular hit "Mercy, Mercy, Mercy," written by Austrian pianist Josef Zawinul, incorporated a funky rock beat throughout.

THE BLUES IN FUNKY/SOUL JAZZ

The funky jazz tunes recorded in the 1950s by such groups as Art Blakey's Jazz Messengers and the Horace Silver Quintet were infectious blues-based works steeped in the gospel tradition. As noted in Chapter 5, gospel singing and blues-based music provided two significant influences for funky jazz. One important influence for the funky jazz players of the 1950s and 1960s was the blind singer-pianist Ray Charles (b. 1930), who injected heartfelt soulful singing into rhythm and blues. Charles also recorded with jazz artists such as vibraphonist Milt Jackson, and he earned commercial success with hits that included "What'd I Say" and "Georgia on My Mind."

In stark contrast to the avant-garde wing of jazz, some of the funky/soul jazz of the 1960s was commercially quite successful. After his 1963 hit "Watermelon Man,"

Singer-pianist Ray Charles. Charles's earthy, blues-based music influenced many of the funky/soul jazz players.

Courtesy Morgan Collection

which reached the Top 100 of the popular-music charts, Herbie Hancock later recalled that on his subsequent albums he tried to include at least one tune with the even eighth notes of funky/soul jazz.[32] Also in 1963, hard bop trumpeter Lee Morgan recorded a successful hit with "The Sidewinder," a catchy, instrumental blues with a funky/soul-jazz feel.

The 12-bar blues was the mainstay of much funky/soul jazz, particularly the music played by the jazz organists who sprang up during the late 1950s. Although Fats Waller recorded wonderful jazz solos on the pipe organ in the late twenties, musicians generally thought that the organ was not well suited to jazz because the attack of the notes was extremely smooth and lacked the bite usually heard in jazz phrasing. Beginning in 1935, the Hammond company manufactured an electronic organ, which, though imposing, was portable—unlike the traditional pipe organ, which was usually found only in churches and theaters. By the fifties the electronic organ had become a mainstay in black churches and the backbone of modern gospel music. As a result of its practicality and popularity, the electronic organ soon found its way into black neighborhood clubs, where it was often heard in a trio setting with saxophone and drums. Instead of using a bass player, the organist could play bass lines with either the feet or the left hand.

Courtesy Morgan Collection

Jimmy Smith, organist, in a smooth publicity pose.

JIMMY SMITH AND JAZZ ORGANISTS

One of the most influential jazz organists to emerge in the late 1950s was Jimmy Smith, who was born in Norristown, Pennsylvania, in 1925. His New York debut took place at the Cafe Bohemia in 1956, but his international career lifted off after a performance at the Newport Jazz Festival in 1957. Even the titles of Smith's albums, such as *The Sermon* and *Prayer Meetin',* emphasized the gospel origins of the music.

Smith's approach to the organ set the standard for the instrument. Although Smith used bebop tunes on his earliest albums, he gravitated toward the blues, combining blistering right-hand runs against bass lines played by his left hand and feet. He made abundant use of idiomatic organ sounds, often sustaining a single high note above rapid-fire, sixteenth-note lines. Smith influenced virtually all subsequent jazz organists. Many, such as Brother Jack McDuff, Richard "Groove" Holmes, and Jimmy McGriff, maintained Smith's strutting approach to the blues.

GUITARISTS

Organists also showcased their guitarists, many of whom were strongly rooted in the blues. Kenny Burrell (b. 1931) had a mellow guitar sound; although he played fluently, he often preferred simple, singable lines, as heard on Jimmy Smith's recording *Midnight Special.* George Benson (b. 1943) created a major impact with his 1976 album *Breezin',* which became quite popular thanks to the hit recording of "This Masquerade." Benson began his career with organist Jack McDuff, whose bluesy orientation strongly influenced the guitarist:

> That was a value I learned in Jack McDuff's band, the value of playing everything with a little blues touch. You know, adding a bended note here and there, a little cry over there, a little glissando here. It really helped to give me a concept, something to build on.

Benson also acknowledged how jazz organists helped highlight guitarists:

> I think that's what really helped the guitar to come to the front . . . as far as jazz music is concerned, because there was never any real, dynamic guitar playing, except for exceptional guys like Wes Montgomery, and even he came by way of the organ at first. And Kenny Burrell and just a couple of others, but I think the organ gave the guitar a form. . . . It featured the guitar so much. Guys could really test themselves, and night after night they had to come with some interesting solos, so it was a good format for guitar players.[33]

Wes Montgomery (1923–1968) may have performed with organ trios, but he worked principally with mainstream jazz groups. Montgomery became known in the fifties from several albums recorded for Riverside. He later played with John Coltrane. During the mid-1960s, Montgomery became one of the best-known jazz guitarists with hit pop-jazz records, such as *Goin' Out of My Head* (1965) and *A Day in the Life* (1967).

The Hard Bop Legacy

During the 1960s, many jazz artists continued the tradition of hard bop, established in the 1950s. Here we look at four key players.

LEE MORGAN AND FREDDIE HUBBARD

Many of the artists who recorded on Blue Note in the 1960s began their careers with the Art Blakey and Horace Silver bands. Trumpeter Lee Morgan, born in Philadelphia in 1938, had a major hit, "The Sidewinder," in 1963; he wrote other important compositions as well. His album *Cornbread* contained a beautiful Latin-based composition, "Ceora." Morgan experimented with other tangents in modern jazz as well. For example, the title track from his *Search for the New Land*, with guitarist Grant Green, explored modal improvisation. Morgan died in 1972, murdered by his lover at a gig.

Morgan was replaced in the Jazz Messengers by trumpeter Freddie Hubbard (b. 1938), an equally fiery player whose tone was slightly mellower. Interestingly, Hubbard participated in several important free jazz recordings, including Coleman's *Free Jazz* and Coltrane's *Ascension*. Nonetheless, Hubbard's own Blue Note albums made during the early 1960s showed him to be a fundamentally more traditional player than the avant-garde musicians. Hubbard's work as a sideman on two of Herbie Hancock's Blue Note recordings, *Maiden Voyage* and *Empyrean Isles*, contained some of his finest work. After 1970, Hubbard turned to more commercially promising music, recording jazz-rock fusion and funk.

Courtesy Morgan Collection

Trumpeter Lee Morgan (CD 2, Track 5) was one of the many significant players to work with Art Blakey's Jazz Messengers. On his recordings for Blue Note Records, his own compositions touched on hard bop, funky/soul jazz, and modal jazz.

WAYNE SHORTER

Hubbard's band mate in Blakey's Messengers was tenor saxophonist Wayne Shorter. Shorter was born in 1933 in Newark, New Jersey. After earning a bachelor's degree in music education from New York University in 1956, Shorter worked with Horace Silver and Maynard Ferguson. Beginning in 1959, Shorter served as music director for the Jazz Messengers until his defection to Miles Davis in 1964.

Shorter's early Blue Note recordings were in the hard bop mainstream, but as both tenor player and composer he was attracted to the exploratory and experimental. In addition to modal compositions Shorter experimented with a funky/soul-jazz rhythmic feel on the title track to his quartet recording *Adam's Apple,* and he moved decisively toward free jazz playing on *The All Seeing Eye.* In recent years, Shorter has been writing for orchestra, often with pieces that feature himself as soloist. His work with the fusion group Weather Report is discussed in Chapter 7.

Free Jazz Styles

TIMBRE

▸ Emphasis often on hard-edged, tough sound
▸ Use of entire range of instrument, but upper range more prominent
▸ Wide variety of attacks and articulations
▸ Vocal sounds—cries, shrieks, etc.—used
▸ Extended techniques such as multiphonics on individual instruments emphasized

PHRASING

▸ Extremely irregular

RHYTHM

▸ Free use of extreme rhythms, from held notes to *sheets of sound* effects
▸ Syncopations
▸ Often lack of steady pulse

THEMATIC CONTINUITY

▸ Usually motivic

CHORD-SCALE RELATIONS

▸ Outside playing, if a tonal center exists at all

LARGE-SCALE COHERENCE

▸ Gestural, motivic, sometimes based on set theoretical principles

JOE HENDERSON

Another significant tenor saxophonist to emerge in the sixties was Joe Henderson, born in 1937 in Lima, Ohio. Henderson was a member of the Horace Silver Quintet between 1964 and 1966, appearing on Silver's best-known tune, "Song for My Father." On tenor, Henderson combined Coltrane's intensity with Sonny Rollins's motivic approach to improvisation.

In 1963 Henderson made his first recording for Blue Note, *Page One,* which included bebop trumpeter Kenny Dorham. The album featured Dorham's "Blue Bossa," which became a jazz standard, as well as Henderson's own Latin-based "Recorda Me." Henderson's subsequent recordings for Blue Note blended traditional hard bop instrumentation with modally based compositions, such as his 1966 *Mode for Joe.* He died in 2001.

Questions and Topics for Discussion

1. Which principal jazz pianists matured in the 1960s? Compare and contrast their styles.

2. How did the 1960s avant-garde overturn traditional practices in jazz? Cite factors that include instruments, repertory, melody, harmony, and rhythm.

3. How did the social movements that called for integration and the greater acceptance of blacks into mainstream society affect avant-garde jazz works? Can the word *freedom* be applied to both musical and political relationships? How?

4. Who were the principal musicians of the jazz avant-garde? How did these musicians differ in terms of their level of political involvement? Was this evident in their music?

5. What were John Coltrane's three stylistic periods? In a brief biographical outline, show how his musical evolution paralleled his spiritual and professional life.

Key Terms

Free jazz (avant-garde, New Thing) 189

Harmolodics 198

Legato 221

Microtones 212

Motivic cells 204

Multiphonics 193

Nontempered intonation 208

Ostinato 205

Pedal point 219

Pentatonic scale 220

Sheets of sound 200

Sound fields 206

Staccato 221

7

JAZZ-ROCK, JAZZ-FUNK FUSION

Jazz-rock, *jazz-funk*, or *fusion* is a form of jazz that combines elements of rock (or R&B funk) and jazz.

THE DEVELOPMENT of *jazz-rock* and *jazz-funk* fusion during the seventies remains controversial—even some thirty years later. *Fusion* involved the incorporation of rock, soul, and funk elements into jazz, and it drastically altered the musical directions of the postbop era. The key elements of jazz-rock and jazz-funk include the following:

- Replacement of the 4/4 swing feel with rock or funk rhythms
- Harmonies and progressions that were usually simpler and often characterized by a slow harmonic change or the use of long vamps
- Electric and electronic instruments as the norm; specifically:
  - ▶ Replacement of the acoustic bass with the electric bass guitar
  - ▶ Replacement of the piano with electric piano and synthesizers (so that "pianists" became "keyboardists")
  - ▶ Rise to prominence of the electric guitar as perhaps the most characteristic instrument of the fusion ensemble
- Intense amplification and use of electronic effects

An important element in fusion was the addition of the synthesizer to the ensemble. As synthesizers underwent development in the seventies and became less expensive and more convenient to play (smaller and more portable), the typical fusion ensemble became more likely to adopt them. (See the box "Synthesizers" at right.)

The Vietnam War and the space race between the United States and the former Soviet Union dominated headlines in the 1960s. In October 1957 the Soviets launched *Sputnik I*—the first satellite in space—and in April 1961 sent a capsule carrying Yuri Gagarin—the first man in space. Spurred by President John Kennedy, NASA intensified its efforts, and on July 20, 1969, Neil Armstrong landed the *Apollo 11* module on the moon. Meanwhile, 58,000 U.S. service personnel died in the Vietnam War between 1961 and 1973. Here, in an interesting conjunction of the two themes, Neil Armstrong greets troops in Vietnam on Christmas 1969. The soldier in the crowd is waving a copy of the *Moon Flight Atlas,* which Armstrong signed.

Synthesizers

Synthesizers were originally developed for musical use in the early 1950s. Unlike acoustic instruments, the synthesizer produced sound electronically: In analog synthesizers, an oscillator supplies a voltage to an amplifier, from which it is routed to a speaker. The earliest models—pioneered by RCA, Bell Laboratories, and European companies—were cumbersome; they did not have attached keyboards and were unsuitable for live performance.

In the sixties, manufacturers produced the first synthesizers that allowed keyboardists to conveniently control and manipulate the sound during live performances. During the seventies, synthesizers became cheaper and more compact, leading to the familiar sight of the rock band multi-keyboardist surrounded by stacks of electric pianos, synthesizers, mixers, and other gear. The Minimoog was perhaps the first widely used synthesizer, a standard keyboard accessory in rock bands and fusion groups in the early seventies.

The mid-seventies witnessed the dual breakthroughs of polyphonic and digital synthesizers. Polyphonic models enabled the keyboardist to play chords. Digital synthesizers were even more flexible: Their numerical translations of complex sound waves allowed for the creation of a greater number of timbres or sound qualities for each note.

In addition to synthesizers, *samplers* were gradually developed: When acoustic instrumental sounds (or in fact any kinds of sounds) are recorded and reproduced for musical use, the practice is known as *sampling*. These electronically stored recordings are referred to as *sound modules*.

Sampling is the practice of recording sounds for musical use in playback. Any kind of sound can be sampled, from a note on an acoustic instrument, to natural sounds, to a passage of music already recorded. For playback, the sound is usually activated by computer or by pressing a key on a keyboard. *Sound modules* play back prerecorded samples, which can be digitally stored in a computer for playback. *Samplers* are used both to sample and to play back sounds.

Curiously, even early jazz synthesizer solos reflected the instrument's potential. The synthesizer was then at the forefront of the developing jazz-rock and jazz-funk styles. Musicians were intrigued by the expressive qualities of the new instrument, and many imaginative solos were created.

In addition to adopting the new timbre of the synthesizer, jazz musicians began modifying the role of the electric guitar. The traditional mellow timbre of the hollow-body electric guitar had been defined by such players as Charlie Christian in the late 1930s and maintained in jazz through the sixties. In fusion, this sound was superseded by the steely, cutting timbre; the sustained notes; and often the distortion obtained from the solid-body electric guitar. (Listen to Tracks 39 and 40 of CD 1 🎧 to compare these sounds.) A common form of distortion was created by intentional *feedback*. Musicians such as Jimi Hendrix in the rock world showed how feedback could be controlled and used as a musical quality.

The radical changes of instrumental timbre associated with fusion were accompanied by changes in the roles of the players themselves. In particular, the concept of solo accompaniment was radically modified: Instead of the improvised comping of the pianist or guitarist, the group often relied on repeated vamps or ostinato figures (an *ostinato* is a repeated melodic or harmonic idea that forms the basis for a section or an entire composition).

For the most part, seventies jazz fusion can be broken down into either jazz-rock or jazz-funk. The latter term, though less common, was often more accurate because the music incorporated elements of R&B and funk more often than rock.

In a very general sense, differences between rock and funk are perhaps best understood by their rhythmic underpinning. Music Example 7-1 compares a rock drum pattern with a funk drum pattern.

Feedback is a distorted effect created when the sound coming from a speaker is picked up by the electronic sensing device of an instrument (or a microphone) and routed back to the speaker. As this process multiplies, harsh electronic wails are created. Feedback commonly (and annoyingly) occurs in PA systems when the microphones pick up the sound coming from the speakers.

Music Example 7-1
A rock drum pattern and a funk drum pattern.

The funk drum pattern is more complex because it is based on a sixteenth-note subdivision and incorporates more syncopation, whereas the rock rhythm is based on an eighth-note subdivision. As a result, funk music is more likely to be syncopated and rhythmically complex; rock music is generally less syncopated and often characterized by the use of "straight" or "even" eighth notes. Both drum patterns incorporate a heavy use of *backbeats,* almost always played on the snare drum.

The first experiments in fusion took place in the late sixties. Much of the impetus for and early development of the style came from Miles Davis and his sidemen. Davis's watershed albums *In a Silent Way* and *Bitches Brew,* both from 1969, helped introduce both electric keyboards and rock/R&B rhythms and harmonies to the jazz audience.

The first wave of popular jazz-rock groups in the early seventies—Mahavishnu Orchestra, Weather Report, Return to Forever, and Herbie Hancock's Headhunters— were formed by former Miles Davis sidemen. These groups earned extensive critical and popular acclaim. Using electronic instruments and the rhythmic grooves of rock

Backbeats are heavy emphases on beats 2 and 4, as played by the drummer (usually) on the snare drum. (Other drums or the hi-hat can be used for quieter backbeats.) Backbeats can be added to a 4/4 swing rhythm as well. Backbeats increase danceability by clarifying the rhythm and adding to the visceral excitement of the music.

and funk, these new groups displayed first-rate improvisational skills and strongly defined compositional structures. Recordings by these groups sold well, too, surpassing many of the musicians' expectations for commercial success. For the first time since the swing era, a form of jazz had become popular again.

Despite the potential of these early fusion groups, two trends occurred that helped, as musician/critic Bill Laswell described, "assassinate the promise of fusion"[1] during the second half of the seventies. The first negative trend was an overreliance on flashy but largely empty technique. Some of the fusion players relied on faster and faster playing in their improvisations. As guitarist Al DiMeola candidly admitted, "I really wanted to become the fastest guitarist in the world. Just like the track stars want to become the fastest runner in the world."[2]

The second negative trend in fusion's evolution was its commercialization. Whereas a typical jazz record might sell 10,000 to 20,000 copies, some of the most popular fusion records sold more than a million. To tap into this market, record companies put subtle—and sometimes not so subtle—pressure on musicians to simplify their music. The more commercially oriented fusion products gravitated toward slickly packaged, danceable, ingratiating music, with catchy melodic hooks replacing the substance of an improvisational or compositional core.

Because of these commercial trends, fusion musicians soon began to earn withering critical scorn for "selling out." For example, in a telling interview with keyboardist George Duke in 1977, *Down Beat* interviewer Lee Underwood soundly reprimanded Duke for his commercial leanings: "There are some artists who shoot for immortality," Underwood lectured, "not just for a heated swimming pool and a house in the Hollywood hills."[3]

Although some fusion artists continue to break new ground, one of the legacies of fusion—*smooth jazz*—is unabashedly oriented toward extensive radio airplay (see Chapter 8). Although it can be argued that smooth jazz is simply satisfying popular demand—much like the cookie-cutter swing tunes of the late 1930s—it can also be argued that latter-day fusion has not fulfilled its earlier artistic promise. Its detractors disdainfully refer to the music as "lite jazz," "hot-tub jazz," or "fuzak" (a contraction of *fusion* and *Muzak*).

Smooth jazz is a popular form of fusion jazz that is common today. It combines rock or funk grooves with an electronic ambience to create an "easy listening" feel. Although improvisation may be present, the pleasant quality of the groove and melody are its dominant features.

The Appeal of Rock and Funk

Many jazz musicians developed a fascination with rock and soul music as these styles developed during the sixties. These types of music were popular with youth to an unprecedented degree and largely embodied the rebellion of the sixties against the mores and values of the previous generation. The new generation of jazz musicians grew up listening to rock and funk; it was natural for them to incorporate these elements into their experimentation with jazz.

Soul and, later, funk developed out of rhythm and blues, which itself was the offspring of the so-called race records of prewar African-American music. The rhythm and blues of the 1940s embraced a danceable style with a heavy beat and often syncopated rhythms. As the sounds of the swing-era big bands faded away and bebop proved to be uncommercial, rhythm and blues filled the demand for popular music among black audiences.

The soul and funk groups of the sixties and early seventies strongly influenced the development of fusion. The band of singer James Brown, the self-proclaimed "hardest-working man in show business," featured horns, electric guitar, electric bass, and drums. Brown's hits such as "Papa's Got a Brand New Bag" and "I Feel Good" made prominent use of harmonies heard in jazz, such as ninth chords. Brown's music was also rhythmically complex, with a strong backbeat and highly syncopated, rhythmically interlocking parts. The dense interplay of the rhythm-section instruments in funk suggested a way for upcoming jazz-fusion players to integrate their jazz-oriented harmonies with syncopated rhythms.

Herbie Hancock made the connection between Brown's funk rhythms and the new jazz fusions explicit:

> In the popular forms like funk, which I've been trying to get into, the attention is on the interplay of rhythm between the different instruments. The part the Clavinet plays has to fit with the part the drums play and the line that the bass plays and the line that the guitar plays. It's almost like African drummers where seven drummers play different parts. They all play together and it sounds like one part. To sustain that is really hard.[4]

Another influential soul band, particularly admired by Miles Davis and Herbie Hancock, was the group Sly and the Family Stone, whose hits in the late sixties and early seventies included "There's a Riot Going On," "I Want to Take You Higher," and "Everyday People." The group's electric bassist was Larry Graham, who developed *slap bass,* a technique of thumping the low strings while plucking the higher strings, creating a percussive funky sound. This style was picked up by other funk players and by fusion electric bassists such as Stanley Clarke, Alphonso Johnson, Marcus Miller, and Jaco Pastorius, who made the "slapping and popping" sound an important component of their playing.

In addition to soul and funk, rock also made an impact on the development of fusion. Rock, which came of age in the 1950s, developed out of a complicated mix of 1940s R&B, country and folk music, and Delta and electric blues, among other elements. With the "British Invasion" of the mid-1960s, groups such as the Beatles and the Rolling Stones earned phenomenal popularity by covering compositions by African-American blues and R&B artists such as Chuck Berry, Muddy Waters, and Robert Johnson.

After first performing in the United States in 1964, the Beatles became cultural icons impossible to ignore, with many popular hits. Jazz guitarist Wes Montgomery's albums *Michelle* and *A Day in the Life* were titled after the Beatles compositions included on each record. Ultimately, covering popular rock tunes in a jazz setting proved to be relatively infertile. As fusion developed, the music retained the rhythms, harmonic concepts, and electric ambience of rock music but used these elements to support improvisation. Covering hit tunes became far less common.

Early fusion artists expressed admiration for the solos of rock guitarist Jimi Hendrix (1942–1970). Hendrix was a self-taught guitar virtuoso who used feedback, distortion, and electronic devices in his extended and flamboyant solos. His hits included "Purple Haze"—the title based on a nickname for the hallucinogenic drug LSD. He also had an interest in jazz. For example, he recorded with fusion guitarist John McLaughlin and organist Larry Young late in his career, and he had several discussions with Miles Davis about recording an album, which sadly never materialized. Hendrix died in 1970 from a drug overdose.

Slap bass is a technique in which the bass player percussively hits the low strings of the instrument while picking melodies on the higher ones. This style was created by Larry Graham and subsequently imitated by jazz, funk, and popular bass players.

Other rock-oriented bands of the late sixties and early seventies managed to fuse jazz with rock while appealing to a wider public. Blood, Sweat, and Tears thrived on a formula of horns and jazz-based solos to augment their rock compositions, which featured the soul-based singing of David Clayton-Thomas. The group penned a string of Top 40 hits, as did the band Chicago, which used similar instrumentation. Some experimental rock groups, such as the British bands Soft Machine and King Crimson, featured even more extended improvisation.

The Fusion Music of Miles Davis

In a remarkable life in which he was always at or near the center of the action, Miles Davis managed to pioneer jazz development yet again with his groundbreaking work in fusion. His watershed albums *In a Silent Way* and *Bitches Brew* were important for their adoption of electric keyboards, rock-based rhythms, dense percussion textures, and simplified harmonic foundations often based on repeated ostinato figures. As we shall soon discuss, Davis's sidemen on these recordings formed the first wave of the major fusion groups in the early seventies.

Davis never turned back. After his fusion experiments in the late sixties, he continued to explore creative, improvised music within rock, funk, and computer-controlled synthesizer frameworks. In doing so, he gained an even higher degree of popularity and commercial success. After releasing *Bitches Brew,* Davis began playing at rock music venues, such as the Fillmore East in New York and the Fillmore West in San Francisco. In this astute professional move, Davis tapped into a wider audience

Miles Davis on stage with his jazz-rock ensemble, 1987, JVC jazz fest, New York.

© Bettman/CORBIS

Miles Davis in the Early 1970s

With Davis's move to fusion and accompanying popularity, jazz traditionalists such as singer Betty Carter accused him of selling out by cashing in on a popular trend: "It's all about money. . . . They [Davis, Herbie Hancock, and Donald Byrd] have a 'reasonable' excuse for the why of what they're doing, but the only excuse is money."*

Nevertheless, a review of Davis's early 1970s recordings shows just how uncompromising and uncommercial much of his music actually was. In contrast to the well-rehearsed, high-octane precision of fusion groups like the Mahavishnu Orchestra and Return to Forever, or to the dance-floor grooves of Herbie Hancock, Davis's groups often performed dissonant, atmospheric, seemingly free-form medleys stitched together loosely by a rock or funk beat. With a loose approach to performance, many of the pieces seemed to rewrite themselves each night: "Friday

---
* Linda Prince, "Betty Carter: Bebopper Breathes Fire," *Down Beat,* May 3, 1979, p. 14.

Miles" (named for the night the group performed), from his 1970 recording *At Fillmore,* combined versions of "Pharoah's Dance," "Sanctuary," "Bitches Brew," "Miles Runs the Voodoo Down," "I Fall in Love Too Easily," and "The Theme." The record-side length of each composition on the double album was created by splicing together chosen segments of longer, live performances.

Captivated by the guitar playing of Jimi Hendrix, Davis began incorporating guitar into his ensembles in the seventies, at times recording with two and sometimes even three guitarists. He soon dispensed with acoustic bass by hiring Michael Henderson, an electric bassist who had played R&B and soul in the Motown studios with songwriter-vocalist Stevie Wonder. Al Foster was often the drummer called on to set the groove with Henderson.

In contrast to the funk-based rhythm sections, Davis's horn lineup was more in keeping with his bands of the past. For his saxophonist, Davis often used a player

strongly influenced by John Coltrane, such as Dave Liebman, Gary Bartz, or Sonny Fortune. These players usually played soprano saxophone. Davis himself played both trumpet and organ. Like the rock guitarists and keyboardists of the era, he often used a *wah-wah pedal* on trumpet. During live performances, Davis would stalk the stage, often directing the musicians from the organ with cues that were sometimes overt, sometimes imperceptible.

A **wah-wah pedal** is a pitch-frequency filter operated by the foot that is usually used by guitarists or electric keyboardists. When the pedal is depressed, the note or chord being held makes a "wah" sound. (An acoustic "wah" sound can be achieved by brass players using their left hands or mutes over the bells of their instruments.) The up-and-down movement of the pedal creates the repeated "wah-wah" effect.

---

by opening for rock acts such as the Grateful Dead, the Band, Santana, and Crosby, Stills, and Nash. (See the box "Miles Davis in the Early 1970s" above.)

Davis stopped performing between 1975 and 1981 because of declining health. He had developed problems from cocaine addiction, an arthritic hip, and stomach ulcers exacerbated by alcoholism. He returned from seclusion with the 1981 album *The Man With the Horn,* which included saxophonist (not pianist) Bill Evans, bassist Marcus Miller, drummer Al Foster, and guitarist Mike Stern. In the 1980s Davis continued to show his flair for hiring some of the rising young stars of jazz by picking up guitarist John Scofield in 1982. Scofield inspired Davis to return to his blues roots: The trumpeter featured a 12-bar blues on "It Gets Better" from *Star People.*

As in the past, these newer sidemen continued with prominent careers after their association with Davis. Guitarists Stern and Scofield are among the important players of today; Miller flourished with an accomplished career as a bassist, synthesist, composer, and producer; and Bill Evans has remained in the forefront as a saxophonist.

Although Davis continued to tour and perform, he turned more often to the studio for his albums rather than recording live as he had in the early seventies. For example, Davis created a landmark album in 1985—*Tutu*—which was named after Archbishop Desmond Tutu, winner of the Nobel Peace Prize for his work in ending apartheid in South Africa. *Tutu* made extensive use of studio technology. The funk grooves and catchy melodic ideas provided a foundation over which Davis later added his trumpet solos.

Despite the slick studio technology on *Tutu,* Davis's playing was unmistakable. Despite the sometimes radical change of musical circumstances, his style was remarkably consistent throughout his career. Trombonist and composer J. J. Johnson sums up this point neatly:

> Miles is doing his natural thing. He's just putting in today's setting, on his own terms. If you put Miles and his new group in the studio and record them on separate mikes and then you cut the band track and you just played the trumpet track, you know what you'd have? The same old Miles. What's new is the frame of reference.[5]

On his final albums, Davis continued to experiment with studio technology. His work from the late eighties featured sampled, electronically derived soundscapes over which Davis added trumpet improvisations. Davis died of a stroke on September 28, 1991, at age sixty-five. His last recording, *doo bop,* was released posthumously and incorporated hip-hop grooves and rap. He had been an integral part of the jazz scene for more than four decades, always moving and changing. Interestingly, nearly half of his career was dedicated to fusion music after he helped spark the trend in the late sixties.

Speaking of Davis's role in incorporating aspects of R&B, rock, and funk music into the jazz idiom, pianist Ramsey Lewis noted:

> It was not until the late sixties when Miles Davis gave his stamp of approval by incorporating some of these ideas into his albums that musicians accepted the fact that rock rhythms and influences other than the traditional ones could be integrated with jazz. . . . Davis extended the harmonic concept, employed polyrhythmic patterns, added electronic instruments and devices to his trumpet along with his highly unique and creative ability, and set the pace for what has come to be known as fusion music.[6]

Other Fusion Pioneers

Miles Davis was not the only prominent jazz musician responding to rock and funk in the sixties. Jazz guitarist Larry Coryell (b. 1943) was one of the earliest musicians to incorporate rock, blues, and even country elements into his jazz playing. Like some of the other young players in the mid-sixties, he took a wildly eclectic approach. Coryell later remembered, "We were saying, We love Wes [Montgomery], but we also love Bob Dylan. We love Coltrane but we also love the Beatles. We love Miles but we also love the Rolling Stones."[7] In 1966 Coryell was part of the Free Spirits; the following year, he joined the Gary Burton Quartet. Coryell used blues-based licks, playing with sustain and distortion that sometimes approached feedback.

The late sixties also witnessed the formation of an important band called Dreams. Among its players were many of the upcoming stars of the fusion movement, including drummer Billy Cobham (b. 1944); tenor saxophonist Mike Brecker (b. 1949); Mike's brother, trumpeter Randy Brecker (b. 1945); and guitarist John Abercrombie (b. 1944). Abercrombie's use of feedback and distortion on "Try Me," from the 1970 recording *Dreams,* showed the attraction of high-energy rock guitar playing.

Guitarist Larry Coryell was one of the first guitarists to bring a rock-based approach into a jazz idiom.

LIFETIME

One of the most important early fusion bands was Lifetime, a dynamic trio formed by Tony Williams, the drummer who had earned tremendous acclaim with Miles Davis in the sixties. Originally from Boston, Williams had been a drumming prodigy, playing regularly around the city by age fifteen. In 1963, at age seventeen, Williams recorded in New York with saxophonist Jackie McLean (for Blue Note) and was soon asked to join the Miles Davis Quintet.

In addition to Tony Williams, Miles Davis's landmark recording *In a Silent Way* included an astounding British guitarist who had arrived in the United States only two weeks before. John McLaughlin, born in Yorkshire in 1942, had played in British rock and jazz groups during the fifties and sixties. McLaughlin's 1969 album *Extrapolation,* recorded while he was still living in England, demonstrated the guitarist's remarkably fast execution in an acoustic jazz format. Instead of the syncopated phrasing of traditional jazz guitarists, McLaughlin's playing was even, hard, and cutting. He occasionally used *bent pitches* in the manner of rock guitarists.

Invited by Williams, McLaughlin left Britain to come to the United States and join Lifetime. The group began as a trio; along with Williams on drums and McLaughlin on guitar was organist Larry Young. Lifetime not only was indebted to the jazz tradition but also drew inspiration from jam-oriented rock bands such as Jimi Hendrix and Cream.

Blending jazz and rock rhythms and held together by Williams's high-energy "take no prisoners" style of drumming, Lifetime never achieved wide popularity. The group's raucous energy, propelled by the distortion and sheer volume of the guitar and organ, was too extreme for mainstream jazz fans, while its often dissonant and extended improvisations proved too esoteric for mainstream rock fans.

Tony Williams's work with Miles Davis and Lifetime earned him almost legendary status among jazz drummers of the eighties and nineties. He continued with a variety of projects involving both jazz and rock, including reunions with the Miles Davis rhythm section of Herbie Hancock and Ron Carter in a group known as V. S. O. P. The jazz world was greatly saddened in 1997 by his early death from heart failure at age fifty-one. Later that year, Williams was elected to the *Down Beat* Hall of Fame.

MAHAVISHNU ORCHESTRA

Lifetime was short-lived—the group broke up in 1971—but the hard-driving energy of the music was something fresh. John McLaughlin was emerging as one of the important guitarists on the jazz scene. McLaughlin and Larry Coryell were perhaps the two musicians most responsible for bringing the sound of rock guitar into the jazz idiom.

McLaughlin's concept of jazz-rock guitar included elements of non-Western musical traditions, especially classical Indian styles, along with the blues licks typical of the fifties and sixties R&B guitar playing. During this time, McLaughlin adopted as his guru Sri Chimnoy; accordingly, the titles of McLaughlin's solo albums *Devotion* and *My Goal's Beyond* reflected his newly formed spiritual interests.

After Lifetime broke up, McLaughlin began assembling one of the first, and most important, fusion bands of the seventies. The Mahavishnu Orchestra was named by McLaughlin's guru. McLaughlin hired drummer Billy Cobham, who had played with Horace Silver and the band Dreams; Czech keyboardist Jan Hammer, who had been

A **bent pitch** is achieved by pushing against the guitar's string on the fretboard, thus "bending" it. The resulting effect is a tiny glissando or slide from one frequency to a slightly higher one.

John McLaughlin playing with the Mahavishnu Orchestra, August 1975, Orange Rock Festival. Note the double bass drum in the drum set.

© Richard Melloul/CORBIS SYGMA

a member of Sarah Vaughan's trio; Irish bassist Rick Laird; and violinist Jerry Goodman, who had been a member of the rock group The Flock.

The success of the Mahavishnu Orchestra was phenomenal, and their popularity enabled them to play concerts and tour on the rock music circuit. In contrast to the loose, often ethereal jazz-rock improvisations played by Miles Davis, however, the Mahavishnu Orchestra was tightly rehearsed. The group played dazzling unison figures, complex meters, ostinato figures—sometimes indebted to Indian music— and rock rhythms pounded out with ferocious energy by drummer Billy Cobham.

The Mahavishnu Orchestra did not rely exclusively on high-octane, blisteringly fast playing. For example, "A Lotus on Irish Streams," from *The Inner Mounting Flame*, and "Open Country Joy," from *Birds of Fire*, are pastoral, acoustic reveries. Much of the band's impact derived from the dramatic juxtaposition of acoustic works such as these with high-energy electric compositions. Keyboardist George Duke called attention both to the excitement that the Mahavishnu Orchestra generated and to the disappointment brought on later by other derivative groups:

> When fusion was first happening, it was the most interesting music I had heard in my life. It reached its peak with the Mahavishnu Orchestra. . . . But it seemed like after that everybody was copying each other and getting too technically oriented, playing so many notes and scales that the feeling was going out of the music.[8]

The group disbanded in 1973. McLaughlin formed a second Mahavishnu Orchestra in 1974. The short-lived, eleven-piece group included Jean-Luc Ponty, a highly talented French violinist who went on to create his own fusion recordings during the seventies and eighties. After the Mahavishnu Orchestra broke up, much of McLaughlin's work abandoned the fusion directions he had helped chart. He concentrated on acoustic guitar, playing with the Indian-based group Shakti and later in an acoustic guitar trio with Paco de Lucia and Al DiMeola.

HERBIE HANCOCK AND HEADHUNTERS

After leaving Miles Davis's band, Herbie Hancock continued his exploration of electronic media on his recordings *Crossings, Mwandishi,* and *Sextant.* Hancock's group for these recordings—usually a sextet—was booked into rock music venues such as the Fillmore, but their spacey, open-ended improvisations proved unsuccessful, and Hancock was forced to disband the group in 1973.

Before abandoning the rock circuit, however, Hancock experienced opening for the R&B pop group the Pointer Sisters at the Troubadour club in Los Angeles. Hancock was impressed by the direct audience appeal of the Pointer Sisters. He began to think about taking his music in a more popular direction, one rooted in the funk and R&B styles of James Brown, Stevie Wonder, and especially Sly and the Family Stone. Introduced to Nichiren Shoshu Buddhism by his bassist, Buster Williams, Hancock experienced a revelation while chanting:

> My mind wandered to an old desire I had to be on one of Sly Stone's records. It was actually a secret desire of mine for years—I wanted to know how he got that funky sound. Then a completely new thought entered my mind: Why not Sly Stone on one of my records? My immediate response was: "Oh, no, I can't do that." So I asked myself why not. The answer came to me: pure jazz snobbism.[9]

Although Hancock never recorded with Stone, he did achieve a breakthrough into popular culture with his phenomenally successful album *Headhunters.* The album reached number 13 on the *Billboard* chart, then eventually went platinum. His intent, Hancock claimed, was to hire not jazz musicians who could play funk, but funk musicians who could play jazz. *Headhunters* made extensive use of overdubs and studio technology. In addition to playing the Fender Rhodes electric piano, Hancock also played other electronic keyboards.

Hancock's solo on "Chameleon" established him as one of the finest live performers on synthesizer. Much of the success of Hancock's *Headhunters* album was due in fact to "Chameleon," which became a hit largely because of its syncopated, danceable two-measure bass riff and catchy melody.

LISTENING GUIDE

"Chameleon" (excerpt)
CD **2** Track **13**

The Herbie Hancock Group: "Chameleon" (Hancock), from *Headhunters.* Columbia KC 32731.
San Francisco, 1973. Herbie Hancock, keyboards; Bennie Maupin, soprano saxophone,
tenor saxophone, saxello, bass clarinet, alto flute; Paul Jackson, electric bass and marimbula;
Harvey Mason, drums; Bill Summers, percussion.

Because of its infectious funk groove, "Chameleon" was an enormously successful hit for Hancock, earning him a huge crossover audience. Most of the composition is based on a simple riff in the bass texture, played by the synthesizer. This excerpt omits the head so as to include the full synthesizer solo.

Opening riff

0:00   The piece begins with a repeated funk riff played on the synthesizer. This riff forms the backbone of the entire composition. The riff is played twice by itself.

0:12   The other instruments are gradually added to the texture, one by one, beginning with the drums.

0:31   A guitarlike synthesizer sound plays a simple, rhythmic line.

0:51   The clavinet, a percussive keyboard instrument, is now added to the texture. Hancock plays a funky rhythmic accompaniment on the clavinet.

1:11   *(Fade out and back in)*

Synthesizer solo

1:53   The synthesizer solo begins.

3:44   Listen here for Hancock's repeated riff.

4:54   The tenor saxophone/synthesizer melody returns, now stated along with Hancock's synthesizer solo.

Although Hancock was later criticized for "selling out," not all of the compositions on *Headhunters* were overtly commercial. "Sly," a homage to Sly Stone, included several drastic tempo changes and featured daring improvisations by both Hancock and saxophonist Benny Maupin.

Compositional subtlety and extended improvisation faded somewhat in Hancock's later recordings. The group's next project, *Thrust,* used repetitive funk and dance rhythms, although Hancock's composition "Butterfly" was haunting and evocative, reminiscent of some of his earlier impressionistic recordings for Blue Note. Hancock's subsequent recordings were marketed squarely as commercial products. His biggest success came with "Rockit," from the 1983 album *Future Shock,* which stayed on the pop-music charts for more than a year and became a classic MTV video. In response to the sometimes hostile comments from jazz critics, Hancock insisted that his dance music was not jazz:

> Jazz fusion is another idiom. It uses elements of jazz and elements of popular forms, but it established its own idiom. I'm not concerned with changing that idiom, or changing disco. I want to play the music I'm playing and still have it be dance music. Making some music that is fun to dance to and really nice to listen to, some music that has emotion in it. . . . It's funny because many of the elements are simpler than before. For example, a lot of the music happening today has simpler chord structures and simpler harmonies than in the past. The complexity is now in the textures and in keeping the groove going.[10]

Despite success in the pop-funk market, Hancock frequently returned to an acoustic jazz format, playing in a hard bop idiom with the V. S. O. P. Quintet, as mentioned earlier. The group reunited Hancock with bassist Ron Carter, drummer Tony Williams, and saxophonist Wayne Shorter—and included trumpeter Freddie Hubbard. Hancock also returned to the hard bop and modal idiom in recordings with trumpeters Wynton Marsalis and Wallace Roney.

On the 1998 album *Gershwin's World,* Hancock teamed up with an impressive array of players from the jazz, popular, and classical fields, such as jazz pianist Chick Corea, classical soprano Kathleen Battle, the Orpheus Chamber Ensemble, and pop musicians Stevie Wonder and Joni Mitchell. We shall return to Hancock and this album in Chapter 8 because it both embodies the eclecticism of the 1990s and hints at a possible direction for jazz in the twenty-first century.

CHICK COREA AND RETURN TO FOREVER

Herbie Hancock's replacement in the Miles Davis Quintet was Chick Corea, who joined Davis in the fall of 1968. In summer 1970, Corea gave notice to Davis in order to pursue his own projects and an interest in what he called musical "abstraction": a series of recordings that made extensive use of free improvisation. However, with Corea's group Return to Forever, the pianist abandoned free playing, moving decisively toward airy, Brazilian-influenced music. He hired bassist Stanley Clarke, saxophonist and flutist Joe Farrell, drummer Airto Moreira (who often went by his first name only), and Airto's wife, singer Flora Purim. The group made two recordings, *Return to Forever* and *Light as a Feather,* which highlighted Corea's sophisticated compositions. Some of these—such as "Spain" and "La Fiesta"—were playful references to Spanish music. Corea's tunes caught on. "It seemed like after we made that record," saxophonist Joe Farrell related about *Light as a Feather,* "everybody and their brother started playing sambas and songs with melodies. It became very popular."[11] The title *Light as a Feather* characterizes the album as a whole. The lightness is achieved by the relative lack of bass drum in the rhythm section. The prominent Brazilian rhythms and the lively character of the performances imbue the work with a feeling of joy and exhilaration throughout.

Corea reorganized Return to Forever in 1973, converting the group into an electric quartet. As for the repertory and overall style of the group, Corea drew upon his own experiences playing with Miles Davis, but he was equally inspired by John McLaughlin's Mahavishnu Orchestra. "John's band, more than my experience with Miles," Corea admitted, "led me to want to turn the volume up and write music that was more dramatic and made your hair move."[12]

Like the Mahavishnu Orchestra, Return to Forever excelled in playing exciting, impressive unison lines at breathtaking speed. Corea performed not only on electric piano but also on Moog and Arp synthesizers, clavinet, and organ. At its best, Return to Forever's music was compositionally sophisticated: The group effectively blended complex forms, meter and tempo changes, and well-written ensemble passages with dynamic and virtuosic improvisation. Corea broke up the electric group in 1975.

After working with Corea, guitarist Al DiMeola (b. 1954) continued as one of the most successful names in fusion. He released a series of albums in the Return

Stanley Clarke in an early promotional photograph. Clarke made the switch to electric bass as a member of Return to Forever when Corea turned the group electric.

to Forever mold, most notably *Elegant Gypsy* and *Casino*. These emphasized DiMeola's brilliant though flashy technique and were testaments to his desire to become "the fastest guitarist in the world."

Like Hancock, Corea's subsequent career in the 1980s and nineties included work in both electric and acoustic formats. His group, Chick Corea's Elektric Band, with bassist John Pattitucci and drummer Dave Weckl, set the standard for fusion playing in the 1980s. Corea also returned to the acoustic trio format on two recordings: *Trio Music* (featuring the music of Thelonious Monk) and *Live in Europe*. Corea's compositional inventiveness and brilliance has led him to undertake musical projects that combine extensive written composition with improvisation, such as *Three Quartets* and his *Sextet* recording. In the 1990s Corea returned to his earlier musical roots, recording a tribute to Bud Powell and performing with his group Origins.

WEATHER REPORT

One of the longest-lasting and best-known fusion groups, Weather Report formed in 1970. They recorded fifteen albums in their fifteen-year history. The group underwent numerous personnel changes, with only founding members keyboardist Josef Zawinul and saxophonist Wayne Shorter—both of whom worked with Miles Davis in the sixties—remaining through the band's tenure. In addition to changes in personnel, Weather Report also undertook several changes in musical direction. They began as an acoustic group that used collective improvisation that was sometimes

Courtesy Morgan Collection

A 1979 publicity photo of Weather Report (CD 2, Track 14): Joe Zawinul, Wayne Shorter, Peter Erskine, and Jaco Pastorius.

metrically free. However, by their third album, 1973's *Sweetnighter,* keyboardist and composer Zawinul was moving the group toward more strongly defined compositional structures and more rock- and funk-based rhythms and grooves. They reached the high point of their popularity when electric bassist Jaco Pastorius joined the band and they recorded their hit composition "Birdland," from the album *Heavy Weather.*

Born in Austria in 1932, Zawinul was raised in Vienna and studied at the Vienna Conservatory. After arriving in the United States in 1959, he soon found himself with a ten-year stint, from 1961 to 1970, with alto saxophonist Cannonball Adderley that gave Zawinul national exposure. Foreshadowing his later interest in synthesizers and fusion, Zawinul played electric piano with Adderley during the late sixties. His use of the instrument helped bring its sound into the jazz idiom. (Zawinul was not first to promote the electric piano in jazz, however: Earl Hines had both performed and recorded on a "Storytone" electric piano as early as 1940.)

Showing a natural talent for pop-jazz crossover, Zawinul wrote the Adderley band's prominent soul jazz hit, "Mercy, Mercy, Mercy." On this cut, Zawinul played the Wurlitzer electric piano. In 1969 Miles Davis paid the distinct compliment of recording Zawinul's composition "In a Silent Way," while hiring him to play electric piano alongside Chick Corea and Herbie Hancock. On the recording, Davis simplified the piece's harmonic progression.

In 1970 Zawinul and Wayne Shorter formed Weather Report with Czech bassist Miroslav Vitous. The quintet was initially filled out by drummer Alphonse Mouzon and percussionist Airto Moreira. With Zawinul on electric piano and Shorter primarily on soprano saxophone, Weather Report's first two albums, *Weather Report* and *I Sing the Body Electric,* emphasized mood, color, and collective improvisation.

By *Sweetnighter,* the group had moved toward danceable grooves underlying the solos. The album showed new directions that the group would continue to explore: the use of electric bass and short, catchy melodies that were repeated. The latter highlighted Zawinul's ability to write brief melodic ideas as song hooks. *Sweetnighter* was also the first of Weather Report's recordings on which Zawinul also played synthesizer. He would soon become one of the premier synthesists in fusion, mining the vast compositional and coloristic possibilities of the instrument. By the group's next album, *Mysterious Traveller,* Zawinul was behind a stack of Moog and Arp synthesizers as well as electric piano augmented by wah-wah pedal and other electronic effects.

Beginning with the 1976 album *Black Market,* electric bassist Jaco Pastorius joined the band. Pastorius redefined electric bass playing with ripping, staccato funk accompaniments; fast, clean solos; interjections of surprising harmonics and entire chords; and a liquid sound that often incorporated terminal vibrato at the ends of phrases. He played a fretless bass. Born in Norristown, Pennsylvania, in 1951, Pastorius grew up in Fort Lauderdale, Florida, and began his career playing in local soul and jazz bands. He made the trio recording *Bright Size Life* with guitarist Pat Metheny, but it was his own 1975 recording *Jaco Pastorius* that showcased his remarkable abilities, particularly on the Charlie Parker classic, "Donna Lee."

With Weather Report, Pastorius's outgoing exuberance brought more and more fans to the band's live performances, which generally showcased the bassist in a solo feature. Pastorius was "an electrifying performer and a great musician," noted Zawinul. "Before Jaco came along we were perceived as a kind of esoteric jazz group . . . but after Jaco joined the band we started selling out concert halls everywhere."[13]

Pastorius was a talented composer too, writing "Teen Town" and "Havana" for Weather Report's best-selling album, *Heavy Weather*. Largely on the popularity of Zawinul's composition "Birdland," *Heavy Weather* reached 30 on the *Billboard* chart and became a gold record, selling more than 500,000 copies.

L I S T E N I N G   G U I D E

"Birdland"
CD **2**   Track **14**

Weather Report: "Birdland" (Zawinul), from *Heavy Weather*. Columbia PC 34418. North Hollywood, California, 1977. Josef Zawinul, composer, keyboards; Wayne Shorter, soprano and tenor saxophone; Jaco Pastorius, bass, mandocello, vocals; Alejandro Acuna, drums; Manalo Badrena, tambourine.

As do many of Zawinul's fusion compositions, "Birdland" comprises tightly connected sections of brief, singable melodies. The piece is a marvel of ingenuity, with its varied sections uniting in an imaginative and well-crafted whole.

As the following notes show, the piece exhibits a complex structure with numerous sections of unpredictable length, rather than the usual eight-bar units of AABA formats.

Introduction—12 measures

0:00   A four-bar synthesizer bass line is heard three times.

Part I—AAAAB, 24 measures

0:18   A four-bar main thematic idea (A), played by bassist Jaco Pastorius, is added to the four-bar vamp. The idea is played four times: twice in a lower register, then twice in a higher register; an eight-bar B section idea completes part I with a saxophone added.

Transition—4 measures

0:55   A transition pedal point reaffirms the tonality.

Part II—20 measures

1:02   The piano introduces a new four-bar vamp idea. At the end of the third statement of the vamp, a new bass line enters that recalls the earlier bass line but in longer note values.

Part III—9 measures

1:32   A saxophone melody is joined to the next section, which has an unusual nine-bar length.

Transition—9 measures

1:46   The saxophone melody deconstructs into call-and-response funky figures among various timbres.

Part IV—24 measures

1:59   A new four-bar vamp idea appears.

Transition—8 measures

2:36   During the second four bars of the eight-bar section, a backbeat (in part syncopated) is added in the snare and continues into the next section.

Synthesizer solo—12 measures

2:49   The synthesizer solo grows out of the bass line almost imperceptibly.

Saxophone solo—14 measures

3:07   The static bass of the last two sections beautifully sets up the background for the saxophone solo: The synthesizers create a two-bar vamp of chords moving down. This is the climax of the performance. Shorter's saxophone solo shows the group's ability to interweave written and improvised sections seamlessly.

Transition—4 measures

3:29   The texture is again radically simplified for contrast with the preceding section.

Reprise of part I—24 measures

3:35   Over the simplified texture of the preceding section, the melody from part I returns. As it proceeds, the original bass line is added, then the B section returns with heightened energy.

Reprise of part II—8 measures, modified

4:11   The four-bar vamp from part II returns in a modified form.

Reprise of part IV—Fade-out

4:23   The material from part IV returns with a long fade-out combining added texture and improvisation.

5:00–5:56 Sparsely at first, Zawinul adds a synthesizer solo to the texture, which gradually becomes more active. A handclap is added as a backbeat, increasing the energy and adding a jam-session aura during the fade.

On some subsequent Weather Report albums of the late seventies—as with other promising fusion bands, such as the Brecker Brothers—the group turned to more-formulaic disco rhythms. Nevertheless, the group remained enormously popular. In 1980 Weather Report won the reader's poll category in *Down Beat* for the ninth year in a row. Pastorius left the group in 1982, forming his own group, Word of Mouth, which recorded two albums. Unfortunately, alcohol and cocaine addiction brought about severe personal problems for Pastorius, who died after a barroom fight in 1987.

After Pastorius left, Weather Report persisted until 1986. Zawinul then formed Weather Update, a short-lived group that played Weather Report compositions; in 1988 he put together the Zawinul Syndicate with guitarist Scott Henderson.

The Zawinul Syndicate has continued to explore musical styles that blend different cultures. For example, Zawinul's album *Stories of the Danube* (1996) unites orchestral music and jazz in a tapestry linked thematically by the Danube and the cultures touched by the river's course. Zawinul has also been involved in staging multicultural festivals throughout the world.

As mentioned in Chapter 6, Wayne Shorter has also pursued a variety of projects. For example, he recorded an interesting duo record with Herbie Hancock in 1997, *1 + 1*. Other projects include large-scale orchestral works that sometimes feature Shorter on saxophone.

Despite the varied directions of Shorter and Zawinul in the 1990s, Weather Report remains their legacy from the seventies and eighties. During the fifteen years they kept the band together, Weather Report explored a remarkable abundance of compositional styles and approaches. As Stuart Nicholson summarizes:

Despite being routinely described as a "jazz-rock" band, their stylistic outlook was extremely broad, perhaps the most inclusive in jazz. Their range extended from classical influences such as the French Impressionists to free jazz, from World music to bebop, from big-band music to chamber music, from collective improvisation to tightly written formal structures, from modal vamps to elaborately conceived harmonic forms, from structures with no apparent meter to straight-ahead swing. . . . Both Zawinul and Shorter created a large body of work that, outside of Duke Ellington, numbers among the most diverse and imaginative in jazz.[14]

PAT METHENY

Guitarist Pat Metheny was one of the most original and popular fusion artists to emerge in the mid-seventies. Much of his work avoided the cutting, hard-rock sound favored by other fusion guitarists such as John McLaughlin. Instead, Metheny preferred bright, lyrical, and often gentle timbres.

Metheny's distinctive sound was created by his use of electronic devices. He used them not for distortion and power effects, but rather to give his instrument a fatter, richer sound. In addition, Metheny shunned the pyrotechnics of other fusion guitarists, such as John McLaughlin and Al DiMeola. "I'm not," he made clear, "drawn to the athletic approach to the music." Rather, Metheny saw his lyricism as part of the midwestern melodic tradition of Lester Young and Kansas City: "Even today I think of what I'm playing as sort of a Kansas City style, evolved or modernized. It's that melodic, lyrical thing."[15]

Metheny was born in Lee's Summit, Missouri, in 1954. His first album, *Bright Size Life,* was released in 1976. Created with bassist Jaco Pastorius and drummer Bob Moses, it showed Metheny's penchant for clear melodic lines with an occasional country twang. He also displayed his affinity for the music of Ornette Coleman—whom Metheny called "one of the most melodic musicians ever"[16]—by recording two of Coleman's compositions in a medley, "Round Trip/Broadway Blues."

Pat Metheny in the 1970s.

Courtesy Morgan Collection

After *Bright Size Life,* Metheny put together a quartet for touring, consisting of drummer Danny Gottlieb, electric bassist Mark Egan, and keyboardist Lyle Mays. The group built a national reputation by playing one-nighters throughout the country. *Watercolors,* his next album, was followed by the lyrical *The Pat Metheny Group* in 1978. The moody, gentle "Phase Dance," from the latter album, featured simple, spacious, diatonic harmonies, with pianist Lyle Mays capturing the folksy quality sometimes heard in Keith Jarrett's playing.

Metheny's next several albums explored a variety of genres. For example, in contrast to his earlier work, *American Garage* was more rock-oriented and was dedicated to garage bands across the country. Metheny also performed in acoustic jazz settings. His recording *80/81* included Ornette Coleman's former bassist Charlie Haden. On *Song X,* Metheny finally recorded with Coleman himself. The record was an uncompromising enterprise that both enhanced Metheny's status in the jazz world and brought Coleman to a larger listening public.

On subsequent recordings, Metheny merged his neoromantic streak with Brazilian elements, as on the 1987 album *Still Life Talking,* which won a Grammy award. By the late 1990s, Metheny—by now an eminent and respected elder statesman of fusion—was involved in several related projects that built on his previous work and reputation and that sometimes involved nonfusion concepts as well. In 1999, for example, he released albums with his longtime hero, guitarist Jim Hall, and saxophonist Dave Liebman. In a 1998 article, Metheny summed up his beliefs:

> I made a commitment to focus on and bring into sound the ideas I heard in my head that might not have existed until my time, to try to represent in music the things that were particular to the spiritual, cultural and technological potentials that seemed to be actively available to me in the shaping of my own personal esthetic values.[17]

This statement may serve as a general credo for the ideals of jazz-rock fusion. At its best, it is a happy marriage of rock, funk, technology, and jazz. Despite reactions against fusion on the part of some musicians (see Chapter 8), its basic philosophy has provided an important direction for jazz in the twenty-first century.

Jazz-Rock, Jazz-Funk Styles

TIMBRE

▸ Electronic; either:
  ● Very hard-edged, raucous
  ● Smooth, vague
▸ Upper instrumental ranges emphasized
▸ Use of blue note effects, particularly in funky substyles
▸ Ambience of rock with many electric and electronic instruments in addition to more-traditional instruments
▸ High volume in many forms

PHRASING

▸ Highly irregular in improvisation, but thematic heads often composed in two- and four-bar units

RHYTHM

▸ Wide variety of rhythmic values, but eighth notes emphasized in up-tempo improvising
▸ Highly energetic
▸ Very relaxed; sometimes out of tempo

THEMATIC CONTINUITY

▸ Motivic

CHORD-SCALE RELATIONS

▸ Inside, although can become outside in high-energy modal rock performances
▸ Blues scale usages in funky styles

LARGE-SCALE COHERENCE

▸ Motivic

Questions and Topics for Discussion

1. What are the principal differences between rock and funk?

2. What changes in rhythm and instrumentation did fusion bring to jazz? Describe the new instrument that the fusion bands of the 1970s began to use.

3. How did the performance and sound of the electric guitar change in the fusion bands, compared with electric guitar in earlier jazz groups?

4. How does the keyboardist's accompaniment in a fusion band generally differ from that of a pianist in an acoustic jazz group?

5. How can Miles Davis's career be seen as a virtual history of jazz from the late 1940s to the 1970s?

6. What were some of the most significant fusion bands? Who were their key musicians?

Key Terms

Backbeats 230

Bent pitch 236

Feedback 230

Jazz-rock (jazz-funk, fusion) 228

Samplers 229

Sampling 229

Sound modules 229

Slap bass 232

Smooth jazz 231

Sound modules 229

Wah-wah pedal 234

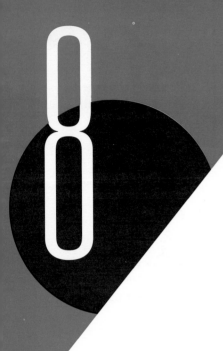

JAZZ SINCE THE 1980s

ALTHOUGH THE SEVENTIES was the decade of fusion, numerous nonfusion artists and substyles prospered then: Dixieland and traditional jazz (Doc Cheatham, Preservation Hall), swing-based styles (Count Basie, Benny Carter), bebop (Johnny Griffin, Phil Woods, Art Blakey), big bands (Toshiko Akiyoshi and Thad Jones/Mel Lewis), and free jazz (Ornette Coleman, Lester Bowie). Fusion gained the most attention, however, by attracting many of the younger players and by generating the most controversy among jazz fans and the media.

The proliferation of nonfusion jazz styles in the seventies is no surprise: Musical styles launched in the course of jazz history almost never disappear. As a result, the history of jazz should be seen not as a linear progression from style to style—with each new style displacing the previous one—but as a profusion, with styles added as younger musicians tinker with, build on, or simplify the work of more-established artists. Hence, jazz history is a rich overlapping of improvisational approaches— a general succession from artist to artist, not from style to style.

Still, because fusion was the big story of the seventies, the eighties has rightly been seen as a return to jazz traditionalism: a revival of the acoustic formats and postbop approaches that were forged in the late fifties and sixties. For many of the younger players of the eighties, this return to traditionalism meant a reconnection with the roots of jazz, roots sometimes neglected by the fusion players of the seventies. For some, such as Wynton Marsalis, this traditional stance became ideological: Marsalis has positioned himself as a forceful, influential, and articulate spokesperson in support of the traditional aesthetic. Traditional values continue to be extremely popular as the twenty-first century begins.

As with other jazz styles since the eighties, fusion has not dropped from the scene; indeed, smooth jazz, fusion's commercial legacy, remains quite popular, with such well-known artists as Kenny G generating interest and impressive record sales. Further, many commercial radio stations are entirely devoted to the smooth-jazz format. In the case of 1970s fusion, there have been three spin-offs: the popular-music connection, the recent jazz avant-garde, and world-beat popular music. Similarly, the 1960s avant-garde also can be seen as having three legacies: a continuation of an acoustic avant-garde scene, an electronic avant-garde scene (intersecting with a legacy of fusion), and a world-music connection. These legacies are in many cases called *crossover* because they combine jazz (or jazz values) with the styles and musics of other cultures.

To summarize, we can think of contemporary jazz as:

- Traditionalist or mainstream
- A legacy of 1970s fusion:
  - ▶ Popular-music connections, electronic or smooth jazz
  - ▶ Electronic avant-garde
  - ▶ Crossover to world-beat popular music
- A legacy of 1960s avant-garde:
  - ▶ Acoustic avant-garde
  - ▶ Electronic avant-garde
  - ▶ Crossover to world-music cultures

The rest of this chapter discusses these three trends in further detail, beginning with an overview of the traditionalists and their return to jazz "classicism."

Classicism and the Jazz Repertory Movement

Jazz since the eighties has witnessed an exploding interest in the history of jazz. This mini-renaissance has had two key results:

- ▶ Increases in the re-creation and live performance of older jazz music
- ▶ Complete works of older jazz artists reissued on digital compact discs (CDs)

The live performance of earlier jazz—usually in concert hall settings—is called the *jazz repertory movement*.

To introduce the repertory movement and its widespread implications for jazz in the twenty-first century, we shall describe the notable appearance of complete-works jazz recordings on CD, a movement parallel to and thematically linked with the repertory movement.

COMPLETE JAZZ-RECORDING REISSUES

After the LP was introduced in the late 1940s, record companies began to learn that profiting from the highlights of their *back catalog* was simpler and cheaper than developing and promoting unknown artists. However, many of the major labels, such as Columbia and RCA, initially failed to capitalize on this idea. Instead, smaller independents—such as Riverside and Original Jazz Library (OJL)—reissued this material, often by drawing on collectors who had meticulously preserved the original

Crossover is the practice of mixing musical styles and cultures. As first seen in the concert jazz of the 1920s and the third-stream practices of the 1950s, crossover can mix different styles within a given culture—for example, bluegrass and classical music—or it can mix entirely different cultures, such as traditional Japanese music and bebop.

The *jazz repertory movement* refers to ensembles devoted to the re-creation and performance of historically significant jazz artists and their work. Just as classical music has an accepted repertory of great works, the jazz repertory movement is trying to establish an official canon for jazz.

A *back catalog* includes the complete recordings that a company holds in its vaults or claims the rights to by having purchased other record labels. Many of these recordings are out of print or were never issued in their original form.

78 recordings. When the major labels realized the profits that could be made by issuing this material, they began their own reissue series, beginning in the late fifties and early sixties and continuing through today.

The digital CD replaced the analog LP as the commercial record format of the 1980s and 1990s. Record companies realized they could sell the same albums that they had issued in the fifties, sixties, and seventies to a new generation of listeners (and in many cases to the same audience who had purchased the LPs originally and now wanted the same material on CD). Also, the development of digital sound *remastering* enabled companies to reissue with superior sound quality much of the material on 78s.

Hence, the 1980s and 1990s witnessed an explosion of CD reissues. *Down Beat* magazine, for example, began a column devoted entirely to reissues. What used to be a difficult collector's task—tracking down every recording made by a particular artist—became much simpler. CD reissues comprise not only studio recordings but also live work.

Complete reissues in jazz arguably began with Charlie Parker, whose collected Savoy studio recordings appeared in 1978 on LP. The company decided to include every scrap of recorded material, no matter how insignificant. Sometimes excerpts were only a few seconds long, with the recording cut off by Parker, the recording engineer, or the producer following a *false start,* technical problem, or other blatant error. No matter—every flub was issued, available for scrutiny. This completist philosophy was subsequently extended to Parker's other two record companies, Dial and Verve, as well as to live performances of Parker, often captured on amateur equipment in informal settings.

Complete issues work fairly well for jazz of the 78-rpm era and perhaps the early LP era, but it is more controversial when modern studio sessions are anthologized. For example, *The Miles Davis Quintet 1965–68: The Complete Studio Recordings* contains fascinating material, but the integrity of the original albums is destroyed because the cuts (and outtakes) are all issued in chronological order. This arbitrary reordering of the material has created further problems. For example, only a portion of Davis's album *Filles de Kilimanjaro* is included in the reissue because the personnel of the band changed while the recording was under way.

This type of reissue disregards the *album* as an aesthetic entity worked up by artist and producer. An album is carefully prepared by an artist who may exclude outtakes and weaker cuts and determines the order of presentation for maximum effect. Still, for those interested in Davis, it is probably better to have this material available for study, despite the problems created by the reissue.

The completist philosophy also has implications for the general direction of jazz. This practice marks a phase of jazz in which the past has overtaken the present in importance because it promotes an art form that is less alive, less immediate, and more self-conscious than jazz has ever been before. Historically, European concert music reached a similar point around the end of the nineteenth century and the beginning of the twentieth century, when listeners and many professional performers de-emphasized contemporary music and made earlier compositions the focus of their repertory. Some have argued that this point marked a downturn in the immediacy and vitality of European concert music. Interestingly, this turn to the past in classical music may have created the opportunity for the success of jazz: The West was ready for something new, a spontaneous art form that could mirror the increased rhythmic pace and speed of industrialization and communication in the new century.

Remastering is the digital enhancement of an original recording's sound quality; it includes such techniques as filtering out extraneous noise and boosting certain frequencies.

A *complete reissue* duplicates an artist's or a group's entire available body of recorded material—including errors, outtakes, and technical problems—that the issuing record company can locate.

A *false start* is an incorrect start of a performance: A musician begins playing a measure or two, then, realizing a mistake, stops abruptly.

What kind of computers will be needed tomorrow?

As man reaches further for knowledge, the problems he meets become more complex. IBM is developing new computers to help solve them.

Some modern electronic computers can make a million calculations a second . . . store information bits in the multimillions.

Even this is not always enough. The problems that computers are being given to solve grow more complex every day. They point to the eventual need for faster speeds and greater capacities. After years of dealing in millionths of a second, IBM scientists now talk of billionths of a second.

How do they hope to achieve such speeds? By tapping completely new principles for the operation of computer circuits. IBM scientists and engineers, for example, are developing computer circuits and high-speed memories of thin magnetic films of metal. They also are investigating the application to computers of tunnel diodes, and of cryogenic circuits which function at temperatures approaching absolute zero.

From these research directions will come new generations of computers. IBM is exploring them all now, to assure businessmen and scientists that computer technology will be ready for new generations of information-handling problems. **IBM**

It's the first thing you should know about personal computers.

A is for Apple.

The era of the personal computer is here. Apple will challenge your imagination for years to come. Thousands of uses, from finances to fun and games. For information, call toll-free (800) 538-9696.* Or write:

*In California, call (408) 996-1010.

apple computer

10260 Bandley Dr., Cupertino, California 95014.

The 1970s witnessed the entrance of the personal computer into U.S. society. Above right, in a 1961 advertisement that shows the former size of computers, IBM wonders what kind of computer people will need in the future. Immediately above is one of the answers—the Apple computer of 1978.

Courtesy Morgan Collection

A refocusing of interest on the jazz past is evident not only in the huge number of CD reissues but also in the repertory movement itself. These practices are mutually related: CD reissues stimulate interest in an artist and lead to more concert performances, while the repertory ensembles stimulate more reissues. Much attention in jazz has been refocused on what has been accomplished, not on what is happening now. It remains to be seen how this preoccupation will affect the second century of jazz.

LIVE PERFORMANCE

The appearance of a book in 1984 by Grover Sales called *Jazz: America's Classical Music* speaks of the impetus of the jazz repertory movement. The idea of jazz as American classical music is not new. Indeed, the U.S. violinist Misha Elman claimed as far back as 1922 that in Europe jazz had "become known as the American classical music."[1] But the difference between current times and the 1920s is that older jazz has now become the preoccupation of major performance organizations, whereas before it was not.

Interestingly, this practice was predicted by stride pianist and composer James P. Johnson in 1947, when he wrote that "jazz musicians of the future will have to be able to play all different kinds of jazz—in all its treatments—just like the classical musician who, in one concert, might range from Bach to Copland."[2]

The idea that jazz should be appreciated and studied alongside the history of Western concert music has generated controversy. Some have argued that such a practice demeans jazz—that by calling it "classical" we are somehow evaluating it through aesthetic and formal criteria developed for European music. Others have countered by claiming that jazz must be appreciated on the same level as European music but not judged by the same aesthetic criteria.

These concerns have helped spark the jazz repertory movement, which is devoted to re-creating older jazz styles and the masterpieces of earlier eras. For example, the Lincoln Center Jazz Orchestra in New York has performed much of the music of major jazz figures at their Jazz at Lincoln Center concerts. Composer and conductor Gunther Schuller has also played a pivotal role in transcribing, performing, and promoting the music of Scott Joplin, Jelly Roll Morton, Duke Ellington, and others. By publishing transcriptions and edited editions of important jazz artists, recent jazz scholarship also supports this historical focus.

A key issue has arisen regarding the performance of jazz repertory: Should a repertory ensemble duplicate recorded performances that were based on improvisation, or does this oppose the jazz spirit? It can be argued that because recordings "freeze" or codify certain solos, they have become so identified with the pieces that it is a disservice not to duplicate them. And we could respond that if John Coltrane himself were performing in concert, he would not duplicate his own well-known solo from an earlier recording.

One commonly held idea about jazz performers is that they improvise all of their solo material. However, by studying alternate takes recorded by the early jazz bands, scholars have shown that performers played some solos more or less identically on each take. A musician always bases his or her improvisation on some notion of the overall shape of the solo; despite variations in individual notes or phrases, this notion usually stays the same. At this point in jazz history, the issue of literal versus imitative duplication of improvisation remains unresolved in practice. Depending on the band, the individual musicians, and the jazz style, repertory ensembles follow a variety of performance techniques ranging from a literal duplication of well-known recordings to much more informal practices based on the spirit of the earlier music.

Of the nation's repertory jazz ensembles, the two most influential are the Lincoln Center Jazz Orchestra (associated with Jazz at Lincoln Center) and the Smithsonian Jazz Masterworks Orchestra in Washington, D.C. During the 1990s, Jon Faddis also directed the Carnegie Hall Jazz Band, which was a third important group, now discontinued. Although the Carnegie Hall Jazz Band was technically a repertory orchestra, the group premiered numerous new works. Nor did Faddis want to perform older music exactly as it was played previously; as he pointed out, "One of our goals is to try and do the classical jazz repertoire in our own way."[3]

The Smithsonian Jazz Masterworks Orchestra was founded by Gunther Schuller and David Baker, a jazz trombonist who has taught at Indiana University for many years. It is associated with the National Museum of American History, where it was established in 1990 by an act of Congress. Baker generally uses a twenty-year benchmark in choosing works for programming—that is, any music played should be at least twenty years old so that its historical importance and musical value are reasonably clear.

The best-known repertory organization is Jazz at Lincoln Center. The director, Wynton Marsalis, is undoubtedly the most visible jazz artist today. The program has enjoyed astounding success: Beginning with three concerts in 1987, the program soon became a department at Lincoln Center, then in 1996 it became a full-fledged member of the arts consortium, equal in stature to the New York Philharmonic and the Metropolitan Opera. In 1998 Jazz at Lincoln Center announced the creation of a new concert space that will include an 1,100-seat auditorium, as well as office suites and rehearsal rooms.

Jazz at Lincoln Center has benefited immensely from the work of its former executive director, Rob Gibson, and writers Stanley Crouch and Albert Murray, but no one has been more important to its success than Marsalis, who has sought to identify and promote a canon of jazz masterpieces. In making Jazz at Lincoln Center an expression of his musical personality and interests, Marsalis is perhaps the primary spokesperson for the traditionalist point of view.

WYNTON MARSALIS

Wynton Marsalis embodies many of the jazz traditionalist values of the eighties and nineties. Many jazz musicians have cited him as one of the main catalysts responsible for the resurgence of jazz since the eighties. Born in New Orleans in 1961,

A 1989 photograph of Wynton Marsalis (CD 2, Track 15) by Ken Frankling. Despite his many Grammy awards for jazz and classical music, Wynton Marsalis may be most widely known for his work promoting music education and his commentary on the Ken Burns *Jazz* series on PBS.

Marsalis at an early age showed extraordinary talent as a trumpeter, in both the European classical tradition and jazz. His father, Ellis Marsalis, is a professional jazz pianist and prominent educator, while his older brother Branford is a well-known saxophonist.

Wynton Marsalis's talent became clear at an early age. He attended the Juilliard School of Music briefly, but dropped out to join Art Blakey's Jazz Messengers in 1980. He subsequently toured with Miles Davis's brilliant 1960s rhythm section of Herbie Hancock, Ron Carter, and Tony Williams. This association led to his first album as a leader, *Wynton Marsalis* (1981). In 1984 Marsalis became the first musician to win Grammy awards in both classical and jazz categories.

In 1991 Marsalis was appointed artistic director of Jazz at Lincoln Center. He has filled this position capably, helping to bring about a greater appreciation of the music. In the latter regard, Marsalis was featured prominently in the Ken Burns multiepisode documentary *Jazz* (2000), which was first broadcast on PBS in January 2001. Largely through the influence of Marsalis, a handful of greats of the jazz past, in particular Louis Armstrong, dominated the Burns film. Not everyone has agreed with Marsalis's pro-traditionalist point of view, yet there is no denying the positive effect he is having on the appreciation of jazz.

In spite of his rise to prominence as a trumpet player, Marsalis has been focusing more and more on composition. His earliest pieces followed a postbop and modal style; however, he disavowed this direction as his interests began to turn to earlier jazz. For example, in 1987 he wrote a song called "In the Afterglow," which appeared on the album *Marsalis Standard Time,* volume 1. About this tune, Marsalis comments:

> That was the first time I wrote something with a certain type of traditional [chord] progression. Before that, I would write stuff that was modal, with no chords on it. But "In the Afterglow" got me to try to break out of writing the typical type of New York–scene tune and trying to experiment with form, with modulations, with developing themes in different keys, with different grooves. . . . That's when my [composed] music really started to evolve.[4]

After this point, Marsalis began to incorporate earlier jazz traditions into his music, as the 1989 album *The Majesty of the Blues* testified. His jazz-roots evolution continued with such albums as *Soul Gestures in Southern Blue* (1991), *Blue Interlude* (1992), and *In This House, On This Morning* (1994), the last a large-scale work based on a traditional Baptist church service.

Marsalis's extended oratorio, *Blood on the Fields,* was his first composition for large ensemble and included a libretto by Marsalis. It premiered in 1994 and in 1997 became the first jazz composition to win the Pulitzer Prize for music. The work examines American slavery and its aftermath. An important result of Marsalis's award is that the Pulitzer Prize in music is now offered for significant, large-scale works of any musical genre, whereas the Pulitzer had previously been restricted to concert music.

Above all, *Blood on the Fields* reveals Marsalis's ambition to create large-scale pieces in the Duke Ellington tradition. Indeed, Marsalis credits Ellington's *Black, Brown, and Beige* as a precedent for his composition and has frequently cited Ellington as his primary compositional inspiration.

"Express Crossing"
CD 2 Track 15

Jazz at Lincoln Center: "Express Crossing" (Marsalis), from *Jazz: Six Syncopated Movements* (1993), *They Came to Swing*. Columbia CK 66379, 1994. New York, January 14, 1993. Wynton Marsalis, composer and trumpet; Marcus Printup, trumpet; Wycliffe Gordon, Ronald Westray, trombones; Todd Williams, tenor saxophone; Wes Anderson, alto saxophone; Kent Jordan, piccolo; Victor Goines, baritone saxophone; Eric Reed, piano; Reginald Veal, bass; Herlin Riley, drums; Robert Sadin, conductor.

"Express Crossing" is from the larger dance work *Jazz: Six Syncopated Movements,* written for the New York City Ballet. The live performance analyzed here is highly spirited and reveals a composer with a fertile imagination that blends influences ranging from early jazz to Ellington to contemporary modernism. The piece can be compared, for example, with Ellington's "Daybreak Express" (1933), a well-known jazz depiction of a train. Though Marsalis is at heart a traditionalist, this piece can be called postmodern in its blending of disparate styles.

Section I—AA, irregular 8 bars repeated, at tempo I

0:00   After three dissonant chords serving to "start the train," the rhythm begins in a rhythmically complex first section. The trombones play first on the beat, then off the beat, before returning back on the beat. (Compare Robert Sadin's comment on pages 256 and 257.) For the last part of the first A, the alto and tenor saxophones trade rapid notes followed by a "train whistle" honk in the tenor to end the part. Despite the rhythmic irregularities, the basic feel of part A is that of an eight-bar thematic statement.

0:15   Part A is repeated.

Section II—B, irregular 9 bars, at tempo I

0:27   The B part maintains the up-tempo drive of section I. Its nine bars are punctuated with occasional meter changes. These odd meters serve to turn the beat around.

Section III—C, 4 bars in 4/4, at tempo II

0:40   The tempo changes abruptly for four bars. Amidst train whistles and honks, the piccolo occasionally interjects the chromatic idea heard in the A section. There is also a new syncopated motive played in lower-register trumpets and in alto and baritone saxophones.

Section IV—D, 32 bars in 4/4 as 16 + 16, at tempo I

0:48   A return to the hectic tempo of sections I and II, with a perpetual motion idea developed in the piccolo, alto, and tenor. The bass walks in double time. The brass punctuate with sharp chords and occasionally sustain longer chords with glissandi and "fall-offs." The last two bars of the first half feature a break with wah-wah chords in the brass.

1:10   The wah-wah chords continue into the second sixteen bars, as the sixteenth notes in the winds return. The chords of the D section are based on the Dixieland classic "Tiger Rag." (Compare earlier selections: CD 1, Track 57; CD 1, Track 61; and CD 1, Track 62.)

Section V—D, 32 bars in 4/4, at tempo I; Marsalis trumpet solo

1:33   Using the "Tiger Rag" chord progression of part D, Marsalis offers a virtuosic muted trumpet solo. Interestingly, the solo is based on bebop-style chromatic lines. The ensemble backs Marsalis with punctuated chords.

1:52–1:54   Bars 15–16 are a break for Marsalis.

2:14–2:16   Bars 31–32 are a break for the ensemble to introduce the next section.

Section VI—D, 32 bars in 4/4, at tempo I

2:17   The ensemble returns for a written-out piccolo solo that alternates in turn with Marsalis's (now open) trumpet, honks, brass punctuation and wah-wah chords, and a short bass solo. The final two bars again serve as a break for the ensemble to introduce the next section.

Interlude—3 bars in 2/4 and 1 bar in 4/4, at tempo I

3:01   The piano repeats the quintuplet runs first heard in the alto and tenor at the end of section I.

Section VII—E, 22 bars in 4/4 + 1 extra beat, at tempo I

3:04   This new section changes key and is largely a duet featuring counterpoint between Marsalis's muted trumpet and the flute. The rhythm continues, and the ensemble punctuates with chords. The last two bars (plus one beat) are a break for the ensemble.

Section VIII—A, 4 bars in 4/4, at tempo I

3:35   This section recalls the opening A material combined with the running sixteen-note idea in the flutes. The trombones, alternating notes, speed up the rhythm of the alternation. The alto and tenor alternate the quintuplets at the end of the section.

Section IX—F, 32 bars in 4/4 at tempo III; 2 beats clipped from last bar

3:46   The mood completely changes as this section features new material in a slower 4/4 swing tempo. The "Tiger Rag" layout remains roughly as thirty-two bars divided into 16 + 16, although the chords are modified.

Section X—A, irregular 8 bars

4:45   In a reprise of section I, A returns. The last couple of beats are clipped from the alto-tenor quintuplet alteration. The piece ends abruptly.

Postmodernism is an attitude toward art and culture that has become common since the 1970s. It disavows some of the cerebral, audience-distancing tenets of modernism and replaces them with a free-wheeling conception of culture. Some postmodernist practices do the following:

▶ Blend styles and cultures
▶ Forgo structural unity as a necessity for art
▶ Incorporate older styles and genres
▶ Project an ironic, even cynical conception of art and expression
▶ Break down barriers between popular and fine art

Marsalis goes beyond traditionalism, however, in works such as "Express Crossing." This piece is a quintessentially *postmodern* work, an imaginative collage of elements that spans twentieth-century jazz and concert music. These elements include the following:

▶ Modernist dissonance

▶ Modernist irregular time signatures

▶ Modernist tempo changes

▶ Dixieland harmonic progressions

▶ Train simulations that recall early jazz and boogie-woogie blues

▶ Bebop-style improvisation

Robert Sadin, who conducted the piece, compares it to composer Igor Stravinsky's *Pulcinella*, a work that similarly weaves in earlier musical elements. Sadin summarizes the impact of "Express Crossing":

> Conducting "Express Crossing" for me was an experience very similar in feeling to conducting Stravinsky's *Pulcinella*. Although Wynton's borrowings are less literal than Stravinsky's, there is a kindred sense of respecting and at the same time revisiting and even refreshing the past.

The blending of elements of Ellington's train music, of Kansas City shuffle, with a sense of the unexpected rhythmic flavor is very characteristic of Wynton (the irregular meters at the beginning, which have the effect of turning the beat around). All of this makes for a very exhilarating musical experience.

Characteristic of Marsalis is that although with the exception of a few solos (and the rhythm section, of course), the music is entirely written out, and yet the players are expected to bring a great deal of personal color and imagination to their parts while also executing the not inconsiderable technical difficulties.[5]

Marsalis's expectation that individual musicians will contribute "personal color and imagination to their parts" recalls the bandleading techniques of Duke Ellington. Clearly, Ellington has provided Marsalis with a potent role model. In a *New York Times* article celebrating the Duke Ellington centennial in 1999, Marsalis described what he admires most about how Ellington handled his own career. The description seems to apply to Marsalis as well:

After his [Ellington's] initial fame, he could easily have escaped into the art world of the "serious composer" and created some very interesting and tongue-twisting theories about harmony and what-not. He could have retreated to the university to rail bitterly against the establishment while creating a distinguished body of work that ran people out of the concert hall. Or he could have become a tired imitator of pop trends, which have proved to be the creative graveyard for so many jazz musicians. He didn't.[6]

Nor has Marsalis. He seems to be patterning both his jazz career and his musical values after Ellington. With the international platform provided by Jazz at Lincoln Center and its ties to public television and other important forums, it is likely that Wynton Marsalis—as both a composer and a performer—will continue to be one of the most significant jazz artists in the decades to come.

THE BLAKEY ALUMNI AND THE HARD BOP RENAISSANCE

In addition to the repertory movement, there has been a significant resurgence of tradition-minded players since the fusion developments of the 1970s. The traditionalists have in many ways rejected fusion in either its commercial or avant-garde legacies. Some traditionalists, such as Marsalis, have returned to classic jazz for their inspiration. Most of the others look back to bebop or the hard bop of the 1950s. Marsalis first gained national recognition as a member of the Art Blakey Quintet; many keepers of the hard bop flame since 1980 also include those who first gained attention playing with Blakey.

Even in the 1950s, drummer Art Blakey showed a knack for hiring musicians who would go on to form important groups of their own and establish a major presence in jazz. Retaining his traditional hard bop orientation and instrumentation through the 1980s, Blakey was something of a university for up-and-coming jazz players, providing them with a rich environment for musical growth. Membership in Blakey's band constantly shifted, but it allowed his later sidemen to trace their lineage back to the hard bop roots of the fifties and sixties. Blakey's sidemen—in particular, "Blakey's class of 1980–89"[7]—played a significant role in the hard bop renaissance of the 1980s and 1990s.

Other Traditionalists

Tradition-minded musicians abound today. Although it is impossible to compare and contrast all of the most important artists, the following table surveys some of the most notable ones.

SAXOPHONISTS		
NAME	*INFLUENCES*	*LIFE AND WORK*
Joe Lovano (b. 1952) Tenor saxophone	John Coltrane	▶ Often works in a trio led by Paul Motian (drums) and Bill Frisell (guitar) ▶ Collaborated with Gunther Schuller on *Rush Hour* (1995), an album featuring elements of third-stream music
Joshua Redman (b. 1969) Tenor saxophone	Son of saxophonist Dewey Redman	▶ Successful records have led to some criticism for playing "accessible" music
James Carter (b. 1969) All saxophones and bass clarinet	Mixes both traditional and free jazz elements	▶ Mixes "inside" and "outside" playing in a popular blend ▶ Anything-goes approach shows influence of postmodernism
Phil Woods (b. 1931) Alto saxophone	Charlie Parker	▶ Since 1974 has worked in a quartet that included bassist Steve Gilmore and drummer Bill Goodwin
Charles McPherson (b. 1939) Alto saxophone	Charlie Parker, Eric Dolphy	▶ First worked with Charles Mingus ▶ Album *Manhattan Nocturne* (1998) displays inspiration in the mainstream tradition
TRUMPETERS		
NAME	*INFLUENCES*	*LIFE AND WORK*
Tom Harrell (b. 1946)	Bebop with more-modern harmonies	▶ Worked with Stan Kenton, Woody Herman, and Horace Silver through the 1970s before moving to New York ▶ *Play of Light* (1982) established him as a significant composer/arranger/leader
Nicolas Peyton (b. 1973)	Fats Navarro, Clifford Brown	▶ Won Grammy for his collaboration with trumpeter Doc Cheatham (nearly seven decades his senior) in 1998 ▶ Regular soloist at Jazz at Lincoln Center
Roy Hargrove (b. 1969)	Clifford Jordan, Jackie McLean, Slide Hampton, Jon Faddis, Freddie Hubbard	▶ First championed by Wynton Marsalis ▶ Traditionalist, with an interest in world music and funk
Ryan Kisor (b. 1973)	Bebop	▶ Won Monk Competition in 1990 ▶ Worked with various bands over the decade and as a solo recording artist, showing proficiency in many different styles

Other Traditionalists

(continued)

PIANISTS		
NAME	**INFLUENCES**	**LIFE AND WORK**
Kenny Barron (b. 1943)	Thelonious Monk, McCoy Tyner	▶ Performed with various groups as a side-man from the 1960s through the 1980s ▶ Founder/member of the group Sphere, honoring Thelonious Monk and his music ▶ Jazz educator at Rutgers University since 1973
Marcus Roberts (b. 1963)	Early jazz pianists from Jelly Roll Morton through stride and bop stylists	▶ Championed by Wynton Marsalis, with whom he recorded/performed from 1985 to 1991 ▶ Has developed jazz interpretations of Scott Joplin's ragtime works, Gershwin's *Rhapsody in Blue,* and James P. Johnson's *Yamekraw*
Cyrus Chestnut (b. 1963)	Gospel	▶ Noted for blending jazz improvisation with gospel stylings and rhythms
Stephen Scott (b. 1969)	Thelonious Monk	▶ Worked as accompanist for Betty Carter
Jackie Terrasson (b. 1965)	Bill Evans	▶ Worked as accompanist for Betty Carter ▶ Likes to work in trio format pioneered by Bill Evans
Brad Mehldau (b. 1970)	Bill Evans, Kenny Werner	▶ Melds jazz and European classical traditions ▶ Draws on harmonies and arrangements in Evans's style
Eliane Elias (b. 1960)	Brazilian jazz	▶ Mixes Brazilian rhythms and harmonies with traditional jazz repertory

OTHER INSTRUMENTS		
NAME	**INFLUENCES**	**LIFE AND WORK**
Joey DeFrancesco (b. 1971) Organ	Jimmy Smith, Groove Holmes, Jimmy McGriff	▶ Discovered at age sixteen by Miles Davis, with whom he toured and recorded ▶ Plays in hard bop and funky-jazz style
Steve Turre (b. 1948) Trombone and conch shells	Eclectic	▶ Originally with rock band Santana in 1970 ▶ Has recorded with many leading jazz musicians and bands
Mike Whitfield (b. 1967) Guitar	George Benson	▶ Worked with a variety of bands/styles, from pop-fusion to traditional postbop

Other Traditionalists

(continued)

VOCALISTS		
NAME	INFLUENCES	LIFE AND WORK
Betty Carter (1929–1998)	Bebop	▸ Major vocal stylist since the 1940s ▸ Mentor to dozens of young musicians
Bobby McFerrin (b. 1950)	Jazz, opera, pop, rock	▸ Widely versatile, able to produce many vocal sounds ▸ Multitracks elaborate arrangements of standards and his own compositions
Cassandra Wilson (b. 1955)	Sixties rock, postbop jazz	▸ Popular singer who has recorded works not normally associated with jazz, including songs by country legend Hank Williams and by the pop group the Monkees
Diana Krall (b. 1965)	Nat Cole	▸ Canadian-born singer in straight-ahead repertory from American popular song
Kevin Mahogany (b. 1958)	Blues	▸ Worked on a number of film sound tracks for Clint Eastwood
Kurt Elling (b. 1967)	Mark Murphy, Tony Bennett, pop-jazz standards	▸ Known for "ranting" style in which he improvises lyrics
Norah Jones (b. 1979)	Etta James, Sade, Nick Drake; influenced by soul, country, and folk pop	▸ Straight-ahead repertory from American popular song

During his stint with Blakey from 1980 to 1982, Wynton Marsalis and his brother Branford helped elevate the group's visibility. After they departed, they were replaced by nineteen-year-old trumpeter Terence Blanchard and saxophonist Donald Harrison.

Also working as a team through the 1980s, Blanchard and Harrison recorded five albums as co-leaders. Blanchard has also maintained an active career as a film composer: His score for *Mo' Better Blues* was nominated for a Grammy in 1990. On the other hand, Harrison has lately been working with merging mainstream jazz with funk, which he calls "nouveau swing."

Blanchard was replaced in Blakey's band by Wallace Roney, whose often spare and thoughtful playing contrasted with many of the busier hard bop trumpeters. Roney's visibility was enhanced considerably after he was chosen to perform with Miles Davis at a tribute sponsored by the Montreux Jazz Festival in July 1991.

Alto saxophonist Bobby Watson (b. 1953)—from Lawrence, Kansas—served as music director for Blakey from 1977 to 1981. Watson earned a music degree from the University of Miami and then went to New York in 1976. In the past two decades, Watson has recorded more than a dozen albums as a leader.

Watson and Harrison are not alone among the fine altoists who have worked with Blakey. For instance, Kenny Garrett is one of the most accomplished players on the scene. In addition to Blakey, Garrett has also performed with the Mercer

Ellington Orchestra, Freddie Hubbard, and Miles Davis. Born in 1961, Garrett worked with Davis through the late eighties for some five years and served as Davis's personal assistant.

Many fine pianists have also been associated with Blakey. Among the preeminent are James Williams (b. 1951), who, like Bobby Watson, was with Blakey from 1977 to 1981, and Mulgrew Miller, from Greenwood, Mississippi, where he was born in 1955.

BIG BANDS

Many of the big bands today are known as *ghost bands,* groups that tour and sometimes record even though the founders who established the band are no longer alive. There is a long tradition of ghost bands. The most important early ghost band was the one associated with Glenn Miller, which continued for many years under such leaders as Ray McKinley.

Ghost bands are groups whose founding leaders have died but who continue to travel and work under new direction.

Of the current ghost bands, perhaps the most important is the Count Basie Orchestra, which has been led by such fine talents as Thad Jones, Frank Foster, and more recently Grover Mitchell. Some of the surviving players who worked with Basie himself are members. Another important ghost band featuring the works of Duke Ellington was led by Ellington's son, Mercer Ellington, until his death in 1996.

A fascinating big band that unites a creative modern unit, a traditional ghost band, and a repertory ensemble is the Mingus Dynasty, which continues the tradition of the bassist and composer. Interestingly, Charles Mingus himself never led a big band. Andy McKee, the band's bassist and one of its musical directors, points out:

> [Mingus] expected musicians to find their own paths through his work. That spirit of improvisation and freedom is entirely characteristic of Mingus's method. This often will determine who will work out well in the band and who won't. A player may be a tremendous musician but needs more structure to frame his work. This band needs musicians who know how to frame themselves. That's my understanding of how Mingus's original groups worked.[8]

Toshiko Akiyoshi has been one of the most successful big-band composers in jazz for many years. She was born in China in 1929 and began studying jazz in Japan in 1947. Encouraged by Oscar Peterson, she studied at Boston's Berklee College of Music during the late 1950s and worked briefly with bassist Charles Mingus. In 1973 she and reed player Lew Tabackin started a big band in Los Angeles, which became one of the most successful groups of the early eighties. Her writing style can be traced to Gil Evans and Thad Jones; it incorporates considerable modernism and occasional influences of Japanese music.

A young Toshiko Akiyoshi.

Steeped in the tradition of composer-arranger Gil Evans, bandleader Maria Schneider is renowned for her subtle and sophisticated compositions.

Courtesy Maria Schneider

While Akiyoshi has been associated with a postbebop musical vocabulary, composer-arranger Carla Bley (b. 1938) has ventured memorably into the avant-garde. She has written for George Russell, Jimmy Giuffre, and Charlie Haden's Liberation Music Orchestra. She is perhaps best known for *Escalator over the Hill,* a jazz opera completed in 1971.

One of the most visible of current big bands is led by composer-arranger Maria Schneider. Born in 1960 in Windom, Minnesota, Schneider studied at the University of Minnesota and the Eastman School of Music. She led the Maria Schneider Jazz Orchestra at New York's Visiones club during the 1990s. After graduating from Eastman, Schneider studied with composer and trombonist Bob Brookmeyer. In 1985 she became Gil Evans's assistant and in 1988 started her first band.

Schneider's first album, *Evanescence* (1994), established her reputation as innovative yet steeped in the tradition of Gil Evans and other composer-arrangers such as Brookmeyer. Schneider's second album, *Coming About* (1996), was even more successful; her third album, *Allégresse,* was released in 2000. Schneider brings to her work a sophisticated compositional palette derived from jazz and Western concert music, and she creates an excellent balance between composition and improvisation.

The Popular Connection

Acid jazz is a fusion style that incorporates sampling of older jazz recordings, rap, and hip-hop grooves and techniques.

Another side to jazz is the development of several popular forms stemming from advances in digital technology. Since the 1980s, smooth jazz and *acid jazz* have carried on the legacy of fusion. Meanwhile, other popular interests have arisen as well, such as the retro fad neo-swing, which reflects an interest in a largely acoustic sound.

DIGITAL TECHNOLOGY

In the early 1980s, the jazz-fusion music of the 1970s began to adopt new technology. In particular, synthesizers became largely digital, and analog instruments took on a vintage status. Synthesizers were combined with the increasingly popular personal computer. The convenience of storing data on the computer increased the variety, complexity, and interaction of the digitally synthesized sounds. Computer memory also enabled the mixing of multiple tracks of digitally produced sound, simulating a multitrack tape recorder. The technology that enabled computers to "talk" to the synthesizers became known as *MIDI*, for Musical Instrument Digital Interface.

MIDI technology is a major part of the work of jazz-pop and avant-garde artists. In general, the widespread use of electronics and MIDI often distinguishes these artists from the traditionalists discussed earlier in this chapter, who tend to rely on acoustic instruments. For example, MIDI-controlled synthesizers and samplers may wholly

MIDI is an acronym for Musical Instrument Digital Interface. This standard language allows computers to control synthesizers or samplers.

Other Pop Jazz Stars

The following table summarizes the careers of popular fusion stars other than the ones already discussed in the text.

NAME	FAME	LIFE AND WORK
Chuck Mangione (b. 1940)	Trumpet	▶ "Feels So Good" (1978) his major hit, featuring a pleasant pop-fusion groove
Bill Frisell (b. 1951)	Guitar	▶ Use of electronic effects ▶ Eclectic style, as shown by his country music crossover in his album *Nashville* (1997), which won the *Down Beat* Jazz Critic's Jazz Album of the Year award in 1998
The Yellowjackets	Fusion band	▶ Popular, long-lived fusion band together since the early 1980s ▶ Plays in both electronic and acoustic styles
Medeski Martin & Wood	Fusion band	▶ Funk-fusion group, particularly popular on college campuses ▶ Exhibits a fascinating blend of styles that is sometimes reminiscent of film music
John Scofield (b. 1951)	Guitar	▶ Worked with Miles Davis in the seventies
Phish	Rock band	▶ Heavily into improvisation, in the tradition of the Grateful Dead
Kenny G (b. 1956)	Saxophone	▶ Probably the most popular of all the pop-jazz artists
David Sanborn (b. 1945)	Saxophone	▶ Has worked with Stevie Wonder

or in part provide a background texture for the principal voices or instruments in an ensemble; or percussionists or other players may enhance the MIDI textures by interacting with preprogrammed synthesizer textures. This kind of work may take place in both live and recorded performances but is obviously easier to control in the recording studio. Smooth jazz has made extensive use of MIDI technology. Some computer-synthesizer technologies that are even more complex and sophisticated than MIDI are also in use.

SMOOTH JAZZ

Smooth jazz has been called "the jazz of the '90s"[9] by its advocates, while its detractors describe it as "smooth like a lobotomy flattens out the ridges on a brain."[10] None can deny its extreme popularity. Radio stations that broadcast the format are among the most listened to in a given metropolitan area. In this sense, smooth jazz can be compared with the wildly popular swing music of the late 1930s and early forties: For perhaps the second time in its history, a jazz style can be looked on as a type of mainstream U.S. popular music.

Many artists have provided consistently interesting performances of popular-jazz fusion. For example, the work of Grover Washington Jr. (1943–1999) could be considered a form of smooth jazz, although it was often quite adventurous and unusually well crafted.

Other extremely popular smooth-jazz artists include Kenny G, who is perhaps the most commercially successful, and Charlie Hunter, Earl Klugh, Al Jarreau, Hubert Laws, and David Sanborn.

ACID JAZZ

A style that had a major impact on the jazz world in the early- to mid-1990s is known as acid jazz, a fusion of jazz and hip-hop. Groups with hits include Buckshot LeFonque (featuring Branford Marsalis; the group's name comes from a nickname for Cannonball Adderley), Incognito, and Us3. Nurtured on the rap and hip-hop of the 1980s, the young musicians in these bands were inspired to sample jazz tracks and vamps to form the basis of their new sound.

One of the biggest acid jazz hits to date was Us3's "Cantaloop (Flip Fantasia)," from the album *Hand on the Torch*. This single consisted of a rap over samples from Herbie Hancock's "Cantaloupe Island"; it reached the Top 20 on the pop charts in 1994. Despite this success and others like it, by the late 1990s the future of acid jazz was unclear, with many of the earlier groups no longer producing records.

THE MASS MARKET: RADIO AND THE INTERNET

The various types of pop-jazz share an important goal: attracting a mass market. Hence, pop-jazz must generate extensive radio airplay to boost record sales and draw in listeners for live performance. Not surprisingly, some radio stations interested in jazz conduct in-depth studies of their listeners' preferences to better understand what the public wants to hear. In this process, the program director of Seattle's KPLU, Joey Cohn, made an unsettling discovery, as Charles Levin notes here:

> Cohn's research breaks down jazz into six modes: lyrical, instrumental, driving improvisation, contemporary rhythms, vintage, swinging singers and blues. On the ratings scale, "driving improvisation was at the bottom of the list," [KXJZ Music Director Gary] Vercelli says. "'Driving improvisation' was driving a lot of our audience away."[11]

Cohn's classifications have little to do with jazz history or stylistic congruity: They depend entirely on split-second reactions from listeners with little or no knowledge of jazz. With some radio stations testing market reactions to jazz so carefully, it seems likely that radio play for jazz will continue to feature smooth jazz and the most popular crossover styles. Radio play for a larger spectrum of jazz styles may continue to decline.

Another potentially significant development in the realm of electronics has been the use of the Internet for selling music and for live broadcasts. The MP3 digital music format allows recorded music to be transferred and stored for reuse, although controversies have arisen regarding appropriate compensation for artists and record companies. Jazz clubs such as the Blue Note and Knitting Factory in New York are also broadcasting shows from their Web sites. The practice of archival broadcasts has arisen as well: A venue can create a video of a performance for later broadcast over the Internet. The long-established Montreux Jazz Festival in Switzerland, for example, has experimented with this practice.

NEO-SWING

During the later 1990s, the big-band swing sound momentarily returned. The music was quite popular, especially among teenagers and young people in their twenties, who became enthusiastic about the jitterbug and the older ballroom dances. Their enthusiasm stems in part from nostalgia for the glamour of the 1930s and 1940s; for example, retro clothing styles played a big part in the revival. The music was reminiscent of 1940s jump-style swing, which itself was a precursor to rock and roll, rather than the more sedate, smoother sounds of many of the 1930s big bands.

Although the relationship of neo-swing to jazz remains controversial, the music offered a distinctive change of pace from the ubiquitous electronic ambience of popular music. While its largely acoustic sound was modernized through amplification, older swing tunes were revived in the process and, according to journalists' reports, interest in traditional 1930s jazz recordings was whetted considerably among much of the audience.

A particularly successful neo-swing artist is guitarist Brian Setzer. In the later 1990s, the Brian Setzer Orchestra, a big band with standard instrumentation, was enormously popular—one of its CDs, *The Dirty Boogie* (1998), sold in double platinum figures (four million CDs). Their live performances have attracted as many as 4,000 people.

The Avant-Garde, Crossover, World Music, and Jazz to Come

Although it seems safe to say that the principal styles of jazz—from Dixieland to swing to hard bop to fusion—will continue to have their fans and proponents, jazz will itself continue to develop in the years to come. It seems likely that future developments will see change regarding such issues as the following:

- Crossover with other musical styles and cultures, including:
  - ▶ Popular music (such as neo-swing)
  - ▶ Non-Western music cultures
  - ▶ Concert music (third-stream experimentation)
- Greater participation of women
- Greater participation of artists from countries other than the United States

We shall conclude this chapter by looking at where these trends might go. We shall also mention some of the most significant artists in each area.

JAZZ AND FEMINISM

A glance back through this book shows that jazz has been a music dominated by men. Apart from talented pianists and composer-arrangers such as Lil Hardin and Mary Lou Williams and some women's big bands from the 1940s, women have largely participated in jazz as vocalists. One important consequence of feminism in the 1960s and 1970s has been a remarkable increase in the number of women with jazz careers. Among the important artists of our time, we have mentioned pianist Eliane Elias and composer-arrangers Toshiko Akiyoshi, Carla Bley, and Maria Schneider. Among others are violinist Regina Carter; drummers Terri Lyne Carrington, Susie Ibarra, and Cindy Blackmon; pianists Geri Allen and Renee Rosnes; alto saxophonist Virginia Mayhew; and trumpeter Ingrid Jensen. The Kennedy Center in Washington, D.C., sponsors a Women in Jazz festival in honor of Mary Lou Williams to showcase the many fine women artists at work today.

For example, Renee Rosnes (b. 1962) has been especially prominent among the pianists. Originally from Saskatchewan, she has worked with Joe Henderson, Wayne Shorter, James Moody, the Carnegie Hall Jazz Band, and the Lincoln Center Jazz Orchestra. Pianist Geri Allen (b. 1957) is comfortable in both traditional and avant-garde settings and in both traditional piano trios and larger ensembles. She has also worked extensively with synthesizers and electronic media. Allen has taught jazz piano at the New England Conservatory and has recorded and performed extensively,

Courtesy of Eliane Elias

Brazilian jazz pianist Eliane Elias.

playing with bassist Charlie Haden, drummer Paul Motian, Ornette Coleman, and vocalist Betty Carter.

Pioneer Jane Ira Bloom (b. 1955) has been one of the first women to carve a major jazz career on an instrument other than piano. As a soprano saxophonist, she has worked in numerous venues, most recently in a quartet. As a composer, she has worked on projects with NASA and the innovative dance company Pilobolus.

The big band Diva (with the slogan "No Man's Band") contains all women. It includes the well-regarded trumpeter Ingrid Jensen and drummer/leader Sherrie Maricle. The group has been getting much attention and many gigs.

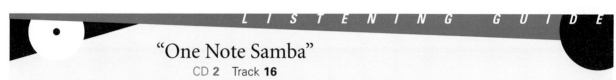

L I S T E N I N G   G U I D E

"One Note Samba"
CD **2**   Track **16**

Eliane Elias: "One Note Samba" (Jobim), from *Eliane Elias Plays Jobim.* Blue Note CDP 7 93089 9.
New York, December 1989. Eliane Elias, piano, leader; Eddie Gomez, bass;
Jack DeJohnette, drums; Nana Vasconcelos, percussion.

Eliane Elias, a gifted Brazilian pianist, displays a fine sensibility for adapting Brazlian music to the demands of the American jazz world. Born in 1960, Elias studied classical piano as a child but quickly developed an interest in jazz. After settling in the United States in the 1980s, she continues to pursue projects that combine jazz with Brazilian music.

In "One Note Samba," Elias interprets the music of Antonio Carlos Jobim, a Brazilian composer who wrote many of the most enduring bossa nova hits, including "Desifinado" and "Girl from Ipanema." Interestingly, according to the liner notes of the original CD, Elias did not meet Jobim in Brazil, but was later introduced to him in New York after she had become established as a rising star in the jazz world.

Introduction—16-bar vamp

0:00   Elias and the trio begin with a vamp in which she features a three-note motive (D-G-B♭). The harmonic and melodic feel of the vamp recalls the blues in contrast to the song itself, which is not blues-oriented. The vamp, as introduction, thus provides a contrast to the elegant harmonic progression of the song. The D-G-B♭ motive begins with the "one note" (D) that is the hallmark of the melody.

1st chorus head—A (16) B (8) A (16)

0:20   The vamp flows directly into a statement of the head without sectional demarcation. The head is an irregular 40-bar structure of 16 + 8 + 16. Elias moves to the higher register for the beginning of the A section with the note D repeated frequently as the principal melodic idea. At 0:30, the second half of the A begins: the D "one note" changes to a G "one note," in following Jobim's song. The G returns to D toward the end of the A section, which then concludes on the high G.

0:39   The B section begins. Here, Jobim contrasts the repeating "one-note" idea of the A section with a running passage moving up and down. This melodic line vividly contrasts the melodic minimalism of the A section.

0:48   Return to the "one-note" idea of the A section.

2nd chorus—ABA improvisation

1:08   Elias's first chorus elegantly continues the sparse texture of her statement of the head. The emphasis is on right-hand melody with the left hand largely inactive.

3rd chorus—ABA improvisation

1:56 Elias gets bluesier at the beginning of this chorus. The left hand is brought in to provide a fuller texture at time. At the return of the A for this chorus, she opens up with greater intensity in the right-hand solo line.

4th chorus—ABA improvisation

2:44 Elias returns to a simpler texture, emphasizing the "one-note" quality of the melody in the A. In the first A section, she sometimes plays the same melody in octaves. In the B section, she stays close to the original melody. This chorus can also be heard as a return to the head.

Return to introductory vamp as coda

3:32 Return to the introductory vamp and its bluesy melodic and harmonic feel. The left hand gets much busier to help add intensity to the texture. The selection fades during this vamp.

JAZZ ABROAD

Superb non-Americans have been involved in jazz virtually since its beginning. Earlier, we discussed the enthusiasm of Europeans for ragtime and how European performers such as Stéphane Grappelli and Django Reinhardt established first-rate jazz credentials as early as the later 1920s (Chapter 2). In addition, a number of U.S. jazz musicians spent extended periods living in Europe, drawn to England and the Continent by the enhanced prestige accorded jazz and jazz musicians there and the less racist atmosphere. Benny Carter worked in England in the 1930s, while saxophonist Coleman Hawkins spent five years in Europe in the 1930s, even recording with guitarist Django Reinhardt. Saxophonist Dexter Gordon spent much of the 1960s and 1970s based in Copenhagen. Other artists, such as Stan Getz, Chet Baker, Steve Lacy, also resided for a time in Europe.

In addition, European jazz artists left Europe, making their careers in the United States by playing with established jazz artists. For example, guitarist John McLaughlin and bassist Dave Holland both left England and began playing with Miles Davis in the late 1960s. Austrian pianist Josef Zawinul gained national attention working with Cannonball Adderley, Miles Davis, and Weather Report.

Jazz musicians have come from all corners of the globe: Canada (Oscar Peterson, Kenny Wheeler, Gil Evans), Brazil (Airto, Flora Purim, Eliane Elias), South Africa (Abdullah Ibrahim), Japan (Sadao Watanabe), Cuba (Gonzalo Rubalcaba), and Norway (Jan Garbarek). Jazz remains an international phenomenon, and jazz clubs in cities such as London, Paris, Amsterdam, Prague, and Moscow provide venues for local musicians playing traditional jazz (Dixieland), bebop, or avant-garde jazz. While most jazz histories tend to stress the music as an American phenomenon, it is important to acknowledge the wide reach of jazz, as well as the innovations of non-American players and composers.

CROSSOVER, POSTMODERNISM, AND WORLD MUSIC

Both the neo-swing and fusion movements can be likened to crossover, or blending one musical style with another to attract listeners of the other style. Because jazz combined aspects of the European and African traditions, one could argue that the original jazz crossover was jazz itself. Forms of jazz have almost always maintained crossover connections to popular music, a connection most commonly forged through vocal and dance music. When jazz splintered into numerous substyles in the late 1940s and 1950s, some substyles such as funky/soul jazz retained a tie to instrumental popular music. Much of today's vocal jazz continues to maintain crossover connections to popular music.

Beyond the vocal connection, some jazz artists are experimenting with the song repertory of the early 1960s and later as a means of expanding the traditional jazz focus on the great popular standards of 1920–1950. Artists are experimenting with tunes by numerous rock groups, including the Beatles; the Grateful Dead; Sly and the Family Stone; Crosby, Stills, Nash & Young; and the Doors. John Zorn (discussed later) has featured the music of pop songwriter Burt Bacharach. Herbie Hancock recently issued a record called *The New Standard*.

In Chapter 4 we discussed another crossover music, Latin jazz, which has been in existence at least since the 1923 recordings of Jelly Roll Morton. It most likely had a significant impact on the formation of the early New Orleans jazz style and came to the forefront with Dizzy Gillespie and Charlie Parker in the earliest days of bebop. The Latin connection has continued unabated since then. The exceptional Latin jazz percussionist Tito Puente was a presence on the scene for many years. He died in 2000. Today the thriving Latin jazz scene includes many fine artists, such as saxophonist-clarinetist Paquito D'Rivera.

Crossover experiments will likely continue to affect jazz in the near future. For example, even mainstream artists such as Wayne Shorter and guitarist Jim Hall are experimenting with writing for orchestra. The development of jazz depends on its capacity for absorbing and integrating new music.

Crossover has been linked to world-music styles since the 1980s at least. Among the most interesting artists are Fred Ho, a baritone saxophonist who unites Asian music sensibilities with jazz; pianist Randy Weston, who created a fine blending of African music and jazz in his album *The Spirits of Our Ancestors* (1991), and pianist Horace Tapscott, who founded the Pan-African Peoples Arkestra in Los Angeles; he died in 1999.

Crossover that ambitiously attempts to link disparate styles and cultures can be likened to postmodernism, which John Zorn virtually personifies in

Contemporary Jazz Musicians in Other Countries

The following table highlights just a few of the outstanding jazz musicians not from the United States who have claimed considerable attention and reputation since the 1980s.

SAXOPHONISTS
▶ **Jan Garbarek** (Norway)
▶ **Evan Parker** (England)

TRUMPETERS
▶ **Hugh Masekela** (South Africa)
▶ **Valery Ponomarev** (Russia)
▶ **Arturo Sandoval** (Cuba)

PIANISTS
▶ **Eliane Elias** (Brazil)
▶ **Abdullah Ibrahim**, a.k.a. **Dollar Brand** (South Africa)
▶ **Adam Makowicz** (Poland)
▶ **Michel Petrucciani** (France)
▶ **Gonzalo Rubalcaba** (Cuba)
▶ **Tete Montoliu** (Spain)

GUITARISTS
▶ **John McLaughlin** (England)

BASSISTS
▶ **Dave Holland** (England)
▶ **George Mraz** (Czechoslovakia)
▶ **Niels-Henning Orsted Pedersen** (Denmark)
▶ **Miroslav Vitous** (Czechoslovakia)

DRUMMERS/PERCUSSIONISTS
▶ **Trilok Gurtu** (India)
▶ **Airto Moreira** (Brazil)

SINGER-SONGWRITERS
▶ **Gilberto Gil** (Brazil)
▶ **Milton Nascimento** (Brazil)
▶ **Flora Purim** (Brazil)

John Zorn directing a performance in London, England, in 1989.

his musical approach. Zorn has emerged as one of the most intriguing figures of the downtown New York scene. Probably more important as a composer and conceptual artist than as an altoist, this prolific musician has worked in numerous media, from his quartet Masada, which shows a blending of Ornette Coleman and klezmer music, to commissions for the New York Philharmonic.

Although it is difficult to pin down Zorn's style, an important quality is its postmodern sensibility of stylistic juxtaposition. Segments of medieval Gregorian chant might segue into a distorted heavy-metal timbre, then into a more conventional jazzlike swing—all within minutes. Zorn's eclecticism virtually defines postmodernism in jazz.

Dave Douglas (b. 1963), who has worked extensively with Zorn, is one of the most interesting crossover trumpet players today. Always involved in a large number of projects, he has recorded extensively, with CDs as both leader and sideman approaching 100 by the late nineties. His numerous projects have included experiments with electronics, Romanian folk music and other eastern European traditions, the twentieth-century styles of Webern and Stravinsky, and Lebanese music. Truly difficult to categorize, Douglas is one of the most adventurous players on the scene.

James "Blood" Ulmer (b. 1942) is a guitarist who played with Ornette Coleman's band Prime Time. Before Ulmer began playing and studying with Coleman in 1973, he was associated with blues and organ groups. Inspired by Coleman's ideas about music, in the late 1970s Ulmer led his own group, which combined funk, avant-garde jazz, and hard rock. The combination of elements have taxed the ability of jazz critics to label Ulmer's music, which has been described as "avant-garde fusion," "jazz-funk," "futuristic jazz-funk," and even "harmolodic diatonic funk."

Ronald Shannon Jackson (b. 1940) worked as the drummer for "Blood" Ulmer; like Ulmer, Jackson also worked closely with Ornette Coleman, playing on the first two Prime Time albums. Jackson's band, the Decoding Society, similarly merges funk, rock, and avant-garde into combinations creatively described as "No-Wave," "funk-jazz," and "punk-jazz."

Anthony Davis (b. 1951) blends jazz with concert music. In particular, he has written several operas, including *X,* which is based on the life of black leader Malcolm X. Premiering in 1985 in Philadelphia, the work—in its use of tailgate trombone and Coltrane-like sheets of sound—made extensive use of jazz elements. Other Davis pieces also refer to African-American history, such as his solo piano work entitled "Middle Passage," named after the harrowing slave-ship voyages from Africa. In the liner notes for *Lady of the Mirrors,* Davis wrote:

> I consider myself fortunate to be part of a long and vital tradition of composer-pianists in creative music. From Scott Joplin to Cow-Cow Davenport, to Jelly Roll Morton, James P. Johnson, Duke Ellington, Fats Waller, Thelonious Monk, Bud Powell, and Cecil Taylor, this is a tradition which has always been at the fulcrum of change and evolution in our music.[12]

Courtesy Steve Coleman/Sooya Arts

George Lewis is another eclectic figure. Like Davis, he has performed extensively as a jazz improviser, while also writing composed music. Born in Chicago in 1952, Lewis began study at Chicago's AACM in 1971 with Muhal Richard Abrams. While a member of AACM in 1976, Lewis performed with two wildly disparate performers—the venerable Count Basie Orchestra and the iconoclastic free jazz saxophonist Anthony Braxton. A recent recipient of a MacArthur Fellowship, he has taught computer music at the University of San Diego, California, and recently joined the faculty of Columbia University.

Steve Lacy (b. 1934) was one of the principal soprano saxophonists of the 1990s. He has spent much time living in Europe because of its openness to the avant-garde. Lacy has been known for his free jazz associations, although lately he has been favoring music that combines free improvisation with composed constraints. Lacy received a MacArthur Fellowship in 1992.

Saxophonist Steve Coleman (b. 1956) is experimenting with combining jazz with rap, funk, and rock grooves. He has been interested in such crossovers since at least the early eighties, when he organized his Five Elements band. He underscores his commitment to crossover when he says, "I'd like to have all those elements in the music, something for people who want to dance, something for people who are intellectual and want to find some abstract meaning, and something for people who just want to forget their troubles."[13]

Steve Coleman's M-Base concept has attracted a number of players. Coleman (CD 2, Track 17) has explored a variety of crossovers since the 1980s.

Coleman has been closely associated with what he calls the M-Base concept, which stands for "Macro-Basic Array of Structured Extemporization." According to Coleman, M-Base should not be considered a stylistic label; it is a "way of thinking about creating music, not the music itself."[14] Coleman has been deeply influenced by non-Western musics, particularly African music and meter. Coleman's ideas have taken hold on a loose-knit community of jazz musicians; among those affiliated with the M-Base concept are saxophonists Greg Osby and Gary Thomas, trombonist Robin Eubanks, keyboardists Geri Allen and Renee Rosnes, and vocalist Cassandra Wilson.

However esoteric his philosophy, much of Coleman's crossover conception is rooted in jazz tradition. For example, in addition to original compositions, he performs jazz standards of the bebop period, such as "Salt Peanuts."

L I S T E N I N G   G U I D E

"Salt Peanuts"
CD **2**   Track **17**

Steve Coleman and Five Elements: "Salt Peanuts" (Gillespie), from *Def Trance Beat (Modalities of Rhythm)*.
RCA-BMG 63181-2. Brooklyn, New York, 1994. Steve Coleman, alto saxophone, leader; Andy Milne, piano;
Reggie Washington, electric bass; Gene Lake, drums and percussion.

A prime example of Coleman's crossover approach is found in his version of "Salt Peanuts," recorded in 1994. Coleman's reinterpretation of the classic Gillespie tune pays homage to the bebop tradition. Yet a comparison with the Gillespie-Parker version (CD 2, Track 1) reveals startling differences, particularly in rhythm. Coleman's 1994 version imbues the composition with driving rock rhythms played by the drums; the use of electric bass further removes it from the bebop tradition.

Most notably, Coleman alters the meter of the composition, pushing the overall metric feel somewhat off-kilter. This metric reinterpretation poses significant challenges for the improviser. In the recording, the group sounds tightly rehearsed, with predetermined ensemble passages as well as improvised sections. Both the original AABA form and the F tonal center are retained throughout.

Introduction
0:00   Coleman plays the introductory riff on saxophone alone.

Melody—AABA
0:06   The group plays the melody of the entire AABA form. Note the driving rhythms on drums and the electric bass.

0:17   The B section begins.

Written ensemble + 16-bar drum solo
0:27   Coleman plays the written-ensemble passage of the tune, and the drummer follows with a 16-bar drum solo.

Stop time melody
0:38   Two bars of the melody are followed by two bars of silence. The "Salt Peanuts" (SP) motive is omitted.

Coleman solo, then "mop-mop" figure

0:59   A brief improvisation by Coleman leads to the repeated-note "mop-mop" figure (from the original arrangement as played by Parker and Gillespie), first by Coleman, then by the drummer.

Milne piano solo

1:09   Milne's piano solo develops motives over two choruses, alternating between short rhythmic ideas and longer linear runs.

1:28–1:30   Drum break takes place between the first and second choruses.

Coleman solo

1:48   The beginning of Coleman's aggressive and energetic solo overlaps with the end of the piano solo. Although the drummer plays very actively with Coleman, during much of the solo the drummer keeps the half-note beat audible on the cymbal.

Coleman 2nd chorus into B

2:29   During the end of Coleman's second chorus, he begins a repeated figure (from the original arrangement) as if to announce the end of his solo. He plays the figure five times, follows with the B section of the composition, then plays the figure two more times.

Reprise of AABA

2:51   The group returns to the melody of "Salt Peanuts." This time the band stops while Coleman plays the SP motive.

Coda

3:11   The group plays the brief coda to the tune, again taken from the original arrangement.

DIRECTIONS FOR CROSSOVER JAZZ

We will close this overview of recent crossover developments in jazz with brief discussions of two fascinating records that appeared in 1998 and 1999 and that presage possible directions for the twenty-first century. One is by an almost legendary older artist, pianist Herbie Hancock, and the other is by Tim Hagans, who has been a visible trumpeter on the New York scene for many years. Both albums are eclectic and heavily produced, embodying crossover to electronic media as well as traditional performance.

Herbie Hancock's 1998 album *Gershwin's World* combines Hancock's interests and accomplishments: the postbop jazz of the sixties, his funk hits of the seventies and eighties, and his long-abiding interest in classical music. For example, some of the tracks are mostly improvised postbop jazz ("Cottontail"), some combine live performance (with touches of African music) and MIDI technology ("Here Come De Honey Man"), some are pop oriented ("St. Louis Blues" with Stevie Wonder), some combine world-music grooves ("Overture"), and some are European classical works given a jazz interpretation (Ravel's *Concerto for Piano and Orchestra in G*). In this last performance, Hancock improvises much of his solo against the original orchestral score as performed by the Orpheus Chamber Ensemble.

Trumpeter Tim Hagans (CD 2, Track 18) is exploring world-music crossovers with his latest work.

Courtesy Tim Hagans

Gershwin's World was a top-selling jazz album and eventually won two Grammy awards. In a *New York Times* article on the album, Hancock said, "Anything I can do to be a force to encourage multiculturalism is what I want to do."[15] It is clear that Hancock's future work will maintain a similar eclectic combination of musical styles and cultures as well as incorporate both electronic and acoustic media.

Tim Hagans (b. 1954) has emerged as one of the most highly respected trumpeters on the New York scene. A native of Dayton, Ohio, Hagans paid his dues in the Stan Kenton and Woody Herman bands. He once lived in Sweden, where he directed the Norrbotten Big Band; he taught at Berklee, and he has worked with some of the most visible groups on the scene, including the Maria Schneider band and the Yellowjackets.

In an album released in 1999, *Animation • Imagination*, Hagans and producer Bob Belden combine the free jazz spirit of the 1960s and electronic fusion sounds of the 1970s with up-to-date studio techniques and grooves derived from hip-hop and rap. The record contains many selections entirely produced by interacting with and overdubbing preproduced electronic tracks. Unlike *Gershwin's World*, *Animation • Imagination* is uncompromising in its exploration of effects and electronics and does not necessarily seek broad-range appeal within a multiplicity of styles.

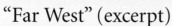

"Far West" (excerpt)
CD **2** Track **18**

Tim Hagans: "Far West" (Hays), from *Animation • Imagination*. Blue Note 7243 4 95198 2 4. New York,
May 6, 1998. Tim Hagans, trumpet; Kevin Hays, composer, Fender Rhodes electric piano, programming;
Scott Kinsey, synthesizers; Ira Coleman, bass; Billy Kilson, drums; Alfred Lion, narration.

"Far West" is a typically interesting track from *Animation • Imagination*. It combines synthesized textures,
sampled sounds, and live improvisation.

Introduction—4-bar groove

0:00   A hip-hop groove begins the track with tabla samples added to the drum texture.

Section I—8 bars

0:09   An acoustic bass line with additional synthesizer textures is added. In the second four bars,
these synthesizer and electric piano textures are elaborated.

Section II—16 bars as 8 + 8

0:26   The North Indian vocal sample defines what might be called the head. The eight-bar unit is
repeated. The electric piano employs wah-wah pedal textures.

Section III—Extended trumpet solo

1:05   Hagans enters with sustained notes in the high register over swirling electronic textures for
eight bars.

1:19   The vocal sample returns twice during Hagans's solo. After the second return, his solo becomes
more active, and drum work on the snare increasingly answers the solo's repeated figures.

Section IV—Electric piano solo

3:48   The electric piano is in the forefront of the texture.

4:14   The vocal sample returns.

Section V—Trumpet returns with rhythmic breakdown

4:24   Hagans returns for the climactic electronic breakdown of the rhythm sounds. The vocal sample
is also treated electronically. Hagans continues to solo over the thick textures.

5:05   The backbeat rhythm returns as the textures blend together for a climax with a fade-out.

Gershwin's World and *Animation • Imagination* present alternative visions for
jazz in its second century. *Gershwin's World* is extremely popular as well as beautifully
crafted and imaginative, displaying a huge stylistic and cultural palette that in no
way panders to the audience in hope of increased sales. The album emphasizes a
multiplicity of crossover combinations. It is also a *tribute* record—a genre that has
become more and more common in jazz. Alternatively, *Animation • Imagination*, by

a relatively unknown but well-established musician, aggressively projects a consistent musical vision, colored by electronics and original compositions with avant-garde free playing.

The exciting musical directions and points of view heard in *Gershwin's World* and *Animation • Imagination* certainly differ from most of the jazz produced in the twentieth century. They may anticipate directions for the music in its second century, while the older, long-established jazz styles will likely continue to attract audiences.

The Future of Jazz

A comparison of the first fifty years of jazz with the second reveals an intriguing difference, one that may have implications for the future of the music. Without question, the first fifty years featured three artists of indisputable greatness and incomparable influence on the development of the music: Louis Armstrong, Duke Ellington, and Charlie Parker. In addition to these three, the first fifty years of jazz included such legendary jazz giants as James P. Johnson, Jelly Roll Morton, Bix Beiderbecke, Earl Hines, Sidney Bechet, Lester Young, Coleman Hawkins, Benny Goodman, Thelonious Monk, Dizzy Gillespie, and Clifford Brown.

What about the second fifty years? John Coltrane and Miles Davis have certainly influenced jazz in long-lasting and far-reaching ways. Arguably, no artists comparable to Coltrane and Davis have emerged since 1970, with the possible exception of Wynton Marsalis. Additionally, the jazz world in the nineties and the early twenty-first century was saddened by the deaths of such major artists as Miles Davis, Dizzy Gillespie, Art Blakey, Sarah Vaughan, Gerry Mulligan, Betty Carter, Joe Williams, Stan Getz, and Benny Carter. Some critics claim that there are now simply no artists of remotely comparable stature.

Examining the jazz section of any well-stocked record store reveals the imbalance of major artists between the first and second halves of the century: The number of available CDs by players no longer living dwarfs the work of contemporary artists. In this respect, jazz-record departments increasingly resemble classical-record departments. Many if not most of the major younger jazz artists receiving attention today are traditionalists of some sort. The end of the first century of jazz may be the first time in its history that middle-aged and older players epitomize the avant-garde, while younger players disavow the new and attempt to refurbish the old. Given this state of affairs, can it be possible that jazz is dying?

The other side can be argued as well: The dearth of decisively influential new artists may be part of a larger historical process. When measured by record sales, attendance at festivals and clubs, interest among scholars, and the creation of repertory ensembles, jazz is thriving. With music in general, and with jazz in particular, a splintering of the market seems an almost necessary by-product of the information age.

With so many disparate substyles and audiences for radically different kinds of music, the emergence in jazz of a dominant figure comparable to Parker, Ellington, Armstrong, Coltrane, or Davis does not seem likely: There are simply too many different tastes to satisfy. A paradox, which has become a cliché of our times, is that as the information age homogenizes culture throughout the world, numerous subcultures have sprung into healthy and even aggressive existence as if in retaliation.

Jazz is no exception. Its many competing substyles reveal the urgency of its message and its ability to reach audiences throughout the world.

As jazz begins its second century, its vital signs are mostly positive. Activity throughout the jazz community remains vigorous as it draws from its own historical tradition, non-Western cultures, electronics, the high-culture avant-garde, and the many formats of popular music. With the easy-listening grooves of Kenny G, the postmodern eclecticism of John Zorn, the popular and blues infusions by Stevie Wonder, the neo-traditionalism of Wynton Marsalis, and the straight-ahead swinging of Charles McPherson, jazz remains vibrant in its stylistic multiplicity and continuing world-class appeal. If the history of the music in the last half-century is any indication, jazz will continue the same complex and paradoxical course begun one hundred years ago. At the same time that new substyles continue to spin off from the center of jazz, reissues of classic jazz will consolidate a greater appreciation of its history and a deeper understanding of its evolution. The outlook is indeed exciting on all fronts.

Questions and Topics for Discussion

1. Why is it important not to think of the history of jazz as one style succeeding or supplanting another? Cite contemporary artists mentioned throughout the chapter to argue the point that the history of jazz is not rigidly linear.

2. How can the 1980s be described as a reaction against fusion?

3. What approach to jazz does Wynton Marsalis personify? How does he personify it? In considering this issue, refer to his life, his role in the jazz repertory movement, and in particular his work as a composer.

4. What traditional prejudices have restricted the role of women in jazz? How have some of these prejudices been overcome in the past two or three decades?

5. Is jazz, most broadly conceived, increasing or declining in either importance or popularity? Cite cultural trends to support your view. Part of your answer may depend on what you consider to be jazz. Another important consideration may be record sales: They measure popularity, but do they measure importance?

6. How do Herbie Hancock's *Gershwin's World* and Tim Hagans's *Animation • Imagination* suggest possibilities for the future of jazz? Which possibility do you prefer? Can you think of any possibilities not discussed in the text?

Key Terms

Acid jazz 262

Back catalog 249

Complete reissue 250

Crossover 249

False start 250

Ghost bands 261

Jazz repertory movement 249

MIDI 263

Postmodernism 256

Remastering 250

NOTES

Chapter 1

1. Olly Wilson, "The Significance of the Relationship Between Afro-American Music and West African Music," *Black Perspective in Music* 2, no. 1 (Spring 1974): 16.

2. Robert Farris Thompson, "Kongo Influences on African-American Artistic Culture," in *Africanisms in American Culture*, ed. Joseph E. Holloway (Bloomington: Indiana University Press, 1990), 149–50.

3. Quoted in Robert L. Hall, "African Religious Retentions in Florida," in *Africanisms in American Culture*, ed. Joseph E. Holloway (Bloomington: Indiana University Press, 1990), 108.

4. See Sterling Stuckey, *Slave Culture: Nationalist Theory and the Foundations of Black America* (New York: Oxford University Press, 1987).

5. Marshall Stearns, *The Story of Jazz* (New York: Oxford University Press, 1958), 19.

6. William Francis Allen, Charles Pickard Ware, and Lucy McKim Garrison, *Slave Songs of the United States* (New York: Peter Smith, 1951; orig. pub., New York: A. Simpson, 1867; reprint, New York: Dover, 1995), vi.

7. Thomas L. Riis, *Just Before Jazz: Black Musical Theater in New York, 1890–1915* (Washington, DC: Smithsonian Institution Press, 1989), 5–6.

8. Frederick James Smith, "Irving Berlin and Modern Ragtime," *New York Dramatic Mirror*, January 14, 1914, p. 38.

9. Edward A. Berlin, *Ragtime: A Musical and Cultural History* (Berkeley: University of California Press, 1980), 12.

10. See Berlin, *Ragtime*, esp. pp. 147–170.

11. Blues lyrics quoted in Paul Oliver, *Aspects of the Blues Tradition* (New York: Oak Publications, 1970), 18.

12. W. C. Handy and Arna Bontemps, *Father of the Blues* (New York: Macmillan, 1941; reprint, New York: Collier Books, 1970), 13.

Chapter 2

1. Lawrence Gushee, liner notes to *Steppin' on the Gas: Rags to Jazz 1913–1927*, New World Records 269.

2. Alan Lomax, *Mister Jelly Roll: The Fortunes of Jelly Roll Morton, New Orleans Creole and "Inventor" of Jazz* (New York: Pantheon Books, 1950), 109. See also 2nd ed. (Berkeley: University of California Press, 1973).

3. Pops Foster, as told to Tom Stoddard, *Pops Foster: The Autobiography of a New Orleans Jazzman* (Berkeley: University of California Press, 1971), 18–19.

4. See William J. Schafer, with Richard B. Allen, *Brass Bands and New Orleans Jazz* (Baton Rouge: Louisiana State University Press, 1977), 8. Lewis Porter discusses the relationship of the brass band instrumentation to frontline Dixieland instrumentation in Lewis Porter, Michael Ullman, and Edward Hazell, *Jazz: From Its Origins to the Present* (Englewood Cliffs, NJ: Prentice-Hall, 1993), 18.

5. Baby Dodds, as told to Larry Gara, *The Baby Dodds Story* (Baton Rouge: Louisiana State University Press, 1992), 17–18.

6. Dodds, *Baby Dodds Story*, 106.

7. Quoted in Donald M. Marquis, *In Search of Buddy Bolden* (Baton Rouge: Louisiana State University Press, 1978), 105.

8. Martin Williams, *Jazz Masters of New Orleans* (New York: Macmillan, 1967), 1.

9. Ernest Ansermet, *Revue Romande*, October 19, 1919; reprinted in John Chilton, *Sidney Bechet: The Wizard of Jazz* (New York: Oxford University Press, 1987), 40. Also in Robert Walser, *Keeping Time: Readings in Jazz History* (New York: Oxford University Press, 1999), 11.

10. Jelly Roll Morton, Library of Congress Recordings, Riverside 9001-12.

11. Lomax, *Mr. Jelly Roll*, 79.

12. Martin Williams, *The Jazz Tradition*, 2nd ed. (New York: Oxford University Press, 1983), 55. See also 1st ed., 1970.

13. William Howland Kenney, *Chicago Jazz: A Cultural History, 1904–1930* (New York: Oxford University Press, 1993), 9.

14. Ibid., 45.

15. Frederick Ramsey Jr. and Charles Edward Smith, eds., *Jazzmen* (New York: Harcourt, Brace, 1939), 51.

16. Kenney, *Chicago Jazz*, 42.

17. Kenney, *Chicago Jazz*, 104.

18. Lawrence Gushee, liner notes to King Oliver, *King Oliver's Jazz Band—1923*, Columbia P2 12744.

19. Max Kaminsky, with V. E. Hughes, *My Life in Jazz* (New York: Harper & Row, 1963), 39–41.

20. Nat Shapiro and Nat Hentoff, eds., *Hear Me Talkin' to Ya: The Story of Jazz as Told by the Men Who Made It* (New York: Rinehart, 1955; reprint, Dover, 1966), 120.

21. Richard Hadlock, *Jazz Masters of the Twenties* (New York: Collier, 1974), 80–81.

22. Gunnard Askland, "Interpretations in Jazz: A Conference with Duke Ellington," *Etude* (March 1947): 134.

23. Many of the ideas in this section are influenced by Samuel A. Floyd Jr. "Music in the Harlem Renaissance: An Overview," in *Black Music in the Harlem Renaissance*, ed. Samuel A. Floyd Jr. (New York; Westport, CT: Greenwood Press, 1990), 1–27.

24. Nathan Irvin Huggins, *Harlem Renaissance* (New York: Oxford University Press, 1971), 5.

25. See Nathan Irvin Huggins, "Interview with Eubie Blake," in *Voices from the Harlem Renaissance*, ed. Nathan Huggins (New York: Oxford University Press, 1976), 339–40.

26. Robert Bartlett Haas, ed., *William Grant Still and the Fusion of Cultures in American Music* (Los Angeles: Black Sparrow Press, 1975), 134.

27. Floyd, "Music in the Harlem Renaissance," 21.

28. Willie "The Lion" Smith, with George Hoefer, *Music on My Mind: The Memoirs of an American Pianist* (New York: Burdge & Co., 1954; reprint, New York: Da Capo Press, 1984), 66–67.

29. Hadlock, *Jazz Masters*, 153.

30. James T. Maher and Jeffrey Sultanof, "Pre-Swing Era Big Bands and Jazz Composing and Arranging," in *The Oxford Companion to Jazz*, ed. Bill Kirchner (Oxford: Oxford University Press, 2000), 264.

31. Hadlock, *Jazz Masters*, 212.

32. Duke Ellington, *Music Is My Mistress* (New York: Da Capo Press, 1976), 419.

33. Shapiro and Hentoff, *Hear Me Talkin' to Ya*, 231.

34. Mark Tucker, *Ellington: The Early Years* (Urbana and Chicago: University of Illinois Press, 1991), 201.

35. Gunther Schuller, *The Swing Era: The Development of Jazz 1930–1945* (New York: Oxford University Press, 1989), 48.

36. Tucker, *Ellington*, 201.

37. John Edward Hasse, *Beyond Category: The Life and Genius of Duke Ellington* (New York: Simon & Schuster, 1993), 92.

Chapter 3

1. James Lincoln Collier, *Benny Goodman and the Swing Era* (New York: Oxford University Press, 1989), 5.

2. "Who Started Swing?" *Metronome* (August 1936): 11.

3. George T. Simon, *The Big Bands*, rev. ed. (New York: Collier, 1974), 4.

4. Transcription adapted from Fred Sturm, *Changes over Time: The Evolution of Jazz Arranging* (Rottenburg, Germany: Advance Music, 1995), 65.

5. Ross Russell, *Jazz Style in Kansas City and the Southwest* (Berkeley: University of California Press, 1971), 72.

6. Nathan W. Pearson Jr., *Goin' to Kansas City* (Urbana: University of Illinois Press, 1987), 119.

7. John Hammond, "Count Basie Marks 20th Anniversary," *Down Beat,* November 2, 1955, p. 11.

8. Teddy Wilson, with Arie Ligthart and Humphrey van Loo, *Teddy Wilson Talks Jazz* (London: Cassell, 1996), 33, 82.

9. Count Basie, as told to Albert Murray, *Good Morning Blues: The Autobiography of Count Basie* (New York: Random House, 1985), 382.

10. Gunther Schuller, *The Swing Era: The Development of Jazz 1930–1945* (New York: Oxford University Press, 1989), 548.

11. Nat Hentoff, "Pres," *Down Beat,* March 7, 1956, p. 9.

12. See Lewis Porter's study in *Lester Young* (Boston: Twayne, 1985), especially chap. 4 (pp. 56–88). Also pp. 175–180.

13. Schuller, *Swing Era,* 547.

14. Benny Goodman and Irving Kolodin, *The Kingdom of Swing* (New York: Frederick Ungar, 1961), 140.

15. Goodman and Kolodin, *Kingdom of Swing,* 198–99.

16. John Edward Hasse, *Beyond Category: The Life and Genius of Duke Ellington* (New York: Simon & Schuster, 1993).

17. Hasse, *Beyond Category,* 215.

18. James Lincoln Collier, *Duke Ellington* (New York: Oxford University Press, 1987), 130.

19. Gary Giddins, "Notes on the Music," in the liner notes for *Giants of Jazz: Johnny Hodges,* Time-Life Records TL-J19, 1981, p. 47.

20. Billy Strayhorn, "The Ellington Effect," *Down Beat,* November 5, 1952, p. 4.

21. Derek Jewell, *Duke: A Portrait of Duke Ellington* (New York: Norton, 1977), 110.

22. Wilson, *Teddy Wilson Talks Jazz,* ix.

23. Wilson, *Teddy Wilson Talks Jazz,* 23–24.

24. Nat Shapiro and Nat Hentoff, eds., *Hear Me Talkin' to Ya: The Story of Jazz as Told by the Men Who Made It* (New York: Rinehart, 1955; reprint, Dover, 1966), 201.

Chapter 4

1. "'Bop Will Kill Business Unless It Kills Itself First'— Louis Armstrong," *Down Beat,* April 7, 1948, p. 2.

2. Marshall Stearns, *The Story of Jazz* (New York: Oxford University Press, 1958), 159.

3. Ira Gitler, *Jazz Masters of the Forties* (New York: Da Capo Press, 1983), 26–27.

4. Dizzy Gillespie with Al Fraser, *To Be or Not . . . to Bop* (Garden City, NY: Doubleday, 1979), 146.

5. Ibid., 135.

6. Miles Davis, with Quincy Troupe, *Miles: The Autobiography* (New York: Simon & Schuster, 1989), 54.

7. Danny Barker, *A Life in Jazz* (New York: Oxford University Press, 1986), 171–72.

8. Budd Johnson, quoted in Gillespie, *To Be,* 218.

9. Gitler, *Jazz Masters,* 22.

10. Gillespie, *To Be,* 208.

11. "My Memories of Bird Parker," *Melody Maker,* May 28, 1955. Reprinted in Carl Woideck, *The Charlie Parker Companion* (New York: Schirmer Books, 1998), 136.

12. "Interview: Charlie Parker, Marshall Stearns, John Maher, and Chan Parker," in Woideck, *Charlie Parker Companion,* 93.

13. Ross Russell, *Bird Lives: The High Life and Hard Times of Charlie (Yardbird) Parker* (New York: Charterhouse, 1973; reprint, New York: Da Capo Press, 1996), 138. For more on Parker's solos, see Henry Martin, *Charlie Parker and Thematic Improvisation* (Lanham, MD: Scarecrow Press, 1996).

14. Davis, *Miles,* 64.

15. "Louie the First," *Time* 53 (February 21, 1949): 52.

16. Gitler, *Jazz Masters,* 120.

17. Gillespie, *To Be,* 137.

18. Davis, *Miles,* 80–81.

Chapter 5

1. Jack Chambers, *Milestones 1: The Music and Times of Miles Davis to 1960* (Toronto: University of Toronto Press, 1983), 129.

2. John Lewis, *The World of Music* (Information Bulletin No. 4, International Music Council, UNESCO House, Paris, May 1958).

3. Chambers, *Milestones 1*, 131.

4. Ted Gioia, *West Coast Jazz* (New York: Oxford University Press, 1992), 143.

5. "What's Wrong with Kenton?" *Metronome* 64, no. 2 (February 1948): 32.

6. Miles Davis, with Quincy Troupe, *Miles: The Autobiography* (New York: Simon & Schuster, 1989), 9.

7. Ross Russell, *Bird Lives: The High Life and Hard Times of Charlie (Yardbird) Parker* (New York: Charterhouse, 1973; reprint, New York: Da Capo Press, 1996), 267.

8. Davis, *Miles*, 219.

9. John Coltrane, in collaboration with Don DeMicheal, "Coltrane on Coltrane," *Down Beat*, September 29, 1960, p. 27.

10. Liner notes to Miles Davis, *Kind of Blue*, Columbia CK 64935 (CD reissue).

Chapter 6

1. Jerry D'Souza, "Richard Davis—Philosophy of the Spiritual," *Coda Magazine* 285 (May–June 1999): 11.

2. Ekkehard Jost, *Free Jazz* (New York: Da Capo Press, 1981), 127.

3. Nat Hentoff, *The Jazz Life* (New York: Dial Press, 1961), 238.

4. Ornette Coleman, liner notes to Ornette Coleman, *Change of the Century*, Atlantic 1327.

5. Hentoff, *Jazz Life*, 241.

6. Jost, *Free Jazz*, 54.

7. Hentoff, *Jazz Life*, 228.

8. John Coltrane, in collaboration with Don DeMicheal, "Coltrane on Coltrane," *Down Beat*, September 29, 1960, p. 26.

9. Ibid.

10. Thomas Owens, *Bebop: The Music and the Players* (New York: Oxford University Press, 1995), 94.

11. Jack Chambers, *Milestones 1: The Music and Times of Miles Davis to 1960* (Toronto: University of Toronto Press, 1983), 249.

12. Coltrane, "Coltrane on Coltrane," 27.

13. Joe Hunt, *52nd Street Beat: Modern Jazz Drummers 1945–1965* (New Albany, IN: Jamey Aeborsold Jazz, n.d.), 44.

14. Quoted in Don DeMicheal, "John Coltrane and Eric Dolphy Answer the Jazz Critics," *Down Beat*, April 12, 1962, p. 20. Originally published in a *Down Beat* review of November 23, 1961.

15. Lewis Porter, "John Coltrane's *A Love Supreme*: Jazz Improvisation as Composition," *Journal of the American Musicological Association* 38, no. 3 (1983): 593–621.

16. Jost, *Free Jazz*, 89.

17. Quoted in Jost, *Free Jazz*, 83.

18. Liner notes to Joseph Jarman, *As If It Were the Seasons*, Delmark 410.

19. Liner notes to Lester Bowie, *Numbers 1 and 2*, Nessa N-1.

20. Jost, *Free Jazz*, 177.

21. Ibid., 190.

22. DeMicheal, "John Coltrane and Eric Dolphy," 21.

23. Ibid., 21–22.

24. Liner notes to Eric Dolphy, *Far Cry with Booker Little*, Prestige 7747.

25. Miles Davis, with Quincy Troupe, *Miles: The Autobiography* (New York: Simon & Schuster, 1989), 241.

26. R. Townley, "Hancock Plugs In," *Down Beat*, October 24, 1974, p. 15.

27. Davis, *Miles*, 270.

28. Townley, "Hancock Plugs In," 14.

29. On Track 2, at 1:02, of Marian McPartland, *Piano Jazz*, with guest Bill Evans, The Jazz Alliance TJA-12004.

30. Conrad Silvert, "Chick Corea's Changes: A Return to Forever Is Not Forever," *Rolling Stone*, July 15, 1976, p. 24.

31. Liner notes to Charles Lloyd, *Charles Lloyd: Love-In,* Atlantic SC 1481.

32. Ben Sidran, *Talking Jazz: An Oral History, Expanded Edition* (New York: Da Capo Press, 1995), 268.

33. Ibid., 324, 327.

Chapter 7

1. Bill Laswell, foreword to *Jazz-Rock: A History,* by Stuart Nicholson (New York: Schirmer Books, 1998), x.

2. Bill Milkowski, liner notes to Al DiMeola, *Electric Rendezvous,* Sony/Columbia 468216-2.

3. Lee Underwood, "George Duke: Plugged-In Prankster," *Down Beat,* March 10, 1977, p. 34.

4. Bret Primack, "Herbie Hancock: Chameleon in His Disco Phase," *Down Beat,* May 17, 1979, p. 42.

5. Liner notes to *Miles Davis at Fillmore,* Columbia CG 30038.

6. Julie Coryell and Laura Friedman, preface to *Jazz-Rock Fusion: The People, the Music* (New York: Delacorte Press, 1978), x.

7. Bill Milkowski, "Larry Coryell: Back to the Roots," *Down Beat,* May 1984, p. 16.

8. Scott Yanow, "George Duke: Dukin' out the Hits," *Down Beat,* November 1984, p. 17.

9. Len Lyons, *The Great Jazz Pianists: Speaking of Their Lives and Their Music* (New York: Da Capo Press, 1989), 276.

10. Primack, "Herbie Hancock," 42.

11. Coryell and Friedman, *Jazz-Rock Fusion,* 239.

12. Josef Woodward, "Chick Corea: Piano Dreams Come True," *Down Beat,* September 1988, p. 19.

13. Bill Milkowski, *Jaco: The Extraordinary and Tragic Life of Jaco Pastorius, "The World's Greatest Bass Player"* (San Francisco: Miller Freeman Books, 1995), 73.

14. Stuart Nicholson, *Jazz-Rock: A History* (New York: Schirmer Books, 1998), 181.

15. Fred Borque, "Pat Metheny: Musings on Neo-Fusion," *Down Beat,* March 22, 1979, pp. 13–15.

16. Nicholson, *Jazz-Rock,* 240.

17. Pat Metheney, "In Search of Sound," *Down Beat,* February 1998, p. 19.

Chapter 8

1. Ann Douglas, *Terrible Honesty: Mongrel Manhattan in the 1920s* (New York: Farrar, Straus, Giroux, 1995), 352.

2. James P. Johnson, "I Like Anything That's Good," *The Jazz Record* (April 1947): 14.

3. Dave Hellend, "Repertory Big Bands," *Down Beat,* January 1997, p. 35.

4. Howard Reich, "Wynton Marsalis," *Down Beat,* December 1997, p. 34.

5. Robert Sadin, personal communication, May 20, 1999.

6. Wynton Marsalis, "Ellington at 100: Reveling in Life's Majesty," *New York Times,* January 17, 1999, Arts and Leisure section.

7. Stuart Nicholson, *Jazz: The 1980s Resurgence* (New York: Da Capo Press, 1990), 227.

8. John McDonough, "Doin' 'em Proud," *Down Beat,* January 1997, p. 20.

9. Radio emcee Don Burns of smooth-jazz station KTWV of Los Angeles, as quoted in Eliot Tiegel, "Smooth Moves on the Air," *Down Beat,* December 1996, p. 10.

10. Record producer Michael Cuscuna, as quoted in Eliot Tiegel, "Smooth Moves on the Air," *Down Beat,* December 1996, p. 10.

11. Charles Levin, "Reconfiguring the Public Radio Puzzle," *Down Beat,* April 1999, p. 44.

12. Liner notes to Anthony Davis, *Lady of the Mirrors,* India Navigation IN 1047.

13. Nicholson, *Jazz: The 1980s Resurgence,* 258.

14. Steve Coleman [Internet home page], available from www.m-base.com/mbase.htm/.

15. David Hadju, "Rhapsody in Black and White: Herbie Hancock Finds a Soul Mate in George Gershwin," *New York Times Magazine,* October 28, 1998, p. 52.

GLOSSARY

AABA song form A musical form that comprises an eight-bar theme (A) played twice. A contrasting melody (B) follows, also usually eight bars long, before the A theme returns. The second and third A sections often vary slightly.

ABAC song form A musical form in which each section is usually eight bars and has three themes (A, B, and C). Musicians often speak of the "first half" of the tune (AB) and the "second half" (AC).

acid jazz A fusion style that incorporates sampling of older jazz recordings, rap, and hip-hop grooves and techniques.

antiphony The trading of melodic figures between two different sections of the band; the formal musical term for *call-and-response.*

arpeggiation (arpeggiated figure) A melodic fragment based on the notes of the chord harmony and played in succession.

arranger The person who plans the form of a band's performance and often notates the parts for the different instruments. *See also* **head arrangement.**

atonality A description of music that avoids the standard chords, scales, harmonies, and keys of *tonality.* It is sometimes associated with free jazz, which flourished in the 1960s.

avant-garde *See* **free jazz.**

backbeats Heavy emphases on beats 2 and 4, as played by the drummer, usually on the snare drum. (Other drums or the hi-hat can be used for quieter backbeats.) Backbeats can be added to a 4/4 swing rhythm as well. Backbeats increase danceability by clarifying the rhythm and adding to the visceral excitement of the music.

back catalog All the recordings that a company holds in its vaults or claims the rights to by having purchased other record labels. Many of these recordings are out of print or were never issued in their original form.

back phrasing A musical technique in which the singer momentarily delays the entry of a new phrase, in effect freeing the rhythm of a composition. Occurring most often in ballads, it generally conveys a loose feeling, as if the singer were delivering the song spontaneously.

balance The ability of a section to blend. In a well-balanced section, none of the players is too soft or too loud relative to the others.

banjo A stringed, strummed instrument that often provided the chords in New Orleans (Dixieland) and Chicago-style jazz.

bass A low-pitched stringed instrument and one of the members of the rhythm section in a jazz band. Listen to Track 43 of CD 1 to hear an acoustic bass.

bebop (bop) A nervous, energetic style of jazz that developed in the 1940s. The terms probably developed from the nonsense syllables used by scat singers to re-create the characteristic melodic phrases of the new style.

bent pitch A small glissando or slide from one frequency to a slightly higher one, achieved by pushing against the guitar's string on the fretboard, thus "bending" it.

big band A large jazz ensemble typically including three to four trumpets, three to four trombones, four to five reeds (saxophones and doublings), and rhythm (typically piano, bass, guitar, and drums).

block-chord style *See* **locked-hands style.**

blue note A bent, slurred, or "worried" note. Most often occurs on the third of the scale, but any note can be made "blue" by varying its intonation in a blues or jazz performance.

blues An African-American folk music that appeared around 1900 and exerted influence on jazz and various forms of U.S. popular music.

blues form A basic 12-bar chord progression that may be varied depending on the blues or jazz style. The basic progression is shown in Music Example I-5 on page 13. Its fundamental harmonies are I (4 bars), IV (2 bars), I (2 bars), V (1 bar), IV (1 bar), I (2 bars). Listen to Track 11 of CD 1 for a modern version of blues form.

blues scale A form of scale that incorporates the principal notes used in the blues. Most often, 1–♭3–4–#4–5–♭7. Listen to the second scale played on Track 1 of CD 1. See the Introduction for a blues scale in music notation.

bossa nova A Latin jazz style that developed from Brazilian music in the late 1950s and early 1960s. Stan Getz was prominent among jazz players with bossa nova hits.

break A short pause in a band's playing—usually one or two bars—to feature a soloist. Often a band will play in stop time while the soloist improvises breaks between the band's chords.

bridge The B section of an AABA popular song. The B section of an ABAC popular song is occasionally called a bridge as well. Older terms for bridge are *release* and *channel*.

cadence The closing strain of a phrase, section, or movement. Also a term used for a common closing chord progression.

cakewalk A dance involving an exaggerated walking step. In exhibitions of cakewalking, the most talented couple won a cake at the end of the evening. The cakewalk may have been a parody of the way members of white "high society" comported themselves.

call-and-response A musical procedure in which a single voice or instrument states a melodic phrase—the *call*—and a group of voices or instruments follows with a responding or completing phrase—the *response.*

chair Each part of a section, as in first trumpet chair, first trombone chair, and so on.

chart A common, informal term for *arrangement.*

Chicago jazz A type of New Orleans–style jazz created by Chicago musicians in the 1920s.

chorus Each time the performers execute or work through the form of a song, it is called a *chorus*—for example, once through a 12-bar blues or once through a 32-bar song.

clarinet A single-reed woodwind instrument. Listen to Tracks 20–21 of CD 1 to hear the clarinet.

coda Italian for "tail," a coda provides an optional, concluding section of an arrangement, added for greater finality. A brief coda is called a *tag.*

comping The chordal accompaniment provided by pianists or guitarists in jazz bands. This accompaniment is often syncopated. The term *comp* is probably derived from a contraction of the word *accompany* or *complement.*

complete reissue The duplication of an artist's or a group's entire available body of recorded material—including errors, outtakes, and technical problems.

cool jazz A reaction against bebop that involved more-complex compositions, slower tempos, and sometimes less emotional involvement.

cornet A medium-range brass instrument much like a trumpet but with a larger bore and hence a mellower sound. Heard mostly in New Orleans and Chicago jazz in the 1920s, where, like the trumpet, it was a lead instrument.

countermelody A separate line that runs in counterpoint to the main melody. Like an obbligato, a countermelody is a secondary melody that accompanies the main melody. A countermelody, however, is generally heard on the trombone or in a lower voice, has fewer notes than the obbligato, and is often improvised. Another word for countermelody is *counterline.* Listen to Track 7 of CD 1 to hear a countermelody.

counterpoint The use of simultaneously sounding musical lines. *See also* **polyphony**.

Creoles of Color People of mixed black and white ancestry, often from New Orleans. Until the late nineteenth century, they enjoyed more freedom and were better educated than the general black population. Musicians from this group generally had classical training and could read musical scores.

crossover The practice of mixing musical styles and cultures. As first seen in the concert jazz of the 1920s and the third-stream practices of the 1950s, crossover can mix different styles within a given culture—

for example, bluegrass and classical music—or it can mix music from entirely different cultures, such as traditional Japanese music and bebop.

cross-rhythms The performance of simultaneous and contrasting rhythms, such as patterns with duple and triple groupings. Superimposing one rhythmic pattern on another causes a cross-rhythm to develop.

Dixieland *See* **New Orleans jazz**.

dropping bombs A technique in which bebop drummers used the bass drum to make sharp, irregular accents in the rhythmic accompaniment.

drums The backbone of the jazz rhythm section. Usually, a drum kit consists of a snare drum, a bass drum, several tomtoms, and various cymbals. Listen to Tracks 26–35 of CD 1 to hear a range of drum sounds.

extended chord tones (tensions) Notes added to seventh chords to make the harmony richer and more pungent. These tones are usually ninths, elevenths, and thirteenths. Extended chord tones will usually resolve to more-stable pitches such as roots, thirds, and fifths.

false start An incorrect start of a performance—a musician begins playing a measure or two, then, realizing the mistake, stops abruptly.

feedback A distorted effect created when the sound coming from a speaker is picked up by an electronic sensing device such as a microphone and routed back to the speaker. As this process multiplies, harsh electronic wails are created.

formula *See* **lick**.

free jazz The 1960s jazz substyle that overturned many of the traditional elements of the music. Also called *avant-garde* and the *New Thing*.

front line The lead (melody) instruments in early jazz bands. The front line usually included trumpet (or cornet), trombone, and clarinet. Use of saxophone was a later development.

full-chord style *See* **locked-hands style**.

funky jazz (soul jazz) A style that combines elements of gospel music and R&B with jazz. It began to emerge in the 1950s as an outgrowth of hard bop and became quite popular in the 1960s.

fusion *See* **jazz-rock**.

ghost bands Groups whose founding leaders have died but who continue to travel and work under new direction.

glissando A technique whereby notes are slurred directly from one to another, producing a continuous rise or fall in pitch.

guitar A string instrument played as either a lead instrument (through picking) or a rhythm instrument (through chord strumming). It can be acoustic or amplified. Listen to Tracks 36–42 of CD 1 to hear examples of acoustic and electric guitar in different settings.

hard bop A jazz movement of the 1950s that drew on the speed, intensity, and power of bebop and sometimes married bop to gospel and blues-influenced music.

Harlem Renaissance A period—roughly 1921 to 1929—of outstanding artistic activity among African Americans. The movement was centered in Harlem, in New York City.

harmolodics A theory of music devised by Ornette Coleman.

harmon mute A hollow metal mute that, when placed in the bell of the trumpet, gives its sound a distant, brooding quality. Miles Davis's adoption of the harmon mute from 1954 onward helped popularize its use.

harmonic substitution The technique of replacing an expected chord with a more unusual one. Listen to Track 6 of CD 1 to hear examples of harmonic substitution.

head An informal term used to designate the original melody on which a jazz performance is based. It usually appears at the beginning of a jazz performance and is often repeated at the end. The A section of an AABA song is also sometimes called the *head*.

head arrangement A musical plan and form worked up verbally by the players in rehearsal or on the bandstand.

hipster A young, often white, follower of jazz who affected the dress, speech, and manner of jazz musicians working in the new jazz styles of the late 1940s and early 1950s.

hot bands Jazz bands that featured fast tempos and dramatic solo and group performances, usually with more improvisation than sweet bands had.

inside playing The jazz technique of playing melodic lines that favor the principal notes of the harmonies. *See also* **outside playing**. Listen to Track 8 of CD 1 to hear examples of inside and outside playing.

intonation The ability of a musician to reproduce a given pitch. Musicians with good intonation are said to be playing "in tune." That is, the players know how to make small adjustments in the pitch of their instruments as they play so that they match the pitches of the other players in the section.

jazz chair A player hired especially for improvisational fluency; spoken of as the jazz chair of a given section. For example, Bix Beiderbecke occupied the jazz trumpet chair in the Paul Whiteman band, as did Bubber Miley in the Ellington band.

jazz-funk *See* **jazz-rock**.

jazz repertory movement A movement since the 1980s in which ensembles devoted themselves to the re-creation and performance of historically significant jazz artists and their work. Just as classical music has an accepted repertory of great works, the jazz repertory movement is trying to establish an official canon for jazz.

jazz-rock A form of jazz that combines elements of rock (or R&B funk) and jazz. Jazz-rock often features rock or funk rhythms, vamps, and electric and electronic instruments. Also called *jazz-funk* or *fusion*.

lead player The player in a section who usually takes the melody or top part and occupies the first chair of the section. The lead player usually plays slightly more loudly than the other players in the section.

lead trumpet The lead chair or first trumpet player of the trumpet section. This player needs to be dominating and capable of precision, power, and control of the high register. A big band is particularly dependent on the lead trumpet.

legato The technique of playing notes smoothly in a connected manner. The opposite of legato is staccato.

library (book) A band's collection of arrangements or pieces. These are usually songs but may also include larger-scale works. A library is necessary for big bands, but smaller groups may also have one.

lick A worked-out melodic idea that fits a common chord progression. Most improvisers develop licks for up-tempo improvisation especially because the rapid tempo does not allow time for total spontaneity. A lick is also called a *formula*.

locked-hands style A mode of performance in which the pianist plays a four-note chord in the right hand and doubles the top note with the left hand an octave below. The hands move together in a "locked" rhythmic

pattern as they follow the same rhythm. This style is also called *block-chord* or *full-chord style*. Listen to Track 9 of CD 1 🎵 to hear an example of locked-hands style.

LP A long-playing record that typically plays at 33⅓ rpm (revolutions per minute). LPs first became commercially available in 1948. LPs were made with polyvinyl chloride (hence the nickname *vinyl* for records) and allowed up to about twenty-five minutes of music per side.

meter A rhythmic pattern arising from regular groupings of two or three beats. These define, respectively, duple or triple meter. Most music has meter.

metronomic sense A steady rhythmic pulse, often associated with drums and music from Africa.

microtones Pitches between the tempered notes of the chromatic scale. Used in nontempered intonation.

MIDI An acronym for *Musical Instrument Digital Interface*. This standard language allows computers to control synthesizers or samplers.

minstrelsy A form of U.S. musical theater and variety show that flourished in the nineteenth century. Traveling troupes performed songs, dances, and skits based on caricatures of African Americans. Performed by both blacks and whites in blackface, minstrelsy is often considered the first distinctively U.S. musical genre.

modal jazz A body of music that makes use of one or more of the following characteristics: modal scales for improvising, slow harmonic rhythm, pedal points, and the absence or suppression of functional harmonic relationships.

moldy figs A term used by younger musicians and fans in the 1940s to describe older jazz fans who clung to the music of the 1920s and 1930s and derided the newer bebop style.

motive (motivic material) A short melodic fragment used as the basis for improvisation or development.

motivic cells Short melodic ideas subject to variation and development. Also called *thematic cells*.

multiphonics A technique of producing more than one note at a time on a wind instrument. Using nonstandard fingering and appropriate embouchure, the player splits the air stream into two or more parts, thus producing a multinote "chordal" effect. The technique is difficult to control, may be strident, and is generally associated with avant-garde playing.

multitracking *See* **overdubbing.**

mute Device played in or over the bell of a brass instrument to alter its tone. Different mutes create different kinds of effects, but a muted brass tone is usually less brilliant than an "open" one.

New Orleans jazz The jazz style that originated in New Orleans and flourished in the late 1910s and 1920s. The New Orleans jazz band often had a front line of trumpet or cornet, trombone, and clarinet, accompanied by a rhythm section of piano, guitar or banjo, bass, and drums. Often called *Dixieland.*

New Thing *See* **free jazz.**

nontempered intonation The use of pitches unrestricted by the "equal-tempered" twelve-note chromatic scale. For example, a nontempered pitch might be a note between D and E♭. *See also* **microtones.**

obbligato A complementary melodic part played at the same time as the main melody. In jazz, the obbligato part is usually improvised. In early jazz, obbligato parts were often florid, usually played by the clarinet, and sometimes improvised.

ostinato A repeated melodic or harmonic idea that forms the basis for a section or an entire composition.

out-chorus The final, usually highly exuberant chorus of a jazz performance. Also called *shout chorus.*

outside playing The jazz technique of playing notes that depart from (or are "outside") the chords of a given piece. *See also* **inside playing.** Listen to Track 8 of CD 1 🎧 to hear examples of inside and outside playing.

overdubbing A recording-studio technique that was generally available by the 1950s. The recording tape has several parallel tracks that enable musicians to record additional performance parts at later times. The added part is called an *overdub.* By wearing headphones, the players follow and play to the previously recorded tracks. Also called *multitracking.*

pedal point A sustained or repeated bass note or drone played to accompany a melody.

pentatonic scale A five-note set that avoids the interval of a tritone and can be arranged as a series of perfect fourths or perfect fifths. The black notes of the keyboard form one such pentatonic scale. Also called *pentatonic set.*

piano The principal Western keyboard instrument. In jazz it functions as a solo instrument and as part of the rhythm section (usually with bass and drums and sometimes added guitar or banjo). The piano trio (with bass and drums or bass and guitar) is a common small jazz ensemble that features the piano.

piano rolls Cylinders of rolled paper punched with holes. When fed through a properly equipped player piano, the holes activate hammers that play the piano automatically.

plagal cadence A type of cadence that contains the harmonic progression IV–I (instead of the more common progression V–I). Sometimes called a *church cadence* or an *Amen cadence,* it is often used at the ends of hymns with the concluding "Amen." Plagal cadences were featured frequently in funky/soul jazz.

player piano A piano equipped with a mechanism that allows it to play piano rolls.

plunger A type of mute derived from a plumber's sink plunger. The rubber cup of the plunger is held against the bell of the instrument and manipulated with the left hand to alter the horn's tone quality.

polyphony Distinct, simultaneous musical parts. Another name for a polyphonic texture is *counterpoint.*

postmodernism An attitude toward art and culture that has become common since the 1970s. It disavows some of the cerebral, audience-distancing tenets of modernism and replaces them with a freewheeling conception of culture.

race record An early recording, usually of jazz or blues and typically performed by and marketed to African Americans.

ragtime An African-American musical genre that flourished from the late 1890s through the mid-1910s. It is based on constant syncopation in the right hand and is often accompanied by a steady march bass in the left hand. Associated now primarily with piano music, ragtime was originally a method of performance that included syncopated songs, music for various ensembles, and arrangements of nonragtime music. Scott Joplin was ragtime's most famous composer.

recomposition The composition of a new melody to fit the harmonic and formal structure of a previously composed popular song.

reharmonization The practice of inserting different chords into the fundamental chord structure of a well-known song to freshen the interpretation and expand harmonic options for the soloist.

remastering The digital enhancement of an original recording's sound quality. It includes such techniques as filtering out extraneous noise and boosting certain frequencies.

rent party An informal gathering in the 1920s, held to help raise money for rent or groceries. At these parties, musicians often gathered and performed, sometimes in competition with one another.

rhythm changes The harmonies of the George and Ira Gershwin song "I Got Rhythm" (1930). (The final two-bar tag of the original song is omitted, so a symmetrical 32-bar AABA plan results.) The bridge in rhythm changes consists of two-bar harmonies following a circle-of-fifths pattern that returns to the tonic. For example, if rhythm changes are performed in B♭, the harmonies of the eight-bar bridge are D7 (2 bars), G7 (2 bars), C7 (2 bars), and F7 (2 bars). The F7, as the dominant of the tonic B♭, leads back to the A section. Extremely popular since the 1930s, rhythm changes are still commonly used by jazz musicians for improvisation and composition. Listen to Track 10 of CD 1 to hear an example of rhythm changes.

rhythm section A part of a jazz band that provides the rhythmic pulse, harmonies, and bass line. It may include any of the following: bass, drums, piano, or guitar. Early jazz bands sometimes included banjo and tuba in place of the guitar and bass.

riff A short melodic idea, usually one or two bars long, that is repeated as the core idea of a musical passage. Different band sections sometimes trade riffs in a call-and-response format. Usually rhythmic and simple, the riff can also provide an effective background for an improvising soloist.

ring shout A rhythmic dance performed in a circular figure, originally derived from African religious practice. Worshipers moved in a counterclockwise direction while singing spirituals and accompanying themselves by clapping and stamping. Some historians describe the ring shout as contributing the essence of African song, dance, and spirit to African-American music.

samplers Electronic devices used both to sample and to play back sounds.

sampling The practice of recording sounds for musical use in playback. Any kind of sound can be sampled, from a note on an acoustic instrument, to natural sounds, to a passage of music already recorded. For playback, the sound is usually activated by computer or by pressing a key on a keyboard. *See also* **samplers** and **sound modules.**

saxophone A single-reed instrument made of brass that is common in all jazz styles except New Orleans (Dixieland). The saxophone comes in many sizes and ranges. Listen to Tracks 16–19 of CD 1 to hear the four most common saxophones.

scat singing A jazz vocal style in which the soloist improvises using made-up or nonsense syllables.

section A group of related instruments in a big band; three trumpets and three trombones might form the brass section.

sheets of sound An expression coined by jazz critic Ira Gitler to describe John Coltrane's method of playing that features extremely fast notes with irregular phrase groupings. Sometimes unusual harmonies are introduced over the given chord change.

shout chorus *See* **out-chorus.**

shuffle A 4/4 rhythmic pattern in which each beat is represented by the drummer's playing a dotted-eighth and sixteenth note, usually on the ride cymbal.

sideman A player who is not a lead player or featured soloist.

slap bass A technique in which the bass player percussively hits the low strings of the electric bass while picking melodies on the higher ones. This style was created by Larry Graham and subsequently imitated by jazz, funk, and popular bass players.

slash notation A method of showing the harmonies (or "chord changes") in jazz and popular music. Each slash in a measure denotes a beat. The arranger places chords over the slashes to show the beats on which the harmonies change. (See Music Example I-4 on page 6 for an example.)

smooth jazz A popular form of fusion jazz that combines rock or funk grooves with an electronic ambience to create an "easy listening" feel. While improvisation may be present, the pleasant, mood-music quality of the groove and melody dominates.

soul jazz *See* **funky jazz.**

sound fields A musical effect created when coinciding melodic lines fuse into a indistinguishable web or mass of sound with irregular accentuation within each line.

sound modules Electronic devices that play back prerecorded samples. *See also* **sampling.**

speakeasy A Prohibition-era nightclub in which liquor was sold illegally.

spirituals African-American songs that arose in the nineteenth century and consisted of religious lyrics with folk melodies. They were often harmonized for vocal choir.

staccato The technique of playing short notes with distinct spaces between them. The opposite of staccato is legato.

step connection The principal means of stringing together the melodic and harmonic elements. The steps are often based on the scale determined by the key of the piece. This is a key element in voice leading.

stock arrangement (stock) An arrangement created and sold by a publishing company to bandleaders. Bands played stock arrangements to keep up with the latest hit songs.

stop time The punctuation of distinct beats, often to accommodate a soloist's improvisations between the band's chords.

stride piano A school of jazz piano playing based on a moving left-hand accompaniment of alternating bass notes and chords with appropriate right-hand figuration that seems to pull at the left-hand rhythm to impart swing.

suite A European classical musical work that has several sections, each with distinctive melodies and moods. The sections may or may not be related thematically. Composers often extract the most popular or most effective sections from extended works such as operas and ballets to create a suite for concert performance.

sweet bands Bands that played relatively less-syncopated, slower pieces, such as ballads and popular songs. *See also* **hot bands.**

swing Generic term for the jazz and much popular music of the mid-1930s through the mid-1940s.

syncopation The unexpected accenting of a "weaker" melody note or offbeat. Syncopation displaces the accent, or emphasis, from an expected to an unexpected position. For example, because the first and third beats are usually emphasized in each bar of a 4/4 piece, emphasizing the second beat would be syncopation. In general, syncopation involves unexpected accents occurring within a regular pulse stream. For an illustration, see Music Example 1-2 on page 29, third measure, and listen to Track 4 of CD 1. The Joplin phrase is played first as it was written (with syncopation), then without.

tag A short, codalike section added to the end of a composition to give it closure.

tailgate trombone The New Orleans style of playing trombone with chromatic glissandos created by a rapid up-and-down motion of the slide. Jazz mythology relates that the trombonist played in the back—on the tailgate—of the New Orleans advertising wagons when the bands traveled during the day to advertise their upcoming dances. Listen to Track 25 of CD 1 to hear an example of tailgate trombone.

tensions *See* **extended chord tones.**

terminal vibrato A vibrato added to the end of a sustained note.

territory band In the swing era, a band that played and toured a region around a major city that served as a home base.

texture The density of musical sound, as determined by the instruments (or voices) heard, the number of instruments, and the number of notes or sounds being played by them. Textures are often described as thick (many notes heard) or thin (few notes).

thematic cells *See* **motivic cells.**

third-stream music A blend of jazz and European concert music. In many instances, third-stream composers create concert works that allow for improvisation within larger-scale structures influenced by both jazz and concert music.

tonality A Western musical system in which pieces are organized according to harmony within some key or with respect to some central pitch.

trading twos, trading fours, or trading eights Improvisational jazz formats common since the swing era. In trading fours, for example, each soloist improvises for four bars before the next soloist takes over for four bars. Any number of soloists may participate, but most typically two to four do. Trading solos is often used to create climactic moments in performances.

transcribe To write in standard, European music notation what the transcriber hears when listening to a piece of music. *See also* **transcription.**

transcription The notated version of a piece of music. Transcriptions of the same piece of music can vary widely, depending on the quality of the original sound source, the skill of the transcriber, and what the transcriber chooses to include in the notation.

trombone A lower brass instrument that changes pitch by means of a slide. (There is also a less common valve trombone that works largely like a lower-pitched trumpet.) In New Orleans jazz, it typically provides countermelodies to the trumpet lead. Big bands often feature sections of three or four trombones. It is also an important jazz solo instrument. Listen to Tracks 22–25 of CD 1 🎧 to hear examples of trombone playing.

trumpet The most important brass instrument in jazz. With its commanding presence, the trumpet often dominates the sound of the big band. Trumpet-like instruments that are more mellow include the cornet and the flugelhorn. Listen to Tracks 12–15 of CD 1 🎧 to hear the trumpet, both open and with various mutes.

tuba A low brass instrument that sometimes provided the bass part in New Orleans (Dixieland) and Chicago-style jazz. Uncommon in later jazz styles.

vamp A repeating melodic or harmonic idea, often one to four bars long, similar to an ostinato. Vamps can provide an introduction to a performance or a background to an improvisation.

vibrato A method of varying the pitch frequency of a note, producing a wavering sound. A vibrato brings a note to life. It is heard mostly on wind instruments, strings, and vocals.

vocalese The technique of setting lyrics to existing jazz solos. Eddie Jefferson was probably the most important pioneer of this technique.

voice leading A means of making logical melodic and harmonic sequences within an improvised solo. *Step connection,* a key element in voice leading, is the principal means of stringing together the melodic and harmonic elements. The steps are often based on the scale determined by the key of the piece.

wah-wah pedal A pitch-frequency filter, operated by the foot, that is usually used by guitarists or electric keyboardists. When the pedal is depressed, the note or chord being held makes a "wah" sound. (An acoustic "wah" sound can be achieved by brass players' using their left hands or mutes over the bells of their instruments.) The up-and-down movement of the pedal creates the repeated "wah-wah" effect.

walking bass A musical technique in which the bass player articulates all four beats in a 4/4 bar. The bass lines often follow simple scale patterns, avoiding too many disruptive leaps between notes. The walking bass is quite common in jazz, heard in all styles since becoming firmly established during the swing era. Listen to Track 43 of CD 1 🎧 to hear a walking bass.

West Coast jazz A jazz style from the 1950s that embodied many of the principles of cool jazz as performed by a group of players centered in California.

whole-tone scale A scale with whole steps only and thus no tonic or dominant, making it impossible to form major or minor triads. A whole-tone scale starts on a note and proceeds up or down by whole step only. There are only two whole-tone scales: C–D–E–F#–G#–B♭ and D♭–E♭–F–G–A–B. Notice that they share no notes. This scale was common among French composers, including Claude Debussy.

SELECTED READINGS

Allen, William Francis, Charles Pickard Ware, and Lucy McKim Garrison. *Slave Songs of the United States*. New York: Peter Smith, 1951. Orig. pub., New York: A. Simpson, 1867. Reprint, New York: Dover, 1995.

Armstrong, Louis. *Satchmo: My Life in New Orleans*. New York: Prentice-Hall, 1954. Reprint, New York: Da Capo Press, 1986.

———. *Swing That Music*. New York: Longmans, Green, 1936.

Balliett, Whitney. *Jelly Roll, Jabbo, and Fats: Nineteen Portraits in Jazz*. New York: Oxford University Press, 1983.

Barker, Danny. *A Life in Jazz*. New York: Oxford University Press, 1986.

Basie, Count, as told to Albert Murray. *Good Morning Blues: The Autobiography of Count Basie*. New York: Random House, 1985.

Bechet, Sidney. *Treat It Gentle: An Autobiography*. New York: Hill and Wang, 1960. Reprint, New York: Da Capo Press, 1978.

Berlin, Edward A. *Ragtime: A Musical and Cultural History*. Berkeley: University of California Press, 1980.

Bethell, Tom. *George Lewis: A Jazzman from New Orleans*. Berkeley: University of California Press, 1977.

Borque, Fred. "Pat Metheny: Musings on Neo-Fusion." *Down Beat*, March 22, 1979, pp. 13 ff.

Brown, Theodore Dennis. "A History and Analysis of Jazz Drumming to 1942." Ph.D. diss., University of Michigan, 1976.

Calloway, Cab, and Bryant Rollins. *Of Minnie the Moocher and Me*. New York: Crowell, 1976.

Carr, Ian. *Miles Davis: A Biography*. New York: Morrow, 1982.

Carver, Reginald, and Lenny Bernstein. *Jazz Profiles: The Spirit of the Nineties*. New York: Billboard Books, 1998.

Chambers, Jack. *Milestones 1: The Music and Times of Miles Davis to 1960*. Toronto: University of Toronto Press, 1983.

———. *Milestones 2: The Music and Times of Miles Davis Since 1960*. Toronto: University of Toronto Press, 1985.

Charters, Samuel, and Leonard Kunstadt. *Jazz: A History of the New York Scene*. Garden City, NY: Doubleday, 1962. Reprint, New York: Da Capo Press, 1981.

Chase, Gilbert. *America's Music: From the Pilgrims to the Present*. 3rd ed. rev. Urbana: University of Illinois Press, 1987.

Chilton, John. *Sidney Bechet: The Wizard of Jazz*. New York: Oxford University Press, 1987.

———. *Who's Who of Jazz: Storyville to Swing Street*. 4th ed. New York: Da Capo Press, 1985.

Collier, James Lincoln. *Benny Goodman and the Swing Era*. New York: Oxford University Press, 1989.

———. *Duke Ellington*. New York: Oxford University Press, 1987.

———. *Louis Armstrong: An American Genius*. New York: Oxford University Press, 1983.

Coltrane, John, in collaboration with Don DeMicheal. "Coltrane on Coltrane." *Down Beat*, September 29, 1960, pp. 26–27.

Coryell, Julie, and Laura Friedman. *Jazz-Rock Fusion: The People, the Music*. New York: Delacorte Press, 1978.

Dance, Stanley. *The World of Earl Hines.* New York: Scribner, 1977. Reprint, New York: Da Capo Press, 1979.

———. *The World of Swing.* New York: Scribner, 1974. Reprint, New York: Da Capo Press, 1979.

Davis, Miles, and Quincy Troupe. *Miles: The Autobiography.* New York: Simon & Schuster, 1989.

DeMicheal, Don. "John Coltrane and Eric Dolphy Answer the Jazz Critics." *Down Beat,* April 12, 1962, pp. 20 ff.

DeVeaux, Scott. "Bebop and the Recording Industry: The 1942 AFM Recording Ban Reconsidered." *Journal of the American Musicological Society* 41, no. 1 (1988): 126–65.

———. *The Birth of Bebop: A Social and Musical History.* Berkeley: University of California Press, 1997.

Dodds, Baby, as told to Larry Gara. *The Baby Dodds Story.* Rev. ed. Baton Rouge: Lousiana State University Press, 1992.

Douglas, Ann. *Terrible Honesty: Mongrel Manhattan in the 1920s.* New York: Farrar, Straus, Giroux, 1995.

Ellington, Duke. *Music Is My Mistress.* Garden City, NY: Doubleday, 1973. Reprint, New York: Da Capo Press, 1976.

Floyd, Samuel A., Jr. "Music in the Harlem Renaissance: An Overview." In *Black Music in the Harlem Renaissance,* ed. Samuel A. Floyd Jr. New York: Greenwood Press, 1990.

Foster, Pops, as told to Tom Stoddard. *Pops Foster: The Autobiography of a New Orleans Jazzman.* Berkeley: University of California Press, 1971.

Gillespie, Dizzy, with Al Fraser. *To Be or Not . . . to Bop.* Garden City, NY: Doubleday, 1979. Reprint, New York: Da Capo Press, 1985.

Gioia, Ted. *West Coast Jazz.* New York: Oxford University Press, 1992.

Gitler, Ira. *Jazz Masters of the Forties.* New York: Macmillan, 1966. Reprint, New York: Da Capo Press, 1983.

———. *Swing to Bop: An Oral History of the Transition in Jazz in the 1940s.* New York: Oxford University Press, 1985.

Goldstein, Gil. *Jazz Composers Companion.* New York: Consolidated Music Publishers, 1981.

Goodman, Benny, and Irving Kolodin. *The Kingdom of Swing.* New York: Stackpole, 1939. Reprint, New York: Frederick Ungar, 1961.

Gridley, Mark. *Jazz Styles: History and Analysis.* 5th ed. Englewood Cliffs, NJ: Prentice-Hall, 1994.

Gushee, Lawrence. "How the Creole Band Came to Be." *Black Music Research Journal* 8, no. 1 (1988): 85–100.

———. "Lester Young's 'Shoe Shine Boy.'" In *A Lester Young Reader,* edited by Lewis Porter, 224–54. Washington, DC: Smithsonian Institution Press, 1991. Originally published as International Musicological Society, *Report of the Twelfth Congress, Berkeley, 1977,* edited by Daniel Heartz and Bonnie Wade. Kassel, Germany: Barenreiter, 1981.

———. Liner notes to King Oliver, *King Oliver's Jazz Band—1923.* Columbia P2 12744.

———. Liner notes to *Steppin' on the Gas: Rags to Jazz 1913–1927.* New World Records 269.

Hadlock, Richard. *Jazz Masters of the Twenties.* New York: Macmillan, 1965. Reprint, New York: Collier, 1974. Reprint, New York: Da Capo Press, 1988.

Hall, Robert L. "African Religious Retentions in Florida." In *Africanisms in American Culture,* ed. Joseph E. Holloway. Bloomington: Indiana University Press, 1990.

Handy, W. C., and Arna Bontemps. *Father of the Blues.* New York: Macmillan, 1941. Reprint, New York: Da Capo Press, 1991.

Hasse, John. *Beyond Category: The Life and Genius of Duke Ellington.* New York: Simon & Schuster, 1993.

———, ed. *Ragtime: Its History, Composers, and Music.* New York: Schirmer Books, 1985.

Hentoff, Nat. *The Jazz Life.* New York: Dial Press, 1961.

Hodeir, André. *Jazz: Its Evolution and Essence.* New York: Grove, 1956. Reprint, New York: Da Capo Press, 1976.

Howlett, Felicity. "An Introduction to Art Tatum's Performance Approaches: Composition, Improvisation, and Melodic Variation." Ph.D. diss., Cornell University, 1983.

Huggins, Nathan Irvin. *Harlem Renaissance.* New York: Oxford University Press, 1971.

———. "Interview with Eubie Blake." In *Voices from the Harlem Renaissance,* ed. Nathan Huggins. New York: Oxford University Press, 1976.

Hunt, Joe. *52nd Street Beat: Modern Jazz Drummers 1945–1965.* New Albany, IN: Jamey Aeborsold Jazz, n.d.

Jewell, Derek. *Duke: A Portrait of Duke Ellington.* New York: Norton, 1977.

Jones, A. M. "African Rhythm." *Africa* 24, no. 1 (January 1954): 39.

———. "Blue Notes and Hot Rhythm." *African Music Society Newsletter* 1 (June 1951): 10.

———. *Studies in African Music.* New York: Oxford University Press, 1959.

Jones, LeRoi. *Blues People.* New York: Morrow, 1963.

———. "The Jazz Avant Garde." *Metronome* 78, no. 9 (September 1961): 9 ff.

Jost, Ekkehard. *Free Jazz.* Graz, Austria: Universal Edition, 1974. Reprint, New York: Da Capo Press, 1981.

Kahn, Ashley. *Kind of Blue: The Making of a Miles Davis Masterpiece.* New York: Da Capo Press, 2000.

———. *A Love Supreme: The Story of John Coltrane's Signature Album.* New York: Viking, 2002.

Kaminsky, Max, with V. E. Hughes. *My Life in Jazz.* New York: Harper & Row, 1963.

Kenney, William Howland. *Chicago Jazz: A Cultural History, 1904–1930.* New York: Oxford University Press, 1993.

Kernfeld, Barry, ed. *The New Grove Dictionary of Jazz.* New York: St. Martin's Press, 1994.

Kirchner, Bill, ed. *The Oxford Companion to Jazz.* New York: Oxford University Press, 2000.

Kofsky, Frank. *Black Nationalism and the Revolution in Music.* New York: Pathfinder Press, 1970.

Levine, Lawrence. *Black Culture and Black Consciousness: Afro-American Folk Thought from Slavery to Freedom.* New York: Oxford University Press, 1977.

Lewis, John. *The World of Music.* Information Bulletin No. 4 of the International Music Council, UNESCO House, Paris, May 1958.

Litweiler, John. *The Freedom Principle: Jazz After 1958.* New York: Morrow, 1984.

Lomax, Alan. *Mister Jelly Roll: The Fortunes of Jelly Roll Morton, New Orleans Creole and "Inventor" of Jazz.* 2nd ed. Berkeley: University of California Press, 1973.

Lyons, Len. *The Great Jazz Pianists: Speaking of Their Lives and Their Music.* New York: Da Capo Press, 1989.

Marquis, Donald M. *In Search of Buddy Bolden, First Man of Jazz.* Baton Rouge: Louisiana State University Press, 1978.

Martin, Henry. *Charlie Parker and Thematic Improvisation.* Lanham, MD: Scarecrow Press, 1996.

———. *Enjoying Jazz.* New York: Schirmer Books, 1986.

Merriam, Allan P. "African Music." In *Continuity and Change in African Cultures,* eds. William R. Bascom and Melville Herskovits. Chicago: University of Chicago Press, 1959.

Milkowski, Bill. *Jaco: The Extraordinary and Tragic Life of Jaco Pastorius, "The World's Greatest Bass Player."* San Francisco: Miller Freeman Books, 1995.

Murphy, Jeanette Robinson. "The Survival of African Music in America." In *The Negro and His Folk-Lore,* ed. Bruce Jackson. Austin: University of Texas Press, 1967.

Nettl, Bruno. *Folk and Traditional Music of the Western Continents.* 3rd ed. Englewood Cliffs, NJ: Prentice-Hall, 1990.

Nicholson, Stuart. *Jazz-Rock: A History.* New York: Schirmer Books, 1998.

———. *Jazz: The 1980s Resurgence.* New York: Da Capo Press, 1990.

Ogren, Kathy J. *The Jazz Revolution: Twenties America and the Meaning of Jazz.* Oxford University Press, 1989.

Oliver, Paul. *Blues Fell This Morning: The Meaning of the Blues.* 2nd ed. New York: Cambridge University Press, 1990.

———. *Savannah Syncopators: African Retentions in the Blues.* New York: Stein & Day, 1970.

Owens, Thomas. *Bebop: The Music and the Players.* New York: Oxford University Press, 1995.

Pearson, Nathan W., Jr. *Goin' to Kansas City.* Urbana: University of Illinois Press, 1987.

Placksin, Sally. *American Women in Jazz, 1900 to the Present: Their Words, Lives, and Music.* New York: Seaview Books, 1982.

Porter, Lewis. *John Coltrane: His Life and Music.* Ann Arbor: University of Michigan Press, 1998.

———. *Lester Young.* Boston: Twayne, 1985.

Porter, Lewis, with Michael Ullman and Edward Hazell. *Jazz: From Its Origins to the Present.* Englewood Cliffs, NJ: Prentice-Hall, 1993.

Ramsey, Frederick, Jr., and Charles Edward Smith, eds. *Jazzmen.* New York: Harcourt, Brace, 1939. Reprint, 1977.

Riis, Thomas L. *Just Before Jazz: Black Musical Theater in New York, 1890–1915.* Washington, DC: Smithsonian Institution Press, 1989.

Russell, Ross. *Bird Lives: The High Life and Hard Times of Charlie (Yardbird) Parker.* New York: Charterhouse, 1973. Reprint, New York: Da Capo Press, 1996.

———. *Jazz Style in Kansas City and the Southwest.* Berkeley: University of California Press, 1971.

Schafer, William J., with Richard B. Allen. *Brass Bands and New Orleans Jazz.* Baton Rouge: Louisiana State University Press, 1977.

Schuller, Gunther. *Early Jazz: Its Roots and Musical Development.* New York: Oxford University Press, 1968.

———. "Sonny Rollins and the Challenge of Thematic Improvisation." *Jazz Review,* November 1958, pp. 6–11. Reprinted in *Musings: The Musical Worlds of Gunther Schuller,* by Gunther Schuller. New York: Oxford University Press, 1986.

———. *The Swing Era: The Development of Jazz 1930–1945.* New York: Oxford University Press, 1989.

Shapiro, Nat, and Nat Hentoff, eds. *Hear Me Talkin' to Ya: The Story of Jazz as Told by the Men Who Made It.* New York: Rinehart, 1955. Reprint, New York: Dover, 1966.

Sidran, Ben. *Talking Jazz: An Oral History, Expanded Edition.* New York: Da Capo Press, 1995.

Simon, George T. *The Big Bands.* Rev. ed. New York: Collier, 1974.

Smith, Willie "The Lion," with George Hoefer. *Music on My Mind: The Memoirs of an American Pianist.* Garden City, NY: Doubleday, 1964. Reprint, New York: Da Capo Press, 1984.

Southern, Eileen. *The Music of Black Americans.* 2nd ed. New York: Norton, 1983.

Stearns, Marshall. *The Story of Jazz.* New York: Oxford University Press, 1958. Reprint, 1970.

Stewart, Rex. *Jazz Masters of the Thirties.* New York: Macmillan, 1972. Reprint, New York: Da Capo Press, 1982.

Strayhorn, Billy. "The Ellington Effect." *Down Beat,* November 5, 1952, pp. 4 ff.

Stuckey, Sterling. *Slave Culture: Nationalist Theory and the Foundations of Black America.* New York: Oxford University Press, 1987.

Sturm, Fred. *Changes over Time: The Evolution of Jazz Arranging.* Rottenburg, Germany: Advance Music, 1995.

Szwed, John. *So What: The Life of Miles Davis.* New York: Simon and Schuster, 2002.

Tallmadge, William. "Blue Notes and Blue Tonality." *The Black Perspective in Music* 12, no. 2 (Fall 1984): 155–64.

Taylor, Art. *Notes and Tones: Musician-to-Musican Interviews.* Liège, Belgium: Taylor, 1977. Reprint, New York: Da Capo Press, 1993.

Thomas, J. C. *Chasin' the Trane: The Music and Mystique of John Coltrane.* Garden City, NY: Doubleday, 1975. Reprint, New York: Da Capo Press, 1976.

Thompson, Robert Farris. "Kongo Influences on African-American Artistic Culture." In *Africanisms in American Culture,* ed. Joseph E. Holloway. Bloomington: Indiana University Press, 1990.

Tucker, Mark. *Ellington: The Early Years.* Urbana and Chicago: University of Illinois Press, 1991.

———, ed. *The Duke Ellington Reader.* New York: Oxford University Press, 1993.

Tucker, Sherrie. *Swing Shift: "All-Girl" Bands of the 1940s.* Durham and London: Duke University Press, 2000.

Washburne, Christopher. "The Clave of Jazz: A Caribbean Contribution to the Rhythmic Foundation of an African-American Music." *Black Music Research Journal* 17, no. 1 (Spring 1997): 75 ff.

Williams, Martin. *The Art of Jazz: Essays on the Nature and Development of Jazz.* New York: Oxford University Press, 1959. Reprint, New York: Da Capo Press, 1979.

———. *Jazz Masters of New Orleans.* New York: Macmillan, 1967. Reprint, New York: Da Capo Press, 1979.

Wilson, Olly. "The Significance of the Relationship Between Afro-American Music and West African Music." *Black Perspective in Music* 2, no. 1 (Spring 1974): 3–22.

Wilson, Teddy, with Arie Ligthart and Humphrey van Loo. *Teddy Wilson Talks Jazz.* London: Cassell, 1996.

SELECTED DISCOGRAPHY

Chapter 1

The Greatest in Country Blues. Vol. 1. 1201 Music 70022.

The Greatest Ragtime of the Century. Biograph BCD 103.

Johnson, Robert. *Robert Johnson: King of the Delta Blues.* Columbia/Legacy CK 65746.

Joplin, Scott. *Scott Joplin: His Greatest Hits.* Richard Zimmerman, piano. Legacy International CD 316.

Ragtime. Vol. 1: 1897–1919. Jazz Archives No. 120 159052.

Ragtime to Jazz. Vol. 1: 1912–1919. Timeless Records CBC 1-035 Jazz.

Smith, Bessie. *The Essential Bessie Smith.* Columbia/Legacy C2K 64922.

Chapter 2

Note: The first three listings are widely available series of recordings reissued as CDs that encompass most of the artists of the 1920s and 1930s, as well as many artists of the 1940s.

The Best of Jazz: A good introductory series in which each CD is devoted to a given artist and includes many of the artist's best or best-known recordings.

The Chronological Classics: This series contains hundreds of CDs that treat the major jazz artists' work in chronological order. CD covers are color-coded to make identification easier. A drawback to the series is that it does not include alternate takes but only principal (master) recordings.

Média 7 Masters of Jazz: Like the Chronological Classics in that major artists' works are presented in chronological order, but with a critical difference: Every known recording is included. That is, these CDs contain all takes from each recording session, live recording (irrespective of recording quality), and radio/TV broadcasts. In instances where previous reissues have already exhaustively covered an artist in question for a given period, the series purposely avoids duplication.

Armstrong, Louis. *Louis Armstrong and His Orchestra 1929–1930.* Chronological Classics 557.

———. *Louis Armstrong: The 25 Greatest Hot Fives and Hot Sevens.* ASV CD AJA 5171.

Bechet, Sidney. *The Best of Sidney Bechet.* Blue Note CDP 7243 8 28891 2 0.

Beiderbecke, Bix. *Jazz Me Blues.* AAD JHR 73517.

Ellington, Duke. *The Best of Early Ellington.* Decca GRD-660.

Henderson, Fletcher. *Tidal Wave—The Original Decca Recordings.* Decca GRD-643.

Jazz the World Forgot: Jazz Classics of the 1920s. Yazoo (Shanachie Entertainment Corporation) 2024.

Johnson, James P. *An Introduction to James P. Johnson—His Best Recordings 1921–1944.* The Best of Jazz 4035.

Morton, Jelly Roll. *Jelly Roll Morton and His Red Hot Peppers.* Vol. 1. Jazz Archives No. 110 158942.

Oliver, King. *King Oliver's Creole Jazz Band 1923–1924.* Retrieval RTR 79007 Jazz.

Waller, Fats. *Turn on the Heat—The Fats Waller Piano Solos.* Bluebird 2482-2-RB.

Chapter 3

Basie, Count. *Count Basie: The Complete Decca Recordings.* Decca GRD-3-611.

Carter, Benny. *Benny Carter.* Vol. 3. Média 7 MJCD 39.

Ellington, Duke. *In a Mellotone.* RCA 07863 51364-2.

Fitzgerald, Ella. *The Jazz Sides.* Verve 314 527 655-2.

Goodman, Benny. *Benny Goodman: Sixteen Classic Performances.* Camden (BMG) CAMCD 192.

Hawkins, Coleman. *In the Groove, 1926–1939.* Indigo Records IGOCD 2037.

Hines, Earl. *An Introduction to Earl Hines—His Best Recordings 1927–1942.* The Best of Jazz 4047.

Holiday, Billie. *Greatest Hits.* Columbia/Legacy CK 65757.

The Real Kansas City of the '20s, '30s, and '40s. Columbia/Legacy (Sony) CK 64855.

Tatum, Art. *The Quintessence.* Frémeaux & Associés FA 217.

Wilson, Teddy. *An Introduction to Teddy Wilson—His Best Recordings 1935–1945.* The Best of Jazz 4044.

Young, Lester. *Lester Young.* Vol. 1, 1936–1942. Blue Moon BMCD 1001.

Chapter 4

Gillespie, Dizzy. *Dizzy Gillespie 1940–1946.* Jazz Archives No. 99 158182.

Monk, Thelonious. *The Best of Thelonious Monk—The Blue Note Years.* Blue Note CDP 7 95636 2.

Parker, Charlie. *The Complete Savoy and Dial Studio Recordings.* Savoy 92911-2.

———. *Complete Live Sessions on Savoy.* Savoy Jazz SVY-17021-24.

Powell, Bud. *The Complete 1946–1949.* Roost/Blue Note/Verve Swing Masters. Definitive Records DRCD 11145.

Chapter 5

Blakey, Art, and the Jazz Messengers. *Moanin'.* Blue Note 7243 4 95324 2 7.

———. *Ugetsu.* Original Jazz Classics OJCCD 090-2.

Brown, Clifford, and Max Roach. *Brown and Roach, Inc.* EmArcy 814 644-2.

Brubeck, Dave. *Time Out.* Columbia CK 65122.

Davis, Miles. *Birth of the Cool.* Capitol CDP 7243 4 94550 2 3.

———. *Kind of Blue.* Columbia CK 64935.

Giuffre, Jimmy. *Free Fall.* Columbia 65446.

Modern Jazz Quartet. *Concorde.* Original Jazz Classics OJCCD 002-2.

Chapter 6

Adderley, Cannonball. *Mercy, Mercy, Mercy.* Capitol CDP 7 72438 29915 2 6.

Coleman, Ornette. *Change of the Century.* Atlantic 7 81341-2.

———. *The Shape of Jazz to Come.* Atlantic 1317-2.

Coltrane, John. *Giant Steps.* Atlantic 1311-2.

———. *A Love Supreme.* Impulse! GRD 155.

Davis, Miles. *ESP.* Columbia CK 65683.

———. *Nefertiti.* Columbia CK 65681.

Dolphy, Eric. *Out to Lunch!* Blue Note CDP 7 46524-2.

Evans, Bill. *Portrait in Jazz.* Original Jazz Classics OJCCD 088-2.

Getz, Stan. *Getz/Gilberto.* Verve UDCD 607.

Hancock, Herbie. *Maiden Voyage.* Blue Note CDP 46339 2.

Henderson, Joe. *Inner Urge.* Blue Note CDP 7 84189 2.

Hubbard, Freddie. *Hub Tones.* Blue Note CDP 84115 2.

Jarrett, Keith. *Arbour Zena.* ECM 1070.

Lloyd, Charles. *Forest Flower.* Sound track. Atlantic/Rhino 71746.

Taylor, Cecil. *Unit Structures.* Blue Note CDP 7 84237 2.

Tyner, McCoy. *The Real McCoy.* Blue Note 7243 4 97807 2 9.

Chapter 7

Corea, Chick. *Light as a Feather*. Verve 314 557 115-2.

Coryell, Larry. *Spaces*. Vanguard VMD79345.

Hancock, Herbie. *Headhunters*. Columbia CK 65123.

Mahavishnu Orchestra. *The Inner Mounting Flame*. Columbia CK UDCD 744.

Weather Report. *Heavy Weather*. Columbia CK 65108.

———. *Weather Report*. Columbia CK 48824.

Williams, Tony, and Lifetime. *Emergency!* Verve 314 539 117-2.

Chapter 8

Hagans, Tim. *Animation • Imagination*. Blue Note 7243 4 95198 2 4.

Hancock, Herbie. *Gershwin's World*. Verve 314 557 797-2.

Lincoln Center Jazz Orchestra. *Portraits by Ellington*. Columbia CK 53145.

Marsalis, Wynton. *Jump Start and Jazz*. Sony SK 62998.

Medeski Martin, and Wood. *Last Chance to Dance Trance (Perhaps)*. Gramavision GCD 79520.

Redman, Joshua. *Freedom in the Groove*. Warner Brothers 9 46330-2.

Schneider, Maria. *Evanescence*. Enja ENJ-8048 2.

Washington, Grover. *Strawberry Moon*. Columbia Records CK 40510.

Zorn, John. *Spy Versus Spy—The Music of Ornette Coleman*. Elektra/Musician 9 60844-2.

INDEX

LISTENING GUIDE CD TRACKS

CD 1

1–49 Audio Primer CD Tracks (see inside front cover)

50 Kasuan Kura (Traditional) People of Dagomba, Ghana
Ⓟ 1990 ROUNDER RECORDS CORP. COURTESY OF ROUNDER RECORDS CORP.

51 Daniel (Traditional) Willis Proctor and group
COURTESY OF ROUNDER RECORDS CORP.

52 Dere's No Hidin' Place Down Dere (Traditional) Marian Anderson
ORIGINALLY RECORDED PRIOR TO 1972. ALL RIGHTS RESERVED BY BMG ENTERTAINMENT. COURTESY OF BMG
ENTERTAINMENT, THE RCA RECORDS LABEL, UNDER LICENSE FROM BMG SPECIAL PRODUCTS.

53 Field Hands' Call (Traditional) Annie Grace Horn Dodson
COURTESY OF SMITHSONIAN/FOLKWAYS.

54 Maple Leaf Rag (Joplin) Scott Joplin
COURTESY OF SHOUT! ENTERTAINMENT, A DIVISION OF RETROPOLIS LLC.

55 Maple Leaf Rag (Joplin) Jelly Roll Morton
ORIGINALLY RECORDED PRIOR TO 1972. ALL RIGHTS RESERVED BY BMG ENTERTAINMENT. COURTESY OF BMG
ENTERTAINMENT, THE RCA RECORDS LABEL, UNDER LICENSE FROM BMG SPECIAL PRODUCTS.

56 Back Water Blues (B. Smith) Bessie Smith

57 Tiger Rag (LaRocca) Original Dixieland Jazz Band
ORIGINALLY RECORDED PRIOR TO 1972. ALL RIGHTS RESERVED BY BMG ENTERTAINMENT. COURTESY OF BMG
ENTERTAINMENT, THE RCA RECORDS LABEL, UNDER LICENSE FROM BMG SPECIAL PRODUCTS.

58 Dippermouth Blues (Oliver) King Oliver's Creole Jazz Band

59 Hotter Than That (Hardin) Louis Armstrong and His Hot Five

60 Singin' The Blues (Robinson-Conrad) Frankie Trumbauer and His
Orchestra featuring Bix Beiderbecke

61 Tiger Rag (LaRocca) Quintette du Hot Club de France
COURTESY OF GNP CRESCENDO RECORDS.

62 Tiger Rag (LaRocca) Art Tatum

63 East St. Louis Toodle-Oo (Ellington-Miley)
Duke Ellington and His Orchestra
ORIGINALLY RECORDED PRIOR TO 1972. ALL RIGHTS RESERVED BY BMG ENTERTAINMENT. COURTESY OF BMG
ENTERTAINMENT, THE RCA RECORDS LABEL, UNDER LICENSE FROM BMG SPECIAL PRODUCTS.

64 Down South Camp Meeting (Henderson-Mills)
Fletcher Henderson and His Orchestra
COURTESY OF THE VERVE MUSIC GROUP, A DIVISION OF UMG RECORDINGS, INC., UNDER LICENSE FROM UNIVERSAL
MUSIC ENTERPRISES.

65 Mary's Idea (Williams) Andy Kirk and His Twelve Clouds of Joy
COURTESY OF THE VERVE MUSIC GROUP, A DIVISION OF UMG RECORDINGS, INC., UNDER LICENSE FROM UNIVERSAL
MUSIC ENTERPRISES.

66 Shoe Shine Boy (Cahn-Chaplin) Lester Young

67 Avalon (Jolson-DeSylva-Rosa) Benny Goodman Quartet
ORIGINALLY RECORDED PRIOR TO 1972. ALL RIGHTS RESERVED BY BMG ENTERTAINMENT. COURTESY OF BMG
ENTERTAINMENT, THE RCA RECORDS LABEL, UNDER LICENSE FROM BMG SPECIAL PRODUCTS.

68 Sepia Panorama (Ellington) Duke Ellington and His Famous Orchestra
ORIGINALLY RECORDED PRIOR TO 1972. ALL RIGHTS RESERVED BY BMG ENTERTAINMENT. COURTESY OF BMG
ENTERTAINMENT, THE RCA RECORDS LABEL, UNDER LICENSE FROM BMG SPECIAL PRODUCTS.

69 Vi Vigor (King) International Sweethearts of Rhythm
ORIGINALLY RECORDED PRIOR TO 1972. ALL RIGHTS RESERVED BY BMG ENTERTAINMENT. COURTESY OF BMG
ENTERTAINMENT, THE RCA RECORDS LABEL, UNDER LICENSE FROM BMG SPECIAL PRODUCTS.

70 Body and Soul (Green-Sauer-Heyman-Eyton) Colman Hawkins
ORIGINALLY RECORDED PRIOR TO 1972. ALL RIGHTS RESERVED BY BMG ENTERTAINMENT. COURTESY OF BMG
ENTERTAINMENT, THE RCA RECORDS LABEL, UNDER LICENSE FROM BMG SPECIAL PRODUCTS.

71 Body and Soul (Green-Sauer-Heyman-Eyton) Billie Holiday

CD 2

1 Salt Peanuts (Gillespie-Clark) Dizzy Gillespie and His All Stars
COURTESY OF DENON CORPORATION (USA).

2 Manteca (Gillespie-Pozo-Fuller) Dizzy Gillespie Big Band with Chano Pozo
ORIGINALLY RECORDED PRIOR TO 1972. ALL RIGHTS RESERVED BY BMG ENTERTAINMENT. COURTESY OF BMG
ENTERTAINMENT, THE RCA RECORDS LABEL, UNDER LICENSE FROM BMG SPECIAL PRODUCTS.

3 Four in One (Monk) Thelonious Monk
COURTESY OF BLUE NOTE RECORDS, A DIVISION OF CAPITOL RECORDS, INC., UNDER LICENSE FROM EMI MUSIC
SPECIAL MARKETS.

4 Jeru (Mulligan) Miles Davis
COURTESY OF BLUE NOTE RECORDS, A DIVISION OF CAPITOL RECORDS, INC., UNDER LICENSE FROM EMI-CAPITOL
MUSIC SPECIAL MARKETS.

5 Moanin' (Timmons)
Art Blakey and the Jazz Messengers featuring Horace Silver
COURTESY OF BLUE NOTE RECORDS, A DIVISION OF CAPITOL RECORDS, INC., UNDER LICENSE FROM EMI MUSIC
SPECIAL MARKETS.

6 Hora Decubitus (Mingus) Charles Mingus
COURTESY OF THE VERVE MUSIC GROUP, A DIVISION OF UMG RECORDINGS, INC., UNDER LICENSE FROM UNIVERSAL
MUSIC ENTERPRISES.

7 Powell's Prances (B. Powell) Clifford Brown–Max Roach Quintet
COURTESY OF THE VERVE MUSIC GROUP, A DIVISION OF UMG RECORDINGS, INC., UNDER LICENSE FROM UNIVERSAL
MUSIC ENTERPRISES.

8 So What (Davis) Miles Davis Sextet

9 Ghosts: First Variation (Ayler) Albert Ayler
COURTESY OF ESP.

10 Street Woman (Coleman) Ornette Coleman Quartet
Ⓟ 1972 SONY MUSIC ENTERTAINMENT, INC.

11 Acknowledgement (Coltrane) John Coltrane Quartet
COURTESY OF THE VERVE MUSIC GROUP, A DIVISION OF UMG RECORDINGS, INC., UNDER LICENSE FROM UNIVERSAL
MUSIC ENTERPRISES.

12 Peri's Scope (Evans) Bill Evans Trio
COURTESY OF FANTASY, INC.

13 Chameleon (Hancock) Herbie Hancock
Ⓟ 1973 SONY MUSIC ENTERTAINMENT, INC.

14 Birdland (Zawinul) Weather Report
Ⓟ 1977 SONY MUSIC ENTERTAINMENT, INC.

15 Express Crossing (Marsalis) Wynton Marsalis
Ⓟ 1994 SONY MUSIC ENTERTAINMENT, INC.

16 One Note Samba (Jobim) Eliane Elias
Ⓟ 1990 SOMETHIN' ELSE RECORDS, A DIVISION OF TOSHIBA-EMI LTD. COURTESY OF EMI RECORDS LTD., UNDER
LICENSE FROM EMI MUSIC SPECIAL MARKETS.

17 Salt Peanuts (Gillespie-Clark) Steve Coleman and Five Elements
Ⓟ 1995 BMG MUSIC. COURTESY OF BMG ENTERTAINMENT, THE RCA RECORDS LABEL, UNDER LICENSE FROM BMG
SPECIAL PRODUCTS.

18 Far West (Hayes) Tim Hagans
Ⓟ 1999 CAPITOL RECORDS, INC. COURTESY OF BLUE NOTE RECORDS, A DIVISION OF CAPITOL RECORDS, INC., UNDER
LICENSE FROM EMI MUSIC SPECIAL MARKETS.